Reshaping Capitalism in Weimar and Nazi Germany

In Weimar and Nazi Germany, capitalism was hotly contested, discreetly practiced, and politically regulated. This volume shows how it adapted to fit a nation undergoing drastic changes following World War I. Through wide-ranging cultural histories, a transatlantic cast of historians probes the ways contemporaries debated, concealed, promoted, and racialized capitalism. They show how bankers and industrialists, storeowners and commercial designers, intellectuals and politicians reshaped a controversial economic order at a time of fundamental uncertainty and drastic rupture. The book thus sheds fresh light on the strategies used by Hitler and his followers to gain and maintain widespread support. The authors conclude that National Socialism succeeded in mobilizing capitalism's energies while at the same time claiming to have overcome a system they identified with pernicious Jewish influences. In so doing, the volume also speaks to the broader issue of how capitalism can adapt to new times.

Moritz Föllmer is Associate Professor of Modern History at the University of Amsterdam. He has previously taught at the University Leeds, the Humboldt University Berlin and the University of Chicago. His publications on Weimar and Nazi Germany include *Individuality and Modernity in Berlin: Self and Society from Weimar to the Wall* (Cambridge, 2013) and *Culture in the Third Reich* (2020). Moreover, he has published a range of articles and chapters, including in *Past & Present, Historical Journal, Journal of Modern History, Central European History* and *German History*, where he has also served as review editor.

Pamela E. Swett is Professor of History at McMaster University. Her publications include *Neighbors and Enemies: The Culture of Radicalism in Berlin 1929–1933* (Cambridge, 2004), *Selling under the Swastika: Advertising and Commercial Culture in Nazi Germany* (2014), and, as co-editor, *Selling Modernity: Advertising in Twentieth Century Germany* (2007) and *Pleasure and Power in the Third Reich* (2011) as well as numerous journal articles and book chapters. She is also the co-editor of the Nazi Germany section of the German Historical Institute's online portal, German History in Documents and Images.

Publications of the German Historical Institute

Edited by
Simone Lässig
with the assistance of Kelly McCullough

The German Historical Institute (GHI) is a center for advanced study and research whose purpose is to facilitate dialogue and collaboration among historians across national and disciplinary boundaries. The GHI conducts, promotes, and supports research in three core fields: German/European and Jewish history, the history of the Americas and transatlantic history, and global and transregional history. The GHI works closely with partner institutions and organizations to provide scholars from around the world with opportunities to extend their professional networks and build relationships across borders.

A full list of titles in the series can be found at:
www.cambridge.org/pghi

Reshaping Capitalism in Weimar and Nazi Germany

Edited by
MORITZ FÖLLMER
University of Amsterdam
PAMELA E. SWETT
McMaster University

German Historical Institute Washington
and
CAMBRIDGE
UNIVERSITY PRESS

CAMBRIDGE
UNIVERSITY PRESS

University Printing House, Cambridge CB2 8BS, United Kingdom

One Liberty Plaza, 20th Floor, New York, NY 10006, USA

477 Williamstown Road, Port Melbourne, VIC 3207, Australia

314–321, 3rd Floor, Plot 3, Splendor Forum, Jasola District Centre, New Delhi – 110025, India

103 Penang Road, #05–06/07, Visioncrest Commercial, Singapore 238467

Cambridge University Press is part of the University of Cambridge.

It furthers the University's mission by disseminating knowledge in the pursuit of education, learning, and research at the highest international levels of excellence.

www.cambridge.org
Information on this title: www.cambridge.org/9781108833547
DOI: 10.1017/9781108985192

First published 2022

A catalogue record for this publication is available from the British Library.

ISBN 978-1-108-83354-7 Hardback

Contents

Illustrations

Contributors

Simone Derix, Department of History, University of Erlangen-Nuremberg

Sina Fabian, Department of History, Humboldt University of Berlin

Moritz Föllmer, Department of History, University of Amsterdam

Martin H. Geyer, Department of Modern and Contemporary History, University of Munich

Molly Loberg, Department of History, California Polytechnic State University–San Luis Obispo

Jan Logemann, Institute for Economic and Social History, University of Göttingen

Kim Christian Priemel, Department of Archaeology, Conservation and History, University of Oslo

Tim Schanetzky, Department of Modern and Contemporary History, University of Jena

Alexa Stiller, Institute of History, ETH Zurich

Pamela E. Swett, Department of History, McMaster University

Dorothee Wierling, Research Center for Contemporary History in Hamburg

Acknowledgments

Writing from the vantage point of January 2021, during a global pandemic, we are reminded how important it is for researchers to meet and share ideas, to collaborate, and to critique one another. The volume compiled here grew out of such a meeting – a workshop hosted by the German Historical Institute (GHI), Washington, DC, in February 2018. We were lucky to hold the event when we did. We were also fortunate to benefit from the support of many institutions and individuals in its planning and in producing this collection of essays.

We want to begin by thanking the Thyssen Foundation, McMaster University, and the GHI. Together they provided the financial assistance needed to host an event that welcomed historians from the UK, the Netherlands, Germany, Switzerland, and Norway as well as the United States and Canada. We also want to thank the GHI team for their deft handling of the preparations for the two-day event and its logistics, and for offering their beautiful space as the venue. In particular, Ines Prodöhl (now at the University of Bergen) helped us select the participants, while GHI director Simone Lässig, David Lazar, Susanne Fabricius, and intern Martin Kristoffer Hamre should be commended for making sure all participants had a productive and enjoyable stay in Washington, DC. We also wish to thank Julia Erol, Steven G. Gross, Claus-Christian Szejnmann, Jonathan Zatlin, and various GHI researchers for their insightful contributions to the discussions.

We also appreciate the guidance of the individuals who assisted with this publication. We were thrilled that the GHI and Cambridge University Press selected the project for their long-standing and highly respected book series. We are grateful to David Lazar and Kelly McCullough at the GHI and to Liz Friend-Smith and Atifa Jiwa at Cambridge University Press for their editorial support. For their work on the manuscript and page proofs, we thank copyeditor Ami Naramor and proofreaders Richard Pettit and Elizabeth Tucker. Additionally, we thank Melissa Ward and Sheik Azharudeen J for their expert support during the production process. We thank GHI librarian Anna Maria Boss for her help with illustrations. Our thanks also go to the two anonymous reviewers who provided us and our contributors with constructive commentary and critique. The National Archives of Norway generously supplied the cover photo free of charge. Stephen Curtis was an excellent and thorough copyeditor, while Christine Brocks did a marvelous job indexing the volume. It has been a pleasure to work with everyone involved in this project from start to finish, and any shortcomings that remain are ours alone.

INTRODUCTION

Historicizing Capitalism in Germany, 1918–1945

Moritz Föllmer and Pamela E. Swett

This volume argues that capitalism had a significant presence in Weimar and Nazi Germany but in a different guise than before World War I. *Kapitalismuskritik* (critique of capitalism), nationalism, and state intervention all grew in importance, as did uncertainty about the direction the economy was taking and the ways in which it was intertwined with politics, society, and culture. We are interested in the question of how capitalism was reshaped in this altered context. To get closer to an answer, the cultural dimension of explicit statements about and implicit framings of economic matters needs to be explored. Furthermore, it is crucial to ask who did the reshaping, a focus that suggests attention not just to the capitalist order's many vocal critics but also to those working within it: bankers and industrialists, storeowners and commercial designers, legal scholars and government ministers. Since there were two camps, capitalism was promoted as well as concealed, contested before 1933 and racialized thereafter. Its reshaping during the Weimar and Nazi periods should therefore be studied as a dynamic and active process, and in so doing we take inspiration from a growing literature within the discipline of history and in the social sciences more broadly.

0.1 HISTORICIZING CAPITALISM

Capitalism stands out for its resilience, and not merely its resilience as an economic system. Neither as a disputed notion in political discourse nor as an analytical concept designed to grasp a complex economic reality does it show any signs of going away. In both regards it is even enjoying a revival. Since the financial crisis of 2008 capitalism has once again been attacked by ferocious critics and defended by staunch advocates.[1] Social theorists from various disciplines are currently reacting to this conjuncture by proposing new definitions and interpretations. The broad approach to economic, social, and cultural dimensions as well as the interest in change over time makes their work highly relevant to historians. In understanding capitalism as a "system of expectations," of "imagined futures,"[2] economic sociologist Jens Beckert comes close to some theoretically inclined historians. William H. Sewell Jr. foregrounds the "temporalities of capitalism" in which long cycles and eventful crises are inseparable,[3] while Jonathan Levy defines capital "as a pecuniary process of forward-looking valuation, associated with investment," and capitalism as the state in which this process has become habitual.[4]

Beckert and Levy both stress capitalism's imaginary features, its orientation toward the future. By foregrounding investment, Levy shifts attention away from industry, long the principal focus of economic and business historians, to finance, retail, real estate, and indeed slavery. He is interested in the various agents involved in the "process of forward-looking valuation." Sewell, by contrast, emphasizes the impersonal, recurrent logic of capitalist cycles and crises. These different but complementary theorizations are highly relevant insofar as imaginations and crises were central to the reshaping of capitalism in the Weimar and Nazi periods, as was the relationship between impersonal logic and human agency. These dimensions were inseparably structural and cultural; they were matters of intellectual debate, government intervention, and popular politics, of business practice and consumption. Capitalism's imaginary character, crisis-ridden experience, and personal and impersonal features raised probing moral questions. This

[1] Compare, for instance, Mark Fisher, *Capitalist Realism: Is There No Alternative?* (London, 2009) with Jason Brennan, *Why Not Capitalism?* (London, 2014) or, among historians, Sven Beckert, *Empire of Cotton: A Global History* (New York, 2014) with Werner Plumpe, *Das Kalte Herz. Kapitalismus: Die Geschichte einer andauernden Revolution* (Berlin, 2019).

[2] Jens Beckert, "Capitalism as a System of Expectations: Toward a Sociological Microfoundation of Political Economy," *Politics and Society* 41 (2013): 323–50; Beckert, *Imagined Futures: Fictional Expectations and Capitalist Dynamics* (Cambridge, MA, 2016).

[3] William H. Sewell Jr., "The Temporalities of Capitalism," *Socio-economic Review* 6 (2008): 517–37; Sewell, "Economic Crises and the Shape of Modern History," *Public Culture* 24 (2012): 303–27.

[4] Jonathan Levy, "Capital as Process and the History of Capitalism," *Business History Review* 91 (2017): 483–510, here 485; on historically variable ways of conceptualizing profit see Levy, "Accounting for Profit and the History of Capital," *Critical Historical Studies* 1 (2014): 171–214.

occurred in many countries and in other eras but with particular intensity in Germany between 1918 and 1945. Even less than elsewhere and before could capitalism be grasped in purely economic terms.[5]

Similar insights emanate from the current upsurge in empirical research by historians of the United States. "In history departments," observed the *New York Times* in 2013, "it's up with capitalism."[6] Practitioners of this rapidly growing subfield of American history, in contrast to cliometric economic historians, pursue qualitative and embedded rather than quantitative and disembedded lines of inquiry. They take up impulses from business history but widen the perspective beyond the firm and the factory, thus drawing fresh connections between economic, social, and cultural aspects within capitalist contexts. They are interested in agricultural markets and the rise of corporations, in systems of mortgage lending, debt securitization, and clerical filing, also in capitalism's aesthetics, narrativity, and gendering.[7] And they study a wide range of agents, from major industrialists to less prominent insurance brokers and street hawkers, from slave traders to counterfeiters and prostitutes.[8]

American historians' recent interest in capitalism has been echoed by specialists in the histories of other countries and students of transnational and global history. As one would expect, this boom has also reached Germany. There, the theoretical debate around 1900, when Max Weber, Werner Sombart, and others provided influential accounts of capitalism's origins, is being revisited and again provides inspiration.[9]

[5] On capitalism's cultural embeddedness see the reflections by Stefan Berger and Alexandra Przyrembel, "Moral, Kapitalismus und soziale Bewegungen: Kulturhistorische Annäherungen an einen 'alten' Gegenstand," *Historische Anthropologie* 24 (2016): 88–107; also see several of the contributions to Christof Dejung, Monika Dommann, and Daniel Speich Chassé, eds., *Auf der Suche nach der Ökonomie: Historische Annäherungen* (Tübingen, 2014).

[6] Jennifer Schuessler, "In History Departments, It's Up with Capitalism," *New York Times*, Apr. 6, 2013.

[7] Michael Zakim and Gary J. Kornblith, eds., *Capitalism Takes Command: The Social Transformation of Nineteenth-Century America* (Chicago, 2012); Sven Beckert and Christine Desan, eds., *American Capitalism: New Histories* (New York, 2018). One important monograph is Jonathan Levy, *Freaks of Fortune: The Emerging Worlds of Capitalism and Risk in America* (Cambridge, MA, 2012).

[8] This interest in agents is especially marked in Brian P. Luskey and Wendy A. Woloson, eds., *Capitalism by Gaslight: Illuminating the Economy of Nineteenth-Century America* (Philadelphia, 2015); Steve Mihm, *A Nation of Counterfeiters: Capitalists, Con Men, and the Making of the United States* (Cambridge, MA, 2007).

[9] See, for instance, Jürgen Kocka, *Capitalism: A Short History*, trans. Jeremiah Riemer (Princeton, NJ, 2016), chapter 1; Friedrich Lenger and Friedrich Wilhelm Graf, eds., "Theorien des Kapitalismus," *Mittelweg 36, Zeitschrift des Hamburger Instituts für*

Another feature is the heavy investment in understanding the ideal type of "German capitalism," also labeled "Rhenish capitalism." This is part of an international debate on "varieties of capitalism."[10] However, discussing the German case acquired particular saliency in the early 2000s, when commentators doubted whether the country's previously successful economic model was still fit for purpose. The emphasis on a national model retained its prominence after 2008, when Germany turned out to have weathered the financial crisis better than other countries. Therefore, the relevant studies focus principally on the Federal Republic, though they also hark back to the previous political regimes. They stress how companies, capital, and personal networks were densely interlocked, and how these interlockings were supported by a specific political and legal framework.[11]

Cultural factors – namely, long-standing reservations about mass production and mass consumption – are by no means left out of the picture, but it is fair to say that they continue to take a backseat to Germany's institutions, networks, and regulations. Here is where this book comes in. It foregrounds capitalism's cultural dimension over a broad front, covering economic practices, discourses, and representations as well as various individual and collective agents.[12] Our aim as editors is to foster the dialogue between economic and business historians on the one hand and cultural historians on the other, a dialogue that is presently further advanced with regard to the history of the United States than to the study of twentieth-century Germany.[13] We also complement the existing

Sozialforschung 26, no. 6 (December 2017): 1–74; Friedrich Lenger, *Globalen Kapitalismus denken: Historiographie-, theorie- und wissenschaftsgeschichtliche Studien* (Tübingen, 2018).

[10] Peter A. Hall and David W. Soskice, eds., *Varieties of Capitalism: The Institutional Foundations of Comparative Advantage* (Oxford, 2001); Uwe Becker, *Open Varieties of Capitalism: Continuity, Change and Performance* (Basingstoke, 2009).

[11] Volker Berghahn and Sigurt Vitols, eds., *Gibt es einen deutschen Kapitalismus? Tradition und globale Perspektiven der sozialen Marktwirtschaft* (Frankfurt, 2006); Ralf Ahrens, Boris Gehlen, and Alfred Reckendrees, eds., *Die "Deutschland AG": Historische Annäherungen an den bundesdeutschen Kapitalismus* (Essen, 2013); Hans Günter Hockerts and Günther Schulz, eds., *Der "Rheinische Kapitalismus" in der Ära Adenauer* (Paderborn, 2016).

[12] This broad scope, we think, constitutes an advantage over attempts to define capitalism by the practices it generates. See Sören Bandes and Malte Zierenberg, eds., "Praktiken des Kapitalismus," *Mittelweg 36, Zeitschrift des Hamburger Instituts für Sozialforschung* 26, no. 1 (2017): 1-97.

[13] In contrast to decidedly "pure" – and as such perfectly legitimate and useful – economic histories, as synthesized by Mark Spoerer and Jochen Streb, *Neue deutsche Wirtschaftsgeschichte des 20. Jahrhunderts* (Munich, 2013).

literature through our choice of period. This is a timely moment to look again at Weimar and Nazi Germany through the lens of a cultural history of capitalism. The former is more easily characterized as capitalist; for a long time, it was controversial to attach that label to the Third Reich owing to this regime's interventions, constraints, and incentives.[14] But since mainstream opinion now sees key tenets of a capitalist economy at work between 1933 and 1945, it seems apt to extend our focus to the Nazi years, thus revisiting the classic question of continuity and rupture.[15]

Such a cultural history of how capitalism was reshaped in Weimar and Nazi Germany provides an alternative to more rigid ideal types. It follows Jens Beckert in assuming that credit, investment, innovation, and consumption hinge on a wide range of images, narratives, and practices.[16] Moreover it implies that there was no single capitalism or culture of capitalism in the country and period at issue.[17] Whether this was ever the case in other countries and periods is not for this book to discuss, but, arguably, Germany's economy and its cultural dimensions were more

[14] Unless one takes the pre-1914 period as the sole yardstick, as Niall Ferguson does when claiming that "the dissolution of the German capitalist system" began during World War I and the inflation that resulted: *Paper and Iron: Hamburg Business and German Politics in the Era of Inflation, 1897–1927* (Cambridge, 1995), 462.

[15] See the debate between Peter Hayes, "Corporate Freedom of Action in Nazi Germany," *Bulletin of the German Historical Institute in Washington, D.C.* 45 (Fall 2009): 29–42, and Christoph Buchheim and Jonas Scherner, "Corporate Freedom of Action in Nazi Germany: A Response to Peter Hayes," *Bulletin of the German Historical Institute in Washington, D.C.* 45 (Fall 2009): 43–50; Buchheim and Scherner, "Private Property in the Nazi Economy: The Case of Industry," *Journal of Economic History*, 66 (2006): 390–416. It is fair to say that most scholars now lean toward Buchheim and Scherner's view, which stresses considerable latitude for private business under Nazi dictatorship. For recent syntheses, see Tim Schanetzky, *"Kanonen statt Butter": Wirtschaft und Konsum im Dritten Reich* (Munich, 2015) and Kim Christian Priemel, "National Socialism and German Business," in Shelley Baranowski, Armin Nolzen, and Claus-Christian Szejnmann, eds., *A Companion to Nazi Germany* (Oxford, 2018), 281–98. The discussion is pursued, with different emphases, in Ralf Banken, ed., "Between Coercion and Private Initiative: Entrepreneurial Freedom of Action in the Third Reich," Thematic Issue, *Business History* 62(3) (2020). On the notion of *völkisch* capitalism see Alexa Stiller (Chapter 11) in this volume.

[16] Beckert, *Imagined Futures*, part II. For a stimulating study of how capitalism's growing complexity was reduced by way of visual representation see Daniel Damler, *Konzern und Moderne: Die verbundene juristische Person in der visuellen Kultur 1880–1980* (Frankfurt, 2016).

[17] The otherwise useful chapter by Alexander Schug, "Werbung und die Kultur des Kapitalismus," in Heinz-Gerhard Haupt and Cornelius Torp, eds., *Die Konsumgesellschaft in Deutschland, 1890–1990: Ein Handbuch* (Frankfurt, 2009), 355–69 is solely focused on advertisement and does not attempt to conceptualize "the culture of capitalism."

diverse between 1918 and 1945 than before or after – which is why the concept of "German capitalism" as a singular entity applies most plausibly to the Federal Republic. The challenge is to turn this insight into a historical argument, to pinpoint overarching tendencies in an otherwise confusing picture. We attempt to do so by foregrounding four crucial tensions. Each of these tensions preoccupied contemporaries, each emerges from a reading of the existing historiography, and each is discussed in greater detail in the contributions that follow.

0.2 FOUR TENSIONS WITHIN GERMAN CAPITALISM, 1918–1945

The *first* tension was between the prominence of *Kapitalismuskritik* and a more tacit spread of capitalist practices and attitudes. Scholars emphasize that a negative stance toward capitalism dominated Weimar-era economic discourse. This contributed to undermining liberal democracy and, as Claus-Christian Szejnmann, in particular, has argued, benefited the Nazis: Hitler and his followers were able to tap into a broad anticapitalist consensus while pushing in a more extreme direction.[18] This is hardly controversial, and this book offers further evidence that a great deal of *Kapitalismuskritik* existed in interwar Germany. But there is another side to the story. In his seminal social and cultural history of the inflation years in Munich, Martin H. Geyer repeatedly cautions against "letting oneself be deceived" by contemporaries' moralistic slogans and outrage at rich racketeers. Exploiting any opportunity for financial gain was no longer the preserve of professional speculators. The rapid buying up and selling of goods, stocks, or foreign currency became widespread; the same goes for indulging in alcohol-fueled festivities to the advantage of Munich's brewers, bar owners, and popular musicians. Anticapitalism, however, made it easier to blame such behavior on foreigners, Jews, or the decadence of the metropolis Berlin than to acknowledge its normalcy.[19]

[18] Jerry Z. Muller, *The Mind and the Market: Capitalism in Modern European Thought* (New York, 2002), 258–87; Claus-Christian W. Szejnmann, "Semantik der Kapitalismuskritik in Deutschland nach dem Ersten Weltkrieg," in Darius Adamczyk and Stephan Lehnstaedt, eds., *Wirtschaftskrisen als Wendepunkte: Ursachen, Folgen und historische Einordnungen vom Mittelalter bis zur Gegenwart* (Osnabrück, 2015), 77–99; Claus-Christian W. Szejnmann, "Nazi Economic Thought and Rhetoric during the Weimar Republic: Capitalism and Its Discontents," *Politics, Religion & Ideology* 14 (2013): 355–76.

[19] Martin H. Geyer, *Verkehrte Welt. Revolution, Inflation und Moderne: München 1914–1924* (Göttingen, 1998), chapter 8, quotation 247, 260, 267. There were some timid

It is interesting to observe how contemporary economic agents navigated this tension between principles and practices. Commercial publishers and breweries alike faced moral censure for supposedly undermining Germany's cultural or physical strength, yet developed innovative ways of marketing their respective products.[20] Another pertinent example can be found in the way that some major industrialists hesitated to present themselves as capitalists to a skeptical public. Some reacted by stressing their patriotic sense of purpose; others preferred to limit their exposure. Heinrich Thyssen-Bornemiza, for example, moved his investment activities abroad and, when in Germany, adopted the role of a nobleman and horse racing amateur. Friedrich Flick, by contrast, remained very active within Germany but managed to cover his traces so shrewdly that even the staff of his own companies had little idea for whom they were working.[21] Local savings banks, the *Sparkassen* that are still a cornerstone of the German economy, strove to reconcile their self-image as a people-friendly alternative to the major banks with the need to return a profit.[22] Companies even called each other out for capitalist behavior. Toward the end of World War II, when forced laborers and, in many cases, concentration camp inmates were deployed across the board, some construction firms leveled the charge of human trafficking against their competitors, whom they accused of inflating their workforces in the interest of obtaining government compensation. In the context of the Third Reich, this proved a more effective discursive strategy than complaining about insufficient profits.[23]

The *second* tension was between a preoccupation with the essence of capitalist development, widely assumed to lie in concentration and "organization," and the experience of capitalism's bewildering complexity. Surveying economic and sociological discourse, Roman Köster has convincingly identified the predominance of one particular notion

attempts to promote a popular capitalism in Weimar Germany, but nowhere near to the extent discernible in interwar Britain. See Kieran Heinemann, "Investment, Speculation and Popular Stock Market Engagement in 20th-Century Britain," *Archiv für Sozialgeschichte* 56 (2016): 249–72, here 254–61.

[20] Gideon Reuveni, *Reading Germany: Literature and Consumer Culture in Germany before 1933* (New York, 2005); see Sina Fabian (Chapter 7) in this volume.

[21] See Simone Derix (Chapter 4) and Tim Schanetzky (Chapter 5) in this volume.

[22] Chapter by Pamela E. Swett (Chapter 10) in this volume.

[23] Marc Buggeln, "'Menschenhandel' als Vorwurf im Nationalsozialismus: Der Streit um den Gewinn aus den militärischen Grossbaustellen am Kriegsende (1944/45)," in Mark Spoerer, Helmut Trischler, and Andreas Heusler, eds., *Rüstung, Kriegswirtschaft und Zwangsarbeit im Dritten Reich* (Munich, 2010), 199–218.

centered on large-scale technology, industry, and bureaucracy. Capitalism understood in these terms was seen to erase human individuality and cultural specificity.[24] Social Democrats, most importantly economic theorist and future minister of finance Rudolf Hilferding, saw similar tendencies at work, although they rewrote them into a more optimistic scenario. They hoped that *organisierter Kapitalismus* (organized capitalism) would facilitate codetermination by the trade unions and thus an eventual shift toward a socialist economy.[25] This was, however, a view characteristic of the calmer years between hyperinflation and depression – and even then some Social Democrats raised doubts about their party's stance. Other observers stressed the dispersed rather than concentrated nature of Weimar-era capitalism, how it tended toward chaos rather than greater political control. Disagreement prevailed over whether it was leveling or fostering individuality, creating homogeneity or causing heterogeneity, about to disappear or stronger than ever. Moreover, uncertainty about capitalism's dynamic was linked to uncertainty about male privilege, which is why women's increasing presence in services and consumption triggered such hostile reactions.[26]

Again, the interesting issue is less which assessment was "right" and more how contemporaries dealt with this tension. The numerous advocates of a gradual or evolutionary transformation from the left were struggling with capitalism's simultaneous predominance and elusiveness. Hence, they found it difficult to imagine what a transition to a new economic order would actually look like and how it could be ushered in, while also being reluctant to scale back expectations of political agency.[27] By contrast, others toiling in the growing commercial sector were more concerned with the practicalities of analyzing consumers and designing or selling products. But they too were unsure about the direction of economic and cultural development, striving simultaneously to rationalize consumption and appeal to popular desires.[28] In general, business owners and managers had a clear stake in a capitalist economy while grappling

[24] Roman Köster, "Transformationen der Kapitalismusanalyse und Kapitalismuskritik in Deutschland im 20. Jahrhundert," *Geschichte und Gesellschaft*, Special Issue 24 (2012), *Kulturen der Weltwirtschaft*, ed. Werner Abelshauser, 284–303.

[25] Historians debated the validity of Hilferding's assessment in the 1970s but have since lost interest in the issue. See Heinrich August Winkler, ed., *Organisierter Kapitalismus: Voraussetzungen und Anfänge* (Göttingen, 1974).

[26] See Geyer, *Verkehrte Welt*; Bernd Widdig, *Culture and Inflation in Weimar Germany* (Berkeley, 2001), chapter 8.

[27] See Moritz Föllmer (Chapter 1) in this volume.

[28] See Jan Logemann (Chapter 8) in this volume.

with its sheer complexity. Some entrepreneurs excelled at exploiting the chaos of the inflation years, whereas a key trend of the stabilization years was to reduce market volatility by forming cartels and syndicates.[29]

Such volatility was again in evidence during the depression of the early 1930s, which triggered calls for further consolidation. Against this backdrop, the Nazis' arrival in power could be seen as an opportunity to reorder a complex economy. For business, participating in the elimination of the Jewish presence in an industry or pushing for its rationalization were ways to simultaneously accommodate the regime's political demands and pursue economic interests.[30] Companies could accept a trade-off by which government control stabilized profit-making, and the rhetoric of *Volksgemeinschaft* (national community) enhanced their status without requiring a drastic change of pre-1933 self-understandings.[31] Jewish entrepreneurs had to bear the brunt of this mix between dynamism and consolidation. As some recent studies have argued, they maintained a degree of agency for some time and should thus not be reduced to mere victimhood. This said, their adaptation strategies in the interests of economic survival were designed in a bewilderingly complex situation and implemented in a context of discrimination and persecution.[32]

During the war German industry continued to aim at a rigidly controlled version of capitalism. Along these lines many companies were keen to apply a Fordist approach to production, increasingly drawing on forced

[29] Gerald D. Feldman, *Hugo Stinnes: Biographie eines Industriellen 1870–1924* (Munich, 1998), chapter 9; Martin H. Geyer, *Kapitalismus und politische Moral in der Zwischenkriegszeit. Oder: Wer war Julius Barmat?* (Hamburg, 2018), chapter 3; Alfred Reckendrees, "From Cartel Regulation to Monopolistic Control? The Founding of the German 'Steel Trust' in 1926 and Its Effect on Market Regulation," *Business History* 45 (2003): 22–51.

[30] Frank Bajohr, *"Aryanisation" in Hamburg: The Economic Exclusion of Jews and the Confiscation of Their Property in Nazi Germany*, trans. George Wilkes (New York, 2002); Christoph Kreutzmüller, *Final Sale in Berlin: The Destruction of Jewish Commercial Activity, 1930–1945*, trans. Jane Paulick and Jefferson Chase (New York, 2015), chapter 6. Anne Sudrow, *Der Schuh im Nationalsozialismus: Eine Produktgeschichte im deutsch-britisch-amerikanischen Vergleich* (Göttingen, 2010), 346–7, 402–3, 444–7, demonstrates that shoe producers, rather than merely adapting to political constraints, had a genuine interest in introducing surrogate materials and limiting consumer choice.

[31] See, for instance, the case of commercial advertisers discussed in Pamela E. Swett, *Selling under the Swastika: Advertising and Commercial Culture in Nazi Germany* (Stanford, 2014), chapters 2–4.

[32] Kreutzmüller, *Final Sale in Berlin*, chapter 9; Benno Nietzel, *Handeln und Überleben: Jüdische Unternehmer aus Frankfurt am Main 1924–1964* (Göttingen, 2012), 99–149.

laborers and concentration camp inmates.[33] The quest for order was thus inextricably linked to violent forms of factory discipline. Yet, given the dire military situation, not even extreme state repression could suppress the chaotic side of economic activity. Long before the defeat, the regulation of scarce resources through rationing had the unintended consequence of fostering black market trading. This has been interpreted as a "radical experience of the free market," one that was later glossed over by a sanitized image of coordinated German capitalism.[34]

Capitalism's oscillation between concentration and complexity was closely related to a *third* tension – namely, between the importance of state intervention and the equally crucial dynamics of the market. Germany boasted a long-standing tradition of expecting profit-seeking to be moderate and order to be guaranteed by the state; Werner Plumpe even speaks of a peculiar economic style that semantically underpinned the German variant of capitalism.[35] The state had massively expanded its influence on the economy during World War I and remained involved to a much larger extent than before 1914. It exerted control over wage settlements and crucial sectors, for instance, tightly regulating the housing market through rent controls and tenant protection.[36] State involvement was not simply imposed but often called for by capitalist agents. Store owners demanded government compensation for the destructive

[33] Rüdiger Hachtmann, "Fordism and Unfree Labour: Aspects of the Work Deployment of Concentration Camp Prisoners in German Industry between 1941 and 1944," *International Review of Social History* 55 (2010): 485–513. On companies' profitable partnership with the SS, see also Marc Buggeln, *Slave Labor in Nazi Concentration Camps*, trans. Paul Cohen (Oxford, 2014), 66–73, 82, 117–35, 245–6, 276–7.

[34] Malte Zierenberg, *Berlin's Black Market*, trans. Jeffrey Verhey (Basingstoke, 2015), 209–14.

[35] Werner Plumpe, "Ökonomisches Denken und wirtschaftliche Entwicklung: Zum Zusammenhang von Wirtschaftsgeschichte und historischer Semantik der Ökonomie," *Jahrbuch für Wirtschaftsgeschichte* 2009, no. 1: 27–51, here 51. Even in the context of the United States, though, recent studies have stressed just how much capitalist development hinged on institutional conditions created by government. See Noam Maggor, "To Coddle and Caress These Great Capitalists: Eastern Money, Frontier Populisms, and the Politics of Market-Making in the American West," *American Historical Review* 122 (2017): 55–84.

[36] Karl-Christian Führer, *Mieter, Hausbesitzer, Staat und Wohnungsmarkt: Wohnungsmangel und Wohnungszwangswirtschaft in Deutschland 1914–1960* (Stuttgart, 1995). Even in this domain, however, the continuing significance of private enterprise after 1918 should not be underestimated; see Christoph Bernhardt, "Vom Terrainhandel zur Weimarer Städtebaukoalition: Unternehmen und Unternehmer im Berliner Eigenheimbau von 1900 bis 1939," in Heinz Reif, ed., *Berliner Villenleben: Die Inszenierung bürgerlicher Wohnwelten am grünen Rand der Stadt um 1900* (Berlin, 2008), 71–91.

consequences of political unrest.[37] Industrialists cultivated political connections, leading to a further growth in the importance of interest representation and lobbying. Many came to expect subsidies and bailouts, so that critical observers could not help noticing the contradiction in business's incessant complaints about government interference.[38]

Ardent free traders, such as Hamburg's coffee merchants, were struggling to find a balance between new arrangements with the interventionist state and the hope of reestablishing the prewar liberal order.[39] Then again, private initiative remained crucial, especially in sectors that could not hope for much state support. The aforementioned breweries and commercial publishers, which found ways to make a profit at a time of scarce disposable incomes, are a case in point.[40] Tourism provides another interesting example. Independent travel agencies prospered during the Third Reich despite the much better-known offerings of "Strength through Joy," while hotel owners benefited from visitors to major attractions – classic sites as well as those associated with Hitler and the Nazi Party.[41]

What made this a tension, rather than simply a coexistence of different sectors with varying degrees of government influence? The answer lies in contemporary discourses of unity and decision, reinforced by media dynamics. These discourses prevented an acknowledgment that state-economy relations were inevitably complex; they also rendered it difficult for the advocates of a return to the liberal past to gain much traction. Thus, various scandals attested to the proximity between business and government, which was less discussed in depth than conveniently blamed on the republican *System* and some prominent Jews.[42] More distant observers were keen to distinguish between a modern, "rational" and an

[37] See Molly Loberg (Chapter 9) in this volume.

[38] See Philipp Müller, "Neuer Kapitalismus und parlamentarische Demokratie: Wirtschaftliche Interessenvertreter in Deutschland und Frankreich," in Tim B. Müller and Adam Tooze, eds., *Normalität und Fragilität: Demokratie nach dem Ersten Weltkrieg* (Hamburg, 2015), 154–76; Philipp Müller, *Zeit der Unterhändler: Koordinierter Kapitalismus in Deutschland und Frankreich zwischen 1920 und 1950* (Hamburg, 2019); Fritz Blaich, "'Garantierter Kapitalismus': Subventionspolitik und Wirtschaftsordnung in Deutschland zwischen 1925 und 1932," *Zeitschrift für Unternehmensgeschichte* 22 (1977): 50–70.

[39] See Dorothee Wierling (Chapter 6) in this volume.

[40] Reuveni, *Reading Germany*; see Sina Fabian (Chapter 7) in this volume.

[41] Kirsten Semmens, *Seeing Hitler's Germany: Tourism in the Third Reich* (Basingstoke, 2005), chapters 2–4.

[42] Martin H. Geyer, "Contested Narratives of the Weimar Republic: The Case of the 'Kutisker-Barmat Scandal'," in Kathleen Canning, Kerstin Barndt, and Kristin McGuire, eds., *Weimar Publics – Weimar Subjects: Rethinking the Weimar Republic* (New York,

older, "political" capitalism, while grudgingly admitting that the wartime and postwar periods had led to a revival of blatant influence-peddling.[43] During the depression, the widespread perception of speculation as the root cause of current economic problems led to calls for government to intervene with an authority that it, in fact, sorely lacked.[44]

Once again the Third Reich brought about a putative solution. While claiming to have eliminated "speculation" and "corruption," it led to mutually profitable synergies between private companies on the one hand and government and party agencies on the other. Often these synergies actually reinforced competition. Even the aircraft industry, where demand was almost entirely state-driven, has been labeled a "playground for entrepreneurial initiative."[45] Such entanglements were often far more questionable than those of the Weimar period, but the difference was that they were now justified by a desirable primacy of politics rather than exposed and condemned by a free press.[46] Academic debate on economic issues was less threatening and thus to some extent tolerated in the Third Reich: contrary to a long-standing myth, the neoliberal vision of a more competitive economic order protected by a neutral state was only partly formulated in exile or opposition.[47] Thanks not least to keen transnational networking, this quite authoritarian brand of neoliberalism later merged with a democratic critique of cartels and trusts that underpinned attempts to demarcate a clean American capitalism from a compromised German one in the immediate postwar period.[48]

2010), 211–35; Geyer, *Kapitalismus und politische Moral*; Cordula Ludwig, *Korruption und Nationalsozialismus in Berlin 1924–1934* (Frankfurt, 1998), chapter 2.

[43] See Martin H. Geyer (Chapter 2) in this volume.

[44] Martin H. Geyer, "What Crisis? Speculation, Corruption, and the State of Emergency during the Great Depression," *Bulletin of the German Historical Institute in Washington, D.C.* 55 (Fall 2014), 9–35; see Moritz Föllmer (Chapter 1) in this volume.

[45] Adam Tooze, *The Wages of Destruction: The Making and Breaking of the Nazi Economy* (London, 2006), 129.

[46] See Tim Schanetzky (Chapter 5) in this volume; Frank Bajohr, *Parvenüs und Profiteure: Korruption in der NS-Zeit* (Frankfurt, 2001), 114–16, 140, 147–9. On the discourse around the primacy of politics over the economy see Stefan Scholl, *Begrenzte Abhängigkeit: "Wirtschaft" und "Politik" im 20. Jahrhundert* (Frankfurt, 2015), chapter 3.

[47] Ralf Ptak, "Neoliberalism in Germany: Revisiting the Ordoliberal Foundations of the Social Market Economy," in Philip Mirowski and Dieter Plehwe, eds., *The Road from Mont Pèlerin: The Making of the Neoliberal Thought Collective* (Cambridge, MA, 2009), 98–138. Among treatments of neoliberal thinkers Jean Solchany, *Wilhelm Röpke, l'autre Hayek: Aux origines du néolibéralisme* (Paris, 2015) stands out.

[48] See Kim Christian Priemel (Chapter 3) in this volume; Priemel, "'A Story of Betrayal': Conceptualizing Variants of Capitalism in the Nuremberg War Crimes Trials," *Journal of Modern History* 85 (2013): 69–108.

A peculiarly German variant of capitalism, widely and conveniently faulted for Nazism after the war, had been a focal point of longing in the Weimar and Nazi periods. However, a predominantly national framework of perceiving, debating, and attempting to steer capitalism sat uneasily with the German economy's transnational entanglements, constraints, and opportunities. This *fourth* tension continued to flare up throughout the period in question. Soon after World War I, companies resumed their attempts to seek investment opportunities beyond Germany's borders, by profiting from the reconstruction of destroyed facilities in northern and eastern France or by camouflaging their activities given the restrictions imposed by the Treaty of Versailles.[49] Captains of industry were simultaneously practicing a form of transnationalism and loudly proclaiming their patriotic credentials.[50] Such activities were difficult to own up to in public given the predominant political atmosphere. Yet, after the French and Belgian occupation of the Ruhr subsided, the optimistic vision emerged that national and transnational orientations would once again be compatible. From 1924 to 1929 Foreign Minister Gustav Stresemann negotiated a consensual reparation regime in the interest of foreign loans and international trade.[51] Much as contemporaries were obsessed with America, especially its Taylorism and Fordism, most thought that quintessentially "German"-quality production and cultured consumption could be maintained even in times of rationalization.[52]

The interplay between German capitalism's national and transnational orientations was always controversial, but it seemed to have reached a dead end during the depression of the early 1930s. Chancellor

[49] Anna Karla, "Westeuropas Wiederaufbau – *Made in Germany*? Baumaterial aus Deutschland im Versailler Vertrag," *Zeithistorische Forschungen* 13 (2016): 426–41; Jan-Otmar Hesse, "Die globale Verflechtung der Weimarer Wirtschaft: 'De-Globalisierung' oder Formwandel?" in Christoph Cornelissen and Dirk van Laak, eds., *Weimar und die Welt: Globale Verflechtungen der ersten deutschen Republik* (Göttingen, 2020), 347–77.

[50] Compare Conan Fischer, "Scoundrels without a Fatherland? Heavy Industry and Transnationalism in Post-First World War Germany," *Contemporary European History* 14 (2005), 441–64, with Moritz Föllmer, "Der 'kranke Volkskörper': Industrielle, hohe Beamte und der Diskurs der nationalen Regeneration in der Weimarer Republik," *Geschichte und Gesellschaft* 27 (2001), 41–67.

[51] Tooze, *Wages of Destruction*, 3–12; Peter Krüger, *Die Aussenpolitik der Republik von Weimar* (Darmstadt, 1985), chapters 3–4; Manfred Berg, *Gustav Stresemann und die Vereinigten Staaten von Amerika: Weltwirtschaftliche Verflechtung und Revisionspolitik 1907–1929* (Baden-Baden, 1990), chapters 5–6.

[52] Mary Nolan, *Visions of Modernity: American Business and the Modernization of Germany* (New York, 1994), chapters 4–6.

Heinrich Brüning's government introduced capital controls and tried in vain to form a customs union with Austria. In contrast to what – fairly or unfairly – appeared to be Brüning's cluelessness, the Nazis loudly promised to restore national sovereignty through sheer willpower.[53] Yet in many ways the tension remained, blamed though it was on alleged Jewish influences. As Adam Tooze stresses, even Hitler's regime could not transcend the structural limitations of the German economy – namely, its twin dependence on imports to bring in commodities and exports to earn much-needed foreign currency. But to a significant extent, it was possible to hide these limitations from the public through complicated arrangements paired with dictatorial secrecy.[54] Some relations continued, particularly those with non-Western partners. Small industrialists in Saxony, representatives of the Leipzig trade fair, and German-Romanian chambers of commerce worked hard to promote exports to southeastern Europe. Chemical concern I.G. Farben ventured out to India: it produced dye in the British colony, appealing to the Indian nationalist project of creating a domestic textile industry.[55] Other activities were hectic and often tacit, owing to the drive toward rearmament and autarky. German companies cloaked their foreign assets, with or without the support of their government, and bought up vital goods – for instance, sesame seeds, vegetable oils, and pig intestines in Japanese-occupied Shanghai.[56]

[53] The predominant view among economic historians now is that there were no clear superior alternatives to Brüning's deflationist stance, although the issue continues to be debated. See the seminal article by Knut Borchardt, "Constraints and Room for Manoeuvre in the Great Depression and the Early Thirties: Towards a Revision of the Received Historical Picture," in Borchardt, *Perspectives on Modern German Economic History and Policy* (Cambridge, 1991), 143–60, and the latest controversy over Brüning in the *Vierteljahreshefte für Zeitgeschichte*: Paul Köppen, "'Aus der Krankheit konnten wir unsere Waffe machen': Heinrich Brünings Spardiktat und die Ablehnung der französischen Kreditangebote 1930/31," *Vierteljahreshefte für Zeitgeschichte* 62 (2014): 349–75; Tim B. Müller, "Demokratie und Wirtschaftspolitik in der Weimarer Republik," *Vierteljahreshefte für Zeitgeschichte* 62 (2014): 569–601; Roman Köster, "Keine Zwangslagen? Anmerkungen zu einer neuen Debatte über die deutsche Wirtschaftspolitik in der Grossen Depression," *Vierteljahreshefte für Zeitgeschichte* 63 (2015): 241–57.

[54] Tooze, *Wages of Destruction*, 35–325.

[55] Stephen G. Gross, *Export Empire: German Soft Power in Southeastern Europe, 1890–1945* (Cambridge, 2015), chapters 2 and 5; Christina Lubinski, "Global Trade and Indian Politics: The German Dye Business in India before 1947," *Business History Review* 89 (2015): 503–30. For similar efforts in China, see Mathias Mutz, "'Ein unendlich weites Gebiet für die Ausdehnung unseres Geschäfts': Marketingstrategien des Siemens-Konzerns auf dem chinesischen Markt (1904–1937)," *Zeitschrift für Unternehmensgeschichte* 51 (2006): 93–115, here 105–11.

[56] Christopher Kobrak and Jana Wüstenhagen, "International Investment and Nazi Politics: The Cloaking of German Assets Abroad, 1936–1945," *Business History* 48 (2006):

During the war, this tension once again appeared to have been resolved. German economic nationalism could now draw on an empire. Exploiting occupied countries and coaxing allied or neutral ones into arrangements that benefited the dominant power created numerous business opportunities. Steel companies could acquire shares in their foreign competitors, secure sites or plants in Western Europe, and begin to take over Soviet state enterprises that were to be privatized after the war.[57] In Poland and the Netherlands major banks, whose domestic activities were restricted, competed to secure a large share of the future credit market and eagerly participated in the confiscation of Jewish assets.[58] Bankers working for the SS resettling apparatus aimed to mobilize ethnic Germans' capitalist potential by fostering their economic self-reliance, to the detriment of the native population.[59] The Nazi empire thus rested on capitalist agents both present and future, German as well as European – the latter insofar as the occupation authorities incentivized companies to produce for the *Wehrmacht* rather than the domestic market.[60]

These four tensions, with a little simplification, yielded a situation in which many Germans critiqued capitalism, searched for its essence, and called for its containment by the state and the nation, while others accepted it, along with its complex, market-driven, and transnational character. But what interests us more than static ideal types are the overlaps and shifts between these two poles, often within the same groups or even persons. The dynamic process of reshaping a preexisting economic

399–427; Frederic Wakeman, *The Shanghai Badlands: Wartime Terrorism and Urban Crime, 1937–1941* (Cambridge, 1996), 7–8.

[57] Ralf Ahrens, "German Steel Industry's Expansion in Occupied Europe: Business Strategies and Exploitation Practice," in Marcel Boldorf and Tetsuji Okazaki, eds., *Economies under Occupation: The Hegemony of Nazi Germany and Imperial Japan in World War II* (London, 2015), 247–61.

[58] Harald Wixforth, "Die Banken in den abhängigen und besetzten Gebieten Europas 1938–1945: Instrumente der deutschen Hegemonie," in Christoph Buchheim and Marcel Boldorf, eds., *Europäische Volkswirtschaften unter deutscher Hegemonie 1938–1945* (Munich, 2012), 185–207; Christoph Kreutzmüller, *Händler und Handlungsgehilfen: Der Finanzplatz Amsterdam und die deutschen Grossbanken (1918–1945)* (Stuttgart, 2005), chapters 3–4; Ingo Loose, "Credit Banks and the Holocaust in the *Generalgouvernement*, 1939–1945," *Yad Vashem Studies* 34 (2006): 177–218.

[59] See Alexa Stiller (Chapter 11) in this volume.

[60] Marcel Boldorf, "European Economies under National Socialist Rule," in Boldorf and Okazaki, *Economies under Occupation*, 7–23, here 13–16; Jonas Scherner, "Europas Beitrag zu Hitlers Krieg: Die Verlagerung von Industrieaufträgen der Wehrmacht in die besetzten Gebiete und ihre Bedeutung für die deutsche Rüstung im Zweiten Weltkrieg," in Buchheim and Boldorf, *Europäische Volkswirtschaften*, 69–92.

and cultural order had different potential outcomes. Capitalism did not "create Fascism," as a classic left narrative has suggested, but, in the cultural context of Germany between 1918 and 1945, it could be harnessed effectively by the Nazi regime, so that its various agents contributed to implementing a racist and imperialist agenda. This is especially evident with regard to antisemitism, which provided ready diagnoses of and "solutions" to all four tensions. Jews could be identified with bewildering complexity, speculative and volatile markets, transnational dependencies, and indeed with capitalism itself. They "became the *personifications* of the intangible, destructive, immensely powerful, and international domination of capital as an alienated social form," as the late Moishe Postone aptly put it.[61] Jewish entrepreneurs were not devoid of agency, but the strategies they designed for economic survival ran up against an increasingly desperate situation. Antisemitism thus underpinned the entire Nazi promise of an economy that preserved crucial advantages of the established system, in stark contrast to Marxism, but that had moved decidedly beyond capitalism.

To stress how capitalism was reshaped in a tension-ridden process furthermore allows us to revisit the issue of continuities and ruptures. Important elements of the Weimar and Nazi periods stemmed from the pre-1914 era and pointed toward future "Rhenish capitalism." Many companies continued to exist for decades or are still in business today. The ways in which they interlocked with capital and personal networks were remarkably persistent, and the same can be said about institutionalized industrial production.[62] The attitudes of these companies' owners and managers, who tended to view society and approach family life through the prism of established middle-class values, were equally long-lived.[63] However, continuities are not simply there for the historian to

[61] Moishe Postone, "Anti-Semitism and National Socialism," in Anson Rabinbach and Jack Zipes, eds., *Germans and Jews since the Holocaust: The Changing Situation in West Germany* (New York, 1986), 302–14, here 311–12 (emphasis in original). See also, more broadly, Jerry Z. Muller, *Capitalism and the Jews* (Princeton, NJ, 2010).

[62] Alfred Reckendrees, "Historische Wurzeln der Deutschland AG," in Ahrens, Gehlen, and Reckendrees, *"Deutschland AG,"* 57–84; Werner Abelshauser, "Umbruch und Persistenz: Das deutsche Produktionsregime in historischer Perspektive," *Geschichte und Gesellschaft* 27 (2001): 503–23. But see also the critical discussion by Volker Berghahn, "Das 'deutsche Kapitalismus-Modell' in Geschichte und Geschichtswissenschaft," in Berghahn and Vitols, *Gibt es einen deutschen Kapitalismus?*, 25–43, who stresses the importance of political shifts and American influences.

[63] Jonathan Wiesen, *Creating the Nazi Marketplace: Commerce and Consumption in the Third Reich* (Cambridge, 2011); Hartmut Berghoff, *Zwischen Kleinstadt und Weltmarkt. Hohner und die Harmonika 1857–1961: Unternehmensgeschichte als*

identify; they are also relevant as matters of construction and contention. The Allies told a long-term story that explained business's involvement in Nazi crimes, while German companies promoted a counternarrative of economic activity fundamentally untainted by political interference.[64]

Moreover, one might argue that the deliberate creation of continuities and ruptures is partly what capitalist agents do. Christoph Buchheim, who made major contributions to the economic and business history of the Third Reich before his premature death, saw the essence of capitalist behavior in a long-term orientation. Companies profited from the Nazi regime while attempting to plan ahead for a postwar future that they expected to be governed by the market.[65] This was doubtless the case. But is it really any less capitalist to exploit short-term advantages, for example, by destroying competitors or peddling political influence?[66] Companies that had managed to survive the interwar decades had grown used to a highly volatile, complex, and state-influenced environment. They, like many policy makers and individual consumers, demonstrated remarkable flexibility in adapting to new circumstances – so much so that Gerald D. Feldman spoke of a gambling mentality and an "economic shortness of breath" during the inflation years and beyond.[67] Both long-term and short-term strategizing marked the reshaping of capitalism in Germany, and they were often inseparable – for instance, when

Gesellschaftsgeschichte (Paderborn, 1997); Cornelia Rauh-Kühne, "Zwischen 'verantwortlichem Wirkungskreis' und 'häuslichem Glanz': Zur Innenansicht wirtschaftsbürgerlicher Familien im 20. Jahrhundert," in Dieter Ziegler, ed., *Grossbürger und Unternehmer: Die deutsche Wirtschaftselite* (Göttingen, 2000), 215–48.

64 Compare Priemel, "A Story of Betrayal" with S. Jonathan Wiesen, *West German Industry and the Challenge of the Nazi Past* (Chapel Hill, NC, 2001) and Sebastian Brünger, *Geschichte und Gewinn: Der Umgang deutscher Konzerne mit ihrer NS-Vergangenheit* (Göttingen, 2017).

65 Christoph Buchheim, "Unternehmen in Deutschland und NS-Regime 1933–1945: Versuch einer Synthese," *Historische Zeitschrift* 282 (2006): 351–89, here 385, 389.

66 See Thomas Welskopp's critique of an overly harmonious view of market competition: "Zukunft bewirtschaften: Überlegungen zu einer praxistheoretisch informierten Historisierung des Kapitalismus," *Mittelweg 36, Zeitschrift des Hamburger Instituts für Sozialforschung* 26, no. 1 (February/March 2017): 81–97, here 91–3. For a case study of a conflict between representatives of a long-term and a short-term orientation, see Boris Gehlen and Tim Schanetzky, "Die Feuerwehr als Brandstifter: Silverberg, Flick und der Staat in der Weltwirtschaftskrise," in Ingo Köhler and Roman Rossfeld, eds., *Pleitiers und Bankrotteure: Geschichte des ökonomischen Scheiterns vom 18. bis 20. Jahrhundert* (Frankfurt, 2012), 217–50.

67 Gerald D. Feldman, "Weimar from Inflation to Depression: Experiment or Gamble?" in Feldman, ed., *Die Nachwirkungen der Inflation auf die deutsche Geschichte 1924–1933* (Munich, 1985), 385–401, here 398.

companies strove to safeguard their assets while simultaneously scrambling to secure forced laborers and concentration camp inmates. In that sense, different "temporalities of capitalism" were at work in the Weimar and Nazi periods, and the "process of forward-looking valuation" assumed a variety of forms, which were compatible both with a parliamentary democracy and a profoundly inhuman regime.[68]

0.3 DEBATING, CONCEALING, PROMOTING, AND RACIALIZING GERMAN CAPITALISM

These four thematic tensions did not work in isolation from one another, as explained earlier, and each of the eleven chapters that follow could be said to provide evidence of at least one – sometimes several – of these elements. We have not, therefore, chosen to use these tensions as a strict organizing tool for the volume. Instead, we have grouped the essays in sections that speak to these tensions but also touch on four ways in which Germans interacted with, lived within, and shaped capitalism across the tumultuous years from 1918 to 1945.

Part I of the volume, "Debating Capitalism," seeks to introduce the topic by laying out the main contours of the lively discussions about capitalism held in these decades. All three of its chapters start out from contemporaries' recognition that World War I had ushered in a new age in which the state had become deeply entwined in the economic order and industry had grown increasingly concentrated (and politically influential) through the establishment of cartels and monopolies. The evaluation of these developments, however, remains deeply contentious.

In the first chapter, Moritz Föllmer accepts the existence of strong anticapitalist currents in interwar Germany but turns his attention toward the ways in which contemporaries understood individual agency with regard to capitalist practice. Across the political spectrum activists struggled to find ways to realize their ambitions to reform or overthrow the capitalist order. While the German Communist Party got its start during an era in which a victorious revolution seemed possible, even likely, capitalism held, buoyed by economic and social structures that kept most workers obedient and by incentives that enticed them to keep the

[68] Sewell, "Temporalities of Capitalism"; Levy, "Capital as Process," 485. Vanessa Ogle also stresses that capitalism combines a general orientation toward the future with varying temporalities ("Time, Temporality, and the History of Capitalism," *Past & Present* 243 [May 2019]: 312–37).

capitalist machinery in place. Other critics had no interest in overthrowing capitalism, but they found even reform, a difficult task. The role of the state in the project of reform was also hotly debated. Some maintained that it provided a necessary brake on the fundamental amorality of capitalism, while liberals believed that state intervention and industrial concentration through cartel formation undermined the individual agency and innovation of earlier decades. Here too, however, there seemed to be limits on what could be achieved in the way of taming its expansion. As Föllmer explains, capitalism was a target of criticism from across the political spectrum, but no one seemed able to nail down this adversary – was it on its last legs, or was it unstoppable in its power and reach? Föllmer offers an important corrective. He reminds us that while many critics of capitalism seemed unable to conceive of a way to rein in, reform, or destroy it, other individuals continued to successfully take advantage of its openings for agency. From small-time entrepreneurs like street hawkers to the wealthiest industrialists, individuals were showing the adaptability and creativity needed to participate in a rapidly changing economy.

Martin Geyer's contribution (Chapter 2) also focuses on the critique of capitalism in the interwar period, and he begins by reminding us that the financial crisis of the early 1930s was to many a sign that capitalism had run its course. Like Föllmer, Geyer examines one key component of the anticapitalist discourse. For him, the dangers of "political capitalism" are identified as fundamental to the criticism across the political spectrum. Various forms of rent-seeking were commonplace in the early modern period, according to Max Weber, but the modern state and accompanying legal frameworks had gone a long way toward weeding out such behaviors. The efforts involved in fighting the first total war, however, had meant that the number of intersections between political phenomena and the economy had grown exponentially by 1918. On the left, the problem was blamed on greedy industrialists; on the right, Jews were targeted more specifically for rigging price controls, supply channels, and other things for their own benefit. Regardless of where blame was laid, the belief was that such profit-seeking political interference had shunted capitalism off its normative track and that what was needed was a purging of these influences to restore capitalism to its natural, "rational" state. For Social Democrats, effecting political change through economic policy-making heralded a great opportunity for reform. For the majority of economists, however, political intentions "overloaded" the economy, as witnessed in 1929. While liberal economists sought to disentangle the state and economy, other voices, including political theorist

Carl Schmitt, argued that the state itself had fallen prey to a politicized economy. By 1930, others echoed Schmitt's call for a strong state that could overcome this submissive and degenerative posture.

In Chapter 3, Kim Christian Priemel follows some of these same debates to their conclusion in the immediate post-1945 period. Like the main characters described in the first two chapters, the jurists at the center of Priemel's study recognized the significance of World War I as marking a whole new level of integration, leaving many wondering "who was in the driver's seat – the state or (big) business?" Despite the revolution that followed defeat, the 1919 constitution kept capitalism on the table but left ample room for jurists to consider the relationship between economic and political interests. What they observed in the 1920s was the growing number and complexity of combines and trusts. Two young republicans, Heinrich Kronstein and Franz Böhm, sought administrative reforms to shift the balance of power in favor of the republic so it could bring capitalism under control. After 1933, Kronstein was forced into exile, but Böhm remained convinced that his critique of classical liberalism promised a stable and confident government that would protect and uphold economic freedom. And indeed Priemel illustrates how Böhm's theories remained relevant, because his vision of economic freedom had its origins in competition and struggle. By 1937 Böhm and his Freiburg colleagues had a clear sense of the role the state should play in setting and policing the rules of the marketplace. Only an authoritarian state could protect economic freedom. From the safety of New York City, Kronstein would become involved in the circles of legal thinkers who believed that the destruction of Germany's cartels was a necessary outcome of the war. On returning to Germany, Kronstein and Böhm contributed to establishing the ordoliberal doctrine that would provide the economic foundation for the Federal Republic. Working with other key figures in academia and the civil service, they highlighted the deep roots of Nazism in Germany's political economy and stressed the necessity of locating "freedom in law."

In Part II, "Concealing Capitalism," Simone Derix, Tim Schanetzky, and Dorothee Wierling examine the behavior of capitalist agents, particularly the very wealthy, and the ways in which they sought to mask their riches and influence. The task, however, was fraught with difficulties. On the one hand, a visible demonstration of wealth and power was required for someone to be perceived as successful. On the other hand, that same visibility opened one up to being lambasted as amoral, immoral, or even criminal. The sets of actors in this section each negotiated this paradox in their own ways.

Simone Derix (Chapter 4) begins by dissecting these very complexities, noting that scholars and other observers have traditionally identified capitalist behaviors as visible ones. By the interwar period, for example, "success" had become the catchword for a new literary genre of (auto) biographies of captains of industry and another of self-help books aimed at the common man. In all of these examples "success" had risen above the concept of high performance as the goal, and the difference between the two, Derix notes, had to do with the capacity for rendering one's abilities visible to the public. Media coverage of financial scandals, however, provided a way for observers and critics to uncover, measure, and condemn practices once kept secret because they skirted or crossed moral or legal boundaries. The tension between visibility and invisibility intensified at the end of the nineteenth century, as new forms of surveillance developed, including an expanding tax system, so that "successful" Germans, in turn, sought increasing levels of protection from prying eyes. Derix examines the Thyssen family and details three avenues by which its members sought to conceal their wealth: the use of trusted middlemen who evaluated risk and moved assets, the crossing of national boundaries to hide these assets, and reliance on the contemporary discourse that cast light on individual success while exploiting the complexities of personal, kin, and business networks to keep certain behaviors and assets shielded from public view. For example, Heinrich Thyssen-Bornemisza was able to travel secretly in the interwar and war years and to maintain a private cosmopolitan lifestyle abroad. Back in Germany, however, he was sure to make himself seen in public at patriotic events, which protected him from further scrutiny. Similarly, cloaking family foundations under names derived from female family members or obscure relations meant that few officials realized the provenance of the holdings.

The example of the Thyssen family is followed by Tim Schanetzky's comparative analysis of Friedrich Flick and Henry Kaiser (Chapter 5). In this chapter, as in the previous one, "success" is put under the microscope as a discursive concept. Schanetzky's analysis sets up the two titans of interwar and wartime industry in Germany and the United States to illustrate the ways their differing semantics of success operated to orient the internal workings of their industrial empires and the external images of both men. Schanetzky points to two key elements in Kaiser's image making – the speed at which his production facilities operated and his personal leadership. In both cases, the media and general public seemed to lap up this image of American can-do spirit, of an individual entrepreneur with limitless talent. What was concealed, however, was the fact that

Kaiser's stake in some of the enterprises was limited and that, particularly during wartime, this industrial empire was managed by an ever-expanding bureaucracy rather than an individual tycoon. Friedrich Flick, though working in very different circumstances in Nazi Germany, was also concerned about his public image, which he cultivated in ways that emphasized his success at overcoming his humble beginnings. In contrast to Kaiser, Flick sought to conceal his own involvement in his empire, after critics voiced their belief that he was little more than a capitalist speculator, divorced from the more honorable labor of production. From then on, his major deals and his own personal life were kept out of the newspapers, in contrast to Kaiser's media saturation. Nonetheless, Schanetzky explains, Flick was willing behind closed doors and in his dealings with the regime to cultivate a personal image that gave his willingness to serve the nation pride of place. He also took steps to shape his industrial holdings in ways that made his allegiance to National Socialist ideology visible by stressing the manufacturing side of the enterprises and the notion that his was a "family business." In both cases what stands out is that these two men took advantage of the special circumstances of state contracts and war to build their fortunes while concealing their capitalist behaviors with skillful semantic strategies.

Dorothee Wierling's study of Hamburg's coffee traders (Chapter 6) takes a longer view of the challenges and opportunities that faced this particular community of capitalist agents. Like the others examined in this part, the members of the exclusive Kaffee-Verein (Coffee Association) protected their (collective) image. In this case, the association nurtured a vision of its members as modest and prudent representatives of the centuries-old Hanseatic trading lifestyle. That they carried on this tradition was evidence of their commitment to the city and to Germany. But this lifestyle and business success were built on exclusivity. They took care to support each other, but also to keep competitors at bay. While this system had worked well for several generations, the arrival of World War I was the first major challenge that confronted the Hamburg traders. Wierling finds that their determination to hold onto their independence meant they lost out as others rushed to cooperate with the state. After the war there was no quick return to earlier freedoms. And yet, the constant vigilance needed to maintain a position in the changing 1920s economy meant that the community itself drew tighter. The coming to power of the Nazi regime in 1933 brought new challenges, and whereas the industry saw stabilization and even growth by 1938, the community lost ground as far as its ability to chart its own course was concerned. After the war, Wierling concludes, the

Western Allies sought to break up what they believed to be a dangerous economy controlled by cartels. While the Kaffee-Verein tried to rebuild, most of its members no longer saw free trade as the answer. Nonetheless, the Hanseatic ideal – the modest and community-oriented capitalist – remains part of the cultural fabric of Hamburg, leading in recent years to public commemoration of this past in the area around the old wharves.

While the chapters in Part II focus primarily on the ways that capitalist agents sought to conceal their business dealings and wealth or minimize the public's perception of their personal imprint on the economy, Part III, "Promoting Capitalism," explores the opposite perspective. It offers examples of actors who sought to confront their critics head-on and demand recognition from the state for their contributions to society. The essays also speak to the growing recognition by capitalist agents of the important role played by individual consumers as powerful participants in the market.

Sina Fabian (Chapter 7) illustrates the strategies employed by brewers in the Weimar era to defend themselves against discourses that tarred beer drinking as unhealthy and wasteful. In other words, Fabian's protagonists provided a counter to the anticapitalist discourses of the early 1920s. According to many, breweries, pub owners, and beer drinkers themselves epitomized the moral failings of capitalism (and of Germany more generally) in the years following its defeat in World War I. Selfish desire and greed overshadowed societal needs and personal health, beer critics argued, which led to the wasteful use of essential crops of barley and wheat in a time of shortage. The industry, however, attempted to provide a scientific defense for beer consumption, relying largely on rather exaggerated health claims. Spokesmen also repeated statistics on the important role the industry played in the struggling economy. As the situation stabilized in the mid-1920s, criticism of alcohol production, sales, and consumption waned to some extent. Nonetheless the Brewers Association remained vigilant, and, as Fabian illustrates, industry leaders took a much more sophisticated approach toward public relations in the years that followed in an effort to stay ahead of their detractors. Reaching out directly to consumers and legislators with the aid of the press, lobbyists, and tradeshow exhibitions, the brewers did not shy away from touting the importance of their products as essential to Germany's overall well-being – economic, social, and even physical – and continued to marshal evidence for this position from recent (beer-friendly) scientific studies and generations-old cultural tradition.

Jan Logemann (Chapter 8) examines how capitalist actors concentrated their efforts during the interwar years on managing consumer perceptions and behavior. His protagonists are the same sort of experts that the beer industry relied upon to craft its image for the consuming public. Among the professionals Logemann examines, the goal was to identify and create consumer desire and to predict or manage consumer behavior in ways that tempered the potential boom and bust cycles – the volatility – that seemed to characterize modern markets. Paradoxically, however, the 1920s ushered in a period in which the desire for standardization and efficiency as tools to make commerce more rational was coupled with greater attention to fashion and innovation. Agents within the creative economy, including those working in marketing, advertising, design, and fashion, sought to marry the two impulses together, but, as these fields were in their infancy, there was still considerable debate as to the location of the keys that would unlock the mysteries of consumer motivation. Did engineers, designers, or psychologists have the answers? By the time business owners and policy makers sought ways out of the global depression that struck at the end of the 1920s, to embrace fashion seemed little more than frivolity and wastefulness. In the decade that followed, particularly under the racist vision of an "organic" commercial marketplace, the individual and her or his wants seemed more of a drain on the community than an aspect of its vitality. Logemann concludes that, regardless of the political caesura of 1933, the overall trend continued in which the consumer's place within capitalism remained paramount and an ever-growing cadre of experts offered tools for unlocking (and managing) their power.

In Molly Loberg's analysis (Chapter 9) of the reemergence of the 1850 Tumult Law in the interwar period, we see even more clearly the links between capitalism and political culture, as business owners worked to assert what they saw as their rights as contributors to the local and national economy in an era of violent political upheaval. As in the previous chapter, despite the changing political and economic fortunes facing commercial interests in the interwar years, there was a growing confidence that the state owed the agents of capitalism a safe and protected environment in which to do business. Historically, the law sought to punish communities by making them financially liable for collective violence against property that occurred within their local area. However, the scale of the violence after 1918 coupled with the economic crises that befell the republic meant that many municipalities sought to shift the duty of compensation to the national government. But revision of the law only fueled debate. The state wanted to limit compensation according to need, but business owners and municipal leaders insisted that those most affected were the bedrock of towns and cities – middle-class taxpayers, who both suffered the destructive violence and paid the taxes that covered compensation. After January 1933, Jewish retailers suffered greatly from the regime-sanctioned thuggery of the SA. But Loberg shows that Jewish Germans fought for their rights under the Tumult Law, and in some early cases, received compensation. Ultimately, it was easier for the regime to find legal workarounds than it was to rein in their most violent supporters, which meant that after *Kristallnacht*, in which thousands of Jewish-owned businesses suffered significant damage, the regime found itself again in legal jeopardy. This time, however, Jewish property owners were fashioned as the perpetrators and the state forced private insurers to provide restitution for theft and fire (not "tumult") to non-Jews caught up in the rioting. The chapter thus demonstrates the power of capitalism to shape politics, as both the republic and the dictatorship were held accountable for the protection of businesses and private property.

Part IV, "Racializing Capitalism," includes two chapters that speak to some of the complexities that have led historians to debate whether the Third Reich can even be considered a capitalist system. Alexa Stiller (Chapter 11) opens with a brief synopsis of the major contours of this debate, but ultimately she and Pamela Swett demonstrate through their case studies of racialized thinking in the Reich's financial institutions that certain aspects of a market economy were maintained and private property was upheld, even if the dictatorship and its war aims shaped these elements in significant and oftentimes brutal ways. Both authors refer to this peculiar variety of capitalism as *völkisch* (nationally or ethnically distinctive) in order to draw attention to the specifically racist motivations at its core.

Swett (Chapter 10) examines the unique role that the *Sparkassen* (public saving banks) played in the German economy and national consciousness. Long before the establishment of the dictatorship, these institutions had fashioned themselves as "anticapitalist," even while they supported small businesses with loans and individuals with their dreams of homeownership and capital accumulation. Drawing from the examples of two *Sparkassen* in Stuttgart, Swett focuses on three local ways in which managers' capitalist thinking was entwined with National Socialist ideals and policy. First, she looks at the decisions made in 1933 with respect to employees with non-Nazi political views. In some cases, republic-supporting employees remained on the staff – not out of a principled aversion to Nazification on the part of their employers, but out of a desire to hold onto skilled colleagues. Even so, in basing their determinations on what was "best for business," the men in question often chose to align their decisions with capitalist virtues as a way to rationalize persecution. Swett then turns to other behaviors that illustrate the prioritization of capitalist ways of thinking, which, while obscuring the era's racism, served the regime equally well. Fierce competitiveness, individual greed, participation in Aryanization, and forgoing past bank policies in search of "better deals" that aided the regime's war aims were normalized by the language of capitalism. She concludes with a brief look at the postwar reckoning these banks faced. The capitalist reasoning of the prewar and war years could now be called upon as evidence that the men acted in the banks' best (business) interests – that racist thinking had not distorted their objective calculations. Swett insists that such claims should be read not solely as postwar apologia, but in line with the reasoning that generated the criminal behavior of the 1930s and early 1940s.

Alexa Stiller's chapter, which brings the volume to a close, demonstrates how the Nazi regime's embrace of capitalism was dependent upon its antisemitism. In other words, her essay brings us full circle with regard to the anticapitalist critiques of the Weimar era. By externalizing all aspects of capitalism that were perceived to have sown societal discord, inequality, and instability as "Jewish," National Socialists could claim to be building a *Volksgemeinschaft* in which private property and market competition were still foundational, though now cleansed of insidious "Jewish" greed and criminality. Stiller's first section focuses on private property and the ways in which the regime upheld (non-Jewish) citizens' rights to property, even when expropriating land for state projects. This procedure was not followed in the annexed territories of western Poland, the so-called Wartheland. Here both residential and commercial property was expropriated without any recognition of the rights of property owners. In order to handle the vast number of financial transactions taking place related to the resettlement of *Volksdeutsche* (ethnic Germans) in the Wartheland starting in 1939, Himmler set up a limited liability corporation, the Deutsche Umsiedlungs-Treuhandgesellschaft (German Resettlement Trust Company) (DUT). The tasks of the bank were to handle the liquidation of assets left behind by those moving to the Wartheland. Compensation for these individuals was also managed by the DUT with racial criteria used as the key feature in decision-making. Stiller's analysis of the DUT and its partner institutions as well as the postwar lives of the DUT's leadership corroborate the arguments put forward by Swett and other authors in the volume: the financial and commercial decisions and deals made during the years of dictatorship were shaped and motivated by racist ideology. That statement, however, is inextricably tied to the assertion that the actions taken by economic actors also conformed to capitalist precepts. As Stiller explains, racism was a driving force in the establishment and daily decision-making of the DUT, yet that racist vision also "promoted central elements of the capitalist social and economic order: property, entrepreneurship, and productivity."

This volume's principal argument regarding the transition from the Weimar Republic to the Third Reich is thus that Nazism was attractive not least for promising to resolve the tensions of German capitalism. It is our hope that other scholars will debate this position critically and differentiate it further, all the more since there are many avenues of exploration that we were not able to pursue. Perhaps the most glaring is that our study is purely urban in focus at a time when about 30 percent of all Germans still lived in rural communities and made their livelihoods in agriculture. Besides farmers and the intermediaries who connected them to markets, additional capitalist agents await further attention – for instance, salesmen and women, creditors, debtors, and white-collar criminals. Finally, given the separate, existing literature on individual consumers and consumption, we did not devote substantial space to these important actors.[69] All of these were "real" enough while also forming part of cultural imaginations. Many of them were also active beyond national borders, a further dimension that our analyses have not fully explored.

Whatever directions this inquiry follows in coming years, we advocate explicit efforts to think through the cultural impact of capitalism and, vice versa, the impact of culture on a specific time and place in capitalism's development – in Germany and beyond. By doing so historians will further understand the resilience of this economic form and the attractions of life within it, despite the inequalities and injustices it has created and continues to create to this very day.

[69] Some titles about individual consumers and consumption in the Weimar and Nazi eras: Nancy R. Reagin, *Sweeping the German Nation: Domesticity and National Identity in Germany, 1879–1945* (New York, 2008); Molly Loberg, *The Struggle for the Streets of Berlin: Politics, Consumption and Urban Space, 1914–1945* (Cambridge, 2018); Claudius Torp, *Konsum und Politik in der Weimarer Republik* (Göttingen, 2011); Swett, *Selling under the Swastika*; Peter-Paul Bänziger, *Die Moderne als Erlebnis: Eine Geschichte der Konsum- und Arbeitsgesellschaft 1840–1940* (Göttingen, 2020); Shelley Baranowski, *Strength through Joy: Consumerism and Mass Tourism in the Third Reich* (New York, 2007).

PART I

DEBATING CAPITALISM

1

Capitalism and Agency in Interwar Germany

Moritz Föllmer

How much space does capitalism leave for human agency? What difference can individual entrepreneurs, employees, and consumers hope to make? What can governments achieve by intervening in the economy? Can capitalism be politically contained or reformed? Is it possible to overthrow it through a revolution or subject it to a nationalist agenda? These questions have been intensely debated from the nineteenth century to the present day. It is fair to say that, at least in continental Europe, *Kapitalismuskritik* (critique of capitalism) has played a prominent role in these debates. This was certainly the case in interwar Germany, where capitalism was an even more central topic of discussion than in the Wilhelmine period. Scathing though it often was, the critique was simultaneously riddled with uncertainty. After World War I and the demise of the German Empire, an alternative economic order seemed possible yet frustratingly elusive. Capitalism had clearly been transformed, but the interpretation of these transformations was less clear. Was it "organized" now or still "wild"?[1] Had it been decisively weakened or was it even more pervasive than before 1918? Had it become easier or more difficult to change through human agency? Or – a rather uncomfortable thought – did capitalism exert an agency of its own?

The present chapter reconstructs how contemporaries grappled with these questions. In so doing, it aims to add to the scholarly treatment of

I would like to thank Christina Brauner, Rüdiger Graf, and Pamela Swett for their criticisms and suggestions.

[1] Julius Kaliski, "Wilde oder organisierte Wirtschaft?" *Sozialistische Monatshefte* 34, no. 6 (June 11, 1928): 485–90.

discourses on German capitalism in the first decades of the twentieth century. Both Claus-Christian Szejnmann, on the basis of a wide range of contemporary publications, and Jerry Z. Muller, focusing on communist literary scholar Georg Lukács and radical-right sociologist Hans Freyer, have argued that anticapitalist views reigned supreme during the Weimar period and that they contributed decisively to undermining liberal democracy and legitimizing political extremism.[2] In contrast to Szejnmann and Muller, Roman Köster has focused on critical observers of capitalism – namely, German economists and sociologists between 1900 and 1970 – rather than its political enemies. They wrote of an economic system driving toward large-scale technology, bureaucratization, and industrial concentration, which was also a powerful leveler of cultural specificity and human individuality. However, Köster notes capitalism's conceptual fluidity, its apparent capacity to act as a shrewd subject, and the difficulty of countering it with an alternative vision.[3] These brief remarks hint at a more subtle history of discourses on capitalism than the emphasis on one overarching concept or broad consensus would suggest.

Even the most perceptive contemporaries were unsure whether they faced a single system engendering clear effects or a bewildering complexity with unclear causalities. While some exuded confidence that an alternative economic and social order was possible, others were haunted by the difficulty of transforming something both powerful and fluid. A focus on the relationship between capitalism and agency brings this fundamental uncertainty to the fore, and it throws the fault lines within contemporary *Kapitalismuskritik* into sharp relief. This relationship preoccupied observers, practitioners, and activists of various ideological persuasions. It was discussed in theoretical journals and popular newspapers, in speeches and pamphlets, at cabinet meetings, and by ordinary people. To explore these discussions is to historicize a crucial issue of Weimar culture and politics. Furthermore, crossing the chronological divide of 1933 allows us to revisit the classic question of how capitalism was related to the rise and rule of the Nazis.

[2] Claus-Christian W. Szejnmann, "Semantik der Kapitalismuskritik in Deutschland nach dem Ersten Weltkrieg," in Darius Adamczyk and Stephan Lehnstaedt, eds., *Wirtschaftskrisen als Wendepunkte: Ursachen, Folgen und historische Einordnungen vom Mittelalter bis zur Gegenwart* (Osnabrück, 2015), 77–99; Jerry Z. Muller, *The Mind and the Market: Capitalism in Modern European Thought* (New York, 2002), 258–87.

[3] Roman Köster, "Transformationen der Kapitalismusanalyse und Kapitalismuskritik in Deutschland im 20. Jahrhundert," *Geschichte und Gesellschaft*, Special Issue 24 (2012), *Kulturen der Weltwirtschaft*, ed. Werner Abelshauser, 284–303.

My contention is that in interwar Germany capitalism was widely criticized and seldom defended, but it proved remarkably capable of confining individual, collective, and governmental agency. Capitalism's ability to constrain the realm of human action posed a major challenge to all political currents – until the Nazis prevailed with their promise to overcome it. The first section focuses on different interpretations of capitalism and the possibility of changing it, ranging from the revolutionary left in 1918/19 to doctrinaire communism, from liberal economists to Christian and Social Democrat reformers. The second discusses how various agents within the capitalist order – namely, investors, small businessmen, and industrialists – were perceived by the public and presented themselves to it. The third deals with policy makers, who were unsure how to act during the depression. It then turns to the Nazis' ideological emphasis on willpower and their attempts to demarcate legitimate economic agency from illegitimate capitalism.

1.1 THE INSURMOUNTABILITY OF CAPITALISM

When the revolution of 1918/19 began, capitalism was one of its obvious targets. Severe pressures on working-class Germans during the second half of World War I had made socialism more desirable than ever before. The strains of continued total warfare were exacerbated by the authoritarian measures taken by the Supreme Command. This made militarism and capitalism seem inextricably linked, capable of victimizing proletarians in trenches and factories alike. In 1917 and 1918 hopes arose that they could be overcome jointly in one single transformation. "I am not prepared to risk my neck for the damned Prussians and big capitalists any longer," a building locksmith wrote to his sister in Munich.[4] Rebelling against an immensely powerful yet suddenly frail system meant regaining personal agency after years of being subjected to multiple disciplinary constraints. Germany's military defeat and ensuing revolutionary transformation thus offered the chance "at long last to take vigorous action to counter the hypotrophy [*sic*; he must have meant 'hypertrophy'] of capitalism," as one Maximilian Schmelk of Kempten in Bavaria vividly put it.[5]

[4] Otto Biegner, Aug. 25, 1917, reprinted in Bernd Ulrich and Benjamin Ziemann, eds., *German Soldiers in the Great War: Letters and Eyewitness Accounts*, trans. Christine Brocks (Barnsley, 2010), 144.

[5] Maximilian Schmelk, District Commissioner for Financial Affairs in Kempten, to the Revolutionary Central Council in Munich, Apr. 8, 1919, Bayerisches Hauptstaatsarchiv München, Arbeiter- und Soldatenrat, no. 30.

Schmelk's sentiment was shared by millions of working-class Germans and turned into a political program by the theorists of early communism.[6] These authors attempted to reconcile the structural and long-term vision of Marxism with the subjective and short-term character of revolutionary action. Being able to blame four years of carnage on capitalism so as to hammer home the existential need for a radical rupture greatly facilitated this endeavor. A far-reaching transformation would not only undermine the basis for any future war but also create the conditions for working-class Germans to lead autonomous lives. "The proletarian masses must learn," argued Rosa Luxemburg, "to stop being dead machines that capitalists put to work in the production process, and turn themselves into thinking, free, and autonomous drivers of this process."[7] In the course of the revolution, strike movements, uprisings, and countless small-scale confrontations with industrialists or managers lent credence to this vision. From the vantage point of capitalism's middle-class defenders, it amounted to a massive threat. One of these defenders even expressed the fear that the myriad activities that together constituted the extant economic system would eventually be driven underground: "All personal initiative and any willingness to make oneself useful if possible would be dismissed as merely self-serving, capitalism would be persecuted, in other words, like the contraband trade in the last few years, it would have to survive as best it could under the surface."[8]

In desiring to personally oppose "the hypotrophy of capitalism," the Bavarian revolutionary Schmelk inadvertently put his finger on a problem. To overcome a complex and deeply rooted economic system through direct human action, however bold, was a daunting task. Communists were understandably reluctant to reflect on this problem, given that this would have called their entire political agenda into question. But the frequent comments on the need to educate the proletarian masses sat oddly with millenarian hopes for an imminent transformation. It was only under the influence of the popular dynamics on the streets of Berlin in January 1919 that Luxemburg began to see a chance to usher in a new

[6] The following passages partly draw on Moritz Föllmer, "The Unscripted Revolution: Male Subjectivities in Germany, 1918/19," *Past & Present* 241 (Aug. 2018): 161–92.

[7] Rosa Luxemburg, "Was will der Spartakusbund?" (Dec. 14, 1918), in *Luxemburg, Gesammelte Werke*, ed. Institut für Marxismus-Leninismus beim ZK der SED and Rosa-Luxemburg Stiftung, 7 vols. (Berlin, 1970–2017), 7: 440–9, here 443.

[8] Siegfried Matheus, Berlin, to Ministry of the Interior, Nov. 24, 1918, Geheimes Staatsarchiv Preussischer Kulturbesitz Berlin-Dahlem, HA I, Rep. 77, Tit. 253a.

society in the here and now.[9] However, revolutionary radicalism was repeatedly defeated, and it was not merely counterrevolutionary violence that accounted for this failure, but the resilience of an economic system that greatly limited the scope for human agency and even appeared to exert an agency of its own. Capital, as Bremen's communists analyzed the situation, threatened to strangle the local council republic within a few days as German banks refused to grant the city any further loans. Only a nationwide mass strike and proletarian dictatorship could solve this problem – but the prospects for these were dim.[10]

Capitalism not only constrained revolutionary agency through its structural power; it also appeared to hinder or derail such agency in the first place. Precisely because of its long-time alliance with authoritarianism, it continued to weigh heavily on proletarians' bodies and souls. Moreover, capitalism had corrupted these proletarians through incentives, so that they pursued individual or group interests rather than collective aims. This moral critique was articulated by many socialists, especially once the revolution had subsided and began to be reinterpreted through the prism of failure. At a gathering of Ruhr miners in the autumn of 1919, one speaker deplored the fact that revolution had failed to bring about the expected "struggle against profit-seeking, against capitalism's exploitative rapacity, against people's baser instincts." Instead, reckless materialism had become crasser than ever before.[11] Even the *Rote Fahne* (*Red Flag*), the voice of doctrinaire communism, was forced to conclude that workers allowed themselves to be pitted against each other through competition on the shop floor and thus reverted to acting as tools of the established system: "Let's not deceive ourselves about the fact that capitalism has at its disposal not only means of coercion but also means of enticement."[12]

These basic perceptions were to underpin Communist political culture, especially after several failed revolutionary attempts in the early 1920s. As stoutly as the party upheld its transformative ambition, it remained unclear how this transformation would eventually be realized. The accusation that capitalism usurped the governmental apparatus and crushed

[9] See John Peter Nettl, *Rosa Luxemburg* (London, 1966), 737–86, and Mark Jones, *Founding Weimar: Violence and the German Revolution of 1918/19* (Cambridge, 2016), 173–209.

[10] "Das Kapital erdrosselt die Räte-Republik Bremen," *Der Kommunist*, Jan. 21, 1919.

[11] "Bericht über die vom Werkmeisterverein-Bezirk Eickel-Wanne am 26. Oktober 1919 im Krupp'schen Saalbau in Hordel einberufene Versammlung," Landesarchiv Nordrhein-Westfalen Münster, B 406, no. 14439.

[12] "Akkordarbeit," *Rote Fahne*, no. 49–50 (early Sept. 1919).

proletarian lives attested to the destructive power it was able to exert even when in severe crisis. The communist future, realized in the Soviet Union and embodied by youthful activists, was juxtaposed with this dire reality rather than logically deriving from it.[13] To the Communist Party's leadership, revolutionary struggle appeared as an ongoing project that required further organization since members were insufficiently rooted in the factories and were held back by their own lack of initiative and ideological clarity.[14] Paul Levi, whose trajectory had led him from chairing the party to rejoining the left wing of the Social Democrats, faulted communists for really thinking of capitalism as "something insuperable"; rather than halting its cataclysms, they were waiting for them to produce further violent crises.[15]

The resilience of a deeply rooted economic and cultural system, while painful to acknowledge for its enemies, should have cheered up its remaining defenders. After all, their initial fear of capitalism's downfall by way of revolutionary transformation never materialized. Yet they too were seldom content with the state of affairs and the forms of agency it stimulated or prevented. From a liberal perspective, the problem lay in the arrangements made between government and business since 1914, and the ways these skewed individual initiative. Moritz J. Bonn, a prominent economist, conceded that industrial capitalism had benefited from the war economy and weathered the storm of 1918–19. But the captains of industry, dizzy with success, had abused their power by creating cartels and trusts, thereby undermining the very basis of the capitalist order. They had massively invested in new equipment, marginalized domestic investors during the inflation, and made themselves dependent on foreign loans. German capitalism had lost its capacity to provide better and more affordable goods, opportunities for small stakeholders, and incentives for technological or commercial innovation. For this stagnant state of affairs, Bonn blamed big business's inclination to protect its own position

[13] See Siegfried Kracauer's astute comment on Bertolt Brecht and Slatan Dudow's 1932 film *Kuhle Wampe oder wem gehört die Welt* in *From Caligari to Hitler: A Psychological History of German Film*, 5th ed. (Princeton, NJ, 1974), 247.

[14] For one of many statements, see Ernst Thälmann, *Der revolutionäre Ausweg und die KPD: Rede auf der Plenartagung des Zentralkomitees der Kommunistischen Partei Deutschlands am 19. Februar 1932 in Berlin* (Frankfurt, 1971).

[15] Paul Levi, *Der Sozialismus ist der Friede; der Kapitalismus ist der Krieg! Über realistischen Pazifismus* (n.d., n.p. [1925]), 15–16. American journalist H. R. Knickerbocker later remarked that Communists had turned Soviet instructions to hold back into the mantra "that the capitalist crisis has not yet gone far enough to justify an attempt at revolution." *The German Crisis* (New York, 1932), 176.

from risk and resort to authoritarian methods: "In the German syndicates and cartels, the idea of power-hungry monopolistic capitalism has harmoniously amalgamated with corporatist values."[16]

This was a widely shared diagnosis, but not all liberals were sure that Germany's current economy no longer qualified as capitalist. Like Bonn, Hans Schäffer, the influential state secretary in the Ministry of Finance, believed that businessmen called for state intervention and used cartels to shield themselves from personal risk, and that corporations were increasingly replacing entrepreneurs with managers whose salaries were decoupled from economic success. Yet Schäffer also mused that the war had led to changes that, while "irrational and uncapitalistic per se," recalled the fast-paced times of early capitalism.[17] Heidelberg economist Arthur Salz went so far as to declare that there had never been a pure capitalism. In its constant and unprincipled evolution and its elastic incorporation of even socialist influences lay "this capitalist system's true pièce de résistance."[18] Trying to "master" an entire economic order revealed a misguided "will to power over the facts." This, he contended, overburdened the state with expectations of virtuosity bound to cause disappointment and undermine legitimacy. Government could at most aim to compensate for the irrationalism of economic agents through carefully calibrated state intervention.

This limited concept of political intervention as a mere corrective to the deficiencies caused by self-interested individuals within the peculiar economic order of post-1918 Germany evidently fit into a liberal worldview. But it was also adopted more widely and tacitly by others. Thus, some religious voices drew on a moral critique of the present system to argue for change from within. They upheld the hope for an alternative order while at the same time acknowledging capitalism's resilience. "One should not be naïvely misled into taking these enormous collapses as evidence that capitalism will be unable to withstand the current crisis," warned Catholic social scientist Paul Jostock. "Its end is likely still a long way off." Moral

[16] Moritz J. Bonn, *Das Schicksal des deutschen Kapitalismus*, new ed. (Berlin, 1930), 83.

[17] Hans Schäffer, "Die Problematik der kapitalistischen Gegenwart," in Bernhard Harms, ed., *Kapital und Kapitalismus: Vorlesungen gehalten in der Deutschen Vereinigung für Staatswissenschaftliche Fortbildung*, 2 vols. (Berlin, 1931), 1: 38–52, here 48–9, 38–9 (quotation).

[18] Arthur Salz, "Wirtschaftsstruktur und Kapitalwirtschaft," in Harms, *Kapital und Kapitalismus*, 2: 3–31, here 16, 28–9. See also Alfred Weber, "Wirtschaftsfreiheit und Kapitalpolitik," in Harms, *Kapital und Kapitalismus*, 2: 423–34, here 434, who compared state intervention to pressing the right button on a machine.

pressure and gradual steps toward corporatism were needed in order to avoid both the advent of a socialist planned economy and the "danger of aligning oneself too much with the cultural image and normative order of capitalism."[19] In a similar vein, Oswald von Nell-Breuning, a Jesuit social philosopher, pursued a moderate line between condemning and accepting the capitalist order. He objected to the importance of "wild speculation," the "economic man of violence" who subjected markets to his own will, the impersonal joint-stock company, and "the lack of consumer discipline" stimulating entire "industries of vice." Still, Nell-Breuning did not plead for capitalism to be done away with but called for its transformation through "strict economic ethics" implemented by public administration and the legal system.[20] Both Catholic authors advocated taming the moral corruption and lack of personal responsibility fostered by capitalism through the gradual introduction of authoritarian or corporatist measures. By contrast, Eduard Heimann, a Christian Socialist, foregrounded its repercussions on the working class, which he wished to see counterbalanced by consumer cooperatives and welfare policies. He even argued that the gradual transformation of the economic system would save it from the threat of revolution, thus forcing it to tolerate the imposition of social policies.[21]

Heimann was a card-carrying Social Democrat, and his post-Marxist vision could easily be read as a theorization of the party's political practice. But it was precisely this that constituted a serious problem. For Social Democratic politicians, it was difficult to acknowledge that they could at best transform capitalism gradually from within rather than hope to put an alternative system in its place. After all, their actual reformism was already exposed to severe criticism not just from Communists and socialist splinter groups but also from the party's own left wing. To a considerable extent, Social Democratic debates on economic issues can be read as often rather tortured attempts to cope with this basic paradox. Time and again, capitalism was chided for reinforcing social inequality

[19] Paul Jostock, *Der deutsche Katholizismus und die Überwindung des Kapitalismus: Eine ideengeschichtliche Skizze* (Regensburg, n.d. [1932]), 206, 137.

[20] Oswald von Nell-Breuning SJ, *Die soziale Enzyklika: Erläuterungen zum Weltrundschreiben Papst Pius XI. über die gesellschaftliche Ordnung* (Cologne, 1932), 214, 187, 216, 217. On Nell-Breuning's moderate stance toward capitalism, see Noah Benezra Strote, *Lions and Lambs: Conflict in Weimar and the Creation of Post-Nazi Germany* (New Haven, CT, 2017), 59–65.

[21] Eduard Heimann, *Soziale Theorie des Kapitalismus: Theorie der Sozialpolitik* (Tübingen, 1929), 212.

and creating the dysfunctionalities that in the future would be avoided through careful economic planning. Yet Social Democrats expended much ink reflecting on how to secure its survival in the face of the narrow-mindedness of so many entrepreneurs, by increasing productivity, attracting foreign loans, or campaigning for trade cooperation with France, among other things. The reformist monthly *Sozialistische Monatshefte* even gave credit where credit was due, for instance regarding the reconstruction of northern France by private business after the war: "Capitalism has now taken the initiative. Is our party justified in attacking it precisely because it is on the right track?"[22]

The *Sozialistische Monatshefte* had no ideological problem with viewing government intervention at times as a means to restore the capitalist principle of free competition and at other times as the path to a mixed economy.[23] But this flexibility did not reflect the party line – namely, the commitment to a socialist alternative: "The capitalist economy is the breeding ground where avarice and egoism run riot," asserted the more orthodox *Neue Zeit*, "the insatiable desire for profit that drives people to hunt for wealth without caring whether the masses degenerate in material and spiritual squalor."[24] But what was the "idea of the global market's reincarnation and expansion," advocated in its successor journal *Die Gesellschaft* in 1926, if not a tacit acknowledgment that there was presently no alternative to the capitalist system?[25] To plead, as trade union theorist Fritz Naphtali did, for a political line that would "begin as crisis therapy and develop into a factor in the restructuring of the economic system" amounted to a contorted effort to reconcile economic pragmatism with Social Democracy's cherished transformative ambition.[26]

The depression of the early 1930s threw the contradictions in the party's stance into painfully sharp relief; the reassuring view that

[22] Julius Kaliski, "Ein Schritt auf dem richtigen Weg," *Sozialistische Monatshefte* 28, no. 13 (Sept. 12, 1922): 777–83, here 781. On trade cooperation through tariff reduction, see, for instance, Ludwig Quessel, "Ein Blick in die Zukunft," *Sozialistische Monatshefte* 32, no. 1 (Jan. 1, 1926): 6–11; "Deutschfranzösische Zusammenarbeit," *Sozialistische Monatshefte* 23, no. 6 (June 14, 1926): 362–7.

[23] Max Schippel, "Die Wirtschaftsprogramme der Industrie und der Arbeiter," *Sozialistische Monatshefte* 32, no. 1 (Jan. 11, 1926): 12–16; Walther Pahl, "Rundschau öffentliches Leben: Staatssozialismus," *Sozialistische Monatshefte* 32, no. 3 (Mar. 8, 1926): 169–74.

[24] Franz Laufkötter, "Der Wirtschaftssozialismus und seine drei Grundformen," *Neue Zeit: Wochenschrift der Deutschen Sozialdemokratie* 40 2 no. 5 (Apr. 28, 1922): 98–105, here 100.

[25] Wladimir Woytinsky, "Die Weltmarktentwicklung," *Die Gesellschaft: Internationale Revue für Sozialismus und Politik* 3, no. 1 (1926): 29–67, here 67.

[26] Fritz Naphtali, "Probleme der Krise," *Die Gesellschaft* 3, no. 7 (1926): 111–23, here 123.

"organized capitalism" was gradually creating a planned economy and hence laying the groundwork for a future shift toward socialism lost its plausibility. At the party conference in Leipzig in the spring of 1931, Fritz Tarnow's opening speech predictably blamed capitalism for having colluded with militarism before and during the war and subsequently failed to make good use of productivity gains and the available funds for investment. Instead, the leading trade unionist argued, business had formed cartels and trusts that had largely eliminated the price mechanism and created overcapacities. Having caused mass unemployment, employers now proceeded to lower wages, thereby reducing purchasing power and undermining capitalism's very basis. The delegates repeatedly applauded Tarnow's speech, all the more since he complemented the sober analysis with occasional jibes against whining businessmen, overpaid corporate managers, and ossified economic thinking. But what caused quite a stir was his frank admission that Social Democrats were standing "beside the sick bed of capitalism." "We are, it seems to me, condemned to be both the doctor who seriously wants to cure the patient while nonetheless continuing to feel like heirs who want to get their hands on the capitalist system's entire legacy sooner rather than later."[27]

Tarnow wanted to have it both ways, but he clearly leaned toward the doctor's perspective, prompted by the social consequences of economic depression: "When the patient struggles for breath, the masses outside go hungry." In other words, a wholesale breakdown as imagined by the Communists would have disastrous consequences for the working class as well as democracy. Consequently, Social Democrats needed to give capitalism the means to recover. Capital flight needed to be prevented and foreign loans secured through diplomatic compromises. Work creation schemes, an expansion of the municipal economy, and a reduction of the workweek promised to counterbalance the depression.[28] Several of Tarnow's fellow delegates strongly objected to his reformist reaction to the crisis. Instead, they advocated exploiting the tendencies toward a breakdown lest the party risk losing mass support. Otherwise, the initiative threatened to remain with the opposite camp: "Since the outbreak of the economic crisis, capitalism has shown the most remarkable activity

[27] *Sozialdemokratischer Parteitag in Leipzig 1931 vom 31. Mai bis 5. Juni im Volkshaus* (Berlin, n.d.), 45. On the party conference and its reception, see Heinrich August Winkler, *Der Weg in die Katastrophe: Arbeiter und Arbeiterbewegung in der Weimarer Republic 1930 bis 1933* (Berlin, 1987), 324–37, albeit without much attention to the capitalism debate.

[28] *Sozialdemokratischer Parteitag in Leipzig*, 46, 48.

while the masses simply have to put up with ... the crisis," lamented one speaker. "We have to show the masses a way out of the contradictions in which we have entrapped ourselves." But Tarnow's critics were caught between their desire "to put capitalism's sick body out of its misery as quickly as possible" and their reluctance to usher in the transformation themselves: "The breakdown will be brought about by capitalism itself."[29]

This brief *parcours* through Weimar's political landscape has demonstrated that capitalism, certainly in the peculiar shape it had assumed since 1918, was widely criticized. But the degree of agency ascribed to it differed. Capitalism often appeared severely weakened, liable to be coaxed into concessions, or in need of therapy and even life support. Then again, it was depicted as a formidable opponent, active to the point of crushing subjects or corrupting them through immoral incentives. Consequently, it was deemed sufficiently strong to constrain the realm of human action. Even the Communists, after their disastrous experiences during the immediate postwar period, were no longer preparing for the violent overthrow of the system. Carefully calibrated government intervention and gradual transformation, by contrast, were the results of acknowledging both the structural limitations of politics and the potential cost of dismantling an entire economic order. However, these measures were difficult to defend given the prevailing critique of capitalism, especially during the depression years. Acting from within capitalist society was likewise hard to defend – although widespread, this phenomenon had a limited intellectual pedigree, as we see in the next section.

1.2 CAPITALISM'S TACIT PROMISE AND FLEXIBLE JUSTIFICATION

Weimar Germany exhibited a wide range of economic activity. Investing money, managing a company, setting up a business, or selling a product to customers were hardly specific to that period and country, but they did, in this case, take place within a peculiar context. All these types of activity were marked by a need to react to scarce resources and drastic shifts, requiring unusual flexibility even by the standards of a capitalist economy. At the same time, they were widely deemed either suspicious or trivial in a cultural atmosphere replete with moral critique, appeals to idealism, and invocations of willpower. Against this backdrop capitalist agency was

[29] *Sozialdemokratischer Parteitag in Leipzig*, 60 (Franz Petrich), 73 (Paul Kirstein), 57 (Otto Jenssen).

itself a difficult sell. In the predominant discourse it was either attributed to foreign influences or repackaged as a nationalist pursuit – both of which often stretched credulity. But capitalist agency was also tacitly defended and in some quarters its ambivalence was recognized.

Since the period of inflation investing money was tainted by its association with speculation. In the early 1920s many Germans adapted to the new conditions and tried to make money quickly by buying and selling goods, real estate, stocks, or foreign currency. Yet it was far easier to blame this phenomenon on immoral materialists, often drawing on antisemitic stereotypes and hostility to the metropolis Berlin, than to acknowledge just how widespread such practices were.[30] In the years between stabilization and depression the lack of domestic investment became a frequent concern since it increased the economy's dependence on foreign loans. This was doubtless due to middle-class Germans' scarce means after losing their savings to inflation. Still, pro-business voices such as the daily *Berliner Börsen-Zeitung* wished for more activity on a stock market depicted as "sluggish," even inert. Due to the "passivity of the domestic capitalist public," the more dubious phenomenon of "professional speculation" remained predominant, leaving the economy without sufficient funds.[31] However, the line between legitimate and illegitimate investment remained blurry and contested. When the Ponzi scheme set up by corrupt Berlin entrepreneur Paul Bergmann (often known by his birth name, Sally Bergmann) came under investigation in 1928, it emerged that those who had purchased his worthless bills of exchange and recommended them to others were mainly noblemen and senior civil servants.[32] The Social Democratic daily *Vorwärts* gleefully pointed out that those who constantly preached about the immorality of the times had fallen prey to their own materialism. By contrast, the *Berliner Nachtausgabe*, a conservative evening paper, showed understanding for those who had hoped to improve their lot through unrealistic interest rates, while taking care to distinguish between work, the healthy basis of the capitalist economy, and the "mass craze" of speculation.[33]

Other forms of economic agency were problematic because they ran counter to vigorously defended notions of cultural continuity and

[30] Martin H. Geyer, *Verkehrte Welt. Revolution, Inflation und Moderne: München 1914–1924* (Göttingen, 1998), 243–56, 265–77.

[31] "Lustlose Börsen: Wieder leichter Geldstand," *Berliner Börsen-Zeitung*, Feb. 12, 1928.

[32] See various statements and reports in Landesarchiv Berlin, A Rep. 358–01, no. 2068.

[33] "Bergmanns Kunden! Adel und Hochbureaukratie," *Vorwärts*, Feb. 5, 1928; "Die Tragödie der Einfalt," *Berliner Nachtausgabe*, Feb. 1, 1928 (copy in Landesarchiv Berlin, A Rep. 358–01, no. 2068, vol. 4).

homogeneity. Publishing tabloids or pulp fiction, much like running a kiosk, a railway bookshop, or a commercial lending library, exploited the huge demand for accessible reading material. In so doing, these forms of profit-seeking threatened to undermine the cherished ideal of *Bildung* (education, especially the formation of a person's knowledge, taste, and character), which all sorts of organizations strove to convey to the lower classes. The same goes for film producers and owners of movie theaters who, moreover, adapted to regionally differentiated preferences to the detriment of Germany's cultural unity. Publicity experts secured a growing number of lucrative commissions, but their poster campaigns attracted the ire of activists for *Heimatschutz*, the visual protection of German identity. Notwithstanding their dubious image, they proudly presented themselves as American-style admen with considerable influence over consumers, whom they imagined as passive and feminine. Ironically, they were later faced with competition from American advertising agencies, which began to enter the German market with their more systematic and comprehensive approach.[34]

Antisemitic invectives against speculators and the admen's self-confident Americanism attest to the difficulty of imagining that Germans could be capitalist agents. Yet some strands of Weimar culture recognized this and even suggested that it might not be a bad thing. Novels set in the crisis-ridden present around 1930 portrayed victims of a merciless economic logic and contrasted their despair with the mean behavior of businessmen, line managers, or real estate agents. But they also featured characters who daringly exploited commercial opportunities, acquired new skills, or cultivated relations with influential people – all the while remaining capable of decency and generosity.[35] Berlin's liberal tabloid press described similarly flexible activities. Reports on a former window cleaner who opened a café, a singer who sold insurance, and a guide who offered a tour of the "world city in crisis" addressed an individualistic readership in need of advice on how to cope in a depressed economy. And

[34] Gideon Reuveni, *Reading Germany: Literature and Consumer Culture in Germany before 1933* (New York, 2005); Corey Ross, *Media and the Making of Modern Germany: Mass Communications, Society, and Politics from the Empire to the Third Reich* (Oxford, 2008), 156–62; Alexander Schug, "Wegbereiter der modernen Absatzwerbung in Deutschland: Advertising Agencies und die Amerikanisierung der deutschen Werbebranche in der Zwischenkriegszeit," *WerkstattGeschichte* 34 (2003): 29–52.

[35] Moritz Föllmer, "Kapitalismus und Geschlecht in Zeitromanen um 1930," in Martin Baumeister, Moritz Föllmer, and Philipp Müller, eds., *Die Kunst der Geschichte: Historiographie, Ästhetik, Erzählung* (Göttingen, 2009), 349–71.

this readership was by no means exclusively male. Tabloid newspapers explained how some women entered fields such as fashion advice or interior design, whereas others competed with men by working as artisans or private investigators.[36] Unorthodox voices on the left, far more negative about the prospects of life under capitalism, as one would expect, still showed empathy with those who struggled with it – not just industrial workers or the unemployed but also the fortune-tellers, small shop owners, and street vendors around the Alexanderplatz in Berlin.[37]

Such modest forms of economic agency received precious little theoretical recognition. Focused as they were on the nation-state in its international context and on large firms, economists paid scant attention to unorthodox forms of self-employment. This said, liberals' aforementioned critique of state interventionism reflected a belief in the aggregation of "squillions of individual decisions and economic actions" through the price mechanism.[38] Walter Eucken denied that entrepreneurialism had become unimportant, even in times of monopolistic cartels and bureaucratic concentration. In the machine, food, and textile industries, the Freiburg economist argued, adaptability and flexibility remained crucial to the success of a business. There was no evidence that these forces of innovation were absent in the Germany of his time; to flourish, they just needed a suitable political framework rather than the interventionism that the "masses" misguidedly demanded.[39] In a similar vein, Alfred Müller-Armack built his theory of capitalism around the notions of dynamism and historicity, which, he contended, were independent of whether companies were controlled by individual entrepreneurs. According to the Cologne economist, open-endedness and adaptability made for the resilience of this economic order, which was sooner or later bound to result in a revival of the "sphere of individual initiative and responsibility."[40] These liberal economists, who would go on to become two of the architects of the theoretical basis for West Germany's Social Market

[36] Moritz Föllmer, *Individuality and Modernity in Berlin: Self and Society from Weimar to the Wall* (Cambridge, 2013), 48–9, 51–3.

[37] Ibid., 85, 88–9; Graf Alexander Stenbock-Fermor, *Deutschland von unten: Reise durch die proletarische Provinz* (Stuttgart, 1931), 144–5. See also, of course, Alfred Döblin's 1929 novel *Berlin Alexanderplatz*.

[38] Wilhelm Röpke, *Krise und Konjunktur* (Leipzig, 1932), 51.

[39] Walter Eucken, "Staatliche Strukturwandlungen und die Krisis des Kapitalismus," *Weltwirtschaftliches Archiv* 36 (1932): 297–321, here 299, 301, 314. See also Röpke, *Krise*, 103–4.

[40] Alfred Müller-Armack, *Entwicklungsgesetze des Kapitalismus: Ökonomische, geschichtstheoretische und soziologische Studien zur modernen Wirtschaftsverfassung* (Berlin, 1932), 127.

Economy, were thus more sanguine than other liberals about the present significance and future prospects of capitalist agency.

Big businessmen, who sought public recognition for reasons of prestige and power, faced both criticism for their deviation from liberal ideals and the predictable ire of anticapitalists. Hence, they were reluctant to present themselves as capitalist agents. Insofar as some explicitly defended a positive view of capitalism, they tended to depict it as a past state, while claiming that the present economic order no longer allowed for much entrepreneurial initiative. "What we have had for the past twelve years," Rudolf Blohm, co-owner of an important Hamburg shipbuilding company and avowed conservative, declared in 1931, "is not capitalism but an intermediate condition made intolerable by the state's half-measures and steps toward a planned economy."[41] Much as they liked to complain, however, industrialists were themselves drivers of change, managing corporations and networking with fellow businessmen and government representatives, often beyond Germany's borders. But this was a difficult profile to own up to given the predominant ideal of the forceful entrepreneurial personality embedded in a strong nation – hence big business's knack for foregrounding larger-than-life figures such as Hugo Stinnes, Gustav Krupp zu Bohlen und Halbach, and Paul Reusch.

When interviewing Reusch during the depression, American journalist Hubert Renfro Knickerbocker expressed a certain astonishment that this confident ruler of a vast industrial empire so insistently spoke the language of national despair.[42] Other observers were less restrained: Austrian economist Ludwig von Mises pointed out that the frequently used notion of a *Wirtschaftsführer* (economic leader) made no sense in a capitalist context. Social Democrats poured scorn on business's contradictory way of simultaneously deploring and requesting government intervention. Communists ranted at the figure of the capitalist who purported to work "not, God forbid, for his own profit but for 'the German people,' or 'Christianity,' or 'European civilization.'"[43] These criticisms reveal

[41] *Stenographische Berichte über die Sitzungen der Bürgerschaft zu Hamburg im Jahre 1931* 444 (May 20, 1931).

[42] Knickerbocker, *German Crisis*, 147–50.

[43] Ludwig von Mises, "Die Legende vom Versagen des Kapitalismus," in Siegfried von Kardorff, Hans Schäffer, Goetz Briefs, and Hans Kroner, eds., *Der internationale Kapitalismus und die Krise: Festschrift für Julius Wolf zum 20. April 1932* (Stuttgart, 1932), 23–9, here 27; Herman Kranold, "Nach dem Youngplan," *Sozialistische Monatshefte* 36 (Jan. 20, 1930): 9–17, here 13; Stenbock-Fermor, *Deutschland von unten*, 115.

a broad irritation with German industrialists' way of understanding and presenting themselves.

Industrialists' self-understanding and public presentation revolved around powerful discursive connections between the individual and the nation. The rhetoric of their speeches, pamphlets, and interest group journals combined bourgeois values stemming from the nineteenth century with a modernist ambition to embody progress. Confronted with revolutionary uprisings and, in the west of Germany, the French and Belgian occupation, industrialists deplored "strife," "disorder," and "sickness." To return to the quintessentially German work ethic and entrepreneurial initiative, as before 1918, was the path to regenerating the *Volk* (people or nation) and restoring its unity.[44] Within this crisis discourse the emphasis soon shifted back from self-victimization to self-confidence. By the mid-1920s industrialists were reclaiming their agency for the common good of the nation; both needed "new room to live and develop freely."[45] The trend toward forming trusts and cartels did not, their representatives argued, undermine the "independent industrial and entrepreneurial personality."[46] On the contrary, the strength of the individual entrepreneur would form the basis for Germany's recovery – if that strength were liberated from constant government interventions and reparation payments. As one factory owner insisted: "We're going to show how things will start looking up again, once we're freed from our shackles."[47]

These quotations also show how crucial gender identities were for working around the discursive problem of capitalist agency. To assert themselves as "personalities" endowed with inner autonomy and strong (but chained) bodies was industrialists' way of countering the contention that they were no longer relevant to an impersonal economy.[48] Their opposite pole was the antisemitic image of the "speculator" with his sly masculinity and knack for

[44] Moritz Föllmer, *Die Verteidigung der bürgerlichen Nation: Industrielle und hohe Beamte in Deutschland und Frankreich* (Göttingen, 2002), 199–204, 256–8; Moritz Föllmer, "Der 'kranke Volkskörper': Industrielle, hohe Beamte und der Diskurs der Regeneration in der Weimarer Republik," *Geschichte und Gesellschaft* 27 (2001): 41–76, here 44–5, 48–9, 53–6.

[45] Föllmer, "Volkskörper," 58–66. Quotation: *10 Jahre Wirtschaftliche Vereinigung der Unternehmerverbände Abt. Baden 1920–1930* (n.d., n.p.), 5.

[46] Carl Duisberg, "Die Verbundenheit der Wirtschaft," *Kölnische Zeitung*, Dec. 20, 1929, reprinted in Duisberg, *Abhandlungen, Vorträge und Reden aus den Jahren 1922–1933* (Berlin, 1933), 326.

[47] Speech by the Barmen factory owner Mittelsten-Scheid, *Mitteilungen des Vereins zur Wahrung der gemeinsamen wirtschaftlichen Interessen in Rheinland und Westfalen*, 1931, no. 1, 17.

[48] See, for instance, Werner Sombart, "Entfaltung des modernen Kapitalismus," in Harms, *Kapital und Kapitalismus*, 1: 85–104, here 89–90.

exploiting good-hearted German virtue. Carving out a legitimate space for capitalist agency in such an adverse cultural context required flexibility – embracing Americanness, as in the case of the confident admen, or transcending established notions of middle-class respectability and female domesticity, as in some contemporary novels and the back pages of Berlin's liberal tabloid press. Having said this, the depression of the early 1930s could be overcome neither through capitalist activity nor through anticapitalist activism – hence the widespread expectation that government should act decisively to solve an all-encompassing crisis.

1.3 CAPITALIST CONSTRAINTS, GOVERNMENT INTERVENTION, AND THE POWER OF WILL

Could the German government exert a positive influence on the dynamics of capitalism, and if so, how? This question was intensely debated throughout the Weimar Republic and assumed an increasingly aporetic character in its final years. The Grand Coalition, formed in late June 1928, set out to pursue a wide range of economic policies reflecting its heterogeneous composition. It intended to reduce tariff boundaries, control monopolistic organizations, and check how the indispensable foreign loans were being used; to democratize the economy, rationalize agriculture, and support small businesses.[49] However, the government was faced with high public expectations, insistent lobby groups, and the semi-internal pressure from the president of the Reichsbank, Hjalmar Schacht. Time and again, Schacht painted a gloomy picture of the German economy due to the fragile mix of scarce domestic funds for investment and the huge public and private demand for capital. Since foreign loans were liable to be withdrawn abruptly and their importance made it impossible to lower the overly high base interest rate, Schacht argued, drastic budget cuts at all levels of government were the only right path to take.[50]

Several ministers retorted that a disastrous downturn was unlikely given how complex and internationally entangled the German economy was, and that severe cuts were "only possible on the basis of an enabling

[49] Chancellor Hermann Müller on June 29, 1928, in Martin Vogt, ed., *Akten der Reichskanzlei: Das Kabinett Müller II, 28. Juni 1928 bis 27. März 1930* (Boppard, 1970), 5–6.

[50] See his reports of July 19, 1928, Nov. 9, 1928, and Feb. 7, 1929, in Vogt, *Akten der Reichskanzlei*, 35–44, 203–11, 417–23.

act or other dictatorial measures concealing a political iron fist."[51] Schacht's opponents were aware that realizing their own objectives was only possible if the economy functioned reasonably well within a continuously favorable international climate. This is why members of government pleaded for the acceptance of the Young Plan, which restructured the payment of reparations. However, they struggled to make heard their argument that the room for maneuver was very limited. The campaign to vote against the Young Plan in a referendum was predicated on the assumption that a categorically different kind of political agency was possible. It contended that signing the treaty would render the efforts of "German men," who since 1924 had restored the "sovereignty of German finances and the German economy," null and void and would lead to an "enslavement of the German people."[52] When Schacht chose to resign from his office and openly attack a plan that he himself had negotiated, he deliberately fostered the impression that, as his successor aptly put it, "the German people have hitherto been governed by fools and cheats."[53]

This was the climate in which the two administrations led by Heinrich Brüning, a widely respected politician from the Catholic Center Party, had to cope with the onslaught of a depression. Even when the expectation of forcefulness was articulated with the best intentions – for instance, when the Duchy of Mecklenburg-Schwerin's minister of finance implored the Reich chancellor to act "like a ruthless dictator" lest "a radical *Führer* from the right or the left" appear – it put the government under undue pressure.[54] Its room for maneuver was even more constrained than that of the preceding Grand Coalition given the dire economic situation combined with a press that demanded decisive steps while triggering panicky reactions when such steps were actually taken.[55] Brüning's austerity stance had its inner logic but was so unpopular that interventions in

[51] Hermann Dietrich on May 2, 1929, in Vogt, *Akten der Reichskanzlei*, 626; Joseph Wirth on May 1, 1929, in Vogt, *Akten der Reichskanzlei*, 618.

[52] "Entwurf eines Aufrufs gegen das Volksbegehren zum Young-Plan," Oct. 10, 1929, in Vogt, *Akten der Reichskanzlei*, 1032–4.

[53] Reichsbank president Hans Luther on March 27, 1931, in Tilman Koops, ed., *Akten der Reichskanzlei: Die Kabinette Brüning I und II. 30 März 1930 bis 10. Oktober 1931. 10. Oktober 1931 bis 1. Juni 1932* (Boppard, 1982–90), 994. On Schacht's rather idiosyncratic turn see Christopher Kopper, *Hjalmar Schacht: Aufstieg und Fall von Hitlers mächtigstem Bankier* (Munich, 2010), 162–84.

[54] Koops, *Akten der Reichskanzlei: Kabinette Brüning*, 1469 (letter of July 30, 1931).

[55] Minister of Labor Adam Stegerwald on May 7, 1931, in Koops, *Akten der Reichskanzlei: Kabinette Brüning*, 1055; Chancellor Heinrich Brüning on Sept. 18, 1931, in Koops, *Akten der Reichskanzlei: Kabinette Brüning*, 1701.

a now crisis-ridden capitalist order could not be dismissed out of hand. Cabinet members discussed all sorts of options, ultimately tending to conclude that these had severe disadvantages or were even likely to backfire. To impose the mixing of wheat with domestic rye would damage noodle factories and bakeries in addition to being impossible to enforce with any consistency. To support export industries would stimulate attempts to coax the government into subsidizing individual deals with foreign business partners. But to restore free competition was also problematic since dismantling the Rhenish-Westphalian Coal Syndicate risked causing a series of bankruptcies that could easily spiral out of control.[56]

The two projects that exemplified the Brüning government's shift to the right – namely, the array of subsidies to East Elbian agriculture known as *Osthilfe* and the abortive attempt to conclude a customs union with Austria – were no exception in immediately raising thorny issues. If farmers received protection from bankruptcy, would this not affect the willingness of private investors to grant them loans?[57] And was it really wise to abolish tariffs with Austria? After all, it was pointed out, that country's market was much smaller than Germany's, and its shrewd bureaucrats would likely exploit the opportunities provided by arbitration. Moreover, there was a risk that the southeastern European countries, which the German government was simultaneously trying to woo, would demand the same market access Austria enjoyed.[58]

Any attempts at regaining the initiative were severely hampered by the banking crisis, which began on May 11, 1931, in Austria.[59] It then spread to Germany, dramatically exposing the frailty of its banking sector. The members of the government initially reassured themselves that they could not act as "mentors of the private economy," which would instead have to

[56] Representatives of the Center Party on Apr. 8, 1930, in Koops, *Akten der Reichskanzlei: Kabinette Brüning*, 38; Minister of Finance Paul Moldenhauer on May 19, 1930, in Koops, *Akten der Reichskanzlei: Kabinette Brüning*, 139; State Secretary of Economy Ernst Trendelenburg on May 29, 1931, in Koops, *Akten der Reichskanzlei: Kabinette Brüning*, 1135–6.

[57] Minister of the Economy Hermann Dietrich on May 6, 1930, in Koops, *Akten der Reichskanzlei: Kabinette Brüning*, 99. On the difficulty of stimulating private investment in the East Elbian regions see also Minister without Portfolio Gottfried Treviranus to Chancellor Brüning, Aug. 29, 1931, in Koops, *Akten der Reichskanzlei: Kabinette Brüning*, 1638.

[58] State Secretary Trendelenburg on March 16, 1931, in Koops, *Akten der Reichskanzlei: Kabinette Brüning*, 954, and May 12, 1931, in Koops, *Akten der Reichskanzlei: Kabinette Brüning*, 1069.

[59] For a recent account focusing on political history, see Tobias Straumann, *1931: Debt, Crisis, and the Rise of Hitler* (Oxford, 2019).

take responsibility for its own mistakes.[60] But the belief that the present problems should be solved "from within the capitalist economy itself" could not be upheld. The textile concern Norddeutsche Wollkämmerei und Kammgarnspinnerei ("Nordwolle") had received such massive loans based on fraudulent accounting that its bankruptcy jeopardized international creditors' confidence in the entire German economy.[61] Very soon, cabinet members felt compelled to decide how many banks were on the brink of collapse and therefore in need of government guarantees, even when the criminal activities of individual entrepreneurs would have made them liable to prosecution.[62] The German banking sector had neither prepared for a crisis nor shown solidarity, Chancellor Brüning fumed, but the government had to remain silent about such severe errors "so as not to unsettle credit." Instead of assigning blame where it belonged, Brüning was forced to listen to the US ambassador reading out a telegram from President Herbert Hoover, who admonished the government to confront its difficulties "with energy, prudence, and optimism," thus improving the economic climate within two to three weeks.[63]

During the last round in the perennial debate on the government's "constraints and room for maneuver," Roman Köster pointedly remarked that Heinrich Brüning has always been a difficult man to like, but this does not mean there was a clear alternative to his approach to the depression.[64] While this is plausible, the clarity of the chancellor's approach also seems

[60] State Secretary Trendelenburg (quotation) and Chancellor Brüning on May 28, 1931, in Koops, *Akten der Reichskanzlei: Kabinette Brüning*, 1130.

[61] State Secretary Trendelenburg (quotation) on June 20, 1931, in Koops, *Akten der Reichskanzlei: Kabinette Brüning*, 1229; Reichsbank President Hans Luther on July 1, 1931, in Koops, *Akten der Reichskanzlei: Kabinette Brüning*, 1267; State Secretary Trendelenburg on July 4, 1931, in Koops, *Akten der Reichskanzlei: Kabinette Brüning*, 1281.

[62] State Secretary Trendelenburg on July 4, 1931, in Koops, *Akten der Reichskanzlei: Kabinette Brüning*, 1281; Chancellor Brüning on July 11, 1931, in Koops, *Akten der Reichskanzlei: Kabinette Brüning*, 1328; Minister of Work Stegerwald on July 15, 1931, in Koops, *Akten der Reichskanzlei: Kabinette Brüning*, 1366; State Secretary of Finances Hans Schäffer on July 27, 1931, in Koops, *Akten der Reichskanzlei: Kabinette Brüning*, 1428.

[63] Chancellor Brüning on Sept. 5, 1931, in Koops, *Akten der Reichskanzlei: Kabinette Brüning*, 1656; meeting on July 29, 1931, in Koops, *Akten der Reichskanzlei: Kabinette Brüning*, 1453.

[64] Roman Köster, "Keine Zwangslagen? Anmerkungen zu einer neuen Debatte über die deutsche Wirtschaftspolitik in der Grossen Depression," *Vierteljahreshefte für Zeitgeschichte* 63 (2015): 241–57, here 248. See the classic article by Knut Borchardt, "Constraints and Room for Manoeuvre in the Great Depression the Early Thirties:

doubtful. Reading through the minutes of his two cabinets' meetings, one is struck by the disjuncture between the pressure to take bold policy initiatives, reform bad states of affairs, and arrive at a "unification of economic policy" on the one hand and occasional admissions of sheer helplessness on the other.[65] The chancellor mused that up to 10 million Germans might have to emigrate seeing that there was "no possibility for quick action." He also told industry representatives that the government "was forced to enter economic territory to an unprecedented extent because the economy had been built on sand. This sand had begun to move. It was difficult to contain these movements."[66] Brüning's drive finally to do away with reparations in the winter and spring of 1931/32 needs to be interpreted more as an attempt to take the bull by the horns and realign himself with nationalist opinion than as the master plan he retrospectively designed in order to defend his record.[67]

In any case, the chancellor's efforts to maneuver through quicksand could not live up to the expectation to solve the conundrum of an economic and political crisis through decisive leadership. With their reluctance to intervene in the economy and then their improvised measures against the banking crisis, his administrations fell short of the ubiquitous calls for manly action. While moderate politicians and Social Democratic theorists despaired over capitalism's simultaneous dysfunction and ineluctability, right-wing authors suggested that the solution came down to willpower. Werner Sombart insisted that the future of the economy lay "at the discretion of humans with a free will." Neither muddling through nor returning to a golden age of free trade were viable options, the prominent sociologist contended, only the autarky of a *Volksgemeinschaft* (national community) driven by either an "individual will" or a "collective will." Sombart's view was praised by one

Towards a Revision of the Received Historical Picture," in Borchardt, *Perspectives on Modern German Economic History and Policy* (Cambridge, 1991), 143–60.

[65] State Secretary Trendelenburg on July 12, 1930, in Koops, *Akten der Reichskanzlei: Kabinette Brüning*, 296.

[66] Chancellor Brüning on Oct. 2, 1931, in Koops, *Akten der Reichskanzlei: Kabinette Brüning*, 1793; Sept. 18, 1931, in Koops, *Akten der Reichskanzlei: Kabinette Brüning*, 1701.

[67] See William L. Patch Jr., *Heinrich Brüning and the Dissolution of the Weimar Republic* (Cambridge, 1998), 11, 150–1, 213–20, 256–8, 323, in contrast to the assumption in Jan-Otmar Hesse, Roman Köster, and Werner Plumpe, *Die Grosse Depression: Die Weltwirtschaftskrise 1929–1939* (Frankfurt, 2014), 71, that the chancellor was "led by the goal of shaking off the reparation regime and creating the conditions for a return to the monarchy."

reviewer for bringing "human sovereignty" back into economic thinking.[68]

More radically, Nazi economic discourse kept hammering home the idea that the dictates to which "high finance" subjected the German people via the reparation payments were unbearable and that all it took to escape such slavery was unswerving resistance.[69] Only "a firm and sensible financial policy offensive driven by strong, responsible decision-making and willpower," proclaimed the Nazi Party newspaper, the *Völkischer Beobachter*, "is able to subdue fate in the final hour." The Nazis felt vindicated in their antisemitic belief that international finance and social democracy were "brothers united under Judah's banner" when leading Social Democrats acknowledged that the party was acting as a doctor working to prevent capitalism's death.[70]

Yet the Nazis also took care to exempt key tenets of the capitalist order from damnation. They joined businessmen uneasy about National Socialism in cherishing entrepreneurial initiative. "Recognition of the *Führer* principle and the value of the distinctive personality," clarified the *Völkischer Beobachter*, "calls for the idea of achievement and the rule of selection to be applied to the entirety of economic life."[71] The Berlin party organ adjusted to the realities of the depression and supported its readers' efforts to muddle through by offering practical advice on how to reclaim taxes or apply for a job.[72] The Nazis' mix of frontal attacks on capitalism and attempts to win over many of those with a material or cultural stake in it was thus highly appealing for its unconditional emphasis on human agency.[73] When Adolf Hitler addressed an initially

[68] Werner Sombart, *Die Zukunft des Kapitalismus* (Berlin, 1932), 5, 41, 45. Ernst Wilhelm Eschmann, cited in Friedrich Lenger, *Werner Sombart 1863–1941: Eine Biographie* (Munich, 1994), 356.

[69] Gottfried Feder, "Betrachtungen zum Youngplan," *Nationalsozialistische Monatshefte* 1, no. 6 (Sept. 1930): 249–62, here 257, 252.

[70] "Die schleichende Transferkrise," *Völkischer Beobachter: Kampfblatt der nationalsozialistischen Bewegung Grossdeutschlands*, Jan. 10, 1931; "Unternehmertum und Youngrevision," *Völkischer Beobachter*, Feb. 10, 1931; "Propagandareden für den Kapitalismus auf dem sozialdemokratischen Parteitag," *Völkischer Beobachter*, June 5, 1931.

[71] "Die Privatinitiative," *Völkischer Beobachter*, Feb. 14, 1931.

[72] "Arbeit und Geld," *Der Angriff*, Jan. 30, 1930; "Ratschläge eines Fachmannes: Was soll ein Bewerbungsschreiben enthalten," *Der Angriff*, May 2, 1931.

[73] This is a different interpretation from the one given in Claus-Christian Szejnmann's "Nazi Economic Thought and Rhetoric during the Weimar Republic: Capitalism and Its Discontents," *Politics, Religion & Ideology* 14 (2013): 355–76, which stresses that the Nazis tapped into an anticapitalist consensus.

skeptical audience at the Industrie-Club in Düsseldorf in late January 1932, he sought common ground by breaking "with the view that our fate is conditional on the world as it is" in favor of an emphasis on "human effort" and, most importantly, "outstanding achievements by individuals in all areas of life."[74]

Even the Social Democrats grudgingly came to acknowledge the effectiveness of Nazi economic discourse. They were initially caught between claiming that its competitor party's supposed anticapitalism lacked any theoretical and political substance and recognizing that its followers were "caught up in anticapitalist activity."[75] Social Democrats even hoped to benefit from the division the movement had created within the formerly procapitalist camp. The lower classes would, it was argued, soon come to the realization "that national socialist ideas are bound to remain forever in the realms of wishful thinking and that a successful fight against capital ... can only be waged from a socialist perspective."[76] Serious doubts notwithstanding, the Marxist belief that being determines consciousness was upheld and led some Social Democrats to expect their own party to become capitalism's heir by profiting from Nazism's destructive energy.

This prospect, of course, was shattered in early 1933. Yet many observers remained convinced that the Third Reich would fail to deliver on its promises due to the structural limitations imposed by capitalism. Such a failure would have vindicated Brüning's prediction, in a letter he had sent to Hitler on January 22, 1932, that his extreme-right challenger would likewise be confronted "with the aforementioned economic facts and would have to continue along the path onto which these facts have forced my administration."[77] However, to a considerable extent, Hitler did manage to create alternative facts. His regime drastically redirected the economy toward the preparation of war. In accordance with its needs, it simultaneously limited the capitalist order – for instance, with regard to the stock market and foreign exchange – and harnessed the corporate

[74] Christian Hartmann, ed., *Hitler: Reden, Schriften, Anordnungen. Februar 1925 bis Januar 1933*, 7 vols. (Munich, 1992–2003), vol. 4, part 3, 77–110, 75, 79.

[75] Walter Pahl, "Der Run zum Nationalsozialismus," *Sozialistische Monatshefte* 1, no. 6 (September 1930): 864–72, here 867.

[76] Alfred Braunthal, "Die ökonomischen Wurzeln des nationalsozialistischen Wirtschaftsprogramms," *Die Gesellschaft* 7, no. 12 (1930): 486–99, here 489. See also *Sozialdemokratischer Parteitag in Leipzig*, 68–9 (Hans Ziegler, Breslau), 95–6 (Rudolf Hilferding).

[77] Koops, *Akten der Reichskanzlei: Kabinette Brüning*, 2217.

structures and entrepreneurial initiative this order offered. In many cases the scope of economic agency expanded after 1933.

Adam Tooze stresses that even Hitler's regime could not transcend the structural limitations of the German economy – namely, its twin dependence on imports to bring in commodities and on exports to earn much-needed foreign currency. But he also explains how these limitations were hidden from the public through complicated arrangements paired with dictatorial secrecy.[78] Notwithstanding periodic dissatisfaction, Germans had reason to believe that the Nazis with their emphasis on willpower were right after all. The press provided one-sided coverage of the Third Reich's economic successes and ample room for its ideological insistence "that the economy is not an unalterable fate, but that everything depends on the spirit and will with which it is infused."[79] Pre-1933 trends such as rationalization continued, but they were no longer matters of controversial debate. Instead, they appeared as part of the "struggle for liberation" or, somewhat less hyperbolically, as a way to make domestic labor more comfortable in the interests of German housewives.[80] Readers uneasy with the regime's emphasis on the collective good were reassured that the Third Reich cherished personalities rather than aiming to subject human life to rigid norms.[81]

While capitalist agency thus retained an important presence in all but name, it was ridded of ambiguities, a process in which antisemitism was paramount. Newspaper stories told of Jews acting as fraudulent salesmen or exploitative bar owners. Classifieds advertised a business's "Aryan" credentials or a position for an "Aryan gentleman."[82] Sometimes directly, at other times indirectly, the minority was thus excluded from the realm of legitimate economic behavior, even existence. Boycotts of Jewish owners of shops or companies and the drive for the "Aryanization" of their businesses implemented this principle with devastating consequences for their targets. Conversely, the most ruthless exploitation of any

[78] Adam Tooze, *The Wages of Destruction: The Making and Breaking of the Nazi Economy* (London, 2006), 35–325.

[79] "Ein Jahr Wirtschaftsumstellung nach der Saarrückgliederung," *Völkischer Beobachter*, Feb. 27, 1936.

[80] "Rationalisierung – eine wirtschaftspolitische Notwendigkeit," *Völkischer Beobachter*, June 14, 1936; "Kraftersparnis bei der Wohnungssäuberung," *Zehlendorfer Anzeiger*, Feb. 22, 1935.

[81] "Normung der Dinge, nicht der Menschen: Reichswirtschaftsminister Funk auf dem Bankett der internationalen Normentagung," *Berliner Lokal-Anzeiger*, July 1, 1938, morning edition.

[82] Föllmer, *Individuality and Modernity*, 119–20.

competitive advantage was now morally justified as long as it took an antisemitic direction. Non-Jewish Germans could acquire a business at a fraction of its value, exploiting its owner's desperate position, sideline a competitor by instigating a boycott, or enter a new branch of industry.[83]

Fraud cases shed further light on how antisemitism was used to justify the dubious activities of those redefining themselves as "Aryans." This is how several Hamburgers who were accused of having tricked their victims into granting them loans without the prospect of repayment argued in court. A woman who had raised money in order to breed aquarium fish claimed that she had been the victim of a Jewish blackmailer; a man who had erected a whole system of import and export companies had allegedly been forced to fend off the attacks of a Jewish consortium.[84] Conversely, a professional usurer tried to disavow his former partner by marshaling several stereotypes at once: he presented himself as a "victim of my own gullibility and good-nature ... which the Jewish legal consultant Rosen skillfully exploited through his knowledge of the law and his cunning ... This, in my view, caused my nobleness of heart and modesty of character to take a backseat."[85] One Dr. Isaak Wohlgemuth struck back, at least rhetorically. Incensed about accusations of fraud when he had only invested funds in the collective interest as treasurer of Hamburg's dental association, he wrote in no uncertain terms what he thought of his former colleagues: "I have no wish to call you colleagues anymore, first because I'm a non-Aryan (thank God) and second you did not exactly treat us, the old committee, in a collegial way."[86]

This section has discussed how in the 1930s, several German governments felt compelled to deal with a crisis-ridden capitalism. The liberal position that state interventions were counterproductive and that the private sector should sort out its own problems soon became untenable in the face of mass unemployment, the banking crisis in the spring of 1931, and, especially, mounting public pressure to intervene forcefully. While

[83] Frank Bajohr, *"Aryanisation" in Hamburg: The Economic Exclusion of Jews and the Confiscation of Their Property in Nazi Germany*, trans. George Wilkes (New York, 2002).

[84] District Court Hamburg, sentence of Nov. 12, 1937, Staatsarchiv Hamburg (hereafter StAH), 213–11, 2253/1938, vol. 1; Lawyer Dr. Drögemüller-Hasse to District Court Hamburg, Feb. 13, 1937; StAH, 213–11, 112/1940.

[85] Ludwig Walsen to District Court Hamburg, Aug. 22, 1935, StAH, 213–11, L 26/1937, vol. 2.

[86] Dr. Isaak Wohlgemuth "to the new powers that be in the pension fund within the Association of Dentists" (an die neuen Machthaber in der Versorgungskasse im Verein der Kassenzahnärzte), June 10, 1933, StAH, 213–11, L 5/1934, vol. 1.

Chancellor Brüning and his ministers struggled to come up with effective policies beyond highly unpopular budget cuts, the Nazis promised to subject putative economic constraints to political willpower and agency. The fact that this remained impossible even under Hitler's dictatorship was hidden behind a rearmament-driven recovery, skillfully narrated success stories, and antisemitic persecution. The tension between capitalism and agency, which had been at the very center of German economic discourse before 1933, appeared to have been resolved.

1.4 CONCLUSION

Public discourse in Weimar Germany was marked by blueprints for radical change, an emphasis on existential decisions, and high expectations of politics – all of which rested on the power of human agency.[87] Capitalism sat oddly with these ambitions. On the one hand, according to most contemporaries, it was socially unjust and morally untenable, therefore in need of transformation. On the other hand, it proved remarkably resilient to outside influence. It possessed its own juggernaut dynamics, even during the depression. Capitalism was widely seen as decadent, deficient, or dysfunctional, but it seemed difficult all the same to usher in its demise – hence a broad if tacit tendency to scale back strong claims to agency. There is no denying the substantial differences between liberal economists' skepticism regarding state involvement; Social Democratic and Catholic admissions that one could only hope to reform capitalism, not replace it anytime soon; endorsements of small-scale entrepreneurialism in some novels and newspapers; the predominant view within the two Brüning administrations that intervention was liable to fail or even backfire; and the Communist shift toward postponing the revolution while remaining committed to its preparation. Yet what united them is the realization that capitalism with both its rigid and fluid structures set narrow limits to what even the most determined subjects could accomplish.

[87] Peter Fritzsche, "Landscape of Danger, Landscape of Design: Crisis and Modernism in Weimar Germany," in Thomas Kniesche and Stephen Brockmann, eds., *Dancing on the Volcano: Essays on the Culture of the Weimar Republic* (Columbia, SC, 1994), 29–46; Rüdiger Graf, "Either-Or: The Narrative of 'Crisis' in Weimar Germany and in Historiography," *Central European History* 43 (2010): 592–615; Thomas Mergel, "High Expectations – Deep Disappointment: Structures of the Public Perception of Politics in the Weimar Republic," in Kathleen Canning, Kerstin Barndt, and Kristin McGuire, eds., *Weimar Publics/Weimar Subjects: Rethinking the Political Culture of Germany in the 1920s* (New York, 2010), 192–210.

The extreme right – the Nazis in particular – drew the opposite consequence from the dilemma that capitalism seemed simultaneously insufferable and ineluctable. They raised claims to agency, drawing on a language of force and willpower. Even their Social Democratic opponents had to concede that this was an immensely attractive vision, notwithstanding its theoretical inconsistency. After 1933 the Nazi assertion that economic structures could be subjected to political will was put to the test. It led to fundamental problems that could only be overcome through future military expansion. However, this did not become apparent before 1938/9 due to the recovery for which the regime credited itself, dictatorial control of public opinion, and new incentives enabling material and symbolic gains, not least at the expense of the Jewish minority. In the Third Reich economic agency was cherished and fostered – but it was redefined, however questionably, as agency beyond capitalism.

2

Aporias of "Political Capitalism" between World War I and the Depression

Martin H. Geyer

It might seem tautological to say that one of the many grave problems of the Great Depression was the state of capitalism itself. Capitalism – its history, its crisis-ridden present, and its uncertain future – was the subject of intense academic and public debate in Germany in the early 1930s. Neither before nor after was the term "capitalism" used in such a wide-ranging and controversial way. Just a few years earlier, Werner Sombart had opened the floodgates of academic debate, most notably in a paper he gave at the Verein für Socialpolitik (Social Policy Association) in 1928, in which he forecast a stagnating and increasingly bureaucratized capitalism, driven primarily by rationalization (as opposed to true innovation), in which entrepreneurs would become corporate bureaucrats.[1] The dramatic banking crisis of 1931 fueled such debates. The Reich not only had to rescue some of Germany's biggest banks and enterprises with what seemed to be outrageously high financial guarantees, but it also took full or partial control over them. Brusque as always, Sombart abandoned his earlier pleas for the "primacy of the economy" and set out a range of possible political solutions instead, from the "reactionary" (a return to the former "artlessness of the free market") and the "conservative" (rule by emergency decree) to the "reformist-revolutionary," but considered only the last option, a vaguely conceived "planned economy," worthy of support. Similar arguments could be heard on the left and the right, from academic economists, and, most prominently, from many outspoken

[1] Werner Sombart, "Die Wandlungen des Kapitalismus," in *Verhandlungen des Vereins für Socialpolitik in Zürich 13. bis 15. September 1928* (Munich, 1929), 23–41; Sombart, *Die Zukunft des Kapitalismus* (Berlin-Charlottenburg, 1932), 5, 12–14.

commentators on the economy. Among the latter was Ferdinand Fried, a writer closely associated with the journal *Die Tat*, the mouthpiece of young conservatives. The title of his widely discussed book, *Das Ende des Kapitalismus* (*The End of Capitalism*), published in 1931, made plain his position that the economic and political theory of liberalism and its institutional forms – namely, capitalism and democracy – were outdated or even relics of the nineteenth century.[2]

Fried's thesis was clearly a reflection of the times. By the summer of 1931, Germany's economic situation was catastrophic. "Crisis" was the word of the day. But was it only a sign of despair? As Moritz Föllmer and Rüdiger Graf have argued with respect to the various crisis debates during the Weimar Republic, the evocation of crisis also offered the chance to propose plans for a different future.[3] "Action," "acts," and "deeds" made such a future possible, even necessary, by circumventing well-trodden paths of historical experience and knowledge. Such words could be heard not only from Sombart but also from economist Alfred Müller-Armack, who was infatuated with Italian fascism: "Every attempt to evade responsibility for continual decision-making through acquiescence in the laws of development has been met by history with the summons to an ever redirectable, shaping and guiding act."[4] But in the climate of the Depression, it was legal theorist Carl Schmitt who most eloquently and influentially promoted the authoritarian state and the politics of acts and deeds on the basis of Article 48 of the Weimar Constitution: liberalism, particularly as represented by pluralism and democratic government, was floundering and threatened to paralyze the state.[5]

Capitalism needed to be tamed, controlled, and regulated, if not totally transformed. There was a consensus that a new, active role needed to be given to the state, meaning the bureaucratic state in the strict sense of the German term (*Staat*), as opposed to and distinct from political government. Yet calling for such a new role during the Great Depression posed its own grave problems. After all, wasn't Germany suffering from a dual crisis – namely, a crisis of both capitalism *and* the state? Moreover, to

[2] Ferdinand Fried, *Das Ende des Kapitalismus* (Jena, 1931).

[3] Moritz Föllmer and Rüdiger Graf, eds., *Die "Krise" der Weimarer Republik: Zur Kritik eines Deutungsmusters* (Frankfurt, 2005).

[4] Alfred Müller-Armack, *Entwicklungsgesetze des Kapitalismus: Ökonomische, geschichtstheoretische und soziologische Studien zur modernen Wirtschaftsverfassung* (Berlin, 1932), 218.

[5] His arguments are well summarized in Carl Schmitt, "Starker Staat und gesunde Wirtschaft: Ein Vortrag vor Wirtschaftsführern," *Volk und Reich* 9 (1933): 81–94.

borrow Sombart's classifications, what was this state supposed to be: reactionary, conservative, or reformist-revolutionary? Was its setup to be parliamentary or corporate, dictatorial or bureaucratic-technocratic? One central aspect of these polyphonic debates was the critical evaluation of the developments of the preceding two decades, ranging from possible missteps taken during the seemingly stable years of the Empire to the outright turbulence prompted by the war economy and its aftermath, including the founding of the Republic in 1918–19, with its subsequent social legislation and empowerment of organized labor. "Monopoly capitalism," "imperialism," "organized capitalism," or the *Wirtschaftsstaat* (economic state) versus the *Sozialstaat* (social state): these were the catchwords contemporaries used to describe the crucial intersection of economic and political developments.[6]

In view of the various efforts to conceptualize the economic development of the interwar period, first by contemporaries and then by historians and social scientists, the term "political capitalism" might seem too general and unspecific for analytical purposes. After all, isn't capitalism by definition always political? Nonetheless, my starting point is Max Weber's cryptic and somewhat peculiar usage of the term "political capitalism," by which he tried to denote what he considered to be specific forms of premodern capitalism, as opposed to modern forms of "rational capitalism." I am particularly interested in some of his central diagnoses, which stem from his engagement with early modern history. The term *Beute* (booty or spoils), which is closely aligned with ideas about early modern "booty capitalism," is one such example, as are the phenomena of "corruption" and "adventure capitalism." How do these phenomena relate to the interwar period? Do they just denote criticism – in other words, strands of "anticapitalism" – or do they address "real phenomena" of the postwar economic system? This essay examines the broad consensus that emerged after the Great War, even among liberal economists (including Weber himself), that economic leaders, their policies – and capitalism itself – had gone astray.[7] Language matters. Far from being a neutral description, the word "capitalism" always carries normative notions

[6] For a concise summary, see Stefan Scholl, *Begrenzte Abhängigkeit: "Wirtschaft" und "Politik" im 20. Jahrhundert* (Frankfurt, 2015).

[7] This essay takes up some aspects of the theme I have pursued in other contexts; see *Kapitalismus und politische Moral in der Zwischenkriegszeit, oder: Wer war Julius Barmat?* (Hamburg, 2018); "What Crisis? Speculation, Corruption, and the State of Emergency during the Great Depression," *Bulletin of the GHI Washington*, no. 55 (2014): 9–35; "Grenzüberschreitungen: Vom Belagerungszustand zum Ausnahmezustand," in Niels Werber, Stefan Kaufmann, and

and critiques of its object and thus often implies remedies or solutions as well. What did critics of Germany's interwar economic order actually mean when they talked about rooting out the phenomena associated with "political capitalism," and what, in turn, were they talking about when they called for the restoration of capitalism? Such formulations were of critical importance because they also informed crucial political decisions. Despite the prevalence of anticapitalist rhetoric (both explicit and implicit) and the implementation of interventionist policies, the restoration of a "rational" liberal economic order, a rejuvenated and at the same time tamed capitalism, became – and remained – an urgent task starting from the Great Depression. This was not merely an abstract theoretical debate about capitalism, for it always addressed certain enterprises, social groups, and individuals, and although not outright antisemitic, the diagnoses and terminology of political capitalism always provided springboards for antisemitic agendas.

2.1 "RATIONAL CAPITALISM" AND "POLITICAL CAPITALISM"

Max Weber's references to "rational" and "political capitalism" in *Wirtschaft und Gesellschaft* (*Economy and Society*) were cryptic and based on a very tenuous comparison between the past and the present. His intention was to characterize what he considered to be a new, genuinely "modern" and "rational," and specifically Western form of capitalism. As "rational" he described what economists call the free-market economy (*freie Verkehrswirtschaft*) with functioning, free, and specialized markets for land, capital, and labor. Ideally these were governed by the rules of a competitive market, which were communicated not least by a stable monetary system like the gold standard and by way of rational (meaning market-compliant) "speculations" on the stock exchanges. The market guided the behavior of its participants, who acted "rationally" through their "'capitalist orientation' of economic activity."[8] This argument was

Lars Koch, eds., *Erster Weltkrieg: Kulturwissenschaftliches Handbuch* (Stuttgart, 2014), 341–84.

[8] With regard to the following, see Knut Borchardt, Edith Hanke, and Wolfgang Schluchter, eds., *Max Weber Gesamtausgabe*, part I, vol. 23: *Wirtschaft und Gesellschaft: Soziologie* (Tübingen, 2013), 379–83; also Richard Swedberg, *Max Weber and the Idea of Economic Sociology* (Princeton, NJ, 1998), 45–53. There are references to political capitalism in the English-language versions – i.e., Max Weber, *Economy and Society: An Outline of Interpretive Sociology*, edited by Guenther Roth and Claus Wittich, 2 vols. (Berkeley, 1978), 1: 166, 2: 100–200, 238, 479–80. However, not all of them wholly convey Weber's original phrasing and meaning. The translations in the present essay are mine.

famously based on Weber's ideas about the Protestant – meaning Calvinist – ethic, which was said to determine and generate certain types of habit and behavior. This "modern spirit of capitalism" was epitomized not only by the entrepreneur who acted as a rational *homo oeconomicus*. The historian and political economist Weber did not forget to emphasize the historical role of the modern state in facilitating this process – namely, the development of the *Rechtsstaat* (legal state) and the *Steuerstaat* (taxation state) – including the guarantee of monetary stability, which is of some importance when we look at episodes of inflation after the war in most countries.[9]

Weber contrasted this modern "rational" capitalism with forms of "political" capitalism. This political capitalism, he noted, was a phenomenon that had existed in societies of antiquity and in the early modern period in the occidental world, on the one hand, and that could still be found in the contemporary, non-occidental world on the other. It was a form of capitalism in which politics and economic interests were closely intertwined and in which all sorts of individuals and groups of entrepreneurs, merchants, and bankers profited from and actually thrived on the exploitation of political power. In Weber's scientific language this was "the pursuit of opportunities for constant economic gains by means of the rule of force (*Herrschaft*) guaranteed by political violence."[10] This included the colonial economic system, slavery, and fiscal privileges such as various forms of tax farming and the lease of offices (*Steuer- und Amtspacht*) – in other words, economic activities based on political privileges. What also falls under this rubric are aspects of what Weber called "booty capitalism," whether in the form of state-sanctioned piracy or the violent takeover of colonial lands.[11] This encompassed various phenomena such as state-sanctioned monopolies and the "pursuit of opportunities for present-day booty acquisition by political or politically oriented associations or persons: the financing of war and revolution or the financing of party leadership through loans and gratuities (*Lieferungen*)."[12] Although veiled behind somewhat opaque terminology, all of these phenomena refer to forms of

[9] Knut Borchardt, ed., with Cornelia Meyer-Stoll, *Max Weber Gesamtausgabe,* part I, vols. 5.1 and 2: *Börsenwesen. Schriften und Reden 1893–1898* (Tübingen, 1999), 5.1: 1–111, see especially the introduction.

[10] Weber, *Wirtschaft und Gesellschaft*, 379.

[11] On booty capitalism in the form of war capitalism, see Sven Beckert, *Empire of Cotton: A Global History* (New York, 2015); Michael Jucker, "Beute," in Christof Dejung, Monika Dommann, and Daniel Speich Chassé, eds., *Auf der Suche nach der Ökonomie. Historische Annäherungen* (Tübingen, 2014), 17–46.

[12] Weber, *Wirtschaft und Gesellschaft*, 379.

booty – more neutrally speaking, what is today called "rent-seeking." This political capitalism smacked of what advocates of the new liberal political economy and eighteenth-century Republicans would have called corruption: an ingrained corruption of both the economic and the political systems. A characteristic manifestation of this corruption was the existence of monopolies – such as, perhaps most famously, the East India Company – that used their monetary power to wield political influence.[13]

As Weber emphasized, these older forms of economic acquisitiveness that thrived on the exploitation of political power had by no means disappeared entirely from the modern occidental world. However, he was convinced that they were economically "irrational" and dysfunctional and that, wherever they existed (also in the non-occidental world), they were being marginalized by the forces of "rational capitalism." This affected different forms of trade and financial transactions – that is, various forms of economic speculation: "trade and speculation in currencies" and "speculative financing of capitalistic enterprises and business associations."[14] Again, these supposedly earlier forms yielded to modern "rational" ones such as modern stock exchanges, the mercantile trade (*Warenhandel*), or the commercialization of investment banking and financing within the framework of the modern constitutional and legal state, which plays a prominent role in Weber's argument on the rationalization of modern life.

One further point is of some importance with respect to our period: Weber left no doubt that in the past, "Judaism stood on the side of politically or speculatively oriented 'adventure' capitalism; its ethos was, in short, *pariah* capitalism."[15] Thus, it was the other of "Puritanism" with its ethos of rational bourgeois enterprise and rational organization of work. Weber's argument was about the past; like all other groups, Jews came to practice rational forms of capitalism and thus abandoned this earlier "pariah capitalism" – an argument the rabid antisemites of the late German Empire and the Weimar Republic certainly would not have agreed with.[16]

[13] Lisa Hill, *An Intellectual History of Political Corruption* (Basingstoke, 2014); Nicholas Dirks, *The Scandal of Empire: India and the Creation of Imperial Britain* (Cambridge, 2006).

[14] Weber, *Wirtschaft und Gesellschaft*, 379–80.

[15] Wolfgang Schluchter, ed., with Ursula Bube, *Max Weber Gesamtausgabe*, part I, vol. 18: *Die Protestantische Ethik und der Geist des Kapitalismus. Die protestantischen Sekten und der Geist des Kapitalismus. Schriften 1904–1920* (Tübingen, 2016), 445 (emphasis in the original).

[16] This topic is pursued in Geyer, *Kapitalismus und politische Moral*. The debates between Max Weber and Werner Sombart about Jews and the origins of capitalism are important in this context but cannot be explored here.

2.2 THE WORLD WAR AND THE HARSH REALITY OF POLITICAL CAPITALISM

Weber conceived both rational and political capitalism as "ideal types." In other words, they are not to be confused with historical reality, even though Weber and his followers considered the progression to "rational capitalism" as both a natural path to and a consequence of modernity. There are many good reasons why historians are uncomfortable with the juxtaposition of "political" and "rational," and with all the underlying assumptions about modernization. As economic historian Barry Eichengreen reminds us, "[i]n models of rational agents efficiently maximizing everything" – that is, what Weber called "rational capitalism" – "little can go wrong unless government makes it go wrong."[17] Economic systems and economic actors are always embedded in political systems, with one always exerting influence on the other. Thus, one might well ask just how far in the past this supposedly outdated "political capitalism" actually lay. Although the nineteenth century has traditionally been depicted as the era of the triumphal march of liberal capitalism, contemporaries, including economists, were already reflecting on capitalism's real or supposed decay. They asked whether this decay was the result of tariff policies, the remnants of "feudal power," or the encroachment of – state-sanctioned – monopolies and cartels ushering in "late capitalism."[18] Likewise, many observers understood Germany's muscle-flexing imperialism and naval fleet expansion from the 1890s on as manifestations of a variant of what Weber perceived as "political capitalism." Rosa Luxemburg and Lenin's theory that imperialism is the most prominent and, in fact, necessary form of modern capitalism was the most powerful contribution to this ongoing controversy. Critics of Marxist explanations, among them many liberal economists, may have objected that capitalism and imperialism were not actually compatible. After all, imperialism inhibited economic exchange between nations. However, this does not mean they were unaware of the threatening encroachment by imperial

[17] Barry Eichengreen, *Hall of Mirrors: The Great Depression, the Great Recession, and the Uses – and Misuses – of History* (Oxford, 2015), 9.

[18] This very common argument may be found among authors such as Werner Sombart in his *Der moderne Kapitalismus* or Walther Eucken, "Staatliche Strukturwandlungen und die Krise des Kapitalismus," *Weltwirtschaftliches Archiv* 36 (1932): 297–321; Wilhelm Röpke, *Die Gesellschaftskrise der Gegenwart* (Erlenbach-Zürich, 1942); Alexander Rüstow, *Ortsbestimmung der Gegenwart: Eine Universalgeschichtliche Kulturkritik, vol. 3: Herrschaft oder Freiheit* (Erlenbach-Zürich, 1957), especially chapter 9, entitled "Capitalist Degeneration of the Economy."

(political) power in the economic field, including the lure political power had for economic actors, who were all too ready to renounce principles of economic liberalism.[19]

However, there was consensus that economic liberalism reached its nadir during and after World War I when "state subventionary, protectionist, and monopoly-fostering measures" proliferated and many entrepreneurs and businessmen eagerly exploited the new political situation to their advantage.[20] After all, political capitalism has always thrived where economic gains were to be made from armaments procurement. This caused considerable and lasting resentment, not only among the population at large but also among economists. One illustrative example was Weber himself, who from early on saw little good coming from the war economy, especially not from the economic planning and regulations that mushroomed during the war. Writing in 1917, he pointed to a "purely *political* economic upturn: a capitalism that lives off of government contracts, war financing, black-marketeering, and all such occasions and opportunities for robbery, which the war has vastly increased, and its speculative profits and risk, [a capitalism] that does not have the slightest notion of the profitability calculations of the middle-class (*bürgerlich*), *rational* enterprise of peacetime."[21] What is more, Weber saw right before his eyes "a wild dance around the golden calf, a hazardous hunt for those chance opportunities that well up through the pores of this bureaucratic system."[22] The result was a proliferation of freeloaders (*Schmarotzer*), idlers (*Tagediebe*), and hawkers (*Ladentischexistenzen*) – the latter an allusion to Berlin historian Heinrich Treitschke, who had coined the antisemitic catchphrase "young Jewish pants-peddlers" (*hosenverkaufende jüdische Jünglinge*). Weber also spoke of the "'Austrianization' of

[19] Most interesting in this respect is historian Otto Hintze, who keenly observed sociological debates on capitalism and the modern state; see, for example, " Wirtschaft und Politik im Zeitalter des modernen Kapitalismus" (1929), in Hintze, *Soziologie und Geschichte: Gesammelte Abhandlungen zur Soziologie, Politik und Theorie der Geschichte*, 2nd ed., ed. Gerhard Oestreich (Göttingen, 1964), 427–52; for a summary of the liberal position, which the author shared, see Arthur Salz, *Das Wesen des Imperialismus* (Leipzig, 1931). (In 1919 Weber saved Salz's neck when the latter was accused of being a supporter of the Munich Soviet Republic.)

[20] Rüstow, *Ortsbestimmung*, 3: 162; Eucken, "Staatliche Strukturwandlungen," 303, argued (without a direct reference to imperialism) that after the demission of Bismarck, the economy began to take the lead in the process of integrating the state and society.

[21] Max Weber, "Wahlrecht und Demokratie in Deutschland," in Gangolf Hübinger and Wolfgang J. Mommsen, eds., *Max Weber Gesamtausgabe*, part I, vol. 15: *Zur Politik im Weltkrieg. Schriften und Reden 1914–1918* (Tübingen, 1984), 347–96, 356.

[22] Ibid., 354.

Germany," which was simply an encoded reference to the Eastern European Jews of Galicia.[23]

The language Weber uses is significant: "business cycle of state procurements and war financing" (*Konjunktur von Staatslieferungen und Kriegsfinanzierungen*), "adventurers' economic gains and risks" (*Abenteurer-Gewinnste und -Risiken*), "illicit trade gains" (*Schleichhandelsgewinnste*), and the "new chances for opportunity and predation" (*neue Gelegenheits- und Raubschancen*). None of these terms, as drastic and morally charged as they are, apply to the realm of "rational capitalism"; rather they describe the phenomenon of "a strictly politically rooted predatory capitalism" (*ein rein politisch verankerter Raubtierkapitalismus*).[24] As in many other instances when Weber comments on general developments of his time, he adopts here the language of popular resentment and contemporary critique of both capitalists and the state that had become quite common by the end of the war. Versions of this argument can be found on both the political left and right, though the conclusions drawn were entirely different. The criticism of this political capitalism boiled down to a denunciation of the intertwining of private, public, and political interests and of the parasitic growth of what appeared to be war-based or, later, inflation-based profiteering.

Such utterances were not peculiar to the academic Weber. The left, especially the radical left, targeted the major economic actors involved in the debates over economic war aims, criticizing their self-serving defense of profit-making and annexation. But the radical right, drawing support from the formerly liberal parties, quickly took up that argument as well, and went further by identifying Jews, by proxy Walther Rathenau, as the real culprits. The focus of these attacks was on the wartime economy, with its *Kriegswirtschaftsgesellschaften* (war economy companies) and *Kriegswirtschaftsstellen* (war economy agencies), which provided powerful forums in which representatives of big business cooperated with (and sometimes even ran) state agencies in the distribution of raw materials and the setting of production quotas, supply contracts, and prices. Self-interested (mis)management, "usurious" price gouging, and other corrupt business practices were hotly contested topics.[25] Staunch advocates of liberalism not only condemned these practices but also rejected the alternatives of the planned economy or any form of *Gemeinwirtschaft*.

[23] Ibid., 354. [24] Ibid., 356.

[25] For the following, see also Geyer, *Kapitalismus und politische Moral*, chapters 1–2.

The problem was not just the structural deviations of economic development; the complicity of the very representatives of "rational capitalism" – the entrepreneurs – was equally worrisome. Everywhere one looked there were "war profiteers" (*Kriegsgewinner*), "economic adventurers" (*Glücksritter*), and "creatures of the war and inflation" (*Kriegs- und Inflationsblüten*) who were thriving on the political upturn of the war as much as on postwar inflation. Tied up in this were allegations of self-interested economic behavior, whether in the case of alleged manipulations of the currency or reparation payments. The scandalous fact that industrialists like Hugo Stinnes and many other postwar "profiteers" thrived on the postwar inflation and its vicious redistribution of property and wealth (the negative consequences of which were also evident in the bourgeois households of both Weber and Sombart) became firmly entrenched in German memory. Were not these entrepreneurs operating extremely close to the edge of legality? Did they not at times engage in deception and fraud, and thus undermine the established standards of business ethics and the principle of acting in good faith (*Treu und Glauben*)? Götz Briefs, a Catholic social theorist, already spoke of their "borderline morality" (*Grenzmoral*) in 1920. "Anyone who believes in the law is stupid" (*Wer an das Recht glaubt, ist dumm*) Weber propounded to his students that same year – the very same Weber who had stressed the importance of the legal state for the development of "rational capitalism."[26] The phenomena rubricized under the label "political capitalism" connoted the decay of legal, religious, and commercial ethics. It was in this atmosphere of resentment that antisemites gained adherents by depicting this capitalism as "Jewish."

After 1923 the crucial question was whether the stabilization of the currency after the Witches' Sabbath of hyperinflation would put an end to all of this. Would it weed out inflation profiteers (*Inflationsblüten*) such as Hugo Stinnes, Julius Barmat, and many others whose names are often remembered today only because they were involved in spectacular political corruption scandals? At first, there were many good reasons to think it would. A return to the normalcy of the prewar period seemed at hand, and this impression lasted until the onset of the global economic crisis. Then,

[26] For Briefs, see Geyer, *Kapitalismus und politische Moral*, 21; Gangolf Hübinger, ed., with Andreas Terwey, *Max Weber Gesamtausgabe*, part III, vol. 7: *Allgemeine Staatslehre und Politik (Staatssoziologie). Mit- und Nachschriften 1920* (Tübingen, 2009), 98; for the crisis of the legal state, see Michael L. Hughes, *Paying for the German Inflation* (Berlin, 1988); Weber, *Protestantische Ethik*, 175.

especially after the banking crisis, the situation in Germany once again changed dramatically: what had seemed to be a return to normalcy appeared in 1931 to be just another *politische Konjunktur* (politically generated economic upturn), fueled, in this instance, by American credit closely linked to the international reparations arrangements of 1924. The raising, distribution, and management of reparations fundamentally shaped the new political capitalism, not just in Germany.[27] Economically, this was mostly welcomed, at least as long as the boom lasted. As a result of the massive influx of capital, Germany had become a haven of volatile credit in which, as critics argued, all sorts of capitalist adventurers had thrived. Many failed with the onset of the Great Depression, only to resurface as the German economy slowly moved toward recovery.

2.3 LIBERAL DIAGNOSES OF POSTWAR CAPITALISM

The argument that Germany's postwar economic development was "unsound" almost always carried implications of degeneration, based on the idea that the paths of economic virtue had been abandoned in favor of some sort of debased and politicized capitalism. Although many contemporary economists did not shy away from crossing disciplinary lines to enter the realms of sociology, history, or philosophy, their arguments within their own professional field were by and large framed in a specific disciplinary matrix rooted in the neoclassical tradition. The focus was on prices: price distortions resulting from political-economic interventions including social policies and tariffs, price manipulations by monopolies and cartels, the artificial prices of the controlled (war) economy, and so on.

An interesting and quite illustrative example is the comprehensive analysis of Germany's *Nachkriegs-Kapitalismus* (postwar capitalism) published by the *Frankfurter Zeitung* (Figure 2.1) in 1931.[28] Originally staunchly democratic, the newspaper had become more conservative by the early 1930s, which was in part the result of I.G. Farben's new indirect ownership of it. The paper's business desk, which had always championed economic liberalism (despite its benign tincture of social liberalism),

[27] See, for example, Eucken, "Staatliche Strukturwandlungen," 309–14; Erich Welter, *Dreifache Krise. Weltkrise / Deutsche Krise / Politische Krise* (Frankfurt, 1931), 51–3.

[28] *Nachkriegs-Kapitalismus. Eine Untersuchung der Handelsredaktion der Frankfurter Zeitung* (Frankfurt, 1931), 58.

presented a diagram that tried to trace the causal connections between political and economic developments, notably the war economy, the war debts, inflation, the British blockade, and the *Friedensdiktate* (dictates of the peace treaties). The diagram further shows how those developments affected other increasingly interrelated phenomena ranging from the rising costs of social welfare benefits, high taxation and public debts, public intervention in the economy, and misdirected capital allocation (in the context of the rationalization drive based on foreign loans, in particular US loans) to the creation of economic monopolies, cartels, and public enterprises. Moreover, it also attempted to identify the negative factors at work in Germany's postwar capitalism, including political radicalization, distrust of the German currency (which was one reason for "capital flight"), and the weakening of the much discussed "entrepreneurial will." The diagram is framed so as to demonstrate that all of these developments culminated in the global economic crisis, triggered by the downturn in the business cycle in the United States at the end of 1929 when loans to Germany were liquidated.

The *Frankfurter Zeitung*'s diagram stressed the structural weaknesses and deficits that had accumulated since the war. Political factors had infused each and every aspect of economic life – the process led, in the end, to the Great Depression. The text that accompanied the diagram was critical in tone and strongly defended rational capitalism, which, in the view of this newspaper, had also become a distorted form of capitalism, the problems of which came fully to light with the economic crisis after 1929. Alongside the international postwar settlement, state interventions into the economy were deemed problematic. However, there were other issues as well. The "excesses" of the war and the inflation period apparently had not been altogether erased with the stabilization of the currency, and the types of misbehavior and misconduct by businessmen were many and varied, ranging from "the megalomania displayed by some of the successful entrepreneurs" and "the payment of outrageously high salaries to top managers" to criminal cases of fraud and corruption whenever "the opportunity arose to secure state subsidies for their own enterprises."[29] The newspaper's diatribe once again makes clear just how deeply postwar capitalism was understood in terms of its politicization, which resulted in the weakening of established business ethics.

This understanding of *Nachkriegs-Kapitalismus* must be seen within the context of a very broad and heterodox debate on the economic

[29] Ibid., 10.

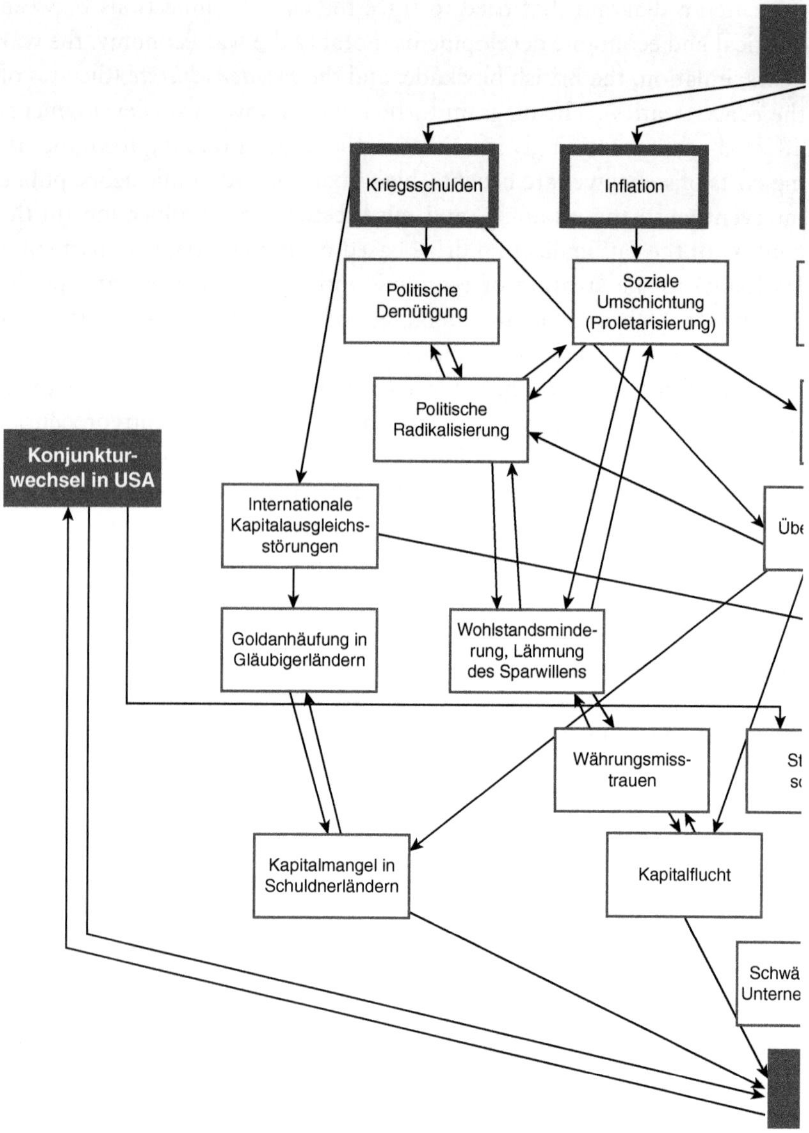

FIGURE 2.1 Postwar capitalism, based on the original diagram from *Nachkriegs-Kapitalismus. Eine Untersuchung der Handelsredaktion der Frankfurter Zeitung* (Frankfurt, 1931), 58. Redrawn for this publication and published with permission.

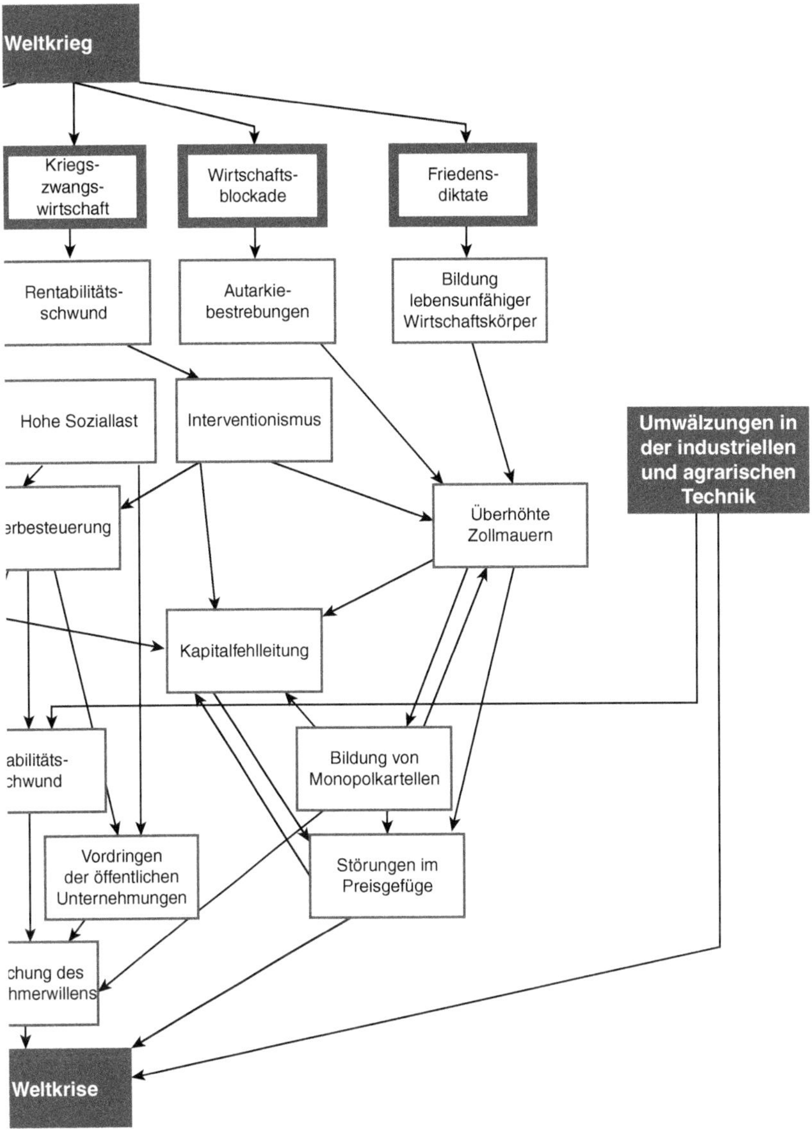

Weltkrieg
Kriegs-
zwangs-
wirtschaft
Wirtschafts-
blockade
Friedens-
diktate
Rentabilitäts-
schwund
Autarkie-
bestrebungen
Bildung
lebensunfähiger
Wirtschaftskörper
Hohe Soziallast
Interventionismus
Umwälzungen in
der industriellen
und agrarischen
Technik
Überhöhte
Zollmauern
Kapitalfehlleitung
Bildung von
Monopolkartellen
Vordringen
der öffentlichen
Unternehmungen
Störungen im
Preisgefüge
Weltkrise

consequences of the relationship between politics and the economy in Germany. Many efforts were made to explain and define the different forms of political capitalism in the broad sense of the term: first, as a system in which *das Politische* (that is, all things political) and *die Politik* (government policy) penetrated the economic sphere; second, as a reverse process in which capitalism penetrated and instrumentalized (economic) politics for its own purposes (such as the war economy or, as some argued, inflation); or, third, as arrangements between industry and labor that constituted forms of corporatism.[30] All of these interpretations were efforts to come to terms with developments that had started during the war (if not before) and had been exacerbated by the revolution of 1918/19. These developments included a vastly expanded system of social welfare policies, with veterans, widows, and orphans as new aid recipients and interested political actors, new fields of social policies like housing, and new institutionalized forms of wage-bargaining and wage-conciliation, as well as protections for the unemployed. Stunning to many were the self-confidence and bargaining power of the various branches of the labor movement with their affiliations not just to the Social Democratic Party but also to the Center Party and even to the conservative German National People's Party. For many this was tantamount to a revolution that overthrew the preceding period of liberal capitalism.[31] By 1927 Social Democratic theorist Rudolf Hilferding had developed the theory of a new "organized capitalism" in which the labor movement would exert political influence on the state apparatus and thereby the economy through its involvement in parliamentary politics. In fact, he envisioned what he called a thoroughly new form of "political capitalism" (which he described as early as 1927), in which the labor movement asserted itself, not least through "political prizes" connected to the issues of wages, social benefits, housing, etc.[32]

Mainstream economists and representatives of the business community were not slow to respond: their critiques first intensified in 1923–24 and

[30] For the following, see especially Scholl, *Begrenzte Abhängigkeit*, chapters 3–4.

[31] This was a widely discussed topic that more often than not was framed in terms of what could be called the social contradictions of capitalism – namely, that the growth and widespread economic benefits of capitalism were the very things that produced its enemies; see Eucken, "Staatliche Strukturwandlungen," 305–39, also Rüstow, *Ortsbestimmung*, 3: 139–94. This issue cannot be pursued further here.

[32] Rudolf Hilferding, *Organisierter Kapitalismus: Referat und Diskussion. Sozialdemokratischer Parteitag* (Kiel, 1927). See also the economist and greatly underestimated sociologist Emil Lederer's *Wege aus der Krise* (Tübingen, 1931), 30–2.

then gained momentum in 1929. The arguments they put forward had been widely voiced since the revolution: political capitalism with its "political wages" and "political labor relations" overburdened the economy, an argument put forward by Alfred Weber, a well-known economist and cousin of Max Weber. Accusations were leveled against *Politisierung* (politicization) and *Parteipolitik* (partisan politics), both of which were seen as transforming capitalism through the pursuit of their own political interests – namely, those of the labor movement.[33] The various forms of political interference in the economy offered distinctive ways of talking about political capitalism. They revolved around micro economic and macroeconomic aspects of "prices," "costs," and "burdens"; it was common to frame all of this in terms of "sickness."

But one should not forget that the authors of *Nachkriegs-Kapitalismus* also had many axes to grind not only with labor but also with the business community and farmers for their self-interested demands (e.g., ever-higher tariff barriers and subsidies for which the larger public had to pay directly or indirectly). As economic historian Roman Köster has demonstrated, it was economists and, one should add, the legions of economic commentators who loudly criticized bureaucratic companies for stifling competition, making the economy inflexible and driving up prices.[34] Large enterprises run by bureaucratically minded "general directors" (as opposed to entrepreneurs running their own companies) were anathema to many old-school economic liberals who diagnosed a loss of capitalist energy and competitiveness along with the spread of rent-seeking.

This mantra of market degeneration implied once again that something had gone seriously wrong not only within the political and economic systems but also with the spirit of entrepreneurialism. Thus the Austrian Ludwig von Mies, a staunch proponent of economic liberalism, condemned the malady of "interventionism" and "state and communal socialism" and also complained that "entrepreneurs and capitalists [were] no longer liberal, but interventionist and statist."[35] Mises

[33] Adolf Weber, "Politische Preise, politische Arbeitsbedingungen, Arbeitslosigkeit (1927)," in Weber, ed., *Sozialpolitik. Reden und Aufsätze* (Munich, 1931), 206–31.

[34] Roman Köster, "Transformationen der Kapitalismusanalyse und Kapitalismuskritik in Deutschland im 20. Jahrhundert," in Werner Abelshauser, David A. Gilgen, and Andreas Leutzsch, eds., *Kulturen der Weltwirtschaft* (Göttingen, 2012), 284–303.

[35] Ludwig von Mises, "Die Legende vom Versagen des Kapitalismus," in Siegfried von Kardorff, Hans Schäffer, Goetz Briefs, and Hans Kroner, eds., *Der Internationale Kapitalismus und die Krise: Festschrift für Julius Wolf zum 20. April 1932* (Stuttgart,

sarcastically criticized those "general directors who negotiate more often with state dignitaries and party leaders than with suppliers or customers." Everywhere he looked, he saw men in business who cultivated good relations with those "above and below" and who knew that clever political maneuvering when shaping tariff policy in arbitration committees or dealing with cartel and other political authorities could "benefit companies more than the greatest managerial prudence."[36] Without addressing specific individuals, Mises delivered an outright attack on entrepreneurs and bankers who played the political game. Similar arguments were put forward by Alexander Rüstow, who retrospectively voiced his criticism of the "monopoly-craving business community" that established itself in a "subsidized-monopolized-protectionist-capitalist" economy. Rüstow spoke of the "capitalist degeneration of the economy" and an *Erbgutverbrauch* (a using up of inherited assets but possibly also values) with respect to the foundational principles on which free market economies were built.[37] This was an unequivocally negative verdict on political capitalism, but there was no clear solution. And the lines of conflict, even among economists, were anything but clear. Mises presented his arguments in an anniversary volume for economist Julius Wolf. Known as a Manchester Liberal (and for having been Rosa Luxemburg's dissertation supervisor), Wolf nonetheless harbored what was considered an unusual "animosity toward booty income" and thus called for all "monopoly-prone" sectors of the economy to be transformed into public corporations.[38]

It is noteworthy that Mises could easily switch his line of attack. This type of new political entrepreneur was a source not only of economic inefficiency but also of corruption – in this case a type of corruption that

1932), 23–9, here 25–6; for a similarly sharp critique of premodern capitalist "feudal economic power," somewhat reminiscent of Max Weber's diagnosis, see also Röpke, *Gesellschaftskrise der Gegenwart*, 181–2. See, for example, the scathing criticism of liberal economist Moritz J. Bonn, *Schicksal des Deutschen Kapitalismus*, 2nd, enlarged edition (Berlin, 1930), 102.

[36] Mises, "Legende," 26–7.

[37] Rüstow, *Ortbestimmung*, vol. 3, headlines of subchapters 1.9 and 1.11; Rüstow's arguments in *Ortsbestimmung* are partially drawn from Rüstow, "Redebeitrag," in Franz Boese, ed., *Deutschland und die Weltkrise: Verhandlungen des Vereins für Socialpolitik in Dresden 1932, 28. und 29. September 1932* (Munich, 1932), 62–9. Likewise, Emil Lederer described the "crisis of the capitalist economy" as resulting from lesser "efforts of will" and a decline in the "elasticity" required to adapt to the new circumstance of a "using up of inherited assets." Lederer, *Wege aus der Krise*, 31.

[38] Erich Petermann, "Julius Wolf," in Kardorff et al., *Der Internationale Kapitalismus und die Krise*, xiii–xxvii, here xxvii.

originated not with entrepreneurs but from the very temptations posed by political capitalism itself. The new public economy, specifically the nationalization and communalization of businesses, was, in Mises's words, not only a "catastrophe for the public finances" but also "a wellspring of filthy corruption." He noted flatly that entrepreneurs who had received political favors had to repay the politicians with comparable "favors" eventually. In fact, he was convinced that it was common practice among big-time entrepreneurs to contribute substantial sums of company money to "campaign funds and charitable institutions and the like."[39] In an altogether different historical context, Max Weber, as noted previously, had already made the connection between political capitalism and the financing of "party leadership through loans and gratuities."

Mises's subtle insinuations fell under the radar of the public outrage expressed in the media and likewise went unnoticed by a good number of journalists and authors of various political persuasions. Fraud and political corruption had been a perennial issue since the war, and both were seen as closely related to political capitalism. The authors of *Nachkriegs-Kapitalismus* at the *Frankfurter Zeitung* spoke of a *Liebesgabenwirtschaft* – that is, an economic and political system that gives handouts to businesses, including farmers, and allows them to offload their entrepreneurial losses on the public. The term *Liebesgaben*, which originally meant "alms," small presents given to the needy, clearly had a second meaning. In the context of the ongoing corruption debates, it meant small presents and favors given on the presumption of a quid pro quo in the form of a return on investment.[40]

Starting in the mid-1920s, charges of political corruption gained traction. Many of the cases brought to public attention involved events going back to the war. By 1930, the case of the Sklarek brothers in Berlin and their supply contracts with Berlin's municipal government was just the latest of such scandals. It was energetically exploited by the political opposition, on both the left and the right, including the Conservatives,

[39] Mises, "Legende," 26, 28. For example, like many similar observations, Röpke's reference to the corruption involved in the Reich's administration of external trade ("Die Intellektuellen und der 'Kapitalismus" [1931], in Albert Hunold, ed., *Gegen die Brandung. Zeugnisse eines Gelehrtenlebens unserer Zeit* [Erlenbach-Zürich, 1959], 87–107, here 98) seems peripheral at first glance; it must, however, be viewed within the context of a wider – and sometimes vicious – contemporary debate, especially after the banking crisis of 1931.

[40] Geyer, *Kapitalismus und politische Moral*, chapter 3; *Nachkriegs-Kapitalismus*, 52.

and, above all, by antisemites of every stripe. The Sklarek scandal was a replay of familiar cases from the recent past connected to the names Sklarz, Barmat, Kutisker, Michael, and Holzmann. These scandals followed more or less the same script: (Jewish) profiteers from political capitalism had supposedly established themselves "parasitically" throughout the political system of the Republic by "buying" its political leaders and judges. They revolved around supply contracts and loans from public credit institutions and various forms of real or supposed bribes. They implicated not just the democratic parties and Jewish businessmen but also heavy industry (and, by implication, the German People's Party), as in the case of restitution for services in connection with reparations in 1923. They also involved the German National People's Party and its connections to bankrupt agrarian financial institutions and later to the *Osthilfe* (aid to the farmers in the eastern provinces of Prussia) of the Brüning government. All these cases smacked of political favors, graft, and corruption. Likewise, Mises alluded to "election funds" in connection with the Reich presidential election of 1932. Although we know little about the details, it was clear that the entrepreneurs and companies rescued by the Brüning government had donated significantly both to Brüning's campaign and to the reelection bid of President Hindenburg. While many of the rumors circulating about "political donations" were exaggerated, they contained grains of truth inasmuch as they focused on the connections between seemingly self-serving economic interests and politics at a time when state finances were in dire straits.[41] With the onset of the Depression, the situation fueled arguments about the decay not only of entrepreneurialism but also of political capitalism – all of this appeared to have become a "systemic question" – that is, an indictment of Weimar's political and economic *System*.

2.4 ECONOMIC CRISIS AND THE CRISIS OF THE STATE

Who was to blame? Capitalism and capitalists (including the farming interests), labor and the political left, or Weimar's system of economic interventionism as it had emerged since the war? In 1929–30 perceptions changed, not least when it became apparent that Chancellor Heinrich Brüning's new government was pursuing a course of austerity and economic reform. He was by no means the only person in Germany who thought that utilizing the emergency powers granted to the Reich

[41] Geyer, *Kapitalismus und politische Moral*, chapter 7.

government by the constitution, in combination with a strong executive state, would be preferable to deadlocked and ineffective parliamentary rule. That view enjoyed wide support among the bureaucratic and technocratic economic elites, who were, however, undecided on the course to take.[42] Most conspicuous was the appeal of the new forms of *Ordnungsdenken* (thinking about or conceiving of order), which became firmly rooted in juridical, economic, and social science thought and thrived on propositions to create new forms of "order."[43] Its mantras were "deeds," "decisions," and "measures to be taken." These catchwords developed a life of their own – in particular, ironically, through their use in attacks on the government's austerity measures. The overarching political aim of *Ordnungsdenken* was to restore the authority of the state and government in the midst of what was conceived at the time not only as an economic crisis but also as a fundamental constitutional crisis – a crisis or emergency of the state.

But it was hard to know where to start: with the remnants of liberal unregulated "Manchester capitalism," in particular the unfettered banks that crashed in 1931? With the costly welfare state? With monopolies and cartels, corruption, and various aspects of the prevalent business ethics? Relying on the state to pick itself up by its bootstraps and restore order by political means was all the more difficult since so much criticism had been directed against those very bootstraps – namely, Weimar's parliamentary state and the legislation enacted over the previous decade. For Social Democratic legal theorist Hermann Heller, it remained unclear "in which areas of public life the state was to act as an authority and which limits on its authority it needed to respect in accordance with the will of its spokesmen." Addressing the government of Franz von Papen, which so obviously rejected the Republic's constitutional-political order and welfare state, Heller declared that the slogan of what he called the new "authoritarian liberalism" was actually "freedom of the economy from the state."[44] At

[42] Moritz Föllmer, "Der 'kranke Volkskörper': Industrielle, hohe Beamte und der Diskurs der nationalen Regeneration in der Weimarer Republik," *Geschichte und Gesellschaft* 27 (2001): 41–67; Geyer, "What Crisis?"

[43] Ernst-Wolfgang Böckenförde, "Ordnungsdenken, konkretes," *Historisches Wörterbuch der Philosophie*, vol. 6 (Basel, 1984), 1312–15; Lutz Raphael, "Radikales Ordnungsdenken und die Organisation totalitärer Herrschaft: Weltanschauungseliten und Humanwissenschaftler im NS-Regime," *Geschichte und Gesellschaft* 32 (2001): 445–66.

[44] Hermann Heller, "Autoritärer Liberalismus?" *Die neue Rundschau* 44 (1933): 289–98, here 292, 295; Heller's essay was an acidic response to Schmitt's speech "Starker Staat und gesunde Wirtschaft." Heller also addressed the book by Walther Schotte, *Der Neue Staat*

a time when the state was being called upon to rescue failed banks and industrial enterprises, the cry for freedom for the economy appeared contradictory indeed.

Using the state to rein in economic interests was not a new idea in Germany. One found it not only on the political left but also among Catholic economists, conservatives, and, especially since the onset of the Depression, among some of the outspoken advocates of economic liberalism. As early as 1923, Wilhelm Röpke, then a rising young star among German neoclassical economists, advocated a new liberalism. His starting point was "the suspension of the market economy" and the inefficiency of public regulations. The entrepreneurial spirit, he argued, was under threat from "the rule of the state-licensed and state-promoted monopolism of the war and transition economy." Against this background, Röpke saw the weakening of liberal positions among the major parties, all of which tried to "pander to the anti-liberal sentiments of the population." The only way out of this predicament, which he believed undermined and weakened political liberalism as much as it did economic liberalism, was to rid liberalism of its image as an ideological advocate of a *Nachtwächterstaat* (night watchman state) that merely guarded the premises of a laissez-faire order. This reputation arose from liberalism's perceived "sterility in social policy" and its opposition to executive power in all its forms and varieties. In order to combat this image, Röpke thought it necessary to put liberalism at the forefront of the defense of the state against economic monopoly interest.[45] In other words, he argued not only against the overpowering regulatory state but also against the "parasitical satrapies of the private sector." Such a defense of the bureaucratic state was all the easier insofar as Röpke considered the state the "embodiment of the common good that stands above the interests of [particular] groups."[46] Like many others, during the hyperinflation Röpke realized that the authority of the state was already just as poorly valued as the German currency and that only vast emergency powers offered a way out.

Carl Schmitt was another voice in the debate on the economic role of the state. An outspoken detractor of liberalism, he adapted like a chameleon to the changing constellations of politics and audiences.

(Berlin, 1932), generally understood as representing Papen's agenda. See also Dieter Haselbach, *Autoritärer Liberalismus und Soziale Marktwirtschaft* (Baden-Baden, 1991), 59–65, 297.

[45] Wilhelm Röpke, "Wirtschaftlicher Liberalismus und Staatsgedanke" (1923), in *Gegen die Brandung*, 42–6, here 42–3.

[46] Ibid., 45.

With his many memorable adages – "Liberalism has its roots partly in economics, partly in ethics and is, moreover, an artful system of methods for weakening the state" – he made himself heard outside of juridical circles.[47] Prima facie, Schmitt did not attack political capitalism for serving the economic interests of either the working class or business, though there can be no doubt that his sympathies lay with the latter. His critique was focused on parliamentarism, which, he believed, transformed "all public affairs" into "occasions for booty and compromise for parties and their loyalty groups." Moreover, he attacked "die argumentierende Öffentlichkeit" (the arguing public), meaning the independent press, which in his mind had become nothing more than a fiction that served to camouflage the power of economic interest groups.[48] Leveling this charge for the first time in 1926, Schmitt did not specify exactly whether he was thinking about social or tariff policies, the *Fürstenteignung* (the expropriation of German princes whose rights he explicitly defended), or the ongoing debates on bribery and corruption in connection with economic scandals. For him, the state was "sometimes a victim, sometimes the product of bargaining, an object of compromise between powerful social and economic groups, an agglomeration of heterogeneous factors, parties, interest groups, economic firms, labor unions, churches, etc."[49]

Echoes of Max Weber's comments on political capitalism are discernable here: *Der Staat* had become a *Wirtschaftsstaat* and subsequently the "booty" of business and political interest groups; these fetters had to be broken.[50] The goal was a strong state that possessed legitimacy and the capacity to govern. Schmitt's argument was that the state had to shed its involvement in almost everything if it was to govern. As he explained to industrialists and merchants in the Ruhr at the end of 1932: "Today's German state, entirely because of its weakness and lack of resistance, its overall incapacity, must endure the onslaught of parties and organized

[47] Carl Schmitt, "Wesen und Werden des fascistischen Staates (book review of Erwin von Beckerath, *Wesen und Werden des fascistischen Staates*, 1927)," *Schmollers Jahrbuch für Gesetzgebung, Verwaltung und Volkswirtschaft im Deutschen Reich* 53/1 (1927): 107–13, here 109.

[48] Carl Schmitt, "Der Gegensatz von Parlamentarismus und moderner Massendemokratie" (1926), in Schmitt, *Positionen und Begriffe: Im Kampf mit Weimar–Genf–Versailles 1923–1939* (Berlin, 1988), 52–66, here 55–6.

[49] Carl Schmitt, "Staatsethik und pluralistischer Staat" (1930), in Schmitt, *Positionen und Begriffe*, 133–45, 136.

[50] For these debates (many of which were inspired by Max Weber) with reverberations also in the later works of Joseph Schumpeter and Friedrich A. Hayek, see William E. Scheuerman, *Carl Schmitt: The End of Law* (Lanham, MD, 1999).

interests. . . . Its expansion is not the result of its strength, but rather of its weakness."[51] Redrawing the boundaries of state activity was the precondition for redrawing political capitalism and installing a new – state-centered – political governmentality.

Schmitt's apodictic statements overlapped with similar ideas and solutions presented not just by academics but also by politicians and bureaucrats. These arguments were fueled by the crisis of parliamentary democracy since 1930, itself exacerbated by a pervasive critique of parliamentarism and what was by then generally considered the narrow-mindedness of interest group politics. Not everyone who used this language was a "Schmittian," yet it is hard to overlook just how much, for example, neoliberal economists Walter Eucken and Alexander Rüstow were indebted to the legal theorist. Whereas, for Eucken, the interventionism of the Bismarckian state had still been characterized by the primacy of politics,[52] state interventionism after Bismarck was characterized by the primacy of economics: business interests had come to dominate the state. This not only led to "the shackling of the state by business," but subsequently undermined "the autonomy of the state's decision-making process." As a result, the state's exercise of power reflected less its own will than the will of interest groups, something that even the best system of civil service could not change substantially.[53] From here, it was only a short step to depicting the state as having become, in the words of Alexander Rüstow, the "booty" of "greedy business interests," or as having been conquered by "an ad hoc mafia-like company."[54] One would have expected to hear such arguments at a Communist Party agitprop event or in a play by Bertolt Brecht, not at a meeting of the Verein für Socialpolitik in 1932.

[51] Schmitt, "Starker Staat und gesunde Wirtschaft," 84.

[52] Eucken, "Staatliche Strukturwandlungen," 303; although without references to Schmitt and this debate, see Martin H. Geyer, "Bismarcks Erbe – Welches Erbe? Die sozialpolitischen Auseinandersetzungen während der Weimarer Republik," in Lothar Machtan, ed., *Bismarcks Sozialstaat: Beiträge zur Geschichte der Sozialpolitik und zur sozialpolitischen Geschichtsschreibung* (Frankfurt, 1994), 280–309.

[53] Eucken, "Staatlicher Strukturwandlungen," 307.

[54] Alexander Rüstow, "Interessenpolitik oder Staatspolitik," *Der deutsche Volkswirt* 6 (1932): 169–72, here 171; see Rüstow's oral contribution in *Deutschland und die Weltkrise: Verhandlungen des Vereins für Socialpolitik in Dresden 1932; 28. und 29. September 1932* (Munich, 1932), 62–9, here 67. Much of this was reprinted in Rüstow, *Ortsbestimmung*, vol. 3, in a chapter on the "pluralistische Zersetzung des Staates." See also Müller-Armack, *Entwicklungsgesetze des Kapitalismus*, 110–11.

2.5 AUTHORITARIAN LIBERALISM AND THE RISE OF NAZI BOOTY CAPITALISM

The appeal of aporias is that they seem to help solve contradictory issues; they call for a turnaround, for far-reaching reforms, possibly even a "revolution" – something that Sombart and other diehard critics of capitalism such as Ferdinand Fried or the *völkisch* (nationalistic) Gottfried Feder were talking about. Or could seemingly degenerate – political – capitalism be tamed and restored to its "rational form"? The challenge facing Germany was not just to find a way out of the Depression; it also needed to reorganize the regulatory framework of its economic system (including the institutional setup of its welfare state) and, not least, to restore the once vibrant capitalist ethic among its entrepreneurs. These challenges were all the greater given the rejection of "economic rationality," not just among large parts of the proletariat but also by the likes of Ferdinand Fried.[55]

Given the overlap between the ideas and critiques put forth in the debate on political capitalism, it is not easy to sort out and identify the various actors and their interests. Although discredited, liberalism, in the guise of a "new liberalism," had its defenders.[56] Opponents spoke of an "authoritarian liberalism" (Hermann Heller), which others then called "neoliberalism."[57] Others voiced similar ideas. A prime example is economist and keen social observer Franz Eulenburg, who in 1932 evaluated recent state interventions into the economy by means of emergency degrees. All of those measures, he concluded, aimed "to save and improve the market economy." Such interventions, in his view, did not exclude forms of state economic regulation in areas ranging from social to fiscal policy – on the contrary. "Starker Staat," a strong state, was Eulenburg's mantra[58]

[55] For a broad (and somewhat pessimistic) liberal take on the question of whether "economic rationality" has ever determined human behavior, see Richard Behrendt, "Wirtschaft und Politik im 'reinen Kapitalismus': Zur Problematik des Zusammenhanges zwischen Politik und Wirtschaft (parts I and II)," *Schmollers Jahrbuch für Gesetzgebung, Verwaltung und Volkswirtschaft im Deutschen Reich* 57 (1933): 223–45, 337–72. This point is very prominent among Eucken, Röpke, and Müller-Armack. It let them delve deeply into issues of cultural history and, in the case of Eucken, issues of religion.

[56] Rüstow, "Oral Contribution," 69.

[57] Heller, "Autoritärer Liberalismus?" 297. Only in the early 1950s was this label used as an autonym to define what came to be called "Ordo-liberalism" and its version of the so-called social market economy; see Ralf Ptak, *Vom Ordoliberalismus zur Sozialen Marktwirtschaft: Stationen des Neoliberalismus in Deutschland* (Opladen, 2004).

[58] Franz Eulenburg, "Ne Laissez Pas Aller!" in Kardorff et al., *Der Internationale Kapitalismus und die Krise*, 30–42, here 37. Erich Welter of the *Frankfurter Zeitung* was also optimistic about the return to a functioning "market economy," thanks to the

Such reasoning was reflected in the actions of the various presidential cabinets after 1930, even if, as one high official in the Reich Ministry of Finance noted, the cabinet often resembled a fire brigade racing from one fire to another as it tried to save capitalism from capitalists.[59] By 1931 an overarching consensus had emerged to obliterate the various forms and consequences of postwar political capitalism: reparations (which were widely held to be the root of all Germany's political problems), "political" wages and social welfare benefits, unregulated banks, various forms of corruption, and hundreds of other issues. More often than not, each of these issues was diagnosed as a contemporary "sickness," the cause of which often appeared to lie in the wartime origins and postwar setup of the Weimar constitutional and federal state.

If the return to forms of "rational capitalism" is understood as an effort to regulate the economy (including social policy, for example) in order to restore the framework for what contemporaries considered a competitive market economy, it becomes easier to understand the middle- and long-term effects of the economic crisis in Germany. These efforts undertaken since the onset of the Depression overlapped with others, especially after 1936, to engineer the war economy. However, more recent studies have convincingly argued that the 1930s witnessed a thriving, competitive – authoritarian – capitalism that also offered new promises of consumerism.[60] As Pamela Swett's (Chapter 10) contribution to this volume illustrates, even publicly owned savings banks were run as profit-seeking enterprises in the capitalist spirit, despite laws and institutional mandates prohibiting such behavior.

The new official rhetoric incessantly proclaimed a new – National Socialist – economic ethics. Individual interests would be subordinated to the common interest; rapacious capitalism and capitalists would be

Geburtshelferdienst (midwifery) of the state, all of which he attributed to a large extent to the Brüning government, which had also solved the reparation issue, Erich Welter, *Ende und Lehren der Krise* [a series of articles published in the *Frankfurter Zeitung* 1932/3 under the title "Land"] (Frankfurt, 1933), 9, 50, 72.

[59] Geyer, "What Crisis?" 19.

[60] For the ongoing debate on this issue, see Jochen Streb, "Das Nationalsozialistische Wirtschaftssystem: Indirekter Sozialismus, gelenkte Marktwirtschaft oder Vorgezogene Kriegswirtschaft?" in Werner Plumpe and Joachim Scholtysek, eds., *Der Staat und die Ordnung der Wirtschaft: Vom Kaiserreich bis zur Berliner Republik* (Berlin, 2012), 61–84. Dieter Ziegler, "'A Regulated Market Economy': New Perspectives on the Nature of the Economic Order of the Third Reich, 1933–1939," in Hartmut Berghoff, Jürgen Kocka, and Dieter Ziegler, eds., *Business in the Age of Extremes: Essays in Modern German and Austrian Economic History* (Cambridge, 2013), 139–52. Johannes Bähr and Ralf Banken, eds., *Wirtschaftssteuerung durch Recht im Nationalsozialismus: Studien zur Entwicklung des Wirtschaftsrechts im Interventionsstaat des "Dritten Reichs"* (Frankfurt, 2006).

brought under control. Adolf Hitler never tired of preaching the "primacy of politics" and the "life interests" of the people and the nation: the state, not "the economy," was to take the lead in pursuing the ultimate aim of restoring Germany to a position of power; this was to end the *Verwirtschaftlichung der Nation* (economization of the nation) that, according to Hitler, had started the moment Bismarck left office.[61] After 1933 such incessant rhetoric swiftly and thoroughly silenced any critical commentary on the new economic status quo, including the ongoing power of cartels and monopolies. Such diagnoses were now relegated to history (like the word "liberalism") – namely, to the history of the *Systemzeit* (time of the system – a Nazi designation of the Weimar Republic), which was painted in the bleakest of colors.

Censoring and even erasing the language used to describe phenomena in the economic sphere is a powerful instrument. But erasing that language does not erase the phenomena. In fact, there are many good reasons to question the assumption that the phenomena of political capitalism actually vanished under the Nazis. Instead, one needs to look both at the persistence of long-established practices and the emergence of new forms. Some of the most brutal forms of political capitalism existed under Nazi rule. The Nazi leadership and the party apparatus claimed to represent the nation but acted as a self-serving interest group – a *Verband* in the Weberian sense of the term – and were ready to seek and seize "booty," first at home and then, once the war started, abroad. One should not forget that the death knell for "pluralism," which Schmitt and others had talked about incessantly, was the rapid and effective destruction of the German labor movement in 1933. Its confiscated property sparked the voracious greed not only of the state but also of various party organizations and individuals and in fact unleashed a booty mentality of the worst sort. Like many other laws and ordinances, the National Labor Law of 1934 had the fingerprints of industrial and bureaucratic interests all over it (notwithstanding the complaints about the purportedly outrageous demands of the German Labor Front). Wages and social welfare benefits were frozen at the low levels of the Depression, which explains why wage labor made up a declining percentage of production costs and national income in the 1930s.[62] It was hardly the freedom of industrial and business interests

[61] For a good summary of Hitler's arguments, see Scholl, *Begrenzte Abhängigkeit*, 185–93, here 186.

[62] Akihiko Amemiya, "Neuer Liberalismus und Faschismus: Liberaler Interventionismus und die Ordnung des Wettbewerbs," *Jahrbuch für Wirtschaftsgeschichte* 49/2 (2008): 173–95.

that was most affected by the emergency decrees issued by the presidential governments. Rather it was labor that suffered.[63]

What is true with respect to the treatment of organized labor is even more valid with respect to other new "enemies of the state," namely the Jews. "Aryanization" of Jewish-owned property became one of the most conspicuous aspects of – state-sanctioned – plunder. In fact, "Aryanization" is probably the most significant aspect of the new booty society, for it benefited individuals, party organizations, and a broad range of private and business interests. Once the war started, the occupied territories promised an influx of new booty.[64] All of this has been extensively described in terms of its bureaucratic mechanisms and the underlying mentalities of the perpetrators. The politics of Jewish exclusion was first and foremost a cornerstone of National Socialist racial politics. But it was also bound up with the regime's response to the debate about capitalism. From the very start, the National Socialists had put forward a very simple position. All of the phenomena associated with "political capitalism" ultimately boiled down to one single problem: the presence of Jews in the German economy. For the *völkisch* right and many others across the German political spectrum, including the left, "financial capitalism" was understood as a form of pariah and adventure capitalism that thrived on exploiting "host societies" through political corruption and various types of dishonest business practice. As we have seen, this was a diffuse, yet widely shared conviction. The German *völkisch* movement and the political right thrived on these resentments and this diagnosis. For others, including industrialists and bankers, the position was sometimes unpleasant, but offered a convenient distraction from their own involvement in the old and new political capitalism. It should come as no surprise that the systematic elimination of Jews from German economic life that started in 1933 went hand in hand with erasing the term "capitalism" from the German vocabulary – at least when depicting Germany. This was one way to replace the much-decried decayed form of political capitalism and to restore capitalism to its – supposedly – "productive" and truly German form.

[63] See also the perceptive observations in Ernst Fraenkel, *The Dual State: A Contribution to the Theory of Dictatorship*, trans. E. A. Shils in collaboration with Edith Lowenstein and Klaus Knorr (New York, 1941).

[64] Dieter Ziegler, "'Entjudung' und Nazifizierung 1933–1937," in Johannes Bähr, ed., *Die Dresdner Bank im Dritten Reich*, Bd. 1: *Die Dresdner Bank in der Wirtschaft des Dritten Reichs* (Munich, 2006), 85–100; Götz Aly, Hitler's *Beneficiaries: Plunder, Racial War, and the Nazi Welfare State*, trans. Jefferson Chase (New York, 2008). See also Alexa Stiller's chapter in this volume.

3

Searching for Order

German Jurists Debate Economic Power, 1919–1949

Kim Christian Priemel

A year after the Third Reich had capitulated, modest signs of reconstruction began cropping up. A number of Allied proclamations between autumn 1945 and early 1947 (re)established the German states, and in July 1946 the creation of the British-American Bizone paved the way for overcoming the severe infrastructural impediments that had been vexing much of western Germany. Although agrarian production was insufficient, and hunger would continue to haunt the occupied territories, industrial output was slowly increasing (if from an all-time low).[1] Material reconstruction was accompanied by cautious efforts to reboot political, academic, and intellectual discourse. While the publication of daily newspapers was sanctioned by the Allies in their respective zones during the first year of occupation, academic publishing began in earnest only in 1946 and differed strongly from discipline to discipline. Whereas historical journals did not resume publication for several years, jurists and some economists moved much more quickly, both anticipating and reflecting a demand for more forward-looking analyses. Among the new periodicals, two journals stood out, the *Süddeutsche Juristen-Zeitung* (*Southern German Jurists' Journal*) (*SJZ*) and the *Deutsche Rechts-Zeitschrift* (*German Law Magazine*), not least because they stressed discontinuity with their discredited forerunners and called for a fresh

I am very grateful to Stefanie Middendorf, Franz Hederer, Moritz Föllmer, and Pamela Swett for their suggestions and comments on earlier drafts of this chapter.

[1] Mark Spoerer and Jochen Streb, *Neue deutsche Wirtschaftsgeschichte des 20. Jahrhunderts* (Munich, 2013), 211–19.

start in German jurisprudence.[2] As the earliest juridical journals to run off the printing presses after the war, they enjoyed a wide readership and became highly influential fora for debating Germany's future. By 1950 the two would merge into the fortnightly lawyers' newspaper the *Juristen Zeitung* (*JZ*), Germany's leading professional legal publication to this day.[3]

A large proportion of the articles in the first issues to appear dealt with economic matters or, more accurately, with the shape of economic things to come. Notably *SJZ*, with its stable of prominent jurists, among them returning exiles, provided space for a host of voices and opinions on economic theory and practice. Not a few of these were drawn from the German variant of neoliberalism, the so-called ordoliberal school, and overlapped with the brains behind another addition to Germany's academic scene, *Ordo*. As the principal outlet for neoliberal thinkers from economics, law, and sociology, *Ordo*'s first editorial acknowledged 1945 as a historical turning point. However, the editors underlined that not everything had to start again from scratch. In fact, they asserted, the guiding principles for the future social and economic order were already available: over the previous decades these had been elaborated by academics both within and outside Germany – a nod to their émigré colleagues.[4]

Though evidently promoting their own brand, the ordoliberals, led by economist Walter Eucken and jurist Franz Böhm, were right. The postwar years saw the continuation of a discussion that had begun thirty years earlier in the wake of another defeat. Throughout the Weimar era, but also under the Nazi regime, debates on economic matters that ran the gamut from socialization and soviets to competition and social security had occupied economists' and jurists' minds. Rather than inaugurating a debate, the years from 1946 to 1949 would see the conclusion of one, with contentious issues being settled in favor of a capitalist market economy, the freedom of which was restricted by the protection of competition, collective bargaining, and welfare state provisions.[5] These debates

[2] See the editorials in *Süddeutsche Juristen-Zeitung* 1 (1946) and *Deutsche Rechts-Zeitschrift* 1 (1946).

[3] Rolf Stürner, "Der Juristenzeitung zu ihrem siebzigsten Geburtstag. Siebzig Jahre deutsche Rechtsgeschichte im Spiegel der Juristenzeitung," *Juristenzeitung* 71 (2016): 1–18.

[4] "Vorwort," *Ordo. Jahrbuch für die Ordnung von Wirtschaft und Gesellschaft* 1 (1948): viii–ix.

[5] See Knut Wolfgang Nörr, *Die Leiden des Privatrechts. Kartelle in Deutschland von der Holzstoffkohlenentscheidung zum Gesetz gegen Wettbewerbsbeschränkungen* (Tübingen,

were tightly interconnected and reverberated around the triangle of law, economics, and politics, allocating different roles and functions to markets, states, and their institutions and agents. Ultimately, though, they were all about power and its distribution and the search for order.[6]

Continuity, of course, did not mean that there were no interruptions. Weimar-educated lawyers like Heinrich Kronstein, Arthur Nussbaum, and Franz Neumann, along with economists and sociologists such as Wilhelm Röpke and Alexander Rüstow, went into exile, where they had more pressing matters, such as survival, to attend to, but where they also took ideas from their new environments and wove these into their own thinking. On their return, they sought out old colleagues and new associates, some of whom had managed to adapt fairly smoothly to the Nazi regime in the relative security of German universities. Böhm, Eucken, and Werner Hallstein numbered among them, as did Paul Josten, a long-time official at the Reich Ministry of Economic Affairs.

The present chapter follows these debates and transatlantic crossings, notably by tracing the parallel careers and intertwined thoughts of Böhm and Kronstein, though also taking into account other contributions that help illuminate the emergence of the Federal Republic of Germany's eventual legal-economic paradigm and the set of lawyer-intellectuals who were instrumental in its establishment. The focus is on legal rather than economic thinking, as German jurists played a pivotal role in conceptualizing notions of the "economy" and rendering them systematic, just as they did with ideas of the "state," "society," and the "body politic." In so doing, they effectively added a sense of public-mindedness to economic proposals that might otherwise have remained sectarian and disputed.[7] Their appeal was twofold: the jurists' emphasis on state authority, their innate belief in rules and regulations, and the dialectic twist that enabled them to reconcile private liberties and public intervention made for a brand of liberalism that was palatable to a much broader audience skeptical of unfettered economic freedoms; jurists provided a degree of legitimacy that economists could not offer. At the same time their peculiar type of *Kapitalismuskritik* (critique of capitalism) had the immense benefit

1994), and Mathias Schmoeckel, *Rechtsgeschichte der Wirtschaft seit dem 19. Jahrhundert* (Tübingen, 2008).

[6] The notion of a "search" has recently also been stressed by Jens Hacke, *Existenzkrise der Demokratie. Zur politischen Theorie des Liberalismus in der Zwischenkriegszeit* (Berlin, 2018), 39–40, 65–70, 355–60.

[7] For an overview see Roman Köster, *Die Wissenschaft der Außenseiter. Die Krise der Nationalökonomie in der Weimarer Republik* (Göttingen, 2011), 269–305.

of not being anticapitalist, thereby ridding regulation and intervention of their socialist flavor.

For these debates, which converged on issues such as competition, concentration, and cartelization, the three decades between the end of one German state and the birth of another formed a distinct, integrated period.[8] And it was the confluence of domestic and émigré thinking – here personified by Böhm and Kronstein – that ultimately helped ordoliberal ideas become the principal, if mitigated, theory underlying the Federal Republic's governance when it came to curbing economic power.

3.1 JURIDIFYING THE ECONOMY: ORGANIZATION AS ZEITGEIST

By the time World War I was coming to a close, German economic law had been on an upward trajectory for several decades. The second half of the nineteenth century had seen both massive growth and deep crisis, the evolution of increasingly large and complex corporate organizations, intensifying conflicts between capital and labor, and tentative steps toward the welfare state.[9] At the same time, a flurry of legal norms and judicial decisions had emerged whose systematization in the commercial codes of 1861 and 1897 echoed the general trend of juridification. Stock exchanges and credit, company law and contractual law, legal liability and labor relations were regulated; there was no dearth of fields in which legal expertise was in growing demand. Unsurprisingly, questions of competition and cartelization also appeared on the agenda of jurists and economists who congregated at the Juristentage (Conferences of German Jurists), the German legal discipline's conventions, of 1902 and 1904 or the venerable economic and sociopolitical association, the Verein für Socialpolitik, as early as 1894.[10]

In a broader perspective, the economic sphere's juridification was another sign of how modernity tended to erode the divisions between state and society as well as between individuals and society. Cultural conservatives were not alone in critically observing that individual lives

[8] The present chronology therefore differs from the one proposed – though from a different vantage point, that of a history of liberal thinking – by Hacke, *Existenzkrise*, 25, who casts the 1920s and 1930s as a second *Sattelzeit* (Saddle Period).

[9] See Spoerer and Streb, *Neue deutsche Wirtschaftsgeschichte*, and Toni Pierenkemper, *The German Economy during the Nineteenth Century* (New York, 2004).

[10] Rudolf Piepenbrock, *Der Gedanke eines Wirtschaftsrechts in der neuzeitlichen Literatur bis zum Ersten Weltkrieg* (Cologne, 1964); Nörr, *Leiden*, 1–2, 18–24.

and liberties were increasingly contingent upon state regulation and intervention: civic life unfolded in intensely regulated contexts, from the workplace to the consumption of public goods, from education to the old age pension, and from legal business conduct to public corporations. As Ernst Forsthoff later noted, the state both expanded and diversified into a multitude of self-administering, law-setting entities and corporations, covering everything from municipalities to health insurance bodies, each with its respective bylaws.[11] These processes implied a growing overlap between civil law and public law, and the German terminology of *Privatrecht* and *Öffentliches Recht* stressed the sea change that was taking place: increasingly, private life was defined in communal terms. In contrast to nineteenth-century liberal ideas of individual spheres protected *from* the state, individual liberty was now enabled, structured, and guaranteed *by* the state.[12] Yet, at the same time, jurists specializing in economic matters like Heinrich Göppert and Karl Geiler (whose political inclinations shared little common ground) wondered who was in the driver's seat – the state or (big) business. Combining academic interest with practical experience – Göppert was a seasoned civil servant in the Prussian administration and a professor of commercial law at the University of Bonn, while Geiler was a prominent attorney-at-law and professor of commercial law at the University of Heidelberg – the two jurists realized that familiar binary oppositions between liberty and regulation, private and public, state and economy were rapidly disintegrating.[13]

If this sense of ambiguity continued unabated, the intensity of public–private entanglement in the economic sphere grew massively during World War I. All-out war demanded an unprecedented degree of economic mobilization and, indeed, of reorganization. Under the aegis of AEG's Walter Rathenau, the German economy underwent substantial change. So-called *Kriegsrohstoffgesellschaften* (wartime corporations tasked with procuring and distributing raw materials) coordinated access to resources, syndicates distributed products, prices were increasingly checked by administrative bodies, and all this was accomplished by an

[11] Cf. Florian Meinel, *Der Jurist in der industriellen Gesellschaft. Ernst Forsthoff und seine Zeit* (Berlin, 2011), 65, 121, 153–4.

[12] Ibid., 56–7, 102.

[13] Karl Geiler, *Gesellschaftliche Organisationsformen des neueren Wirtschaftsrechts*, 2nd ed. (Mannheim, 1922); Heinrich Göppert, *Staat und Wirtschaft* (Tübingen, 1924); Göppert combined statist, dirigiste notions with a deep skepticism of cartels, see Clemens Zacher, *Die Entstehung des Wirtschaftsrechts in Deutschland* (Berlin, 2002), 88–91.

ever-growing bureaucratic apparatus that co-opted private managers into (quasi) public offices.[14] For many observers, World War I therefore amounted to an economic paradigm shift. While Geiler pointed to continuities from the prewar era, most jurists found that these were dwarfed by wartime changes. The war, Arthur Nussbaum firmly stated in 1920, had heralded a "new era in the civilized world's legal evolution." Nussbaum's volume took stock of how far economic legislation as well as regulatory practice had come over the past years and found that civil law had largely been superseded by its public corollary.[15] This was in line with observations other colleagues made, among them Justus Hedemann, who considered the academic separation of the two fields obsolete. Hedemann seized the opportunity to draw attention to his pet subject. In 1919 he established the Institute of Economic Law at the University of Jena, which would soon become an influential hub for legal scholars with an interest in economic matters and, indeed, a largely positive take on cartels.[16]

While the likes of Nussbaum and Hedemann started from what Georg Jellinek, the dean of the positivist school, had famously dubbed "die normative Kraft des Faktischen" (the normative force of the factual) the war also inspired constitutional controversy. The move toward organization and interventionism pointed in a direction that appealed to various parties in the political arena. While conservatives saw the opportunity to morph the authoritarian brand of "wartime socialism" into a corporatist postwar order, rather than returning to the economic liberalism they so disliked, Marxists were eager to seize the opportunity to make the step to full-scale socialization and soviet-style

[14] Gerald D. Feldman, *Army, Industry and Labor in Germany 1914–1918* (Oxford, 1992); Regina Roth, *Staat und Wirtschaft im Ersten Weltkrieg: Kriegsgesellschaften als kriegswirtschaftliche Steuerungsinstrumente* (Berlin, 1997). Cf. the contributions to *Jahrbuch für Wirtschaftsgeschichte* 56, no. 2 (2015).

[15] Arthur Nussbaum, *Das neue deutsche Wirtschaftsrecht: Eine systematische Übersicht über die Entwicklung des Privatrechts und der benachbarten Rechtsgebiete seit Ausbruch des Weltkrieges*, 2nd ed. (Berlin, 1922), 1. See also Christian Eckert, "Staat und Wirtschaft," *Weltwirtschaftliches Archiv* 35 (1932): 357–85, here 367. Cf. Zacher, *Entstehung*, 64–9, and Schmoeckel, *Rechtsgeschichte*, 7–8.

[16] See Zacher, *Entstehung*, 54–6, and Christine Wegerich, *Die Flucht in die Grenzenlosigkeit: Justus Wilhelm Hedemann (1878–1963)* (Tübingen, 2004), 17–19, 26–44; Johannes Bähr, "'Recht der staatlich organisierten Wirtschaft'. Ordnungsvorstellungen und Wandel der deutschen Wirtschaftsrechtslehre im 'Dritten Reich,'" in Johannes Bähr and Ralf Banken, eds., *Wirtschaftssteuerung durch Recht im Nationalsozialismus. Studien zur Entwicklung des Wirtschaftsrechts im Interventionsstaat des "Dritten Reichs"* (Frankfurt, 2006), 445–72, here 448–50.

government.[17] Ultimately, the Weimar Republic's constitution committed the state neither to a liberal nor to a socialist order (of whatever stripe). But in "organization" the various views found a common denominator for how to achieve economic order. Whereas Social Democrats would continue to deduce from the constitution at least a mandate for *Wirtschaftsdemokratie* (economic democracy),[18] their liberal antipodes insisted on constitutional liberties such as private property and contractual freedom; antirepublicans, meanwhile, considered the state of indecision itself to be a fundamental flaw that delegitimized the entire democratic order.[19]

The closest the Weimar constitution came to a corporatist order was the *Reichswirtschaftsrat*, a peculiar type of national economic parliament whose most prominent feature, many thought, was its provisional character.[20] Yet, despite its limited role, the institution was clear evidence that Weimar's economic politics struck a new note. The quasi-parliamentary *Rat*, along with the newly created Reich Ministry of Economic Affairs and a new economic court, originally a wartime body with specific jurisdiction over economic administrative matters, set about establishing an ancillary constitution – a specific "economic constitution" (*Wirtschaftsverfassung*). Indeed, the economic constitution became one of the buzzwords of interwar legal-economic discourse.[21] The point was to establish principles of what the economy should look like, how its components were to be organized, and which powers were to be distributed among whom. Power accordingly would be a key category in any debate on the economy.

3.2 REGULATING MARKET POWER: TECHNIQUES OF COMPETITION

Organization and power were two subjects close to Karl Geiler's heart. In the 1920s the lawyer-cum-professor published several studies of how business and government were increasingly intertwined, and

[17] Feldman, *Army, Industry and Labor*, 279–81, 530; Knut Wolfgang Nörr, *Zwischen den Mühlsteinen: Eine Privatrechtsgeschichte der Weimarer Republik* (Tübingen, 1988), 17–19.

[18] On the concept, its genesis, and the debate see Zacher, *Entwicklung* 63, 230–2; cf. Thilo Ramm, "Juristensozialismus in Deutschland," *Quaderni Fiorentini* 3/4 (1974/5), 7–23, here 14–18.

[19] See, for example, the critique by Ernst Rudolf Huber, *Das Deutsche Reich als Wirtschaftsstaat* (Tübingen, 1931), 6–9, 25.

[20] See Franz Hederer, "How to Handle Economic Power? Law-Making and the Reich Economic Council in Weimar Germany," *Management & Organizational History* 14 (2019): 366–81.

[21] Zacher, *Entstehung*, 50–2, 87–95.

he appreciated that any attempt at organizing the economy implied the regulation of market power. Of particular interest to his analysis were market-regulating syndicates and cartels – precisely because they were private in character, endorsed by state institutions such as the parliament and the courts, and able to establish rules of general validity.[22] Two younger scholars took the torch from Geiler and emerged as astute observers – and, indeed, articulate critics – of German competition law and its shortcomings: his former student and one-time candidate for *Habilitation*, Heinrich Kronstein, and the latter's childhood friend, Franz Böhm.[23] These two lawyers, both raised in the comparatively liberal prewar duchy of Baden, published a handful of essays in the late 1920s in which they took on what they considered fundamental deficits and dead ends in the evolution of German economic law and specifically in securing fair competition in an age of conglomerates.[24]

Both knew what they were talking about from firsthand experience. After studying in Heidelberg and Bonn as well as earning his doctorate from the University of Berlin (supervised by Martin Wolff) with a dissertation on real estate property law, Kronstein had become an attorney who specialized in economic matters.[25] While his lawyering included working for the national wire syndicate, his academic interests turned toward the general trends he observed in the German economy, notably rationalization, horizontal coordination, and vertical integration in industry, trade, and finance. The ever-growing number of cartels and the rise of enormous trusts such as IG Farbenindustrie or Vereinigte Stahlwerke in the mid-1920s illustrated his observation.[26] This concern

[22] Geiler, *Gesellschaftliche Organisationsformen*; cf. Zacher, *Entstehung*, 62f., 162–4, and Nörr, *Zwischen den Mühlsteinen*, 4.

[23] Cf. Eckard Rehbinder, "Heinrich Kronstein (1897–1972)," in Bernhard Diestelkamp and Michael Stolleis, eds., *Juristen an der Universität Frankfurt am Main* (Baden-Baden, 1989), 252–67, here 255, and Zacher, *Entstehung*, 160–1. According to Kronstein's memoirs, the two fell out over Geiler's refusal to support Kronstein's application in 1930, but the exact circumstances of their dispute are unclear at best; Heinrich Kronstein, *Briefe an einen jungen Deutschen* (Munich, 1967), 124–5.

[24] On their respective biographies see the sketches in Rehbinder, "Kronstein," and Rudolf Wiethölter, "Franz Böhm (1895–1977)," in Diestelkamp and Stolleis, *Juristen*, 208–51. Cf. David Gerber, "Heinrich Kronstein and the Development of United States Antitrust Law," in Marcus Lutter, Ernst C. Stiefel, and Michael H. Hoeflich, eds., *Der Einfluss deutscher Remigranten auf die Rechtsentwicklung in den USA und in Deutschland* (Tübingen, 1993), 153–69.

[25] Heinrich Kronstein, *Die Heimstätteneigenschaft* (Berlin, 1925).

[26] Kronstein, *Briefe*, 113–21. But cf. Köster, *Wissenschaft*, 276, 282–3.

was shared by many civil servants in the economic and treasury offices. Career bureaucrats like Paul Josten witnessed how private actors maximized the benefits of conglomerate structures when it came to taxation while employing social and foreign policy concerns to force the state's hand when it came to subsidies and bailouts.[27]

Against this backdrop Kronstein's *Habilitation* manuscript inquired into the more technical aspects of business hierarchies and the legal consequences of combines and trusts. His particular interest was in the extent to which affiliates depended on their corporate parents, raising doubts as to the reasonability of their legal separation.[28] His three shorter articles were much more penetrating and pointed to the political implications of ever-growing organization. Kronstein conceded that technological progress and economies of scale accounted for the appeal of trusts and, to some extent, also of cartels, but he was acutely aware as well of the dangers these brought. Not only did the power that such business entities accumulated go increasingly unchecked by political and legal institutions, trusts and cartels themselves established rules that competitors and consumers – in fact, even the state – had to abide by. In other words, for all practical purposes private capital deprived the sovereign of his prerogative.[29] "The cartel," Kronstein contended, "creates law out of itself," and control over the means of production determined "the distribution of power."[30] Moreover, the state was losing the ability to determine its own policies in crucial fields such as monetary policy, tariffs, and customs, or the framework of security-sensitive markets such as that for

[27] Josten (1883–1974) had studied law and received his doctorate from the University of Würzburg (Paul Josten, *Deutschlands Stellung im Welthandel* [Cologne, 1908]). Joining the Ministry of Economic Affairs in 1920, he soon became a significant figure; see the contributions to Carl-Ludwig Holtfrerich, ed., *Das Reichswirtschaftsministerium der Weimarer Republik und seine Vorläufer. Strukturen, Akteure, Handlungsfelder* (Berlin, 2016). For Josten's encounters with business power see Josten to AA, May 2, 1921, Bundesarchiv, R 3101/4586, fol. 5; Tagebuch Schäffer, May 5, 1926, Institut für Zeitgeschichte (IfZ), ED 93, vol. 2, and Josten to Reichsrechnungshof, June 1, 1933, Russian State Military Archive, 1458–3–2025. (I am grateful to Harald Wixforth for sharing this document with me.)

[28] Heinrich Kronstein, *Die abhängige juristische Person* (Berlin, 1973).

[29] Heinrich Kronstein, "Wirtschaftsrecht – Rechtsdisziplin und Zweig der Rechtstatsachenkunde," *Die Justiz* 3 (1927/8): 215–25, reprinted in Heinrich Kronstein, *Recht und wirtschaftliche Macht. Ausgewählte Schriften* (Karlsruhe, 1962), 3–13; Kronstein, "Zum Problem: Staat und Wirtschaftsmacht. Bemerkungen anlässlich der Großbankenfusion," *Die Justiz* 5 (1929/30): 137–46; Heinrich Kronstein, "Konzentration und Technik," *Die Justiz* 6 (1930/1): 3–19. Cf. Rehbinder, "Kronstein," 263–4.

[30] Kronstein, "Konzentration," 15, 18.

nitrogen products. Even with an eye to taxation, public administration was no longer a match for the resources mustered by big business.[31]

Kronstein's critique chimed with (and in his 1929 piece also quoted from) that voiced by Böhm. Böhm had likewise gained practical insights into the increasing centralization of economic power. From 1925 to 1931, he was employed by the still young Reich Ministry of Economic Affairs, working closely with the head of its cartel office, Josten. However, despite the 1923 *Kartellverordnung*, an executive regulation that enabled the ministry to rein in cartels that harmed the general welfare and economy, Böhm found public offices fairly powerless vis-à-vis business interests. The 1923 regulation continued a "policing" approach that positively allowed cartels, curtailed only excessive behavior – which was less than precisely defined – and had next to nothing to say on trusts. If anything, the regulation confirmed Böhm's doubts as to the state's capacity and, indeed, its willingness to act.[32]

While still in the Reich's employ, he fired a broadside against the state of affairs in competition law. In a long article published in 1928, he lambasted the pitiful efforts to restrict market infringements and specifically his fellow jurists' failure to appreciate – and their complicity in legitimizing – corporate might. "Das Problem der privaten Macht" ("The Problem of Private Power") argued that the economic constitution that had emanated from the previous century was based on free competition. This basic principle, Böhm stipulated, was not up for negotiation – either by the state or through private agreements. It was a misappropriation of contractual freedom to use it to curtail competition and market access or establish monopolies of various kinds. Parliaments and courts had the duty to protect this economic constitution – no different from its political equivalent – and these institutions, though staffed with well-trained lawyers, had failed to do their job.[33]

That all four articles by Kronstein and Böhm appeared in *Die Justiz* was no coincidence. The prorepublican organ of liberal and social democratic lawyers represented the margins rather than the mainstream

[31] Kronstein, "Problem," 142–3.

[32] Information on Böhm's spell at the ministry is scarce; cf. Wiethölter, "Böhm," 218, and Ernst-Joachim Mestmäcker, "Franz Böhm," in Stefan Grundmann and Karl Riesenhuber, eds., *Deutschsprachige Zivilrechtslehrer in Berichten ihrer Schüler: Eine Ideengeschichte in Einzeldarstellungen*, vol. 1 (Berlin, 2007), 31–54, here 31–2. Incidentally, Böhm entered the Reich administration just after Alexander Rüstow, another aspiring academic and future ordoliberal thinker, had quit, presumably out of frustration with inept efforts to regulate competition infringements; see Alexander Rüstow, *Das Versagen des Wirtschaftsliberalismus*, eds. Frank P. and Gerhard Maier-Rigaud (Marburg, 2001), 307–15.

[33] Franz Böhm, "Das Problem der privaten Macht," *Die Justiz* 3 (1927/8): 324–45. Cf. Zacher, *Entstehung*, 240–4.

of German jurisprudence at the time.[34] The vast majority of lawyers, both practical and academic, inclined neither toward the Weimar order nor toward criticism of trusts and cartels, especially as the latter were held to be legitimate business choices and were credited with stabilizing an economy that seemed perpetually in trouble. The two young jurists' articles, while far from anticapitalist in spirit, were therefore far removed from what German lawyers considered the prevailing opinion on competition law.

It was also more than mere coincidence that both men began publishing in 1928. That year, the Juristentag in Salzburg was to tackle the question of cartels once more, and it came out in overwhelming support of the institution, leading to a downright "reactionary" drawback. While Josten, as his ministry's official representative, remained conspicuously silent, the advocates of organized business enlisted German jurisprudence into the services of the cartelized economy and set the tone for an all-out defense of cartelization.[35] Influential practitioners like Rudolf Isay, a veteran of Rathenau's wartime organization, successful Berlin attorney, and key figure in the cartel office of the Reichsverband der Deutschen Industrie (Reich Association of German Industry), joined hands with respected scholars such as Hans Carl Nipperdey, a graduate of Hedemann's Jena Institute and an intellectual force. To Nipperdey, the combination of contractual freedom and contractual ties that marked cartels represented the capitalist zeitgeist: modern economic development pointed in their direction, and it was not the lawyers' task to stand in its way.[36]

On the other hand, Böhm and Kronstein articulated worries that echoed the critiques of legal scholars on both the left and right of the political spectrum, with whom they shared the conviction that traditional economic liberalism had led down the wrong path.[37] With Hugo Sinzheimer (who was coeditor of *Die Justiz*) and the emerging figures Franz Neumann

[34] The journal was jointly edited by Gustav Radbruch, Hugo Sinzheimer, and Wolfgang Mittermaier. See Zacher, *Entstehung*, 182, and Wiethölter, "Böhm," 215.

[35] Oswald Lehnich, "Der gegenwärtige Stand der Kartellfrage," *Zeitschrift für die gesamte Staatswissenschaft* 87 (1929): 501–44; Hugo Sinzheimer, "Der 35. Deutsche Juristentag in Salzburg," *Die Justiz* 4 (1928/9): 95–8.

[36] Nörr, *Leiden*, 67–71, here 69; Nörr, *Zwischen den Mühlsteinen*, 15. Cf. Felix Gaul, *Der Jurist Rudolf Isay (1886–1956): Ein verantwortungsbewusster Vermittler im Spannungsfeld zwischen dynamischer Rechtsschöpfung, ökonomischem Wandel und technischem Fortschritt* (Frankfurt, 2005), 35–47, and the unabashedly hagiographic recollection of Nipperdey's student Klaus Adomeit, "Hans Carl Nipperdey als Anreger für eine Neubegründung des juristischen Denkens," in Grundmann and Riesenhuber, *Zivilrechtslehrer*, 148–65.

[37] For the fluid dividing lines in Weimar's intellectual scene see Hacke, *Existenzkrise*, 32–70.

and Ernst Fraenkel they agreed that the state risked becoming demoted to a mere clerk for business.[38] To the right, the two competition-minded jurists found common ground with the crisis diagnoses of Carl Schmitt and his disciples. Kronstein cited approvingly Schmitt's alarmist warnings against the increasing influence of vested interests, which threatened to undermine and ultimately destroy the state proper. Böhm and Ernst Forsthoff converged in their decisionist reasoning that the constitution determined first principles and could not tolerate its own abrogation; the state could not grant liberties that undermined the constitution's political or economic integrity.[39] However, Schmitt, along with Forsthoff, Ernst Rudolf Huber, and Otto Kirchheimer (despite their heading into opposed political camps), drew very different conclusions from this problem. While the Schmittians found the Republic already delegitimized and therefore called for its replacement by a strong nationalist state, Kronstein and Böhm were open to reforms that would strengthen the existing state: Weimar was not beyond salvation.[40] As Kronstein put it, calls for the return of the old authoritarian state (or a new, total one for that matter) were misguided: it was not more state that was required but a more efficient administration and one that took seriously its responsibility for a "freely organized society." In both an elegant rebuff to Schmitt and a premonition of what was to come, Kronstein added, "the doctrine of the sovereign state misses its own target" (*die Lehre vom souveränen Staat führt nicht zu ihm*). As it turned out, the proponents of state sovereignty paved the way for something quite different.[41]

3.3 ORDER, FINALLY? REPHRASING COMPETITION CONCEPTS VIS-À-VIS THE THIRD REICH

The challenge to the procartelist mainstream and the dialectical reconceptualization of state regulation and economic liberty for which Böhm and Kronstein stood were only just beginning when they seemed to meet an untimely end. The search for a viable economic order that had begun in the

[38] On Neumann's contributions to the 1928 Juristentag, which were consistently rejected as socialist attempts to employ cartel law for socialization purposes, see Lehnich, "Stand," 521–2, 531, 534–6.

[39] Kronstein, "Problem," 141–2; Forsthoff to Schmitt, January 23, April 8, and May 7, 1932, in Dorothee Mussgnug, Reinhard Mussgnug, and Angela Reinthal, eds., *Briefwechsel Ernst Forsthoff Carl Schmitt (1926–1974)* (Berlin, 2007), 39–42. On the relation between Böhm's and Schmitt's concepts cf. Wiethölter, "Böhm," 230–2. See also Sean Irving, "Limiting Democracy and Framing the Economy: Hayek, Schmitt and Ordoliberalism," *History of European Ideas* 44 (2018): 113–27.

[40] Huber, *Wirtschaftsstaat*, 25–9.

[41] Kronstein, "Problem," 145.

waning days of Imperial Germany and had marked Weimar's one and a half decades was first winding down in the face of depression and the dying Republic's executive government by emergency decree. Then it was out of tune with the ushering in of the Nazi dictatorship. Some observers noted as much, among them Huber, who, in a 1934 review of Böhm's book, acerbically commented that his colleague had erred in his judgment of the "National Socialist revolution." This in turn would lead future observers to conclude that liberal legal-economic thinking went into a lull or at least a sort of inner exile in the remote and protected provincial town of Freiburg.[42] However, other university towns like Jena, Marburg, and Tübingen were no less provincial; nor did Huber's work escape criticism. His own *Habilitation* (mentored by Heinrich Göppinger), the first systematic effort to take stock of, categorize, and organize economic administrative law, was lauded as magisterial and a pioneering achievement upon its publication in 1932.[43] Yet it also gave Justus Hedemann the opportunity to note that with the definition of "private" and "public" set by the Nazi *Volksgemeinschaft* (people's community), Huber's entire subject was coming apart. Moreover, the book – written, after all, with the possibility in mind that its author's career would continue within a republican framework – placed the primacy of politics next to the terminology of *freie Verkehrswirtschaft* (free exchange economy), strongly associated with Eucken, and repeatedly emphasized the rule of law (though without emphatically embracing it).[44]

In fact, neither Böhm nor Huber had the impression that their work was no longer in demand; both soldiered on, if in different circles and with different ambitions. Back from his stint at the Ministry of Economic Affairs, Böhm completed both his doctorate and his *Habilitation* at Freiburg in a mere two years, mostly because the subject of both dissertations was the same; accordingly, they were published as parts of one monograph, *Wettbewerb und Monopolkampf* (*Competition and Monopolistic Struggle*) in 1933. Böhm's book, together with a shorter piece that he published a year later in Eucken's journal *Die Tatwelt*, has

[42] Wiethölter, "Böhm," 229; Nörr, *Leiden*, 101; David Gerber, "Constitutionalizing the Economy: German Neo-Liberalism, Competition Law and the 'New' Europe," *American Journal of Comparative Law* 42 (1994): 25–84, here 30.

[43] Matthias Maetschke, "Ernst Rudolf Huber. Im Schatten Carl Schmitts – Ernst Rudolf Hubers Bonner Jahre 1924–1933," in Mathias Schmoeckel, ed., *Die Juristen der Universität Bonn im "Dritten Reich"* (Köln, 2004), 368–86, here 375–6.

[44] Ernst Rudolf Huber, *Wirtschaftsverwaltungsrecht. Institutionen des öffentlichen Arbeits- und Unternehmensrechts* (Tübingen, 1932), 2, 43, 203, 295; cf. the thorough discussion by Zacher, *Entstehung*, 258–91. For Hedemann's comment see Bähr, "Recht," 455.

been called "untimely" and out of sync with the new era – liberal thinking in a profoundly illiberal world.[45] But Böhm begged to differ. In the preface to his monograph he confidently asserted that his book, although written in the final years of the Republic, could stand unchanged. Indeed, some of the "old ideologies" he was critical of had lost their "political and public relevance," which was a polite way of saying communist and social democratic positions no longer mattered. Still, Böhm could hardly have foreseen the radical political changes the new regime would bring, and his reference to "the *current* government" partly vindicated Huber's jibe. In his 1934 essay on "Law and Power," there were more than a few lines that sat ill with the Nazi dictatorship's consolidation, including the declaration that true ethics were only possible in a state of freedom.[46]

Both publications were marked by a strong ambiguity, a tension between affirming individual rights and freedom, on the one hand, and obligations to the community, the nation, and the state on the other. To Böhm, however, there was no contradiction. His dialectical reasoning found fault with traditional liberalism precisely because of its stark opposition between individual liberties and state regulation. Rather than being mutually exclusive, he argued, they were interdependent, and only a determined government could guarantee economic freedom. It had been precisely the failure to establish and enforce an economic constitution that had led to the rise of unchecked private power in the shape of trusts and cartels or, more generally, monopolistic might that undermined individual freedom just as much as state sovereignty. In short, Böhm provided a theoretical foundation for reconciling liberal and regulatory ideas, the detached state with its strong, interventionist alternative.[47]

At the same time, Böhm phrased his synthesis in a vernacular that also spoke to an audience outside the circle of reformist liberalists like Eucken in

[45] Franz Böhm, *Wettbewerb und Monopolkampf. Eine Untersuchung zur Frage des wirtschaftlichen Kampfrechts und zur Frage der rechtlichen Struktur der geltenden Wirtschaftsordnung* (Baden-Baden, 2010); Franz Böhm, "Recht," *Die Tatwelt* 10 (1934): 115–32 and 169–93; quote Mestmäcker, "Einführung," in Böhm, *Wettbewerb*, 5–14, 5, and Nörr, *Leiden*, 101. See also Edith Eucken-Erdsiek, "Franz Böhm in seinen Anfängen," in Heinz Sauermann and Ernst-Joachim Mestmäcker, eds., *Wirtschaftsordnung und Staatsverfassung. Festschrift für Franz Böhm zum 80. Geburtstag* (Tübingen, 1975), 9–14. A slightly different twist is offered by Hans Zacher's interpretation "Aufgaben einer Theorie der Wirtschaftsverfassung," in Helmut Coing, Heinrich Kronstein, and Ernst-Joachim Mestmäcker, eds., *Wirtschaftsordnung und Rechtsordnung. Festschrift zum 70. Geburtstag von Franz Böhm* (Karlsruhe, 1965), 63–109. Zacher argues that Böhm managed to pursue his path by ignoring issues that were of secondary concern to his theory or could not realistically be influenced.

[46] Böhm, *Wettbewerb*, 17–18; Böhm, "Recht," 189 (my emphasis).

[47] Böhm, "Recht," 117–18, 175, 188–9; Böhm, *Wettbewerb*, 17, 131–2, 173–8.

Freiburg, Hayek in London, or Röpke and Rüstow in Istanbul. The linchpin was his understanding of free commerce (*Gewerbefreiheit*), the positively constitutional basis – formulated in explicitly Schmittian terms – of the economy he envisioned. Free commerce was not defined by the absence of the state but by its essence, and that was "struggle" (*Kampf*). Struggle, in the shape of competition, had been a constant principle of economic evolution "for thousands of years," Böhm wrote; its purpose was to select those economic actors and structures that increased output and efficiency and to breed optimal performance.[48] Keeping the state out of economic affairs was just as wrong as having it take over the economy since neither of the two options would produce the Social Darwinist mechanism Böhm envisioned. In the latter case, private initiative was altogether stifled by bureaucracy whereas in the former, cartels and trusts undermined competition. Their members ran the economy on the basis of the principles of private egoism and *Nichtleistungskampf*, a "non-struggle," at the expense of consumers and community, and threatened to ensure the "victory of the worse over the better."[49]

Not only the vocabulary of *Auslesekampf*, *Entartung*, or *Züchtung* (survival of the fittest, degeneration, or breeding) but also the very spirit of Böhm's book justified his perception that he was not entirely out of tune with the new times. It also helped gloss over passages in which he sarcastically commented on "nationalist-pedagogical economic moralists" who failed to understand that neither dictatorial power nor the "gallows" would keep business from wanting to make profits.[50] These thoughts, as well as Böhm's idea of "powerlessness" as the ideal state for all market actors, might have raised Nazi eyebrows. But they were soothed by the jurist's willingness to make concessions in economic areas or at political times when and where competition was inopportune.[51]

Böhm found himself in line with some of his new collaborators in Freiburg, notably his lawyer colleague Hans Großmann-Doerth and economist Walter Eucken. Together the three men set out to campaign for an overhaul of the German economic system that would neither revert to Manchester-style, socially carefree liberalism nor fall into the trap of socialism and a planned economy.[52] While the legal concepts used by

[48] Böhm, *Wettbewerb*, 91, 108, 121, 120. [49] Ibid., 91–2, 147–9, 330–2, quote at 149.
[50] Ibid., 238. [51] Ibid., 107.
[52] Literature on the so-called ordoliberal school is endless; for a recent overview see Josef Hien and Christian Joerges, eds., *Ordoliberalism, Law and the Rule of Economics* (Portland, 2017).

Großmann-Doerth and Böhm provided the nascent movement with syntax, Eucken contributed much of the semantics and the vocabulary, not least the binary opposition of *freie Verkehrswirtschaft* and *Zentralverwaltungswirtschaft* (centrally directed economy), along with his manifest cultural conservatism. His journal *Die Tatwelt*, which would continue publication until 1943, served as an outlet for many of these ideas, but the three Freiburg scholars also sought a more strictly academic platform to promote their ideas. They found this in a new book series, launched in 1936, that assembled a handful of founding texts of the as yet nameless ordoliberal school. Programmatically christened *Ordnung der Wirtschaft* (*Economic Order*), the series established a design for the future German economy. The inaugural volume, penned by Böhm himself, set the tone.[53]

If the monograph was to provide the philosophical basis for the Freiburg school, the editors' preface, "Our Task," came in the shape of a manifesto. Taking no prisoners, it denounced the two historical schools, the legal and the economic, for having led to "relativism and fatalism," it chastised the German Supreme Court for its endorsement of cartels, and it stipulated the demand for an economic constitution as "a fundamental political decision (*politische Gesamtentscheidung*) on the ordering of the nation's economic life."[54] The subsequent chapters took up the thread, with Böhm not mincing his words. With an eye to first principles, the 1937 book covered familiar ground. Readers of his previous book would find little material change in Böhm's argument. However, there was a shift in emphasis as well as a further development in his terminology, which echoed the changes the German political scene had undergone in the meantime. While Böhm continued to praise competition as the mechanism for selecting the most capable, as long as it followed "strict rules on how to play and how to fight," he went to greater lengths to explain how this concept fit into the

[53] The four published volumes were Franz Böhm, *Die Ordnung der Wirtschaft als geschichtliche Aufgabe und rechtsschöpferische Leistung* (Stuttgart, 1937); Friedrich August Lutz, *Das Grundproblem der Geldverfassung* (Stuttgart, 1936); Hans Gestrich, *Neue Kreditpolitik* (Stuttgart, 1936); and Leonhard Miksch, *Wettbewerb als Aufgabe. Die Grundsätze einer Wettbewerbsordnung* (Stuttgart, 1937). Böhm's volume went into print after the monographs by Lutz and Gestrich.

[54] Franz Böhm, Walter Eucken, and Hans Großmann-Doerth, "Unsere Aufgabe," in Böhm, *Ordnung*, viii–xxi, at ix–xiv, xviii–xix. Cf. Tamara Zieschang, *Das Staatsbild Franz Böhms* (Stuttgart, 2003), 15–18. Alexander Nützenadel, *Stunde der Ökonomen: Wissenschaft, Politik und Expertenkultur in der Bundesrepublik 1949–1974* (Göttingen, 2005), 40–2, has noted the irony that the critics entirely shared the historical school's underlying premise – to integrate economics, society, and history.

new political order.[55] The state's role was now expounded in considerable detail, and public power to regulate and intervene appeared much more prominently than had been the case in his earlier writings. The study's entire premise was that "the political leadership must be the master of the entire economy, both in total and in all its details; it is necessary for public economic policy to get a handle on economic matters in terms of both spirit and actual power."[56]

Böhm's demand for firm action was in line with the regime's self-perception, and so were his concessions in major policy fields. Both agriculture and labor law were taken out of the competition-based equation. Protecting German peasants on one hand and overcoming the class divide on the other, Böhm reasoned, were perfectly good reasons for dispensing with competition and relying on authoritarian orders instead. Likewise, a state of emergency – the Four-Year Plan was one such case – effectively suspended economic liberties.[57]

Still – and here lay Böhm's hope for the future – in the long run a stable economic constitution would have to be found. Although the regime had not yet "finalized the new structure of their polity," the principles on the basis of which that constitution was to be organized were plainly in force: a mutually complementary system that combined freedom of commerce with regulation and straightforward state intervention.[58] Only insofar as competition led to order, Böhm posited, was private economic freedom viable; if it did not, "the economy ought not to be free." This preference for authority over anarchy included circumscribing private consumption. Beyond the bare necessities, any freedom to spend was unacceptable because "the *Volksgemeinschaft* cannot be indifferent" to how consumers use their income. "From the community's perspective, any consumption that is detrimental to health, adverse to culture, a danger to morality, even plain thoughtless and impulsive deserves not support but suppression." (*Gesundheitsschädlicher, kulturwidriger, die Sittlichkeit gefährdender, ja auch bloß gedankenloser und nervöser Bedarf verdient vom Standpunkt der Gemeinschaft nicht Förderung, sondern Bekämpfung.*)[59]

Whether Böhm embraced the Third Reich's premises or accommodated them is not easy to discern.[60] But the jurist clearly found enough in the

[55] Böhm, *Ordnung*, 32, 100. [56] Ibid., 10. [57] Ibid., 75–7, 82–4, 87–8.

[58] Jan-Werner Müller, *Contesting Democracy: Political Ideas in Twentieth-Century Europe* (New Haven, CT, 2011), 119.

[59] Böhm, *Ordnung*, 87, 103, 181–9, quotes at 108, 111.

[60] On the debate about how ordoliberal thinking lined up with National Socialist ideas see Dieter Haselbach, *Autoritärer Liberalismus und soziale Marktwirtschaft* (Baden-Baden,

Third Reich's political economy to work with and connect to, not least the notion of a strong state that promised to infuse the economy with an unprecedented degree of authority. That the actual economics of Nazi Germany did not adhere to these abstract principles could be explained by citing the special conditions of rearmament and war. More difficult and ultimately impossible to rationalize, however, were the regime's brutally racist and antisemitic policies. It was because of these traits that Böhm – to his credit – failed to make peace with National Socialism and saw his career slow down considerably; in the racializing of German capitalism he would have no part.[61] Still, his opposition to the regime's politics did not prevent him from participating in discussions of cartel law. In 1942 Böhm joined a panel of economists and lawyers who, under the umbrella of the Akademie für deutsches Recht (Academy for German Law), laid out their plans for a postwar order that was marked by distinctly liberal characteristics, yet in the context of a presumably victorious Third Reich.[62] Here again, Böhm, Miksch, and their associates conceptualized competition, at times drawing on biological analogies, as a means of selection and struggle.[63]

1991), 77–95, and Caroline Harth, "Der 'richtige Vertrag' im Nationalsozialismus: Wettbewerb als Instrument staatlicher Wirtschaftslenkung," in Dieter Gosewinkel, ed., *Wirtschaftskontrolle und Recht in der nationalsozialistischen Diktatur* (Frankfurt, 2005), 107–32, here 130–2. Cf. also Wolfgang Seibel, "Steuerung durch Recht im Nationalsozialismus? Juristische Methodenlehre und ökonomische Dogmengeschichte zwischen Kontinuität, Effektivität und Verbrechen," in Gosewinkel, ed., *Wirtschaftskontrolle und Recht in der nationalsozialistischen Diktatur*, 15–38, and Bähr, "Recht," 453, 462–4.

[61] On Böhm's connection to the German conservative resistance see Michael Klein, *Westdeutscher Protestantismus und politische Parteien: Anti-Parteien-Mentalität und partei-politisches Engagement von 1945 bis 1963* (Tübingen, 2005), 86–8; Traugott Roser, *Protestantismus und soziale Marktwirtschaft. Eine Studie am Beispiel Franz Böhms* (Münster, 1998), 111–23.

[62] The Akademie also operated a separate committee on cartel law. Led by Oswald Lehnich, a National Socialist of long standing, and joined by Hedemann, the committee did little actual work and during its two brief spurts in 1934–5 and 1941–2 found itself overtaken by events. Heavily dominated by business representatives, the committee was clearly cartel-friendly in its inclinations; see the protocols in Werner Schubert, ed., *Akademie für Deutsches Recht: Ausschüsse für den gewerblichen Rechtsschutz (Patent-, Warenzeichen-, Geschmacksmusterrecht, Wettbewerbsrecht), für Urheber- und Verlagsrecht sowie für Kartellrecht (1934–1943)* (Berlin, 1999), 613–27, 667–77, 718–36. Hedemann was more intensely involved in the committee in charge of the law of obligations; cf. Wegerich, *Die Flucht*, 49–50, 53–64.

[63] Günter Schmölders, ed., *Der Wettbewerb als Mittel volkswirtschaftlicher Leistungssteigerung und Leistungsauslese* (Berlin, 1942). Cf. Haselbach, *Autoritärer Liberalismus*, 94–9; Jan-Otmar Hesse, "Zur Semantik von Wirtschaftsordnung und Wettbewerb in nationalökonomischen Lehrbüchern der Zeit des Nationalsozialismus," in Bähr and Banken, *Wirtschaftssteuerung*, 473–508, here 494–6.

The discussions within the Akademie were both close to (in terms of their subject matter) and remote from (when it came to rhetoric) the issues Heinrich Kronstein was worrying about at the time. Against the backdrop of the regime's antisemitic persecution, Kronstein emigrated to the United States in 1935, along with many other colleagues now categorized as Jewish, among them Franz Neumann. Without a law degree that would have gotten him admitted to the bar, Kronstein decided to study once again, this time at Columbia, where as a practically inclined lawyer he felt an affinity to the teachings of Karl Llewellyn, a leading legal realist in American academia. In 1939 Kronstein earned his LLB, and the following year he submitted another JD thesis, this time to Georgetown University, a move in his professional career that coincided with his personal conversion to Catholicism. The dissertation built on his great expertise in the matter of trusts and took up the thread of how to bring order to an increasingly complex transnational economy: who was legally liable for what and which laws applied when the nationality of trusts' decision-making institutions was in doubt? Although Kronstein's thesis abstained from partisan views, the reference to Cordell Hull's advocacy of an international liberal trade regime with direct competition by private companies was both in line with his German writings and made his thoughts on the subject available to a larger audience.[64]

The organization of international trade and the role cartels and trusts were to play – or, rather, not play – would preoccupy Kronstein for much of his remaining career.[65] Yet during World War II his expertise in competition law was called upon for other purposes. By 1940 Kronstein – like Neumann and other exiles – had been drawn into the dense Washington nexus of wartime agencies engaged in enemy studies. Recruited to the Antitrust Office by its short-lived yet influential head Thurman Arnold, a freewheeling libertarian, the German jurist was asked to render the German economy's intricate structure intelligible to US observers, who were particularly interested to learn how trusts and cartels figured in the regime's overall structure. Starting from the widespread observation that Germany was "the

[64] Kronstein, *Briefe*, 188–92, 196–201; Heinrich Kronstein, "The Legal Relationship between American Parent Corporations and Their Foreign Subsidiaries. A Symptom of Anarchy in International Law and Conflict of Laws," PhD dissertation, Georgetown University, 1940. Cf. Rehbinder, "Kronstein," 256.

[65] See, for example, his crowning achievement: *The Law of International Cartels* (Ithaca, NY, 1973).

classical land of cartels,"[66] not a few American economists and lawyers suspected that the Nazi rise to power and the early successes of the German military campaigns and effective domination of Europe could be explained by the corporate structures that tied together the Reich's economy, public administration, party offices, and military organization. Kronstein explained these organizational links, the capacities for mobilization and control, and addressed the likelihood of fifth-column threats in the United States.[67]

However, he stayed clear of conspiracy theories that held German companies and cartels responsible for the regime. Kronstein was also at pains to stress that cartelization, although particularly enshrined in Germany's legal institutions and business practices, was an international and especially a European phenomenon. In his memoirs he would blame his left-leaning colleagues for overgeneralizing and vilifying German business.[68] Such views were indeed fairly commonplace in the enemy studies field, and Kronstein's own work actually fit in better than he would admit. Despite his insistence on wider international trends, to readers looking for an innate Germanic cartelism, his writings offered enough evidence that a distinct tradition had led German capitalists away from free trade and unfettered competition to protectionism and monopoly power. A 1942 article brought such historical continuities to the fore and correlated Prussian authoritarianism with societal illiberalism and antipluralism, the rise of the organized economy of the Rathenau type, and the descent into the maelstrom of two world wars.[69] And, most of all, Kronstein and his American collaborators, many of them seasoned trustbusters, agreed on one salient, eminently practical issue: something had to be done about cartels and

[66] Louis Domeratzky, "Cartels and the Business Crisis," *Foreign Affairs* 10 (1931): 34–53.

[67] Berle to Kronstein, December 24, 1942, and J. Burke Knapp to Boyd, July 20, 1945, Kronstein Papers, www.ili.org/about/528-heinrich-kronstein-documents-and-publications-archive.html (all references to Kronstein's papers are from this site unless indicated otherwise); Memorandum for Mr. Edward Levi, Chairman Interdepartmental Committee on International Cartels, September 24, 1942; Kronstein, *Briefe*, 205–9.

[68] Kronstein notably took issue with Arnold's successor, Wendell Berge, and Joseph Borkin, an antitrust firebrand whom he considered a Germanophobe; see Heinrich Kronstein, "European Cartels," *Commonweal* 38 (1943): 170–3; Kronstein, *Briefe*, 218–21.

[69] Heinrich Kronstein, "The Dynamics of German Cartels and Patents, I," *University of Chicago Law Review* 9 (1942): 643–71, here 645–9, 652–8; Heinrich Kronstein, "The Dynamics of German Cartels and Patents, II," *University of Chicago Law Review* 10 (1942): 49–69, here 51–2. See also his draft for one of Arnold's speeches, "Cartels," July 22, 1942, University of Wyoming, American Heritage Center, Thurman Wesley Arnold Papers, Box 3, Folder 3.

concentration, and Germany was the obvious place to start. The approaching Nazi defeat was considered an opportunity to create a postwar order in which restrictive business practices would be reduced to a minimum.[70]

3.4 POSTWAR PARADIGM: REINING IN CORPORATE POWER (IF NOT QUITE)

Whether or not he was always correctly understood, by the end of the war Kronstein had become a sought-after expert and had "participated in all discussions of the German cartel and monopoly problem." It was therefore not surprising that he was dispatched to occupied Germany, his "first love," as he noted in his diary in mid-August 1945.[71] As he was deeply distrustful of legal retribution and declined an invitation to work at the Nuremberg war crimes tribunal, Kronstein focused on industrial reconstruction, the denazification of business, and economic institution building.[72] Based at the I.G. Farben office in Frankfurt-Hoechst, Kronstein looked out for Germans he trusted among prominent industrialists, labor leaders, and academics. Meeting "many old friends, [s]ome of them real heroes of the anti-Hitler fight," the returned émigré soon found that his views were shared by like-minded scholars, and none more than Böhm. After a long conversation in October, Kronstein confided to his diary that "Franz is wonderful." He would henceforth advertise his friend far and wide as the key thinker to rely on for reestablishing economic order in the US zone.[73] To his superiors, he praised Böhm as "the excellent leader of the German anti-trust movement," confirmed his friend's resistance credentials, and familiarized American readers with the Freiburg faculty's standing as a genuine mainstay of economic and political

[70] Kronstein, "European Cartels," 173; Heinrich Kronstein and Gertrude Leighton, "Cartel Control: A Record of Failure," *Yale Law Journal* 55 (1946): 297–335.

[71] Quotes from Kronstein, Report of German Reaction to the Operation of Deconcentration and Decartelization, no date [ca. 1950], Kronstein Papers; Kronstein, *Briefe*, 14.

[72] Ibid., 25, and diary, July, 23, 1945, Georgetown University Library, SCRC, Rev. Edmund A. Walsh Papers, Box 2, F.126. Via Edmund Walsh, Kronstein was in contact with the US prosecution and must, at least briefly, have been attached to their staff; see the letter, cc'd to Kronstein, by Brodnitz to Deinard, July 3, 1945, National Archives and Records Administration, RG 238, Entry 52E, Box 7, Folder 250.1.

[73] Fuchs to Fahy, July 20, 1945, Franklin Delano Roosevelt Presidential Library, Charles Fahy Papers, Box 66, Folder "Personnel: German Staff – Correspondence with Mr. Fahy"; Devereux to Kronstein, October 15, 1945, and Report on Conditions in Germany Industry (1945), Kronstein Papers; Kronstein, *Briefe*, 42.

liberalism. Moreover – and this would prove important – Kronstein bridged the gap between the liberal protestants of Böhm's stripe and the Catholic Christian Social faction ("very strong" in "its anti-cartel and combine thinking," he noted), anticipating their merger in the Christian Democratic Union.[74]

For Böhm, Eucken, and others, Kronstein's access to American authorities was a great boon. He privileged them vis-à-vis the Allies, gave voice to virtually unknown figures, and would later take them to the United States by establishing an exchange program for aspiring legal scholars from Georgetown and Frankfurt. Kronstein's views were not wholly identical to Böhm's – for instance, in their priorities. Böhm placed greater emphasis on competition as a moral force than Kronstein's belief in social justice and protection of society's weaker members allowed for. Yet they shared enough common ground to reassure the German neoliberals that there was substantial backing for their ideas on the Allied side. Amid the rubble and the ruin, the times seemed propitious for the ordoliberal paradigm.[75]

Kronstein soon built close relations to several key figures in the legal field. Besides Böhm, these included Werner Hallstein, whom Kronstein knew from his spell in Martin Wolff's circle in the 1920s, and Paul Josten, the old ministerial hand who was now put in charge of price controls (and soon of decartelization) and was widely considered "one of the more important civil servants."[76] Hallstein, in his capacity as rector of Frankfurt University, would first offer Böhm a chair and later recruit Kronstein, too. And while his fame now rests mostly on the eponymous doctrine meant to isolate the German Democratic Republic (GDR) diplomatically and on the key role he played in the early stages of European integration,[77] Hallstein was also a pivotal figure in reconstituting West Germany's intellectual liberal-conservative camp.[78] He helped establish

[74] Section 2. Cartels and Combines (Decentralization of Economic Structure), no date [1946], Kronstein Papers.

[75] Cf. Rehbinder, "Kronstein," 262; Nörr, *Leiden*, 120–1, fn. 59.

[76] Walter Vogel, *Westdeutschland 1945–1950. Der Aufbau von Verfassungs- und Verwaltungseinrichtungen über den Ländern der drei westlichen Besatzungszonen. Teil II. Einzelne Verwaltungszweige: Wirtschaft, Marshallplan, Statistik* (Boppard, 1964), 54. Quote from Kempner to Schäffer, October 31, 1947, Leo Baeck Institute Berlin, Roll 1040, Reel 12, Contents 4/6–4/11.

[77] See Wilfried Loth, William Wallace, and Wolfgang Wessels, *Walter Hallstein: The Forgotten European?* (New York, 1998).

[78] This he understood broadly, also reaching out to Forsthoff, with whom he was familiar from one of the many circles that sprang to life under presumably apolitical Christian

the *Süddeutsche Juristen-Zeitung*, which he coedited with Karl Geiler and Hans Ehard, now the prime ministers of Hesse and Bavaria, respectively, as well as with Gustav Radbruch (of impeccable anti-Nazi pedigree). The *SJZ* instantly became the most influential jurisprudential journal in occupied Germany, providing a sounding board for many voices that would come to mark the early Federal Republic. Hallstein himself penned the inaugural issue's lead article, which drew a firm line between the Third Reich's legal system and the one he hoped to build. Significantly, the Frankfurt professor did not place all the blame on Hitler's shoulders but pointed out that things had gone wrong much earlier as a result of the historical school, which had ended in "relativism and fatalism" – a sound bite that echoed Böhm's 1937 manifesto as much as it did Friedrich Hayek's *Road to Serfdom*. Hallstein's recipe for protecting the two pillars of civil law – property and family – combined good conservative thinking with the liberal credo, now phrased in the ordoliberal vernacular of "freedom in law" rather than freedom from the law.[79]

The *SJZ* also provided an arena for fending off *Kapitalismuskritik* from the left and its demands for economic democracy. While offering the Social Democratic Party's Adolf Arndt the space to formulate his vision of a constitution that would oblige not only the state but also capital to respect basic rights, it was Böhm's sharp rejoinder that expressed the journal's editorial line. In a lengthy article that more than once crossed the boundary of fairness, Böhm's portrayal of Arndt as a legal amateur dabbling in economics was one of the lighter charges. In a condescending tone, the Frankfurt professor claimed that Arndt misunderstood the very concept of *Wirtschaftsdemokratie*, dealt in simplistic dichotomies of planned versus free economy, and – this was the gravest part – represented an antiquated, drill-sergeant style authoritarianism that prized command and obedience. Indeed, Böhm added, Arndt was perilously close to Carl Schmitt, the *bête noire* of postwar German jurisprudence.[80] The article was impertinent, not least because its author conveniently ignored his own

banners. However, the Hessian prime minister barred Forsthoff's appointment in Frankfurt; Forsthoff to Schmitt, February 22 and May 9, 1950, in Mussgnug et al., *Briefwechsel*, 65–6, 70–2; cf. Klein, *Protestantismus*, 182; Meinel, *Jurist*, 308–9; Dirk van Laak, *Gespräche in der Sicherheit des Schweigens: Carl Schmitt in der politischen Geistesgeschichte der frühen Bundesrepublik* (Berlin, 1993), 45.

79 Walter Hallstein, "Wiederherstellung des Privatrechts," *Süddeutsche Juristen-Zeitung* 1, no. 1 (1946), 1–7, here 6.

80 See Laak, *Gespräche*, and Jan-Werner Müller, *A Dangerous Mind: Carl Schmitt in Post-War European Thought* (New Haven, CT, 2003).

previous leanings toward authoritarian solutions, and prompted an angry reply from Arndt.[81]

If Böhm's tone was unusual, it was not gratuitous. Casting himself and his collaborators in the role of modernizers, he sought to gain hegemony in a public discourse just beginning to reconstitute. With the realization that social democracy had both the organizational means and the moral credibility to push for a more socialist economic constitution, it seemed all the more important to undermine the standing of the likes of Arndt. Böhm's postwar hopes went so far as to suggest that collective bargaining might not be reintroduced in industrial relations; trade unions, he posited, would do well to consider individualized, liberal alternatives to "the bilateral monopolies" of employers' and employees' organizations.[82]

But Böhm also reached out to his adversaries. As early as autumn 1945 he had, as a member of a Christian discussion circle, formulated an agenda that centered on three principles: a free and democratic constitution, the rule of law, and the "social state."[83] The prominence of the latter point (and that of equity in another article of his) marked a shift away from the previous decade but also served as a translation of the "community" terminology that Böhm had employed earlier and that was no longer opportune. Likewise, "struggle" effectively disappeared from his vocabulary and was replaced by "exchange" and "competition" plain and simple. The strong state, meanwhile, was still where he had left it in 1942. In rigorous language Böhm demanded the "firmest state supervision," which would, if necessary, "prescribe prices, disassemble trusts, and subordinate recalcitrant companies."[84]

If that implied coercion and force, Böhm was keen to point out that this was how "freedom-loving peoples" dealt with private power and that – a nod to Kronstein's wartime studies – power-ridden economies inevitably threatened war.[85] This concept invoked the authority of US occupation

[81] Adolf Arndt, "Das Problem der Wirtschaftsdemokratie in den Verfassungsentwürfen," *Süddeutsche Juristen-Zeitung* 1 (1946): 137–41; Franz Böhm, "Die Bedeutung der Wirtschaftsordnung für die politische Verfassung," *Süddeutsche Juristen-Zeitung* 1 (1946): 141–9; Adolf Arndt, "Planwirtschaft. Erwiderung auf den Aufsatz von Prof. Dr. Franz Böhm über 'Die Bedeutung der Wirtschaftsordnung für die politische Verfassung,'" *Süddeutsche Juristen-Zeitung* 1 (1946): 169–71.

[82] Böhm, "Bedeutung," 149.

[83] Klein, *Protestantismus*, 165–7.

[84] Böhm, "Bedeutung," 146–7, quotation at 148; Franz Böhm, "Kartellauflösung und Konzernentflechtung: Spezialistenaufgabe oder Schicksalsfrage?" *Süddeutsche Juristen-Zeitung* 2 (1947): 495–505, here 498 and 502 (quotation).

[85] Böhm, "Kartellauflösung," 496, 504.

policies of decartelization and deconcentration,[86] which Böhm hoped would back his position against the other group he expected to resist a competition-based economic order without market-rigging institutions – business and business associations and their legal representatives. In his contribution to the ordoliberal school's new journal, *Ordo*, Böhm underlined that, ever since the famous 1897 Reichsgericht (German Supreme Court) decision, the majority of German lawyers had gone down the wrong path. "For half a century and eight days," both jurisdiction and jurisprudence had divested themselves of responsibility and had allowed private power free rein. As a result, "a badly organized economy, hamstrung by ever worse crises and marked by social inequality and increasingly opaque cases of exploitation" had emerged.[87]

Accordingly, the advisory council, which was appointed by the western zone governments in 1946 to prepare an antimonopoly statute, was conspicuously free of cartel proponents. Chaired by his erstwhile boss, Josten, the committee was dominated by Böhm. The eventual recommendations handed to the Federal Ministry of Economic Affairs's rising star Ludwig Erhard in 1949, the so-called Josten draft, would bear Böhm's imprint.[88] Eventually the suggestions for a strict antimonopoly legislation outlawing both cartels and trusts with monopolistic power, and enforced by a distinct, powerful office, would be whittled down to the much less stringent competition law passed in 1957; Böhm's fears that his more radical intentions would be subverted by organized business proved correct. Still, it represented a massive step forward when compared to the "50-years-and-eight-days" era of cartel impunity.[89]

[86] Wyatt Wells, *Antitrust and the Formation of the Postwar World* (New York, 2002), 146–63; Lisa Murach-Brand, *Antitrust auf Deutsch: Der Einfluß der amerikanischen Alliierten auf das Gesetz gegen Wettbewerbsbeschränkungen (GWB) nach 1945* (Tübingen, 2004), 41–97.

[87] Franz Böhm, "Das Reichsgericht und die Kartelle: Eine wirtschaftsverfassungsrechtliche Kritik an dem Urteil des RG. vom 4. Febr. 1897, RGZ. 38/155," *Ordo* 1 (1948): 197–213, here 212.

[88] Heinrich Kronstein, "German Cartels," Lecture, American Foreign Law Association, 1957, Kronstein Papers; Gutachten des Wissenschaftlichen Beirats bei der Verwaltung für Wirtschaft, July 24, 1949, ibid.; Eberhard Günther, "Die geistigen Grundlagen des sogenannten Josten-Entwurfs," in Sauermann and Mestmäcker, *Wirtschaftsordnung*, 183–204. cf. Murach-Brand, *Antitrust*, 107–12; Gerd Hardach, "Wettbewerbspolitik in der Sozialen Marktwirtschaft," in Werner Abelshauser, ed., *Das Bundeswirtschaftsministerium in der Ära der Sozialen Marktwirtschaft. Der deutsche Weg der Wirtschaftspolitik* (Berlin, 2016), 193–264, here 202–7.

[89] A key figure in undermining the original draft was a long-time lobbyist for industrial associations, former member of the Akademie's cartel committee, and now a high-ranking civil servant in Erhard's department. See Wells, *Antitrust*, 163–74; Philip Plickert, *Wandlungen des Neoliberalismus: Eine Studie zur Entwicklung und Ausstrahlung der*

Following the West German parliament's decision, Erhard sent a note of thanks to Kronstein, even though the latter had not formally been a committee member.[90] But the minister correctly credited the German-American jurist with an important contribution. Kronstein had not only facilitated Böhm's ascendance; he had also served as a commentator and intellectual sparring partner as well as a link to US antitrust thinking. He invited Hallstein to Georgetown in 1948, and two years later took a group of German colleagues, among them Böhm and Eberhard Guenther, the first president of the FRG's antimonopoly office, on a fact-finding mission to the USA. There, he introduced the German competition law experts to their American peers, who included Kronstein's wartime associates Thurman Arnold, Walton Hamilton, and Corwin Edwards. Even if he sometimes floundered in his role as "interpreter of minds," Kronstein found support for those like Böhm who considered the distinction between the power of cartels and that of trusts of secondary importance.[91] In his own publications, as well as in his professorships at Frankfurt (where he took over Hallstein's chair) and Georgetown, Kronstein continued along the lines of comparative law and academic exchange, sending some of his and Böhm's star students like future Christian Democratic politician Kurt Biedenkopf abroad.[92] Both lawyers eventually made their peace with the FRG's competition law – if, as Kronstein put it, understood "not [as] the end of development but rather a stop on the road"[93] – and Böhm could take extra pride in the fact that some of his most persistent academic antagonists now had to eat their words. In 1950 it was none other than Hans Carl Nipperdey who disowned his teachings from the 1920s and embraced the principle of free competition as unalienable and superior to contractual freedom and the freedom of association. Only if this was guaranteed, Nipperdey asserted in

"*Mont Pèlerin Society*" (Stuttgart, 2007), 272–5; Volker Hentschel, *Ludwig Erhard: Ein Politikerleben* (Berlin, 1993), 128–33.

[90] Kronstein to Böhm, Josten, Veit, Nell-Breuning, Ilau, Köppels, Müller, Heimerich, June 22, 1949, and Erhard to Kronstein, September 16, 1967, both Kronstein Papers.

[91] Kronstein, *Briefe*, 254; Heinrich Kronstein, "Antitrust – Rückblick und Ausblick," *Wirtschaft und Wettbewerb* 11–12 (1971): 827–30, here 827–8. One of Kronstein's friends, however, overstated his influence on US foreign policy; Fabian von Schlabrendorff, *Begegnungen in fünf Jahrzehnten* (Tübingen, 1979), 380–1.

[92] Heinrich Kronstein, *Neue deutsche wirtschaftsrechtliche Entscheidungen im Lichte des amerikanischen Antitrustrechts* (Karlsruhe, 1953); Kurt Biedenkopf, "Heinrich Kronstein," in Grundmann and Riesenhuber, *Zivilrechtslehrer*, 187–205, and Ernst-Joachim Mestmäcker, "Franz Böhm," in Grundmann and Riesenhuber, *Zivilrechtslehrer*, 31–54. Cf. Rehbinder, "Kronstein," 252.

[93] Heinrich Kronstein, "'Cartels' under the New German Cartel Statute," *Vanderbilt Law Review* 11 (1958): 271–301, here 301.

Rooseveltian terms, would German and European reconstruction succeed and "freedom from want and from fear" be attained.[94]

3.5 CONCLUSION

When neoliberal thinkers reflected on their rise after 1945, it was a common staple to describe their place in academia as marginal. Even when a host of professors from prestigious universities and research institutions began congregating at the exclusive resort on Mont Pèlerin, their self-perception as outsiders fighting an overwhelming, authoritarian-minded mainstream remained ubiquitous.[95] For all its obvious self-stylization there were grains of truth in this narrative, notably from the perspective of lawyers like Franz Böhm and Heinrich Kronstein (who would have rightly refused the label of a "neoliberal"). When it came to competition law and, more generally, to the question of how power was distributed in markets, it was indeed a minority position to doubt conventional liberal wisdom that the markets would sort themselves out. That the two lawyers also refused corporatist and socialist views that considered tightly regimented, state-controlled markets as an inevitable step in economic evolution, if not a hallmark of modernity itself, did not make them any more popular either.

Yet the very fact that debates about competition, concentration, and cartelization never vanished from the agenda between the 1920s and the 1950s illustrated that all was not well. Not only Böhm and Kronstein, but also Geiler and Göppinger, Neumann and Nipperdey observed that private economic power had grown exponentially and that governments and public administrations were either unable to rein it in or resorted to interventionist, authoritarian measures to assert their authority. Germany was hardly the only place where these processes could be observed, but here they were particularly prominent, due both to the legal endorsement by the Reichsgericht that Böhm so loathed and to the recurrent economic problems caused by war and rearmament, inflation, and depression. As a result,

[94] Hans Carl Nipperdey, "Die Grundprinzipien des Wirtschaftsverfassungsrechts," *Deutsche Rechts-Zeitschrift* 5 (1950), 193–8. Not everyone, of course, was won over. Forsthoff, for one, remained deeply antipluralist in his creed and rejected the neoliberals' free-market ideas; Müller, *Dangerous Mind*, 75; Meinel, *Jurist*, 355–6.

[95] This narrative is often merely reproduced – for example, in Plickert, *Wandlungen*, 1, 102. For corrections see Hagen Schulz-Forberg, "Rejuvenating Liberalism: Economic Thought, Social Imagination and the Invention of Neoliberalism in the 1930s," in Schulz-Forberg, ed., *Zero Hours: Conceptual Insecurities and New Beginnings in the Interwar Period* (Frankfurt, 2013), 233–68.

the three decades between the end of one world war and the end of another were characterized by a continuous debate about which order would be optimal and how it was to be achieved. If this was in line with the broader temporal patterns of an "organized modernity," the peculiarity of Böhm and Kronstein's era (and that of Hallstein, Huber, and Nipperdey) was that this may have been the last time jurists rather than economists held sway in directing fundamental economic debates.[96]

The argument about the *Wirtschaftsstaat* in general and competition in particular did not simply follow party lines, in fact not even the line between democrats and autocrats. Democratically inclined liberals like Böhm and Kronstein found common ground with their legal colleagues to the right while publishing in *Die Justiz*, which leaned distinctly to the left of the political spectrum. This mirrored their own perception of themselves as proponents of a third-way solution: positively capitalist in its general outlook yet without any naïve expectations as to private business interests.[97] Corporate strategies often, if not as a rule, undermined the market's invisible, price-driven hand. This is not to say that the two jurists distrusted each and every businessman. But they feared precisely the most successful because their drive and energy threatened to pervert the free economy. Thus, if liberal capitalism was unable to guarantee the preconditions for its own existence, something else had to, and that was the law. Only a clearly thought through, precisely formulated, and effectively protected economic constitution could guarantee economic liberties in perpetuity.

The groundwork for these ideas was laid in the late stages of the Weimar Republic, and to a large degree Böhm and Kronstein remained faithful to them through the 1950s, though in different contexts. Inside Nazi Germany Böhm finally saw the opportunity for a truly strong state to accomplish the goal of reining in private power without toppling into economic dictatorship. Precisely because there was no genuinely National Socialist economic system, Böhm found considerable room for maneuver and offered for consideration the nascent ordoliberal concept – rephrased in authoritarian jargon that catered to his audience. The regime's very opportunism provided substantial room for fantasy regarding the future order. And the Freiburg scholars' vision was not an oppositional Cloud Cuckoo Land tucked away in the remote corners of the Black Forest, but

[96] Peter Wagner, *Modernity: Understanding the Present* (Cambridge, 2012).

[97] The "third way" was a common trope; see, for example, Köster, *Wissenschaft*, 299–300.

a take on capitalism that squared with some, though not all, Nazi concepts of economy and community, of business and the state.

Meanwhile, Kronstein – always more of a practical man than his theorizing friend – found a receptive audience in American exile. With the US antitrust office moving to investigate international cartel arrangements that were believed to subvert the Allied war effort, experts in German trusts, syndicates, and cartels were highly welcome. Kronstein therefore joined the rapidly growing field of enemy studies, while also adopting views on how business deconcentration and decartelization were to be handled in practical terms. As a US representative in occupied Germany, Kronstein would apply these concepts while, even more importantly, building bridges to German ordoliberal thinking. His personal contact with Böhm, soon expanded to a significant number of jurists and economists in universities, municipalities, and state administrations, gave the nascent ordoliberal school an advantage when it came to determining the course of German capitalism. Its personnel – Böhm, Kronstein, Geiler, and Hallstein, as well as their disciples such as Ernst-Joachim Mestmäcker and Kurt Biedenkopf – overlapped strongly with the protagonists of Christian Democracy who, as Jan-Werner Müller has argued, were to dominate the political scene in postwar Western Europe. Culturally pessimistic, but also "chastened Weberians" in their understanding of politics (a notion rather in tune with Kronstein's pragmatic style), these jurists provided a grammar and a lexicon for the efforts to reshape German capitalism.[98]

Here, competition was one of the two key catchwords, while the notion of a determined, assertive state was the other. The Josten draft for the FRG's competition law marked the high tide of this line of conceptualizing the future republic's economic constitution. Yet the academics' power, even when they held public office as Hallstein and Böhm did in the 1950s and 1960s, went only so far. The eventual competition law bore all the signs of compromise with vested interests, represented by able corporate lawyers, and notably failed to tackle trusts with the same rigor meted out to cartels. But when compared to thirty years earlier, the move from private organization to state regulation had come a long way. The next stop would be European integration.[99]

[98] Müller, *Contesting Democracy*, 129–30.

[99] On the (ordo)liberals' rather different takes on regulation and control on the European level (and Böhm's incremental move toward Hayekian views) see Gerber, "Constitutionalizing," 69–74; Zieschang, *Staatsbild*, 93–4, 218–19; Plickert, *Wandlungen*, 24–50.

PART II

CONCEALING CAPITALISM

4

Capitalism, Wealth, and the Question of (In)Visibility

The Thyssen Family and Its Investments

Simone Derix

Having been left to economists for a long time, capitalism is now back at the center of sociological and historical research on modern societies.[1] Although tendencies to limit capitalism to "a particular kind of economy" continue to exist, a growing number of sociologists and historians call for a broader understanding of capitalism as denoting "both an economy and a society."[2] German sociologist Wolfgang Streeck holds that we "must" study "contemporary society as [a] capitalist society."[3] A capitalist society is one that has "on a current basis to work out how its *economic social relations*, its specific relations of production and exchange, are to connect to and interact with its *non-economic social relations*" (italics in original). Since economic social relations tend to "expand into and become dominant relative to their social context," capitalism cannot be considered "a static and timeless ideal type of an economic system." On the contrary, it "must be studied … as a *historical social order* that is precisely about the relationship between the social and the economic," a social order that emerged in Western Europe at the beginning of the nineteenth century and "has been continuously evolving

I wish to thank Moritz Föllmer, David Lazar, Pamela Swett, and Helen Wagner for their thoughtful comments and careful editing. I am also grateful to Moritz Föllmer for translating some sections from German.

[1] For an overview see Friedrich Lenger, "Die neue Kapitalismusgeschichte: Ein Forschungsbericht als Einleitung," *Archiv für Sozialgeschichte* 56 (2016): 3–37.

[2] Wolfgang Streeck, "How to Study Contemporary Capitalism?" *European Journal of Sociology* 53 (2012), no. 1: 1–28, quotes 1–2.

[3] Ibid., 1.

since" (italics in the original).[4] In a similar vein, social historian Thomas Welskopp argues that capitalism is deeply linked to modern societies, which he defines per se as capitalist societies. For capitalism is not "an isolatable subset of things and structures" that limits itself to "the economy"; rather capitalism exhibits strong tendencies to pervade every realm of society.[5] For Streeck, Welskopp, and others, such as Eva Illouz, it is the pervasiveness of a particular set of economic actions that permeates modern societies.[6] Thus, historical and sociological research cannot limit itself to studying the capitalist mechanisms of producing, distributing, and consuming goods but has to trace how they affect the social and political fabric.

In the ongoing debate about how best to approach capitalism, various suggestions have already been made, such as distinguishing between its "varieties" or highlighting its "commonalities."[7] Despite their differences, most approaches have a blind spot in common: the assumption that capitalism is deeply intertwined with visibility or at least that visibility is much more important than invisibility for the historical development of capitalism. Of course, one may counter this by pointing out that historical research has also focused on corruption as the dark side of capitalism or on business failures and the subsequent disappearance of their protagonists.[8] Nonetheless, hidden or invisible practices are considered peripheral to capitalism.

This chapter explores how a focus on the interplay of visibility and invisibility can improve our understanding of capitalism in Germany in the 1920s and early 1930s. For capitalist societies are shaped by the interaction not only between economic and noneconomic social actions but also between visible and invisible actions. First, I discuss how the understanding of capitalism in the first half of the twentieth century is closely linked to the notion of economic action as visible action. Second, I focus on the investments of the Thyssens, an ultra-wealthy industrialist

[4] Ibid., 3.

[5] Thomas Welskopp, *Unternehmen Praxisgeschichte: Historische Perspektiven auf Kapitalismus, Arbeit und Klassengesellschaft* (Tübingen, 2014), 7.

[6] See, for example, Eva Illouz, *Consuming the Romantic Utopia: Love and the Cultural Contradictions of Capitalism* (Berkeley, 1997).

[7] Peter Hall and David Soskice, eds., *Varieties of Capitalism* (Oxford, 2001); Wolfgang Streeck, "E Pluribus Unum? Varieties and Commonalities of Capitalism," in Marc Granovetter and Richard Swedberg, eds., *The Sociology of Economic Life* (Boulder, CO, 2011), 419–55.

[8] See, for example, Ingo Köhler and Roman Rossfeld, eds., *Pleitiers und Bankrotteure: Geschichte des ökonomischen Scheiterns vom 18. bis 20. Jahrhundert* (Frankfurt, 2012).

family, thereby highlighting the specific interplay of visibility and invisibility in the interwar period and its meaning for understanding capitalist societies.[9]

4.1 CAPITALISM AND THE REGIME OF VISIBILITY

The heyday of industrialization before 1914 was also a period of intense theoretical and public reflection on the visibility and invisibility of economic or economically grounded actions – in Germany and beyond. As early as 1899 American economist and sociologist Thorstein Veblen dedicated his *Theory of the Leisure Class* to conspicuous consumption as a means for the public display of economic and social power.[10] For Veblen, it seemed obvious that economic actions such as the consumption of luxury goods shape social relations. While Veblen neglected the historical implications of his theory, in 1913 German sociologist and economist Werner Sombart stressed, with reference to Veblen, how important the consumption of luxury goods had been for the development of capitalist societies. In his study *Luxury and Capitalism* Sombart tried to establish an explanatory link between the consumption of luxury goods, on the one hand, and the breakthrough of capitalism by boosting new translocal markets on the other. But, more important in our context, he assumed that the consumption of luxury goods is a visible action and that the markets that provide luxury goods are visible markets.[11] These early twentieth-century reflections considered visibility crucial for market action as well as for social action, thereby placing it at the very core of capitalism.[12]

A second set of texts matters when it comes to understanding the connection between capitalism and visibility: the remarkable number of early- and mid-twentieth-century articles and books focusing on the lives

[9] Sections 4.2 and 4.3 are partly based on Simone Derix, "Fortune internationale, philanthropie et patrimoine: le cas de la famille Thyssen," *Relations Internationales* 157 (2014): 41–54, and *Die Thyssens: Familie und Vermögen* (Paderborn, 2016).

[10] Thorstein Veblen, *The Theory of the Leisure Class: An Economic Study of the Evolutions of Institutions* (New York, 1899).

[11] Werner Sombart, *Studien zur Entwicklungsgeschichte des modernen Kapitalismus, vol. 1: Luxus und Kapitalismus*, trans. W. R. Dittmar (Munich, 1913) (first English edition: *Luxury and Capitalism* [Ann Arbor, 1967]). He refers to Veblen on page 70.

[12] In this perspective economic and social participation is deeply interrelated with competition, a central element of capitalism then and now. Jens Beckert bases his theory of capitalism on the "four Cs of capitalism": credit, commodity, competition, and creativity; see " Capitalism As a System of Expectations: Toward a Sociological Microfoundation of Political Economy," *Politics & Society* 41 (2013): 323–50.

and achievements of successful men.[13] Like the theoretical works mentioned before, these texts contributed to shaping contemporary knowledge and notions of capitalism by classifying certain actions and features as successful. Narratives of individual men who succeeded by founding big companies and amassing wealth have been attributed with similar functions to the exempla and vitae of saints in the Middle Ages. While their medieval counterparts provided guidance for a life agreeable to God, the exempla of the early twentieth century served as role models for taking the right steps to succeed in capitalist societies. The emergence of large companies was reduced to the achievements of a few men and at the same time described as the essence of their individual careers. Biographical narratives were a means to make these life courses accessible to everyone. By reconstructing the decisions and values of protagonists such as Andrew Carnegie or Alfred Krupp, (auto)biographies fostered the stereotype of self-made men who controlled not only their companies but also their own destinies. Although these biographical narrations kept the reader at a distance by portraying these men as geniuses who were by definition difficult to imitate, they paradoxically promised to enable the attentive reader to follow their example by shedding light on the secrets of success. Successful life courses were often ascribed to a specific set of capitalist virtues (for instance, high risk tolerance, leadership skills, creativity, or readiness for innovation), thereby providing blueprints for future capitalists. While the ranking of the virtues that were promoted shifted over time, the genre of the entrepreneurial success story remained very popular throughout the 1920s and 1930s.[14]

[13] See, for example, Franz Otto, *Männer eigener Kraft: Lebensbilder verdienstvoller, durch Thatkraft und Selbsthülfe emporgekommener Männer* (Leipzig, 1875); with a focus on entrepreneurs: Herbert Casson, *The Romance of Steel: The Story of a Thousand Millionaires* (New York, 1907).

[14] While Andrew Carnegie managed to control the narrations of his life by publishing posthumously an extremely popular autobiography, Andrew Carnegie, *The Autobiography of Andrew Carnegie* (Boston, 1920) (first German edition: Andrew Carnegie, *Geschichte meines Lebens*, trans. J. A. Sauter [Leipzig, 1921]), Alfred Krupp – as well as his father, Friedrich – became a popular topic of biographies from the 1910s onward: Dietrich Baedeker, *Alfred Krupp und die Entwicklung der Gussstahlfabrik zu Essen*, 2nd ed. (Essen, 1912); *Männer eigener Kraft: Heinrich Schliemann und Alfred Krupp* (Berlin, 1913); F. Wessel, *Alfred Krupp* (Berlin, 1913); Gustav Koepper, *Alfred Krupp* (Leipzig, 1916); Albert Tesch, *Alfred Krupp* (Leipzig, 1923); Wilhelm Berdrow, *Alfred Krupp*, 2 vols. (Berlin, 1926–7); Max Fischer, *Alfred Krupp* (Dresden, 1927); Jakob Strieder, *Alfred Krupp* (Lübeck, 1933); Wilhelm Hofmann, *Alfred Krupp: Der deutsche Schmied an der Ruhr* (Bamberg, 1934); Wilhelm Berdrow, *Alfred Krupp und sein Geschlecht* (Berlin, 1937) (translated into Italian, Spanish, French, and Swedish).

In addition to (auto)biographies, a growing advice literature instructed men (and occasionally women) on how to become successful and/or rich. Recent research has pointed out that advice literature, which at the end of the nineteenth century lavishly used biographical exempla, was more and more supplemented by explicit instructions on how to achieve an objective. Especially in Germany, from the 1920s onward "success" became a real buzzword in public discourse and was the topic of many guidebooks.[15] Simultaneously, there was an increasing tendency to differentiate between "performance" and "success" – the latter not necessarily resulting from performance but from the ability to render individual performances and capacities visible.[16] Success manifested itself in public performance.

Both biographies and advice literature focused on the individual, as did millionaires lists, a further type of document that can provide helpful insights into the linkage between capitalism and visibility. From 1911 to 1914, Prussian civil servant Rudolf Martin, a lawyer by training who worked at the Statistical Office, published lists of the fortunes and incomes of ultra-wealthy individuals in every federal state of the German Empire, which can be considered the root of contemporary billionaires lists.[17] Martin thereby fundamentally altered how wealth was perceived in public. By listing names, addresses, and branches of business alongside figures, wealth could be assigned to specific individuals and places and to a history of how it had been achieved. By personalizing assets and rendering them public, the lists allowed the people and careers they featured to be assessed, rated, compared, and criticized.[18] Furthermore, by demonstrating the economic power of nonaristocratic elites they modified ideas about who could be considered a member of the German upper class and implicitly presented German society as a capitalist one. The impact of the yearbooks reached far beyond the

[15] Stephanie Kleiner and Robert Suter, "Konzepte von Glück und Erfolg in der Ratgeberliteratur (1900–1940): Eine Einleitung," in Stephanie Kleiner and Robert Suter, eds., *Guter Rat: Glück und Erfolg in der Ratgeberliteratur 1900–1940* (Berlin, 2015), 9–40, here 20–1.

[16] Gustav Ichheiser, *Kritik des Erfolgs: Eine soziologische Untersuchung* (Leipzig, 1930).

[17] The first publication was Rudolf Martin, *Jahrbuch des Vermögens und Einkommens der Millionäre in Preußen* (Berlin, 1911). See Eva Maria Gajek, "Sichtbarmachung von Reichtum: Das Jahrbuch des Vermögens und Einkommens der Millionäre in Preußen," *Archiv für Sozialgeschichte* 54 (2014): 79–108, generally Simone Derix, "Zwischen Meritokratie und Heritokratie: Reiche Familien und große Vermögen in der Moderne," *ZeitRäume: Potsdamer Almanach des Zentrums für Zeithistorische Forschung* (2014), 32–42.

[18] Gajek, "Sichtbarmachung," 84–9.

end of the German Empire. They were a summary of the economic and social effects of the heyday of industrialization and established a specific tradition of disclosing information on economic and social inequality that continued after 1918. Although Martin stopped publishing his yearbooks in 1914, he resumed making lists in the Weimar period, and his yearbooks inspired other authors who took up his method of rating the wealthy.[19] The lists were complementary to the aforementioned biographies and guidebooks in that they responded to the fascination with capitalist success by nourishing a growing skepticism toward its moral implications.[20] The yearbooks established a new public interest in singling out the profiteers of capitalism, to be not only cheered and followed but also observed and judged. At the same time biographies, guidebooks, and lists were all grounded in the belief that revealing capitalist values, actions, and effects could facilitate social participation – either by imitating them or by controlling, criticizing, and sanctioning them.

Scandals were a further way of publicly responding to the "transgression of certain values, norms, or moral codes" involving the "disclosure and condemnation" of elements of "secrecy and concealment."[21] Now that the political scandals that had rocked the political culture of Imperial Germany have been thoroughly analyzed, in recent years the focus of academic attention has shifted toward the Weimar and Nazi eras.[22] The relevant studies use scandals as a means to explore the political culture of the period as well as "the shadier sides of capitalism."[23] Like the lists of millionaires, scandals tended to render actions visible that had previously been kept in the dark. Quite literally, they shed light on hidden practices. In the 1920s and the 1930s this was true not only for political scandals but also for scandals concerning economic practices, thereby reflecting that "[m]ore often than

[19] Ibid., 105. See, for example, Georg Wenzel, *Deutscher Wirtschaftsführer: Lebensgänge deutscher Wirtschaftspersönlichkeiten. Ein Nachschlagebuch über 1300 Wirtschaftspersönlichkeiten unserer Zeit* (Hamburg, 1929).

[20] Rudolf Martin, like many authors of guidebooks to success such as Dale Carnegie, managed to become – at least temporarily – affluent through his publications; see Gajek, "Sichtbarmachung," 99–101.

[21] John B. Thompson, *Political Scandal: Power and Visibility in the Media Age* (Cambridge, 2000), 13–14.

[22] Martin Kohlrausch, *Der Monarch im Skandal: Die Logik der Massenmedien und die Transformation der wilhelminischen Monarchie* (Berlin, 2005); Frank Bösch, *Öffentliche Geheimnisse: Skandale, Politik und Medien in Deutschland und Großbritannien 1880–1914* (Munich, 2009).

[23] Martin H. Geyer, "What Crisis? Speculation, Corruption, and the State of Emergency during the Great Depression," *Bulletin of the German Historical Institute Washington* 55 (2014): 9–35, here 10.

not, bankers, entrepreneurs, and financiers operate close to the edge of what is legal and moral." Thus, "[f]or every political scandal there were legions of similar cases about dubious business practices, wrongdoings, and speculative moves on the stock market."[24] Weimar Germany experienced several scandals concerning business practices and failures. These were broadly discussed in public and became a means of social exclusion merging smoothly with antisemitic stereotypes, as Martin Geyer has demonstrated.[25]

4.2 KEEPING CAPITAL INVISIBLE

Biographical narrations, guidebooks, lists of millionaires, and scandals linking capitalism with a regime of visibility had one thing in common: they focused on how wealth and success were achieved. That is true for the interwar period as well as the previous decades. While those still hoping to become rich were mainly interested in such recipes for success, the preoccupations of those who had already accumulated capital shifted. Their concern was not only how to make money but also how to keep it safe and stay affluent. Consequently, contemporary cultures of capitalism were shaped by complex processes of handling risk: perceiving, assessing, taking, or avoiding it – depending on expectations for the future.

German sociologist Jens Beckert has highlighted the fictional character of expectations, which depend on "cultural frames, dominant theories, the stratification structures of a society, social networks, and institutions," as well as attempts at "manipulation by powerful actors."[26] Implicitly, there is a historicity of expectations, as their framings, their "conditions of uncertainty," change over time.[27] From the perspective of wealthy and ultra-wealthy people, the German state had increasingly demanded to participate in their wealth by imposing asset and income taxes from the 1890s onward and by introducing inheritance taxes in 1906. Already at that time debates arose on how to spread the tax burden across German society. Wealthy citizens in particular began to avoid taxes

[24] Ibid., 10 and 12.

[25] Ibid. See also Geyer, *Kapitalismus und politische Moral. Oder: Wer war Julius Barmat?* (Hamburg, 2018), and " Contested Narratives of the Weimar Republic: The Case of the 'Kutisker-Barmat Scandal,'" in Kathleen Canning, Kerstin Barndt, and Kristin McGuire, eds., *Weimar Publics/Weimar Subjects: Rethinking the Political Culture of Germany in the 1920s* (New York, 2010), 211–35.

[26] Beckert, "Capitalism," 326; Beckert, *Imagined Futures: Fictional Expectations and Capitalist Dynamics* (Cambridge, MA, 2016).

[27] Beckert, "Capitalism," 326.

whose impact on their fortune was, in actual fact, fairly limited.[28] The tendency to perceive taxes and other demands of the state as an unjust burden and even as a threat grew stronger after the end of the German Empire, when the new minister of finance, Matthias Erzberger, centralized taxation at the federal level and reorganized the German tax system in favor of citizens with low and moderate incomes. The measures Erzberger introduced encompassed levies on war profits and capital gains, the emergency capital levy (*Reichsnotopfer*), taxes on inheritance, and transfers of landed property, as well as a "highly progressive" tax on income that became the "most important source of income for the German Reich."[29]

Among ultra-wealthy citizens, these measures were perceived as additional attacks on their fortune at a time already riddled with uncertainty.[30] While inflation had been suppressed during the war, in 1919 it became evident and more and more acute. Simultaneously facing the new tax system, a highly unstable currency, and the limitations on economic activity stipulated in the Versailles Treaty, banks and companies as well as bankers, entrepreneurs, and investors were eager to transfer assets to more secure and financially prosperous countries such as the Netherlands and Switzerland.[31] Therefore, the 1920s can be seen as a catalyst for the proliferation of wealth management practices still used today that rely heavily on complex financial constructs encompassing holdings, foundations, trusts, etc. These practices of wealth management presumed the mobility of assets and people across borders.

The case of the partly German Thyssen family of steel magnates can provide insights into peculiar economic activity of this kind that took

[28] Hans-Peter Ullmann, "Die Bürger als Steuerzahler im Deutschen Kaiserreich," in Manfred Hettling and Paul Nolte, eds., *Nation und Gesellschaft in Deutschland: Historische Essays* (Munich, 1996), 231–46.

[29] Carl-Ludwig Holtfrerich, "Rüstung, Reparationen und Sozialstaat: Die Modernisierung des Steuersystems im Ersten Weltkrieg und in der großen Inflation," in Uwe Schultz, ed., *Mit dem Zehnten fing es an: Eine Kulturgeschichte der Steuer*, 3rd ed. (Munich, 1992), 200–8, here 207–8; Gerald D. Feldman, *The Great Disorder: Politics, Economics, and Society in the German Inflation* (New York, 1997), 160–3.

[30] See, for example, Derix, *Thyssens*, 56.

[31] Youssef Cassis, *Capitals of Capital: A History of International Financial Centres, 1780–2005* (Cambridge, 2006), 176–7; Johannes Houwink ten Cate, "Amsterdam als Finanzplatz Deutschlands (1919–1932)," in Gerald D. Feldman, ed., *Konsequenzen der Inflation* (Berlin, 1989), 149–79; Houwink ten Cate, *De mannen van de daad en Duitsland, 1919–1939: Het Hollandse zakenleven en de vooroorlogse buitenlandse politiek* (The Hague, 1995); Marc Frey, *Der Erste Weltkrieg und die Niederlande: Ein neutrales Land im politischen und wirtschaftlichen Kalkül der Kriegsgegner* (Berlin, 1998), 349–61.

place in the 1920s and early 1930s.[32] Like many wealthy contemporaries, the members of the Thyssen family spread their assets – business and private assets being often difficult to distinguish – across borders. They discovered the "benefits of holding companies" and foundations in the interwar period, which allowed them to spread assets almost invisibly so that they became difficult to trace back to a specific country or an individual owner.[33] By establishing a network of interlinked holdings in the Netherlands and the United States as well as (noncharitable) family foundations in Switzerland, they strove to benefit from the aforementioned "shadier sides of capitalism."

The history of these investments and their organization is difficult to trace. Most of the available information was gathered by the British and Americans during the 1940s in cooperation with the Swiss authorities, in an attempt to gauge the Thyssens' assets and clarify whether they should and could be seized. One central aim of these inquiries was to disaggregate the structure of this cross-border financial braid. The transnational dispersal of the Thyssens' assets was virtually unknown beyond these experts, although it contributed decisively to the continuation of the family's ultra-wealth after 1945. This raises the question of which frames enabled and supported this durable invisibility. Three factors are discussed here: first, the invisibility of transnationally mobile asset managers; second, the invisibility of prominent family members' transnational activities; third, the invisibility of the less prominent family members.

First, while there was an institutional and organizational dimension to transnational financial transactions, their success depended on choosing the right advisors and middlemen. Such people needed to be trusted with assessing risks, inventing appropriate vehicles for moving and saving assets, and handling these vehicles inconspicuously. Bankers and lawyers involved in the business scandals of the second half of the 1920s can be viewed as *Grenzgänger* (border-crossers), with an allusion to the moral sense of the word.[34] Contemporaries widely regarded them as adventurers who, by transgressing laws and social norms, caused damage not only to the German state and society but also to the clients whose assets they put at risk. In a way they represented an inverted version of the microfoundations of capitalist actions as

[32] Derix, *Thyssens*, 323–78.

[33] Willi Redelmeier quoted in Houwink ten Cate, "Amsterdam," 155.

[34] Geyer, "What Crisis?" 10.

described by sociologist Jens Beckert.[35] In avoiding the "risks" of inflation and taxation, they ran the risk of moral decline, thereby creating their own way of "success seeking by risk taking."[36] Furthermore, the relationship between investors and their middlemen was strongly based on trust, especially since neither the clients nor their agents wanted the transactions to become public. Thus, as I have suggested elsewhere, these middlemen should be viewed as "hidden helpers."[37]

Second, literal border-crossing, the practice of moving assets across frontiers, can help differentiate between other forms of border-crossing in the interwar period. Whereas Streeck has specified "border-crossing" as a "metaphor for the dynamics of capitalist growth" in contemporary societies, describing the power of "profit-pursuing actors seeking to extend economic exchange across demarcation lines," the practices of the 1920s and 1930s reveal a more ambivalent picture of human and financial mobility.[38] The period appears very ambiguous when it comes to economic or economically grounded activities trespassing national borders. On the one hand, Germans maintained a deep fascination with economic success and the high standard of living it allowed, including extensive traveling and the consumption of imported goods. On the other hand, there was a strong pressure to commit to one's nation. People who were identified as "international" were increasingly eyed with suspicion. This was especially true for those men who were, in addition, classified as important capitalist actors.

This skepticism started before World War I. The late nineteenth and early twentieth centuries were a period of heightened mobility of both people and commodities across borders and intensified nationalization of people and things. Virtuousness was closely related to patriotism. Unsurprisingly, in the run-up to the war, Rudolf Martin, the inventor of the millionaires lists, promoted paying taxes as a patriotic duty.[39] Although with fluctuations, after World War I wealthy economic actors continued to be suspected of using the state, nation, and national economy to increase their own profits or hide assets from the state.[40] This climate of suspicion

[35] Beckert, "Capitalism." [36] Ibid., 329.

[37] Simone Derix, "Hidden Helpers: Biographical Insights into Early and Mid-Twentieth Century Legal and Financial Advisors," *European History Yearbook* 16 (2015): 47–62.

[38] Streeck, "How to Study Contemporary Capitalism?" 6.

[39] See, for example, Rudolf Martin, *Jahrbuch des Vermögens und Einkommens der Millionäre in Bayern* (Berlin, 1914), 1–5.

[40] For critical accounts of the German industrialist Hugo Stinnes's putative patriotism, see, for example, Edmund Stinnes, *Ein Genie in chaotischer Zeit* (Bern, n.d.), 18–19.

reached a further climax at the end of the 1920s and early 1930s before and during the unfolding of the Great Depression. The German government took measures to control the transnational financial transactions of its citizens by introducing foreign exchange controls in 1931.[41]

This discrepancy between practices and required attitudes resulted in contradictory behavior on the part of wealthy citizens, who often staged a pronounced nationalism while at the same time leading a transnational life. For instance, during the 1920s Heinrich Thyssen-Bornemisza, a Prussian citizen by birth who additionally adopted Hungarian citizenship in 1906, was traveling between several luxurious properties and rented hotel suites in, among other countries, Hungary, the Netherlands, and Germany. In 1932 Thyssen-Bornemisza, the third son and heir of steel magnate August Thyssen, moved to Switzerland following the large share of his mobile assets that, without German authorities noticing, had been transferred step by step to Swiss family foundations interlinked with holdings in the Netherlands.[42] By establishing holding companies and foundations in different countries through middlemen and giving the new entities obscure names, he managed to create a certain institutional distance between himself and a large portion of his assets. Moreover, during the 1930s Heinrich led a reclusive life in Switzerland, continuing his habit of traveling extensively throughout Europe even after the beginning of World War II. In contrast to this mobility of man and money, which he tried to make as inconspicuous as possible, he limited his public appearances to Germany, hiding his transnational way of life and adapting his public life to the expectations of his country of origin – for instance, by participating in the German horse racing milieu where he was re-Germanized and addressed as "Baron von Thyssen."[43] These public appearances within a national framework may have enabled a lifestyle that was in fact decidedly international but for a long time went unnoticed as such.

Third, the case of Heinrich Thyssen-Bornemisza echoes the aforementioned basic link between capitalism and visibility, including the focus on the individual. As in (auto)biographies and millionaires lists, public attention

[41] See Ralf Banken, "Das nationalsozialistische Devisenrecht als Steuerungs- und Diskriminierungsinstrument 1933–1945," in Johannes Bähr and Ralf Banken, eds., *Die Wirtschaftssteuerung durch Recht im Nationalsozialismus: Studien zur Entwicklung des Wirtschaftsrechts im Interventionenstaat des "Dritten Reiches"* (Frankfurt, 2006), 121–236.

[42] Derix, *Thyssens*, 162–70, 346–51.

[43] Felix de Taillez, *Zwei Bürgerleben in der Öffentlichkeit: Die Brüder Fritz Thyssen und Heinrich Thyssen-Bornemisza* (Paderborn, 2017), 108–88.

as well as the attention of the authorities was focused on individual persons, actions, and moorings.[44] However, a closer look at the "shadier sides" of economic action brings networks – family and kin in particular – into the picture. It is easily overlooked that economic actors were constrained by multiple responsibilities and commitments, including their personal relations, and that these personal relations could play an important role in wealth management. This certainly goes for Heinrich Thyssen-Bornemisza, who throughout the 1930s was financially bound to a family network, although he desired to cut off all financial ties with his elder and to this day much more prominent brother, the firstborn Fritz. In 1926 Heinrich and Fritz had inherited equal parts of their father's assets (37.5 percent each), encompassing shares in companies, banks, etc., that were difficult to disentangle and divide.

Moreover, the case of the Thyssen family illustrates how family and kin could actively take part in and shape the dubious networks to which the discourse on business scandals often refers in a very abstract way. Family and kinship networks seem to have been a blind spot for both the public and the authorities. The tendency to narrate success stories around selected individuals and their outstanding achievements created a large group of family members and kin who remained in the shadows.

A case in point are the Thyssens' family foundations in Switzerland, which became especially attractive during the economic crises of the 1920s and 1930s. Germany's neighbor enjoyed the reputation of a fairly safe financial center offering favorable tax conditions. The Thyssens located several family foundations there, carefully designed to safeguard their assets: the Kaszony-Stiftung in Schwyz (from 1926), later Chur (from 1945), the Familienstiftung Sammlung Schloss Rohoncz in Schwyz (from 1931), later Chur (from 1945), and the Pelzer-Stiftung in Ennenda, Glarus (from 1931). The Kaszony-Stiftung and the Familienstiftung Sammlung Schloss Rohoncz were founded by Heinrich Thyssen-Bornemisza. He transferred large parts of the inherited shares of the family's steel business to the Kaszony-Stiftung, while a couple of years later he made over his valuable art collection to the Familienstiftung Sammlung Schloss Rohoncz. The Pelzer-Stiftung nominally originated with Hedwig de Neuter, August Thyssen's divorced wife, who figured as its founder and a member of its supervisory board. The assets transferred to the foundation, however, can be traced back to her son Fritz and her granddaughter

[44] For an account of changing notions of individuality, see Moritz Föllmer, *Individuality and Modernity in Berlin: Self and Society from Weimar to the Wall* (Cambridge, 2013).

Anita. Moreover, the Pelzer-Stiftung's financial transactions and decisions suggest that she acted as a front for Fritz Thyssen and his family.

That these foundations barely attracted contemporaries' attention was due not least to the names they had been given. Thus rendered invisible, they were arguably an inversion of the philanthropic foundations that the Thyssens had founded in the Ruhr area during the second half of the 1920s in order to fund orphanages and old age homes.[45] These proudly bore the family's name, whereas the Swiss foundations' names could only be deciphered by those in the know. Kaszony was the noble predicate of the Bornemisza family, into which Heinrich had married in 1906 and whose baronial title was transferred to him after his adoption by his father-in-law. The name thus had a connection to the family while at the same time, owing to its Hungarian connotation, being distanced from the German origin of the foundation's assets. The name Sammlung Schloss Rohoncz also pointed to Hungary. Until 1919 Heinrich and Margit Thyssen-Bornemisza had lived at Rohoncz Castle in western Hungary, which remained in the family's possession until 1945. Both names thus drew on familial contexts whose knowledge required close acquaintance with the Thyssens.

The same goes for the Pelzer-Stiftung,[46] which was given Hedwig de Neuter's maiden name. The fact that in twentieth-century society women generally received less attention than men came in handy when the aim was to keep a low profile. Moreover, few contemporaries would have known the maiden name of August Thyssen's former wife. Intentionally or not, the foundation's name facilitated unimpeded activity and, once the authorities of various countries had begun to take an interest, made it nearly impossible for them to reconstruct how it worked and what it was doing. In this case the Thyssens were also able to make use of Hedwig de Neuter's Belgian nationality, which she had acquired in 1893 and again in 1899 by marrying Belgians (her third and fourth marriages). Beside herself, a Belgian, the foundation's supervisory board consisted of a Dutch banker and lawyer and it was administered by a Dutch trust connected to the Bank voor Handel en Scheepvaart (BHS). Not only that, but having been founded in Switzerland, the Pelzer-Stiftung operated under Swiss law.

These arrangements rendered the Pelzer-Stiftung's national categorization difficult, obscured its workings, and thwarted the identification of its

[45] See Stiftungsurkunden, April 4, 1927, Bundesarchiv Berlin-Lichterfelde, N2307/11, 55–61.

[46] Derix, *Thyssens*, 351–5.

assets with any state. This constituted a big challenge for tax authorities as well as the agencies tracing enemy assets after the two world wars. These institutions were geared toward connecting wealth to particular nations, an objective family foundations were purposely designed to undermine. Such activities have been analyzed with respect to corporations under the headings of "cloaking," "camouflage," or "concealment," but they were also pursued by family foundations.[47] A further factor was that Switzerland did not force these foundations to publish reports of their activities, which impeded any attempt at observation and analysis. German tax authorities and the German foreign exchange control office had started investigating the finances of the Thyssen family before World War II, including making inquiries with the Swiss authorities, while US and British authorities became interested in the Thyssen assets only during the war in conjunction with questions of war financing and enemy property legislation. However, all investigators found it difficult to find out about the foundation's activities in the first place, had to invest significant resources in tracing them, and needed real perseverance to arrive at any kind of result. In this case the involvement of a lesser-known family member facilitated the invisibility of economic action and inverted the notion of success: it was not the individual who succeeded but a network, and not by staging success but by hiding it.

4.3 THE PRICE OF INVISIBILITY

The case of the Pelzer-Stiftung, however, shows that the deliberate construction of invisibility also carried risks for the wealthy. The invisibility of assets could come at the cost of limiting agency and control; moreover, it could not always prevent the loss of assets. On September 3, 1939, two days after Germany had invaded Poland and thus entered into war with the United Kingdom, it transpired that 1,100 gold bars were kept at the City Safe Deposit in London. It was surmised that these belonged to German owners; the suspicion fell

[47] See Christiane Uhlig, Petra Barthelmess, Mario König, Peter Pfaffenroth, and Bettina Zeugin, eds., *Tarnung, Transfer, Transit: Die Schweiz als Drehscheibe verdeckter deutscher Operationen 1939–1952* (Zurich, 2001); Gerard Aalders, *Operatie Safehaven: Kruistocht tegen een Vierde Rijk* (Amsterdam, 2006); Gerard Aalders and Cees Wiebes, *The Art of Cloaking Ownership: The Secret Collaboration and Protection of the German War Industry by the Neutrals* (Amsterdam, 1996); Christopher Kobrak and Jana Wüstenhagen, "International Investment and Nazi Politics: The Cloaking of German Assets Abroad, 1936–1945," *Business History* 48 (2006): 399–427. On the visual dimension of the perception of trusts, see Daniel Damler, *Konzern und Moderne: Die verbundene juristische Person in der visuellen Kultur 1880–1960* (Frankfurt, 2016).

first on the Stinnes family, then on the Thyssens.[48] After the British Parliament passed the Trading with the Enemy Act on September 5, it appeared possible for the Board of Trade to seize the gold, which would have been a welcome addition to public finances during a costly war.[49] However, the plan proved impossible to implement since the deposit had been commissioned by an American citizen, Cornelis Lievense, the director of the Union Banking Corporation (UBC) in New York; there was no blacklist on which to put him.[50] While the British learned only later that Lievense and the UBC were acting in the Thyssens' service, the fact that the BHS, a Dutch bank founded by the family, had rented the safes for the gold bars made the connection apparent. Although the Treasury got involved and argued that the gold constituted an enemy asset, the intended seizure never took place.[51] As it turned out, the Thyssens' transnational asset management, including their family foundations, contributed to the reluctance of the British authorities.

The first problem for the British was that – in line with the contemporary custom of individualizing achievement and wealth – they suspected Fritz Thyssen to be the owner of the gold in question but lacked compelling evidence. Hence, the Custodian of Enemy Property refused to authorize a seizure. The second hindrance was that the Foreign Office, which was also involved, did not deem it opportune to declare him an enemy when he had openly pronounced himself against the Nazi regime with his recent flight into exile.[52] For these reasons the British preferred to negotiate a sale. They recruited Sir William Firth, a steel industrialist and Thyssen acquaintance, for a tricky mission.[53] In early March 1940, Firth went to see the industrialist in Switzerland in order to present him with an offer to purchase the gold. At first Thyssen only agreed to discuss the issue as a hypothetical case before he slowly opened up to his visitor's arguments. It seems as though he wanted to forestall public knowledge of his assets and hence showed himself prepared to sell.[54]

[48] Siepmann, Bank of England, to Fass, Custodian for Enemy Property, September 14 and 19, 1939, The National Archives, London (TNA), T 236/6780; Minute, June 1949, TNA, T 236/6781.

[49] See Fass to Siepmann, September 20, 1939, TNA, T 236/6780.

[50] See Stopford to Rowe-Dutton, September 28, 1939, TNA, T 236/6780.

[51] See Speed to Rowe-Dutton, October 24, 1939, TNA, T 236/6780.

[52] See Rowe-Dutton, Treasury, Minute, April 10, 1940, TNA, T 236/6780.

[53] See Jebb, Foreign Office, to Cobbold, Bank of England, January 1 and February 19, 1940, TNA, T 236/6780.

[54] See Firth, Report, March 5, 1940, TNA, T 236/6780.

However, when he signaled his willingness to enter the proposed deal, Fritz Thyssen had to admit that it was not up to him to make the decision. He possessed property rights over no more than 318 of the 1,100 gold bars (585 belonged to the BHS). And even these he could not dispose of freely since they legally belonged to the Pelzer-Stiftung. Thyssen had to point Firth to Hendrik J. Kouwenhoven, the Dutchman who sat on the foundation's supervisory board, participated in its administration as the director of the BHS, and was one of the family's key "hidden helpers."

Negotiations turned out to be protracted.[55] On May 8, 1940, Kouwenhoven and new British negotiator Nigel Campbell seemed close to finalizing the deal – two days before Germany occupied the Netherlands, a coincidence of almost tragic quality. At the Treasury, the occupation instigated a change of strategy. It now hoped to treat the gold as an "asset of a person in enemy territory," a position that prevailed despite the objection that an American citizen had made the deposit in London.[56] On July 3, 1940, the Custodian of Enemy Property confiscated the gold based on the Trading with the Enemy Act of 1939. Now that Germany occupied the Netherlands, the BHS counted as an enemy of Britain, which meant that the gold lay in an enemy deposit and could be seized.[57] Three weeks later all 1,100 bars were sold for £3,098,693.[58]

Fritz Thyssen learned of these events only after the war. Although the decision to sell was nominally the foundation's to make, he had emphasized from the outset that "all transactions are subject to my approval."[59] In early June 1940 he had inquired about the state of affairs.[60] This letter, however, reached the ministry after the seizure had been decided. Internally the civil servants pondered the option of cutting Thyssen in on the proceeds, but he was officially told that the purchase offer had ceased to be valid.[61] This letter appears not to have reached the industrialist, who was staying in France at the time. As late as 1947 he told his daughter Anita of the

[55] See Jebb, Foreign Office, to Cobbold, Bank of England, March 20, 1940, including Annex Report C by William Firth, March 16, 1940; Fritz Thyssen to William Firth, March 30, 1940; Minute, May 4, 1940; Nigel Campbell, Report, May 10, 1940, TNA, T 236/6780.

[56] Rowe-Dutton to Barnes, May 14, 1940; see Speed to Rowe-Dutton, May 24, 1940, TNA, T 236/6780.

[57] See In the Matter of the Familienstiftung Pelzer, TNA, FO 192/220; Minute Abbott, July 9, 1948, TNA, T 236/6781; Speed, Board of Trade, to Beckett, March 8, 1950, TNA, FO 192/220.

[58] See TNA, T 236/6780.

[59] Fritz Thyssen to Firth, May 4, 1940, TNA, T 236/6780.

[60] See Fritz Thyssen to Treasury, June 3, 1940, TNA, T 236/6780.

[61] See Speed, Treasury Solicitor, to Secretary of the Treasury, June 11, 1940; Dansey to Jebb, June 15, 1940; Treasury to Fritz Thyssen, June 21, 1940, TNA, T 236/6780.

purchase, whose proceeds ought to be available to the Pelzer-Stiftung "for uncontrolled use."[62] Although the attempt to safeguard assets abroad had worked, the story reveals the limits of financial planning and risk calculation. That it was not for Fritz Thyssen alone to decide about the sale of the family's gold had been clear to him, but he could not anticipate the occupation of the Netherlands and the consequences resulting from it.

The case of the Thyssens' gold furthermore reveals the difficulties of government action. Even though the proceeds of the sale were no longer accessible to the family, they were with the Custodian of Enemy Property after the war and constituted a difficult problem ("just dynamite") for the British authorities.[63] From a postwar perspective it seemed morally questionable to have negotiated with Fritz Thyssen about gold that was retrospectively classified as an enemy asset. Not only that, the Treasury's letter cancelling the deal had conferred official status on the negotiations.[64]

The Thyssens put the issue back on the agenda in 1948 with the help of Ernst J. Cohn, a German émigré practicing law in London. Cohn recognized the gold deal's argumentative potential. In correspondence with the Treasury he characterized it as a "sacrifice of extraordinary magnitude."[65] He elevated the Thyssens and the Pelzer-Stiftung to Britain's secret partners and funders, at a time when Fritz Thyssen's financial and ideological contribution to the erection of the Nazi dictatorship was being debated controversially. Only then did Cohn and the Thyssens learn that, while the deal with the family had not materialized, the gold had still been sold, so the proceeds were legally recoverable.[66] They refrained from exploiting this, instead aiming for an out-of-court settlement.[67] Such a settlement finally came about in June 1952. In July 1951 the British High Court of Justice had held that the BHS, at that time mainly owned by the Thyssen-Bornemisza family, should be restituted the outcome of the sale of its 585 gold bars stored in the City

[62] Fritz Thyssen to Blass, May 5, 1947, including a letter to Anita Zichy, The National Archives at College Park, Maryland (NARA), RG 59, CDF 1945–1949, Doc. 862.20235/6–1847; see Cohn to Abbott, Treasury, June 4, 1948, TNA, T 236/6781.

[63] Gregory, TWE, to Playfair, Treasury, October 25, 1945, TNA, T 236/6780.

[64] See Gregory, Summary Thyssen Gold, October 25, 1945, TNA, T 236/6780.

[65] Cohn to Waley, May 5, 1948; Weston, Minute, May 13, 1948; Cohn to Weston, Treasury, May 18, 1948, TNA, T 236/6780.

[66] See Cohn to Abbott, Treasury, June 8, 1948; Abbott, Minute, June 9, 1948, TNA, T 236/6781.

[67] See Hodgson, Board of Trade, to Abbott, Treasury, July 29, 1949, TNA, T 236/6781; Cohn to Ellscheid, October 25, 1949, ThyssenKrupp Konzernarchiv, Duisburg (TKA), NEll/97.

Safe Deposit, thereby facilitating the negotiations for the Pelzer-Stiftung. Furthermore, the Pelzer-Stiftung was granted additional support from the Dutch government, which considered the foundation "a Netherlands resident legal entity" rather than a Swiss foundation, given that two of its trustees were Dutch citizens.[68] The eventual outcome was that 55 percent of the proceeds remained with the British and the rest, £520,000, went to the Pelzer-Stiftung.[69] At this point Fritz Thyssen had already died, but the money was kept in the family, as his wife and his daughter profited from the settlement.

4.4 CONCLUSION

I began this chapter by showing how capitalism has been intertwined with visibility in both public and scholarly discourse. Since success is manifested in its public performance, visibility has been declared a key resource under capitalist conditions. The visibility of capitalist values realized in biographies, advice books, and millionaires lists also enables the public to control, criticize, and sanction capitalist practices. This angle, however, can easily obscure the fact that invisibility is an equally central element of capitalist societies. There is a hidden or downright shady side to commodification, creativity, risk-taking, and trust, which are connected to their visible counterparts in intricate ways. Many of the invisible practices that helped shape German society as a capitalist society remain to be analyzed.

By way of example, this chapter has explored the investments of the Thyssen family. It has elucidated the opportunities for keeping capital invisible by first employing transnationally mobile asset managers, second using the invisible transnational connections of prominent family members, and third installing lesser-known family members in crucial positions of a hidden financial network. To a large extent, it proved possible to steer and shape the attention of the public and the authorities. Attention could thus be concentrated on specific persons, while new options emerged for less prominent family members as well as the circle of financial advisors, all of whom remained in the background. The logic of visibility that governed theories of capitalism, biographies, advice literature, millionaires lists, and

[68] Dutch Embassy, Aide-mémoire, July 18, 1951, TNA, BT 271/596.

[69] See MacKenzie to Symons, March 10, 1952, TNA, T 236/6783; Brown, Board of Trade, to Eggers, Treasury, May 16, 1952, TNA, T 236/6783; Memorandum of Agreement, The Custodian of Enemy Property for England, the Administrator of German Property and Pelzerstiftung, June 24, 1952, TNA, BT 271/596.

scandals foregrounded individuals.[70] Therefore, it left much wiggle room for complex networks acting out of the limelight. This shows the power of figures in narratives and discourses that construed, established, and disseminated logics.[71] This also includes the mental framing of (capitalist) actions within the bounds of a nation or Europe while de facto networks and actions could extend their reach globally.[72]

Moreover, the chapter has highlighted the pitfalls of discreet asset management as, for example, in the loss of discretion with respect to assets that had been transferred to foundations designed to be as invisible as possible. The Thyssen family simultaneously avoided and exploited the logic of individual visibility. Hence, it managed to safeguard most of its assets through decades of political turmoil.

The chapter has also shed new light on the complex and sometimes contradictory interplay of visible and invisible actions. On the one hand, these actions emerged within a specific historical context that shaped their execution and perception. The ambiguity of a publicly displayed nationalism and a hidden transnational way of life and distribution of capital situated these hidden capitalist practices in the specific political and economic context of the interwar period and World War II. On the other hand, these practices are still relevant today. The invisible practices of wealth management, risk diversification, and tax avoidance are still in use – and have increasingly evoked public vigilance over the past decade. However, it is remarkable that in public debate these practices are often identified as recent developments, thereby neglecting their long-standing history. But taking a closer look at their long history highlights the importance of lines of continuity in capitalist societies, despite many political and economic changes. Turning attention to the invisible practices within capitalist societies can thus provide a key to understanding what helped uphold economic and social inequality within capitalist societies in the twentieth century.

[70] This focus on the individual is also brought out by Yves Cohen, *Le siècle des chefs: Une histoire transnationale du commandement et de l'autorité (1890–1940)* (Paris, 2013).

[71] For a sociological approach to storytelling, see Sophie Mützel, "Geschichten als Signale: Zur diskursiven Konstruktion von Märkten," in Rainer Diaz-Bone and Gertraude Krell, eds., *Diskurs und Ökonomie: Diskursanalytische Perspektiven auf Märkte und Organisationen* (Wiesbaden, 2009), 225–44.

[72] For the current debate on the European or global/colonial roots of capitalism, see Werner Plumpe, *Das kalte Herz. Kapitalismus: Die Geschichte einer andauernden Revolution* (Berlin, 2019), and Friedrich Lenger, "Eine eurozentrische Geschichte des Kapitalismus. Gefangen in der Kritik der Kapitalismuskritik," *Merkur* 73, 838 (2019): 59–67.

5

Semantics of Success

The Cases of Friedrich Flick and Henry J. Kaiser

Tim Schanetzky

This chapter discusses the careers of two businessmen regarded as outstanding symbols of the corporate world's capacity for adaptation in an age of big government.

Friedrich Flick, sentenced to a seven-year prison term in the first Subsequent Nuremberg Trial, active in the mining and steel-producing industry, can be seen as the prime example of a National Socialist businessman. He was a member of the National Socialist German Workers' Party (NSDAP), honored as a *Wehrwirtschaftsführer* (leader in the defense economy), and in close contact with men like Hermann Göring, Hjalmar Schacht, Wilhelm Keppler, and Heinrich Himmler. Flick greatly expanded his business in the Third Reich; he profited significantly from the "Aryanization" of Jewish-owned industrial enterprises and took over several businesses in the occupied territories. Up to sixty thousand forced laborers were exploited in the factories and mines he owned.

The career of American Henry J. Kaiser was no less symbolic, as he became successful as a contractor in New Deal civil engineering, involved in the construction of the Hoover Dam and many other major projects of the 1930s. In the early 1940s he also made a name for himself as the operator of shipyards on the Pacific coast and went on to build an industrial empire whose factories produced steel, magnesium, aluminum, and aircraft parts. Kaiser respected labor unionists as negotiation partners. He set up a corporate health insurance and embodied the consensus capitalism established by the New Deal. By summer 1944 Kaiser had become so popular with the

American public that leaders in Washington considered him a possible candidate for the vice presidency.[1]

The two men were about the same age, both were adept social climbers, and both controlled rapidly growing companies that employed almost half a million people combined. This chapter does not focus on their rather different business strategies, which have been researched in the same great detail as the organization of their companies or the mechanisms of their political lobbying.[2] Instead, it foregrounds the semantics of their success. My point of departure is the supposition that business owners who were exceptionally successful in an age of big government – especially in the war economy – adapted particularly well to its conditions and used them effectively for their own interests.[3] Narratives about the meaning of the company, its founding, or the personality of its owner fulfilled a dual function: within the company they facilitated confident decision-making, and outwardly they created an image of the company that contributed to its success.[4] Therefore it is important to be aware of this dual function of internal orientation and external representation in order to go beyond the level of a public relations history or a mere history of lobbyism.[5] I thus hope to prove my hypothesis that semantic maneuvers of adaptation and concealment

[1] Tim Schanetzky, *Regierungsunternehmer: Henry J. Kaiser, Friedrich Flick und die Staatskonjunkturen in den USA und Deutschland* (Göttingen, 2015).

[2] Kim Christian Priemel, *Flick: Eine Konzerngeschichte vom Kaiserreich bis zur Bundesrepublik* (Göttingen, 2007); Johannes Bähr, Axel Drecoll, Bernhard Gotto, Kim Christian Priemel, Harald Wixforth, *Der Flick-Konzern im Dritten Reich* (Munich, 2008); Norbert Frei, Ralf Ahrens, Jörg Osterloh, and Tim Schanetzky, *Flick: Der Konzern, die Familie, die Macht* (Munich, 2009); Steven B. Adams, *Mr. Kaiser Goes to Washington: The Rise of a Government Entrepreneur* (Chapel Hill, NC, 1997); Mark S. Foster, *Henry J. Kaiser: Builder in the Modern American West* (Austin, TX, 1989).

[3] John A. Garraty, "The New Deal, National Socialism, and the Great Depression," *American Historical Review* 78 (1973): 907–44. Wolfgang Schivelbusch, *Three New Deals: Reflections on Roosevelt's America, Mussolini's Italy, and Hitler's Germany 1933–1939* (New York, 2006).

[4] Per H. Hansen, "Organizational Culture and Organizational Change: The Transformation of Savings Banks in Denmark 1965–1990," *Enterprise & Society* 8 (2007): 920–53, esp. 922–7; Cornelia Hegele and Alfred Kieser, "Control the Construction of Your Legend or Someone Else Will: An Analysis of Texts on Jack Welsh," *Journal of Management Inquiry* 10 (2001): 298–309; Fabiola H. Gerpott and Alfred Kieser, "It's Not Charisma That Makes Extraordinarily Successful Entrepreneurs, but Extraordinary Success That Makes Entrepreneurs Charismatic," *Managementforschung* 27 (2017): 147–66.

[5] Niklas Luhmann, "Gesellschaftliche Struktur und semantische Tradition," in Luhmann, *Gesellschaftsstruktur und Semantik. Studien zur Wissenssoziologie der modernen Gesellschaft, vol. 1* (Frankfurt, 1980), 9–71, esp. 44–6.

played an essential part in the success of both Friedrich Flick and Henry J. Kaiser.

5.1 KAISER'S SPEED

During World War II Kaiser's shipyards employed some two hundred thousand workers and built 1,490 ships with a contract volume of more than $5 billion. The United States' entry into the war in December 1941 turned these "Liberty Ships" into symbols of the Allied war effort. Early on German U-boats were so successful in the North Atlantic that they destroyed more tonnage than American and British shipyards could replace – a severe shock for the United States. The US Maritime Commission (USMC) massively expanded its shipbuilding program in order to build more cargo ships in a shorter period of time. While the building of the first "Liberty Ship" took 244 days, the average construction time at Kaiser's shipyards soon dropped to 40 days – and kept dropping. He sharpened his profile with two publicity stunts: in Portland, Oregon, workers laid the keel of the *Joseph N. Teal* on September 13, 1942. Ten days later the ship was launched in the presence of President Roosevelt. Soon after that, workers in Richmond, California, welded the *Robert E. Peary* together in only four and a half days.[6]

These stunt ships and the resulting media coverage made Kaiser famous overnight. The public was largely unaware of the fact that it was mainly government incentives that led to this record production speed. The USMC procurement contracts guaranteed Kaiser's companies a fixed profit per ship and used productivity comparisons as their basis for the reimbursement of production costs. If all shipyards operated in a more efficient manner, the estimate of costs to be reimbursed decreased accordingly. Moreover, it was determined that faster and more efficient production would result in a significant increase in profits. Kaiser's was far from the only example of a success story focusing on a production miracle, and wartime production as such came to communicate patriotic messages.[7]

[6] Frederick C. Lane, Blanche D. Coll, Gerald J. Fischer, David B. Tyler, and Arthur Donovan, *Ships for Victory: A History of Shipbuilding under the U.S. Maritime Commission in World War II* (Baltimore, 2001, originally 1951); Christopher J. Tassava, "Launching a Thousand Ships: Entrepreneurs, War Workers, and the State in American Shipbuilding 1940–1945," PhD Thesis, Northwestern University (Evanston, IL, 2003).

[7] Mark Wilson, *Destructive Creation: American Business and the Winning of World War II* (Philadelphia, 2016), 92–108.

Yet Kaiser set himself apart from this overall pattern through two specific factors: personalization and speed.

First of all, the extent to which Kaiser the man embodied the messages he sought to communicate was striking, as was his willingness to engage in symbolic public actions. It was Kaiser who connected business activities that were in fact disparate, unrelated in terms of production, and overall more of a symbol for expansion opportunities created by the government. There had been a logical connection between the construction of dams and canals, the quarrying of sand and gravel, and the production of cement. Shipbuilding, however, did not fit this pattern; the extraction of magnesium and the production of airframe components and ammunition even less so. Yet all of them were sectors in which Kaiser became active within two years. In addition, the ownership structure in his ventures was much more complicated than the public focus on Kaiser's person suggests. Ever since the construction of the Hoover Dam, he had repeatedly appeared as a kind of entrepreneurial figurehead for consortia in which he actually held only minor shares. One typical case is that of the three operating companies that ran the West Coast shipyards: Kaiser's share in their capital was less than 14 percent in 1941.[8] Therefore the public and political success of Kaiser's strategy of personalization illustrates particularly well how attractive his message must have been at the time: *Time*, *Life*, and *Fortune* enthusiastically reported on Kaiser's biography because they could describe him as the protagonist of a return to American values: an entrepreneur whose individual drive helped the entire society move forward. This image stood in stark contrast not only to the actual distribution of shares in Kaiser's company but also to the actual parameters of the war economy, which brought with it an enormous bureaucratization both on the side of the state and in company headquarters.[9] Anachronistic as the idea of the ingenious entrepreneur was in the face of growing boards and committees, the apparent need for such a narrative remained just as great.

Closely tied to this personalization strategy was Kaiser's use of the speed narrative, which mainly served to conceal matters of funding and profits from the public. For many years he had acted on the principle that speedy progress during construction was paramount for the success of

[8] Henry J. Kaiser Papers, Bancroft Library, Berkeley (HJKP), Box 287, Folder 2, Hearings before the Committee on the Merchant Marine and Fisheries, House of Representatives, 79th Congress, Second Session, Sept. 23–26, Washington, 1946: Kaiser Affiliated Shipbuilding Companies, 1941–6.

[9] Adams, *Government Entrepreneur*, 100–18, 123–44.

a project. Yet only when construction of the Hoover Dam was already quite advanced did Kaiser begin to cultivate the speed narrative through symbolic actions. The construction of his summer home in the Sierra Nevada in the spring of 1934 set the tone. Eleven months later his younger son recounted at the Hoover consortium's victory celebration how his father had been shown a property on the western shore of Lake Tahoe that many considered of no value due to its swampy ground. In contrast, Kaiser "saw: a road winding in and out with thousands of wildflowers, a bubbling brook running along under picturesque bridges, a pretty beach with a snug bay for the boats, four stone houses, and a boathouse." Once his father had decided on the location, everything went very fast, "like all of his work," the son asserted. Proof of his claims about his father's abilities lay in the fact that construction on the estate was complete after only two months. The speech in which Henry Jr. praised his father's drive was printed and distributed to business partners, politicians, and journalists.[10]

Kaiser's systematic cultivation of this image was initially only directed at a relatively small audience, as in the example just cited. He was used to making a name for himself among partners, competitors, suppliers, political experts, and bureaucrats, but did not aim his efforts at a larger public until the war years. When the press became aware of Kaiser due to the shipyards' speed records in 1941, almost every profile of him picked up on the summer home story. The *Saturday Evening Post* set the tone, liberally embellishing the story: "Kaiser bought the land on Saturday, had power shovels, dump trucks and bulldozers at work on Sunday, was draining the land and dredging a speedboat harbor by Monday, had an architect down from Portland, Oregon, by Tuesday, began building a lodge, boathouse, and four stone cottages by Wednesday, with a crew of 100 men at work." The article went on to state that, due to the noise the machines made, Kaiser's neighbors had sought an injunction to stop the men from working at night. But "before the sheriff could serve the papers the project was finished and the machinery was gone." While construction was previously reported to have taken two months, we now read that "it had taken twenty-eight days to turn the swamp into a landscaped show place."[11] This is not the only instance where it is hardly possible to separate character and stylization, reality and staging. Kaiser was reportedly a terrifyingly dashing driver, though there is no evidence to this effect.

[10] HJKP, 255/1, Testimonial Dinner, May 9, 1935.
[11] HJKP, 259/13, *The Saturday Evening Post*, June 7, 1941: Builder No. 1 (Frank J. Taylor).

The records do show that he engaged in speedboat racing with his neighbors in Tahoe. A constant phone user with supposedly the largest long-distance phone bill in the American West, owner of the largest cement factory in the world, inventor of the longest conveyor belt in the world – whenever the press was hungry for superlatives, Kaiser obliged. Even the fact that he was an immoderate eater (confirmed by the cholesterol values in his medical file) readily fit into this picture of a restlessly energetic man of action.[12]

Although this is hardly possible to determine exactly, Kaiser's case provides some evidence for the advantages his company was able to draw from such a success story. We do know that the narrative of speed had a major share in obscuring the connection between government contracts and Kaiser's capitalist pursuit of profit. The experience of World War I in particular was still very present in early 1940s Washington. At the time, politicians and journalists had criticized the armaments industry because it had made high profits without risk. This time too there was a wealth of scandalous news about armaments firms: during a tour of the country Senator Harry S. Truman had publicized many cases of bureaucratic inefficiency and nepotism in the awarding of government contracts. His initiative led to the formation of the Senate Special Committee to Investigate the National Defense Program, soon known as the Truman Committee.[13] Kaiser's narrative of speed has to be seen in this context as well. Not only did it fit perfectly into an armaments economy focused entirely on output and production, it also distracted the public from thinking about his profits.

Within the company, however, speed was a medium that rendered financial opportunities and risks visible. Going back to the construction of the Hoover Dam, progress charts provided information about whether construction was on schedule. When preparing a bid for a government contract, engineers and financial officers calculated not only material and labor costs but also the points in the process at which they would accrue, translating their planning into graphic diagrams. These could later be used to measure the actual construction progress, which also indicated the

[12] HJKP, 260/9, Medical Records Henry J. Kaiser; The Earth Movers, Part I–III, in *Fortune*, Aug.–Oct. 1943. Albert P. Heiner, *Henry J. Kaiser, American Empire Builder: An Insider's View* (New York, 1989), 361–74.

[13] Donald H. Riddle, *The Truman Committee: A Study in Congressional Responsibility* (New Brunswick, NJ, 1964); Theodore Wilson, "The Truman Committee 1941," in Arthur M. Schlesinger and Roger Bruns, eds., *Congress Investigates: A Documented History 1792–1974, vol. IV* (New York, 1975), 3115–261.

financial status of a project. Although budgeting and liquidity planning were professionalized in the course of the 1930s, the advantage of progress charts lay in the up-to-date control of costs and risk. While the financial indicators were put together at the end of the month, supervisors could measure the speed and progress of construction projects based on the amount of material used on a day-to-day basis.[14]

Moreover, the government contracts contributed to the internalization of the semantics of speed. Fixed-price contracts with binding delivery dates and high fines for breach of contract in case of delay created economic incentives, as did the strongly delivery-oriented salaries of construction superintendents who thereby directly shared in profits. The fact that Kaiser passed on a portion of his company's financial success directly to his inner circle had a similar effect. Measures to increase work speed had neither to be invented in a central place nor ordered by headquarters. Young site managers came up with the idea of having different teams of workers compete with each other on construction sites, which was certainly not a Kaiser invention. The same principle was adopted by the shipyards, where entire locations soon competed against each other. In fact, it was the competition between Kaiser's shipyards in California and Oregon that resulted in the building of the two stunt ships.[15]

The narrative of Henry J. Kaiser as someone who constantly pushed forward was not only familiar to anyone within his company, it also provided guidelines for organizational behavior. This became obvious in summer 1939 when a management position became vacant and men in the second and third tiers of the company hierarchy reflected on the skills a member of management at Kaiser should have. They agreed that the candidate needed to be "aggressive." On the one hand, this meant the ability to recognize an opportunity to rise through the ranks and to stand out through one's achievements as "a producer and a real money maker." On the other hand, creativity was considered important in order to make "productive, helpful suggestions from the management side either as to personnel, credits, or any other administrative work." Requirements like these illustrate an organizational culture essentially based on emulating Kaiser's personal example. His sons internalized this early on. Echoing his

[14] HJKP, 269/15, Estimate of Cost, Revenue Forecast for Boulder Canyon Project, June 10, 1933; Construction Program, May 1, 1933.

[15] Kevin Starr, *Embattled Dreams: California in War and Peace, 1940–1950* (Oxford, 2002), 147; Adams, *Government Entrepreneur*, 112–13.

father, Henry Jr. emphasized: "The success and the gains from it mean nothing." What counted instead was "the courage and the fight to come there."[16]

It seems fair to conclude that the semantics of speed played a significant role in shaping the company's organizational culture. The war economy created excellent conditions for the company's expansion into ever more areas, yet it took the string of successes between 1938 and 1941 to explain the optimism among the Kaiser management. After three decades of working in civil engineering and road construction and despite considerable opposition, the company had managed to set up its own cement works and not only enter shipbuilding but immediately beat all the competition in productivity. Kaiser's staff were now confident that they could achieve anything: apply a completely new and untested process for extracting magnesium on a large industrial scale; build and operate an industrial complex consisting of coal mining, blast furnaces, steel works, and rolling mills in the West; or enter the chemical and aircraft industries. Actual successes, their media echo, and public expectations mutually reinforced one other. This in turn resulted in an overestimation of the company's capabilities that caused projects such as the magnesium extraction to fail, or it led to bold dreams like the 1942 cargo plane proposal to send supplies to Great Britain by airlift.[17] The prospect that the Kaiser shipyards might be building aircraft in the near future met with disapproval among politicians, defense bureaucrats, and aircraft manufacturers. No expert believed in a rapid conversion of the shipyards to the tight production tolerances of the aircraft industry; the media, by contrast, reacted with enthusiasm to Kaiser's plan.[18]

Kaiser probably derived just as much satisfaction from his name being mentioned as a possible US vice president in 1944 as from the fact that his political ideas on questions of codetermination, postwar planning, or the peacetime conversion of the arms industry, spread in numerous speeches, now met with resounding public approval. Though rhetorically untrained and more persuasive as a salesman in a small circle, the entrepreneur now became a sought-after speaker. While he had delivered only three notable

[16] HJKP, 3/5, Waste to Reis, Aug. 3, 1939; Waste to Trefethen, July 24, 1939.

[17] Mark Wilson : "Making 'Goop' out of Lemons: The Permanente Metals Corporation, Magnesium Incendiary Bombs, and the Struggle for Profits during World War II," *Enterprise & Society* 12 (2012): 10–45.

[18] *Hearings before a Special Committee Investigating the National Defense Program.* United States Senate, 77. Congress, 2. Session purs. to S. Res. 71, Part 14, July 28–Aug. 11, 1942 (Washington, DC, 1942), 5760–8.

speeches in 1940–1, in 1942 that number rose to fourteen, and between 1943 and 1945 he gave some eighty-eight addresses. This great popularity indicates just how well the narrative Kaiser cultivated fit the times and how eager Americans were for stories like his.

5.2 FOUNDING MYTHS AND INFERIORITY COMPLEXES

Despite the fundamental differences between a democracy and a dictatorship, there were some similarities in the messages Henry Kaiser and Friedrich Flick issued about themselves. This becomes particularly evident when we examine the founding myths that both only started cultivating in 1940–1. In Kaiser's case this was the progressively embellished story of his arrival in California. When bids were sought for a major road construction project in Redding in 1921, Kaiser and his confidant Alonzo B. Ordway boarded a train to travel there. En route they realized that their train was not scheduled to stop in Redding. This is how Ordway told the story:

> We went up to the middle of the train where there wasn't any brakeman and opened the vestibule to jump off. I used to do a little hoboing in my time and was pretty good at hopping off moving cars, but Henry was a little heavy and we both had suitcases ... Henry decided to grab his suitcase and jump. He let go near the little Cottonwood station house and tumbled head over heels, skidding headfirst into a pile of railroad ties ... The station master came out just as we got to our feet and were examining our skinned hands and legs. "You damn fools," he said, and of course he was right. We lost a little skin and ruined our suits but we did get the job at $527,000, our biggest one up until then, and we've been in California ever since.[19]

Although the facts alone raise certain doubts about this story (at this point Kaiser had already won far bigger contracts, including in California), it served the purpose of a founding myth.[20] It testifies to Kaiser's strength of purpose and quick decision-making, his courage and his ability to persuade his staff to follow his ideas. The connection to California was especially important. Yet it was not enough for Kaiser to be perceived as a brilliant organizer or a determined contractor. He also claimed exceptional technical achievements for himself. As early as 1941

[19] Kaiser Engineers, *Henry J. Kaiser – the Legacy Continues* (in my possession, originally retrievable online http://home.earthlink.net/~peterferko/keweb/aboutke/history.htm); similarly, *Kaiser Industries: The Kaiser Story* (Oakland, 1968), 10–12; Heiner, *Empire Builder*, 21–2; Foster, *Kaiser*, 35; Adams, *Government Entrepreneur*, 21.

[20] HJKP, 2/6, Kaiser Paving Company, undated.

he boasted of having been the first contractor to have used wheelbarrows with pneumatic tires on his construction sites. Soon the increasing use of diesel engines in construction machinery was also said to be a Kaiser innovation. Even at the time it was hard to check the veracity of such details in Kaiser's public relations stories, and nobody seems to have felt the need for investigation. Thus they mainly illustrated that financial success alone did not suffice to construct a public image of an entrepreneur that was likely to meet with social acceptance.[21]

The inferiority complex of a social climber that shows through this narrative is even more obvious in the case of Friedrich Flick. Dismissed as a "scrap dealer" by the industrial establishment in the Ruhr valley, Flick also felt the need to embellish his biography. The first opportunity for this came on the occasion of his twenty-fifth anniversary as a board member, which he celebrated with his closest circle in early April 1940. In a long and tedious speech he recapitulated the most important events of his career, describing the true founding moment as having occurred during World War I, when he suddenly realized the "significance of scrap metal" and thus had "taken the initiative to start producing basic pig iron from turnings and blast furnace slag."[22] Three years later, on the occasion of Flick's sixtieth birthday, this had already become a narrative picked up in all press articles about him. Journalists highlighted his "gift for combining technical and economic concerns in a particularly successful way." Friedrich Flick united "the engineer and the businessman within himself," wrote the *Deutsche Allgemeine Zeitung*.[23] It is evident that Flick too employed the strategy of personalization. The idea behind it was made even clearer by a justification statement written in 1945. Looking at his numerous company takeovers, one could easily take him for a speculator, but "only by having an expert knowledge of matters such as coal and steel, ore and the scrap metal trade, as well as steel processing, of the entire circumstances of production and sales both in detail and in the big picture," had he been able to build up his company.[24] This point illustrates how strongly industrialists in the mining and steel-producing industries were focusing on the production sphere and how pronounced their

[21] HJKP, 259/13, *Saturday Evening Post*, June 7, 1941: Builder No. 1 (Frank J. Taylor); Heiner, *Empire Builder*, 29.

[22] Bundesarchiv Berlin (BAB), R 8122/80918, Address Flick, Apr. 1, 1940 (NI-3345).

[23] BAB, R 8122/135, *Deutsche Allgemeine Zeitung*, July 2, 1943: "Friedrich Flick zum 60. Geburtstag."

[24] Westfälisches Wirtschaftsarchiv Dortmund (WWA), S. 8/84, Manuscript Kaletsch (undated), 27–8.

prejudice was against merchants, bankers, and stock exchange speculators.[25]

Friedrich Flick certainly did not lack self-confidence, but after the Gelsenberg Affair of 1932 he had found himself in a defensive position semantically. The scandal broke during the run-up to the general election of July 1932. Former chancellor Heinrich Brüning and his minister for economic affairs had bought a company for 100 million Reichsmark to save Flick from bankruptcy – after two years of severe budget cuts and in a situation of mass impoverishment. The cabinet had never been informed and the minister signed the contracts on his very last day in office, days after he had received his certificate of discharge. From then on, the middle-class ideologues within the NSDAP were not the only ones who saw Flick as the embodiment of a capitalism that needed to be fundamentally reconceived. Critics on both the left and the right complained that Flick was not a "true" entrepreneur but a speculator. Political economist Rudolf Aron wrote in 1936 from his Paris exile that in a quarter of a century he had seen Flick make "dozens of stock transactions, but not a single industrial achievement."[26] Aron's judgment hardly differs from the disdain with which *völkisch* intellectuals looked down on Flick. Giselher Wirsing, for example, characterized him as an unscrupulous speculator. During the worst of the Great Depression, he wrote in the magazine *Die Tat* that a "true entrepreneur" was always in touch with his factory and his workers. Meanwhile speculators like Flick were only interested in that world to the extent that "it could be translated into stocks and bonds."[27]

Flick's efforts to control his public image have to be seen in the context of this defensive position. It is particularly striking that his fiftieth birthday in the spring of 1933 was not reported in the press at all. After the scandal following his bailout by the government in the previous year and recognizing the turmoil that accompanied the establishment of the National Socialist dictatorship, Flick chose to disappear from the public eye. Circumstances were favorable for that, as unwanted press coverage was no longer very likely in the strictly regulated public sphere of the

[25] See also Stefan Unger, "Die Wirtschaftselite als Persönlichkeit: Zur Selbstdarstellung von Unternehmern und Managern im Ruhrgebiet während der Zwischenkriegszeit," in Volker R. Berghahn, Stefan Unger, and Dieter Ziegler, eds., *Die deutsche Wirtschaftselite im 20. Jahrhundert: Kontinuität und Mentalität* (Essen, 2003), 295–316.

[26] Joachim Haniel (i.e., Rudolf Aron), "Der Roman des Herrn Flick," *Das Neue Tage-Buch* 4 (1936): 60–4, quotation 60.

[27] Giselher Wirsing, "Herr Flick und Herr Dietrich," *Die Tat* 24 (1932): 347–50.

Third Reich.[28] This can easily be seen in the summer of 1935 when he sought to take over the controlling interest in the Harpener Bergbau AG mining company: a part of its shares was to be exchanged for bonds in order to increase Flick's share from about 40 percent to more than 60 percent. Prior to the decisive shareholders' meeting, Flick personally invited the editors of the business press to a "beer summit" at the Hotel Kaiserhof in Essen. He kindly asked his all male guests to report as little as possible about his plans, and everyone obliged.[29] He may have used this occasion to indicate that he had obtained permission for the transaction from both the Reichsbank (the German Central Bank) and the Reichswirtschaftsministerium (the Ministry of Commerce), and that the authorities would issue a press embargo if they saw the need. Flick used this strategy again in 1936 when he planned the takeover of the Essener Steinkohlenbergwerke AG mining company.[30]

National Socialist press policy and Flick's close connections to Hjalmar Schacht and Hermann Göring allowed him to keep his company invisible to the public. His management even opposed the use of terms such as "the Flick company" or "the Flick group." Instead, the companies in the group were supposed to be treated as independent corporations. Annual reports and financial statements from the different corporations were deliberately published on different dates in order to prevent the press from reporting on several of them at the same time, thus possibly revealing their affiliation with the Flick group. Robert Tillmanns, who was in charge of handling the press during the war, claimed in retrospect that his work consisted mainly of "making sure that the press did not report on Flick. He did not like to be discussed in the press. Every time it happened, I received complaints."[31] Instead of addressing an abstract audience and cultivating his image in public, as Kaiser did systematically from the beginning of the 1940s, Friedrich Flick pursued a strategy of evasion, control, and limitation of media coverage. On the one hand, this was all in line with prevailing concepts of respectability. For decades to come the German corporate world would disapprove of all publicity that could be conceived as indiscreet forms of self-promotion. Exceptions to that rule were men like steel

[28] BAK, All. Proz. 2F, Roll 73, FC 6133 P, Interrogation Tillmanns, Jan. 16, 1947; Bähr et al., *Flick-Konzern*, 282–3.

[29] WWA, F24/49, Philipp to Flick, Aug. 9, 1935; Philipp, Aug. 8, 1935; Questions and Answers; Welcome Address Flick, undated; Steinbrinck, Aug. 14, 1935.

[30] Bähr et al., *Flick-Konzern*, 284–7.

[31] NARA, RG 260, Farben, Box 22, Interrogation Lang, Feb. 18, 1946; BAK, All.Proz. 2F, Roll 73, FC 6133 P, Interrogation Tillmanns, Jan. 16, 1947.

manager Walter Rohland, who was appointed *Vorstandsvorsitzender* (CEO) of the vast Vereinigte Stahlwerke conglomerate in 1943. The forty-five-year-old did not hesitate to accept a celebrity role as "Panzer-Rohland" in Albert Speer's home-front propaganda, which met with a skeptical frown from his colleagues and provided one of the rare cases in which an industrial career came to a halt in May 1945. On the other hand, Flick did more than just adhere to the rules of his trade – he was aware of the fact that a functional public sphere had quickly ceased to exist in the Third Reich. Not least because of the broad and unkind media coverage of the Gelsenberg Affair, he recognized the new conditions and used them to his advantage.

5.3 FLICK'S FAMILY BUSINESS

Hiding from the general public does not mean that Flick eschewed the semantics of success, however. Especially in his contacts with the ministerial bureaucracy and politicians he purposefully constructed his public image. He repeatedly presented his business decisions as a service to the national cause. In doing so he primarily portrayed himself as protecting the nation's interests. For instance, in one of the largest cases of "Aryanization" the state expropriated the heirs of Ignaz Petschek, a Bohemian lignite magnate, and transferred the stolen industrial assets mainly to the state-owned conglomerate Reichswerke "Hermann Göring." Flick, who had helped devise this mode of transferring assets, gave the Reichswerke access to black coal mines that he owned. In exchange, he was able to achieve a market-dominating position in the lignite industry of central Germany. Flick's management was well aware of the unlawfulness of the entire process. One of Flick's intimates frankly mentioned the possibility that the transaction might later "be dragged before international courts." Even when the deal had long been agreed upon, Flick's people continued lobbying for weeks in order to obtain written documentation stating that the company had only agreed to a government-initiated project in light of an "inevitable national-political necessity." A preamble to that effect was added to the notarized contract.[32]

[32] BAB, R 3101/30985, Contract copies, Mar. 6 and 12, 1940. NARA, T 83/64, Agreement, Dec. 9, 1939. Flick to Göring, Jan. 20, 1940, and drafts Göring to Flick, Kaletsch to Flick, Jan. 30, 1940, and Feb. 3, 1940; T 83/63, Flick to Kranefuss, Apr. 23, 1942, and drafts as of Apr. 16 and 23, 1942; Bähr et al., *Flick-Konzern*, 368–70.

Friedrich Flick repeatedly emphasized how the interests of his business plans and the political goals of National Socialism coincided. His most important means of achieving this was to exploit the idea of a family business. As early as 1934 Flick started thinking about restructuring his central holding company into "a private company owned by his family." The company later publicized this intention, claiming that the restructuring was mainly supposed to bring "stable conditions" to the "family company." The Friedrich Flick *Kommanditgesellschaft* (limited partnership), as it was now called, supposedly provided a simpler organizational structure for this "private family company," making Flick an "immediately responsible entrepreneur." It was important to portray the entrepreneur as a manufacturer: "back to being a manufacturing business is our motto."[33] In fact the restructuring was based on two very different ideas. First, it was meant to strengthen Flick's property rights by further increasing his share in the group's most important companies. The remaining small shareholders were subsequently squeezed out. Second, Flick wanted to find a way to use his considerable armaments profits as assets transferred to his heirs in order to reduce his taxable estate.

In light of the widespread resentment against "anonymous" corporations, it is hardly surprising that Flick emphasized his personal liability, and he was not the only industrialist to do so.[34] In addition, the concept of the "family business" resounded with key themes of National Socialist ideology. The elimination of labor unions and the creation of a so-called *Betriebsgemeinschaft* (company collective), the hierarchical roles of *Betriebsführer* (company leader) and *Gefolgschaft* (loyal following) – all this seemed easier to realize in a family business than in a joint stock corporation. For Flick, the language of "family" offered him an attractive alternative to the politically unpopular concepts of combines and corporations, especially for an entrepreneur whose rise would have been unthinkable without financial transactions and stock market maneuvers.[35] Yet

[33] BAB, R 8119 F/P-1364, Mosler, Jan. 15, 1934; *Wirtschaftlicher Ratgeber*, Mar. 27, 1937: "Innere Kräftigung im Flick-Konzern"; *Frankfurter Zeitung*, July 16, 1937: "Umbauten im Familienkonzern Flick"; *Leipziger Neueste Nachrichten*, July 16, 1937: "Familienkonzern Friedrich Flick"; *Liebenwerdaer Kreisblatt*, July 17, 1937: "Neuordnung in der Flick-Gruppe." All in Landesarchiv Sachsen-Anhalt, Merseburg (LASA, MER), Rep. I Mitteldeutsche Stahlwerke Lauchhammer, 499.

[34] Werner Abelshauser, "Rüstungsschmiede der Nation? Der Kruppkonzern im Dritten Reich und in der Nachkriegszeit 1933 bis 1951," in Lothar Gall, ed., *Krupp im 20. Jahrhundert: Die Geschichte des Unternehmens vom Ersten Weltkrieg bis zur Gründung der Stiftung* (Berlin, 2002), 318–22.

[35] Andreas Meyhoff, *Blohm & Voss im "Dritten Reich": Eine Hamburger Grosswerft zwischen Geschäft und Politik* (Hamburg, 2001), 154–9.

Flick went even further. Ever since the founding of the Friedrich Flick KG in summer 1937, he had repeatedly referred to his property in central Germany as an industrial *Erbhof* (hereditary farm) in the press.[36] This comparison also picked up on a genuine National Socialist plan for reform: by issuing the Hereditary Farm Law in September 1933, *Reichsbauernführer* (Reich Farmers' Leader) Richard Walter Darré had changed economic property rights in order to privilege mid-size farms. In the mid-1930s lawmakers considered transferring the law's provisions to the industrial sector as well, but such ideas were unlikely to succeed in practice since they ran counter to rearmament efforts.[37]

Looking at the semantic construction of his own image, which Flick purposefully promoted despite his pronounced aversion to public news coverage, one thing in particular stands out: inside his company the owner remained almost invisible. Certainly, he kept in regular contact with the boards of directors and supervisory boards of the corporations he controlled and regularly visited their plants. Yet, as a person, the owner was entirely missing from annual reports or company newsletters, from anniversary celebrations or staff cafeterias.[38] Thus there are hardly any documented statements by individuals on the periphery of Flick's company from which one would be able to infer that the public image of the entrepreneur served an internal orientation function, as it did in Kaiser's case. So, even if management staff found the organizational structure of their corporation disadvantageous, they did not hold Friedrich Flick responsible for it. For example, the managing engineer of the Lauchhammerwerk plant in Brandenburg considered seeking a new position in 1937. He was dissatisfied with the "odd organization of our company. Our board consists almost entirely of corporate finance executives (*Kaufleute*), specifically almost exclusively gentlemen who have

[36] *Frankfurter Zeitung*, July 16, 1937: "Umbauten im Familienkonzern Flick." Later an integral part of almost all articles on Flick's sixtieth anniversary; see, for instance, *National-Zeitung Essen*, July 9, 1943: "Ein Sechzigjähriger: Friedrich Flick," in BAB, R 8122/135.

[37] Adam Tooze, *The Wages of Destruction: The Making and Breaking of the Nazi Economy* (London, 2006), 182–99; Mark Spoerer and Jochen Streb, "Guns and Butter – But No Margarine: The Impact of Nazi Economic Policies on German Food Consumption, 1933–38," *Jahrbuch für Wirtschaftsgeschichte* 1 (2013): 75–88. Daniela Münkel, *Nationalsozialistische Agrarpolitik und Bauernalltag* (Frankfurt, 1996), 112–19, 258–60.

[38] LASA, MER, Rep. I 01, AKW, XIb Nr. 28, *Der Braunkohlebergmann: Sondernummer zum 60jährigen Bestehen der AKW* (Berlin, 1941); BAB, R 8122/603, *Der Werksbote*. Werkszeitschrift der SGW Döhlen; Bergbau-Archiv Bochum, 45.16 and 17, *Harpen*. Werkszeitschrift. Ownership structure is not reported while Flick as owner is not covered.

practically nothing to do with our plant." As a technical engineer, he himself was only an authorized officer (*Prokurist*) despite his extensive responsibilities, which, he said, led to "a number of difficulties." Friedrich Flick had created that organizational structure – but the technical engineer of the Lauchhammerwerk was neither personally acquainted with the owner nor had he heard that the "difficulties" were a direct result of Flick's views on corporate governance. The notion of inspiring personal loyalty and setting himself up as a figure to be identified with apparently only occurred to him in relation to the closest circle of his corporations' financial boards.[39]

5.4 CONCLUSION

Friedrich Flick's well-judged publicity was mainly directed at an audience within his industry and at the leading figures in the Nazi Party, the military, and the ministerial bureaucracy. It was similar, in some ways, to Kaiser's public relations campaigns about his own person. But while the American businessman also addressed a broader public, at least from the beginning of the war, recognizing the value of spreading messages about himself both within and beyond his companies, Flick used the censored and regulated press of the Third Reich primarily in order to stay out of the public eye as much as possible. And this is not the only difference that cannot be explained solely by the disparate political circumstances of a democracy and a dictatorship.

Particularly striking is Kaiser's willingness to transmit his message in so personal a manner and to unscrupulously exploit his private life to this end – only thus can the special effectiveness of his semantics of speed be explained. He also benefited from the particular conditions of his industry for, at the time of his arrival in the media, Kaiser's plant produced neither arms nor ammunition, but mostly cargo ships. In the context of submarine warfare in the North Atlantic, however, these vessels became of great military-strategic importance and consequently were at the center of public attention. Kaiser seized the convenient opportunities for self-promotion that came with shipbuilding. In comparison, creating this kind of publicity for arms production was completely out of the question for Flick's company. Even inside the organization, the confidentiality the military imposed was reason enough to speak only of so-called

[39] LASA, MER, Rep. I Mitteldeutsche Stahlwerke Lauchhammer NR.558/1: Ries to Siepmann, Oct. 7, 1937.

Sonderfabrikation (special production) when referring to arms manufacturing. Yet even without such restrictions it certainly would not have occurred to Flick to publicize details about his private life. While Kaiser's self-promotion helped establish his brand, Flick trusted in the traditional channels of influence opened up by political lobbyism, thus avoiding any unnecessary publicity. In addition, a striking feature of both cases is what was missing: when creating their legends for the public, neither Kaiser nor Flick had their customers in an abstractly conceived market in mind. In the German tradition of capitalism there was little need for this because cartels and syndicates organized sales. Moreover, Kaiser and Flick did not produce consumer goods and, since the 1930s, government consumption dominated a market that was eventually swallowed up completely by military demand once the war began. Therefore neither had to worry about selling their products – in the circumstances of the 1930s and World War II this was the government's responsibility. All the more important were the advantages they could gain in a political-bureaucratic market. The semantics of success contributed considerably to these.

Limiting the scope of this chapter to these strategies is by no means intended to suggest that suitable narratives alone serve to explain the success of these two businessmen. I have focused on a central element of their success that has to be seen alongside the lobbying power and corruption that have already been well researched. In this area there are remarkable analogies between Kaiser and Flick. Both relied on strong personalization in an age of depersonalized capitalism, both developed a founding myth, and both claimed also to have been influential as technical innovators. And, finally, as government entrepreneurs both used to portray themselves as instruments serving the common good or an abstract national interest. Perhaps the most striking aspect is that both Kaiser and Flick did everything to obscure their own financial interests. In a nutshell, their entrepreneurial strategy was to exploit the short-term advantages of government consumption and transform the ample flow of taxpayers' money into long-term advantages for themselves. One important part of their success consisted in disguising this capitalist process in such a way that their expansion strategies presented less of a political target in a context that was partly influenced by anticapitalist reservations.

The strategies themselves were pretty unimaginative as they aimed at sectorial consolidation and followed the tracks of the Second Industrial Revolution – Flick started his career in the steel industry and used the conditions of the armaments boom (and the dirty business of

"Aryanization") to orchestrate a massive shift toward energy production and coal chemistry. Former road builder Kaiser headed for steel, the extraction of magnesium, and the aircraft industry. And of course other industrialists followed suit when it came to government contracts and public subsidies. What stands out is that the highly personalized narratives of Flick and Kaiser were so successful. Their story was that of the individual entrepreneur, and it was extremely well received – notwithstanding, or actually because of, the processes of managerial professionalization and bureaucratization that had been prevalent for decades.

Insofar as Henry J. Kaiser made sure that only the speed records set by his shipyards were discussed publicly, not the billions these government contracts were worth or the favorable conditions he received, this maneuver worked out very well. Much the same goes for Friedrich Flick, who pulled off the trick of rendering the most expansive private industrial corporation in the Third Reich virtually invisible to the public by semantically transforming it into a mid-size family business. Just how much the semantics of success depended on the specific context and time period became drastically evident when the political circumstances changed. Kaiser was already on the defensive by late summer of 1944, when victory seemed merely a matter of time and the media started asking more critical questions about private wartime profits. Until the end of his life he struggled against the accusation that he was not a "true" entrepreneur because he owed his success to the government. Flick had succeeded in concealing his expansion within the context of the Nazi dictatorship from the German public, but this was never the case outside of the National Socialist state. Consequently, it was not long before he attracted the attention of the German émigrés and American investigators preparing the Nuremberg Trials.[40]

[40] Kim C. Priemel and Alexa Stiller, eds., *Reassessing the Nuremberg Military Tribunals: Transitional Justice, Trial Narratives, and Historiography* (New York, 2012).

6

Hamburg Coffee Importers

From Guild to Class, 1900s–1960s

Dorothee Wierling

6.1 FREE TRADE AND A CLOSED COMMUNITY

In 1911 Hamburg's Verein der am Caffeehandel betheiligten Firmen (Association of Firms Active in the Coffee Trade) (hereafter the Kaffee-Verein) gathered at the Hotel Atlantic to celebrate the twenty-fifth anniversary of its founding. The celebrants included 212 members of 179 Hamburg-based firms along with 13 local dignitaries. The firms represented included so-called *Kai-Firmen* (wharf companies) based on the city's waterfront and "city firms" located in town. Some of the firms were importers that dealt solely in "green coffee" (raw coffee beans); some were trading companies engaged in the import/export business with coffee-producing nations. Some firms served as agents for coffee exporters; some were brokers that served as intermediaries between importers and coffee roasters. What united these firms was not only their involvement with the commodity coffee but also their location in Hamburg, their status as registered partnerships (usually family-based), and their membership in the Kaffee-Verein, which was a prerequisite for authorization to engage in the coffee trade. The association had been established in 1886 when Hamburg became a free port. The founding also coincided with the construction of the city's vast warehouse district, the Speicherstadt; many coffee firms had their offices there along the Sandtorkai (Sandtor Wharf). The newly founded association became the largest tenant of the Hamburger Freihafen-Lagerhaus Gesellschaft

This chapter draws upon Dorothee Wierling, *Mit Rohkaffee handeln: Hamburger Kaffeeimporteure im 20. Jahrhundert* (Hamburg, 2018).

(Hamburg Free Port and Warehouse Company). At the same time it took over responsibility for the organization and oversight of the coffee exchange established in the free port.[1] Its spatial proximity to the waterfront and the proximity of the waterfront to the city center – site of the city hall, the chamber of commerce, and the stock exchange – contributed to the development of a tight community whose exclusivity the Kaffee-Verein safeguarded.

Hamburg's coffee traders belonged to a *bürgerlich* (bourgeois) milieu that to this day is characterized by its shared values and a hard-to-define "Hanseatic" style.[2] In using the term "Hanseatic," we find ourselves dealing with a cultural phenomenon that Pierre Bourdieu tried to grasp through the concept of "habitus," which is manifested in individuals' outward presentation, their internalized frames of reference, their life-styles, and their social practices.[3] Habitus is a matter of ingrained social belonging. The *Hanseat* (citizen of a Hanseatic town) embodies everything that is appealing and morally good in mercantile capitalism; the *Hanseat* is affluent but does not show off, refined but not arrogant, powerful but quiet about it. In business, a Hanseatic merchant is solid, honest, and trustworthy. With such a one, a handshake or promise is as good as a written contract.

These values and practices were guaranteed not only by the "honest merchant" himself but also by the "community" (*Gemeinschaft*) to which he belonged and on whose recognition he was dependent. From the late nineteenth century onward the community of Hamburg coffee traders was made visible, for insiders and outsiders alike, in the Kaffee-Verein. Membership was exclusive: prospective members had to be nominated by two members willing to vouch for them. Other members could voice their objections, and the governing board decided whether nominees would be accepted for membership. The association thus provided an institutional framework for the community of coffee traders, a community best characterized as a guild (*Stand*, often also translated as "estate").

[1] On the Hamburg coffee import trade before World War I, see Julia Laura Rischbieter, *Mikroökonomie der Globalisierung: Kaffee, Kaufleute und Konsumenten im Kaiserreich, 1870–1914* (Cologne, 2011).

[2] Lu Seegers, "Hanseaten und das Hanseatische in Diktatur und Demokratie: Politisch-ideologische Zuschreibungen und Praxen," in Forschungsstelle für Zeitgeschichte in Hamburg, ed., *Jahresbericht 2014* (Hamburg, 2015), 71–83.

[3] Pierre Bourdieu, "Structures, Habitus, Practices," in Bourdieu, *The Logic of Practice* (Cambridge, 1990), 52–65.

According to Max Weber:

> "Status" (*ständische Lage*) shall mean an effective claim to social esteem in terms of positive or negative privileges; it is typically founded on ... style of life [and] hereditary or occupational prestige. In practice, status expresses itself through ... monopolistic appropriation of privileged modes of acquisition or the abhorrence of certain kinds of acquisition, ... status *may* rest on class position of a distinct or an ambiguous kind. However, it is not solely determined by it: money and an entrepreneurial position are not in themselves status qualifications, although they may lead to them; and the lack of property is not in itself a status disqualification, although this may be a reason for it. Conversely, status may influence, if not completely determine, a class position without being identical with it. The class position of an officer, a civil servant, or a student may vary greatly according to their wealth and yet not lead to a different status since upbringing and education create a common style of life.[4]

The Hamburg coffee trade met Weber's criteria to a large extent. Its understanding of itself as a community rested on the closed front it presented to the outside world, regulation of internal competition in favor of cooperation, and acknowledgment of the hierarchy within the community. At the top of that hierarchy stood the *Kai-Firmen*; lowest in prestige were the brokers who dealt with domestic wholesale firms. Adherence to established practices within the trade (*Usancen*) and the sanctions applied when those practices were violated formed the basis for membership of the community. The reputation of individuals and firms was, according to this philosophy, inseparable from the standing of the Hamburg coffee trade itself within the business community of the Free Hanseatic City of Hamburg, in the financial centers of London and New York, and among overseas partners in the coffee-producing countries. Importers based in other cities – Bremen, for example – and wholesalers in the Rhineland, many of whom purchased their coffee beans in Rotterdam, did not belong to this community. Nor did those engaged in the post-import stages of the coffee business (wholesalers, roasters, retailers): the Hamburg importers did not consider them equals because they were not engaged in international trade and focused on the less prestigious – in the importers' eyes – domestic market.

The guild-like community of the coffee trade – and its individual family firms – rested on a self-consciousness of its collective strength, internal

[4] Max Weber, *Economy and Society: An Outline of Interpretive Sociology*, vol. 1, ed. Guenther Roth and Claus Wittich (Berkeley, CA, 1978), 305–6.

equilibrium, and nearly complete control over a business that was otherwise "free." Until World War I free trade was the rule; the tariff on raw coffee beans was 60 marks per 100 kilograms – a modest sum, importers' complaints notwithstanding. That tariff had to be paid, however, only once the beans crossed Hamburg's customs boundary, which meant it did not apply to beans that were stored in waterside warehouses or reexported (to Scandinavia, above all).[5] Hamburg's coffee importers seemed to have found a way of marrying the benefits of liberal capitalism with the cohesiveness of a premodern guild. The mood was thus excellent at the Kaffee-Verein's twenty-fifth anniversary celebration. The evening began with a seven-course meal accompanied by a musical program featuring light classics and military marches. An eight-stanza poem written for the occasion and printed in the program celebrated the Hamburg coffee trade's past. Later in the evening the celebrants loudly sang a song to the well-known tune of Detlev Lilienchron's "Die Musik kommt" ("Here Comes the Band") about life on the Sandtorkai. The song ended on an optimistic note:

> As long as Brazil has coffee,
> That's where this life will be,
> So, despite valorization,
> Hail Brazilian production,
> Hail the coffee trade, the coffee trade, the coffee trade.[6]

The community of coffee traders celebrated itself with a self-confidence that rested on more than just past successes such as the growth in coffee consumption in Imperial Germany.[7] It was not simply proud of its good reputation and its standing in the city and around the world. It was also celebrating its boundless confidence about the future: "So long as Brazil has coffee, that's where this life will be" – life on the Sandtorkai, the good life of the coffee community.

[5] In 1912 about 40 percent of the coffee beans imported to Hamburg were reexported; half of the reexports went to Scandinavia. Wierling, *Mit Rohkaffee handeln*, table on 369.

[6] "So lang Brasilien Kaffee hat,
Da findet wohl dies Leben statt
Darum, trotz Valorisation
Ein Hoch Brasiliens Produktion!"

Staatsarchiv Hansestadt Hamburg (hereafter StAHH) 612–5/8, Sign. 8 (unpaginated). Valorization refers here to the Brazilian government's practice of withholding coffee for export during times of overproduction in order to support prices. Rischbieter, *Mikroökonomie*, 299–301.

[7] Per capita coffee consumption in Germany before the outbreak of World War I was 3.3 kilos; it did not reach that peak again until shortly before World War II.

6.2 THE STATE AS COFFEE TRADER: WORLD WAR I

Brazil still had coffee, but, as soon became clear, that was by no means enough to ensure continued success for the Hamburg coffee trade. The outbreak of World War I three years after the anniversary celebration brought an end – temporarily, many believed – to free trade and led to ever-stricter state regulation of coffee imports. At first, the German government simply claimed the right of first refusal on coffee inventories stored in the German Reich, above all in Hamburg's waterfront warehouses. Within the framework of the Zentrale Einkaufsgesellschaft (ZEG), the wartime agency created to oversee Germany's foreign trade, the government sought to place the coffee trade under state supervision while at the same time supporting private-sector imports. Importers, as the true experts in the matter, were able to preserve a high degree of independence. They successfully defended themselves against the ZEG's taking stock of coffee inventories by promising to prepare a registry of inventories themselves. The coffee trade also pledged itself to make "appropriate purchases at fair prices."[8] The situation quickly became more difficult, however. Coffee beans were in short supply, and, like transportation costs, prices on international markets were rising. As a result of the British naval blockade, Germany could import coffee only from the Netherlands. In March 1916 Britain was able to restrict the Netherlands' coffee sales to the Central Powers to coffee produced in the Dutch colony of Java. In response – and despite strong resistance from the Hamburg importers – the German government established a syndicate to handle imports, the Kriegsausschuss für Kaffee, Tee, Kakao und deren Ersatzmittel (Wartime Committee for Coffee, Tea, Cocoa and Their Substitutes) (KA).[9] Only a single Hamburg importer, the distinguished firm of Hanssen & Studt, joined the KA. The Hamburg Kaffee-Verein did not gain a voice in the KA until May 1916, when Hanssen & Studt applied for and received permission to sign over half of its allocation to the Kaffee-Verein – and even then its influence was very limited.[10] All decisions pertaining to the coffee trade fell to an administrative council that Bremen-based importer Friedrich Roselius was

[8] Minutes of a meeting on supplying Germany with coffee during the war, Berlin, Aug. 6, 1915, StAHH 612–5/8, Sign. 3, Bd. 3.

[9] On Kriegsausschüsse in general, see Hans G. Ehlert, *Die wirtschaftliche Zentralbehörde des Deutschen Reiches 1914–1919: Das Problem der Gemeinwirtschaft in Krieg und Frieden* (Wiesbaden, 1982).

[10] Executive board meeting, Apr. 8, 1916, StAHH 612–5/8, Sign. 3, Bd. 3. Apparently, the firm's share was transferred from the ZEG to the KA. The Kaffee-Verein, however, was denied a seat on the KA's supervisory board.

chosen to head. Roselius, the producer of the decaffeinated Kaffee Hag, had long been hated in Hamburg as an outsider and because the family's firm promoted decaffeinated coffee as healthier than "real" coffee.[11]

The creation of the KA represented a severe setback for the Hamburg importers in several respects. All important decisions regarding the coffee trade would henceforth be made in Berlin and, indeed, by a body in which state actors would, in union with their hated rival from Bremen, have the final say. The Hamburg importers succeeded in having a branch office of the KA established in the city in May 1916, but the person chosen to head it – a representative of the Theodor Wille firm, a Brazilian coffee export company founded by a Hamburg merchant – was selected for his close ties to the retail chain Kaiser's Kaffee, which made him suspect in the eyes of the Hamburg importers. Worse still, the Hamburg branch office was "regarded as completely irrelevant" in Berlin, as the chairman of the Kaffee-Verein reported resignedly after a visit to the capital. He said it seemed "that again Roselius and his scheming comrades have been making plans behind our backs in Berlin to push us onto a dead-end sidetrack. It is a cause for suspicion that Herr Peimann is always in Berlin."[12] Kaffee-Verein member Otto Peimann of the import firm Peimann & Ziegler had aroused suspicion among his peers even before the creation of the KA when he accepted an invitation from Roselius to participate in a "strictly confidential meeting" in Berlin. At that meeting, he was informed of the plan Roselius had already drafted to create a wartime committee to regulate the coffee trade and was sworn to secrecy, as he confessed during a Kaffee-Verein board meeting. The outraged chairman demanded Peimann's immediate resignation, whereupon the latter threatened to stop his work with the KA until the accusations against him were withdrawn.[13] But he did not follow through on that threat, and the first meeting of the KA's supervisory board took place with representatives of the Hamburg firms of Hanssen & Studt, Peimann & Ziegler, and Theodor Wille in attendance. Only the first named of the three, however, still enjoyed the trust of the Kaffee-Verein.

[11] Svenja Kunze, "'Kaffee HAG schont Ihr Herz': Zur Entstehung und Entwicklung eines klassischen Markenartikels in der deutschen Kaffeebranche 1906–1939," *Hamburger Wirtschaftschronik*, new series, 4 (2004): 85–120.

[12] Executive board meeting, June 4, 1916, StAHH 612–5/8, Sign. 3, Bd. 3.

[13] StAHH 371–8 (Deputation für Handel, Gewerbe und Schiffahrt) Pr VII 91 (Kaffeehandel und Kaffeeversorgung), Bd. 1, Vorgang 51.

The fear of "scheming" soon proved warranted. Roselius, the secret master of the wartime coffee trade, attempted with the help of the German consul in Amsterdam – a close personal friend of his – to shut out the Hamburg importers as far as possible, or at least to regulate their activities. At the same time he exploited his position in the KA to secure special shipments of green coffee for decaffeination. The Hamburgers succeeded, however, in having Roselius expelled from the board of the KA in late 1916 along with his partner and fellow native of Bremen Gustav Adolf von Halem of the Reich Ministry of the Interior.[14] The forced departure of the two was a political victory for the Hamburgers, but it did not fundamentally change the situation. In contrast to prewar times, the Hamburgers had no influence worth mentioning in the sole country from which they could still import green coffee and, to their annoyance, they were dependent on networks established by their Bremen competitors and officials in Berlin. The Hamburg importers might have learned a lesson for the future from this situation and given up their opposition to cooperation with governmental agencies, but their difficulties were rendered moot when the coffee trade with the Netherlands was cut off entirely in 1917.

The wartime experience of the Hamburg coffee trade was ambiguous. Beyond the practical impediments to business that arose as direct consequences of the war, they had to contend with the unaccustomed intervention of the government, which not only affected sources and prices but also limited access to the foreign currency needed for the import of raw coffee. State oversight quickly turned into firm control. Hamburg traders could remain active, at least as long as coffee was available, and their expertise was still indispensable to the government. At the same time, however, they were losing their entrepreneurial freedom of decision step by step, above all on account of the framework of the KA – the visible expression of the state's power to dictate the terms on which business would be conducted.

On top of the constraints affecting the coffee trade in general, the Hamburg importers also had to contend with their own particular troubles. State intervention meant the end of their dominance and the shift of control of the German coffee trade to Berlin, where their competitors from Bremen and Cologne wielded more influence. Moreover, the Hamburgers who were successful in Berlin were those who, because of their particular economic position, had never felt

[14] Wierling, *Mit Rohkaffee handeln*, 83–9.

a sense of obligation to the Kaffee-Verein and the coffee trade community: first and foremost, there was the Brazilian-Hamburg export firm of Theodor Wille, which had close ties to roasters and domestic wholesalers, notably Kaiser's Kaffee. The firm had entered into an alliance with Roselius, who used the Hamburgers' initial and continuing refusal to cooperate with the state as an opportunity to forge an anti-Hamburg alliance. Yet it was precisely the threat to Hamburg's geographic advantage and influential personal networks that increased the Kaffee-Verein's value. Reestablishing and securing Hamburg's predominance and defending the community from both external and internal threat became the chief purpose of the Kaffee-Verein.

Given wartime conditions, state interference also had its advantages. The state recognized the necessity of supplying the armed forces, first and foremost, but also the civilian population with as much coffee as possible even if, as a stimulant with no nutritional value, it was not given the same priority as basic foodstuffs. That put Hamburg coffee importers in a strong position to negotiate for state assistance. They were thus able to continue importing, albeit within ever tighter limits. Their profit margins were guaranteed and, through the Kaffee-Verein, they had a say in decision-making. In other words, they eventually learned not only how to hold off the state and defend themselves against it but also how to cooperate with it. This cooperation increased the power of the Hamburg Kaffee-Verein in the long run. It communicated the state's interests to its members and developed a strategy to serve those interests, thereby providing security for the industry and stability for the community. In practice, that meant protecting the existing structures of power and influence within the Hamburg coffee trade community. It also included supporting the brokers who, on account of the KA's monopoly on taking delivery of shipments of green coffee, had to make do with a cut of importers' profits in lieu of their usual brokerage fees. But the community also had to deal for the first time with the suspicion that some of its members were secretly in cahoots with its enemies. A quick return to the prewar status quo would take care of the problem, they hoped. Free trade would set things right again.

6.3 OPENING UP THE COFFEE TRADE AND MAINTAINING THE STATUS QUO: THE INTERWAR ERA

Hopes and fears were held in check at the war's end, defeat and revolution notwithstanding. The radical workers' and soldiers' council that had led the revolution in Hamburg handed power back to the city's established government and legislature, the *Senat* and the *Bürgerschaft*, after only a week. In the first democratic election the Social Democrats did not win a majority. The positions of mayor and minister of commerce (*Erster Bürgermeister* and *Senator für Handel*) were filled by familiar, trusted figures who had been active in politics before and during the war. A businessman who owned coffee plantations overseas was chosen to lead the chamber of commerce in 1919. In response to the demand for the introduction of the eight-hour workday, the board of the Kaffee-Verein argued in December 1918 that the eight-hour day could "absolutely not be enacted within the firms of the coffee trade," and it defended this position by pointing to the different operating hours of the Hamburg firms, their overseas partners, and the coffee exchanges.[15] The coffee industry trade journal advised against "emotionalism" (*Gefühlsduselei*) and encouraged its readers "to contribute to the rebuilding of international trade and to harness all its power for the new Germany."[16]

More worrisome than political developments, in the eyes of Hamburg's coffee traders, were the economic consequences of the war, above all the trade restrictions the Treaty of Versailles imposed and the dramatic shortage of foreign exchange. The state had imposed currency controls in February 1917; in response, the coffee industry established a private purchasing cartel, the Kaffee-Einfuhr-Verein (KEV), to consolidate the limited supply of capital and to serve as the industry's self-regulatory body. With the establishment of the KEV as a "trade association for coffee, tea, and cocoa," the Hamburg traders succeeded in replacing the wartime KA with an organization run by the industry itself and dominated by Hamburgers. The KEV also enabled them to defend their import monopoly against wholesalers. In particular, the importers were battling consumer cooperatives (*Konsumgenossenschaften*), whose size and economic might they feared. Second place in their list of feared rivals went to a handful of large-scale coffee roasters – for example, the firm of Arthur Darboven – who repeatedly threatened to import raw coffee directly themselves. Under the leadership of the Hamburgers the KEV explicitly saw itself as a lobbying group for the strict separation of the different branches of the coffee industry.[17]

The early postwar years were a time of troubles for coffee importers. There was the shortage of foreign exchange, which repeatedly led the state

[15] Letter, Dec. 23, 1918, StAHH 612–5/8, Sign. 3, Bd. 3.
[16] "Die neue Zeit," *Kaffee-Tee-Kakao (KATEKA)*, Nov. 1, 1918.
[17] Executive board meeting, Sep. 17, 1919, StAHH 612–5/8, Sign. 3, Bd. 4.

to impose temporary import bans. The Hamburgers' business suffered the consequences of smuggling across the border with Belgium and the lower import tariffs charged in the occupied Rhineland. The tariff disadvantage was compounded by inflation because tariffs had to be paid in hard currency, which put the Hamburgers at a particular disadvantage because domestic coffee roasters could supply themselves with raw coffee imported less expensively through the Rhineland. In this instance the Hamburgers actually sought state assistance, arguing that the state should ensure identical conditions for cross-border trade throughout the country. At the same time, though, they expected a general policy of nonintervention on the part of the state and a return to free trade. The Kaffee-Verein appointed its own commission to participate in negotiations on reestablishing free trade, but it soon dissolved the commission on the grounds that it had exceeded its authority. Traditional ideas about free trade were clearly no longer relevant in addressing the complex circumstances of international trade in the wake of the war. The end of the war marked the beginning of a period of deglobalization in international trade. The German coffee industry was confronted with numerous restrictions imposed not only by its own government but also by the coffee-producing nations. Moreover, the United States, emerging as a major player in international trade, had become the most important customer for Latin American coffee producers. An expansion of coffee cultivation quickly led to overproduction, and exports were scaled back in order to maintain prices.

Not until 1925 could the Hamburg coffee industry once again participate in the international market on more or less equal terms with its competitors. The Hamburg Coffee Exchange reopened that year, and for a while it seemed as if things had returned to normal – that is, to the way Hamburg traders had envisioned their future before the war. The Kaffee-Verein once again focused on its original tasks: regulating the coffee industry in the city and the Coffee Exchange, informing and advising its members of changes in international markets, supporting them in reestablishing old and building new relations with coffee-producing nations, and punishing violations of the rules of conduct for the good of the community. At the same time it kept a careful eye on developments that might imperil the position of dominance the Hamburg importers had just reestablished vis-à-vis other port cities and other branches of the coffee industry. The old self-confidence had given way to constant vigilance. That strengthened the community on which all members felt they depended.

Before long the community once again had to go on the defensive. The bank crisis that broke out in Germany in the wake of the stock market crash in the United States led to another severe shortage of foreign exchange and in turn to tight regulation of the foreign currency available to the coffee industry. Under the "Order on the Control of Foreign Exchange" (*Verordnung zur Devisenbewirtschaftung*) issued on August 1, 1931, all business transactions in foreign currencies were subject to government approval.[18] Because German coffee importers conducted their business solely in foreign currencies – usually sterling during the first half of the twentieth century – and because the so-called commission system (*Rembourssystem*) meant that they were in effect permanently in debt to London banks, the currency controls posed a direct threat to the coffee trade because most firms had to pay their bankers in London in sterling for coffee they had already agreed to purchase.[19] But, much to the Hamburgers' surprise, the impact of the currency controls proved less drastic than they had feared: all firms that had been conducting transactions in foreign currencies as of October 1, 1930, received blanket approval to continue doing so. In practice, though, the amount of foreign exchange available to them was limited. This time, however, unlike during the World War, the Hamburg coffee industry took the initiative in seeking to cooperate with the state. Together with other trade associations the Kaffee-Verein called for the creation of a Hamburg branch office of the currency control agency, and it also argued for exempting the transit trade from currency controls. With those proposals, the Hamburg importers implicitly accepted import quotas (via quotas on foreign exchange) and, most importantly, agreed to set those quotas themselves through internal regulation. Eligible firms' quotas would be based on the volume of their imports in the years 1928–30 and determined by an "assembly of honorable merchants" – namely, the electoral committee of the chamber of commerce. The committee's decisions would then have to be approved in Berlin, but it planned to "set the quotas as low as possible" in order to avoid protracted negotiations. "It seems advisable at the moment that the trade limits the volume of its business so that the business that is still

[18] *Reichsgesetzblatt*, 1931, 421–3.

[19] In commission transactions (*Remboursgeschäft*), London banks transferred the sum of the purchase price, which the importer had previously secured with a bill of exchange, to the importer upon presentation of a bill of lading. Most of the Hamburg importers met their payment obligations on time, even if they had to go into debt to do so, in order not to jeopardize relations with their London banks. StAHH 612–5/8, Sign. 3, Bd. 6, meeting of Aug. 5, 1931.

possible can be conducted with a certain amount of freedom and in peace."[20] The situation was made simpler by the fact that monthly quotas were reviewed initially on a quarterly and later half-yearly basis and were generally approved by the authorities. The smooth cooperation with the state also rested on favorable circumstances: stable prices on the international market, for example, and a drop in German coffee consumption. As a result of that decline, many firms did not need their full quota and made their unused foreign exchange available to firms that had received very small quotas. The result was that "those firms were thus in the position to conduct a disproportionately large volume of business," the board of the Kaffee-Verein complained, as it sought to maintain stable power relationships among its membership.[21] This point speaks to one of the association's central objectives: the preservation of the guild community by maintaining its existing economic structures and accepted hierarchies. There were, of course, clear and internally recognized differences in the members' business success. But it was an unspoken rule that members who, through no fault of their own, found themselves in trouble could call on the Kaffee-Verein or other members for assistance; that no member would try to profit directly at another's expense; and, finally, that existing differences in profitability would be recognized and not called into question. The system adopted in the early 1930s assigned quotas on the basis of past conditions defined as "normal" in order to reestablish those conditions and thereby ensure their continuation. This policy apparently struck all of the Kaffee-Verein's members as fair.

Parallel to this arrangement, the Hamburg coffee trade and the state embarked on another close collaboration. In September 1931 Wilhelm-Erwin Michahelles met with a representative of the Brazilian subsidiary of the Hamburg firm of Rudolf Petersen, the finance minister of Brazil, and the German ambassador to Brazil to consider a proposal. The Brazilian government would buy a total of half a million tons of German coal, priced in US dollars, in monthly installments. "In exchange for this purchase, a corresponding volume of high-value Santos coffee will be stored in the Hamburg free port on the basis of the current market price." One year after the first coal shipment, the warehoused coffee would be sold on behalf of the Brazilian government in lots of between thirty thousand and forty thousand sacks. This proposal was subsequently

[20] Undated discussion paper (Nov. 1931) for a meeting of the Hamburger Warenvereine, StAHH 612–5/8, Sign. 3, Bd. 6.
[21] Meeting of Apr. 24, 1933, StAHH 612–5/8, Sign. 3, Bd. 6.

enshrined in a "Coffee-Coal Treaty" (*Kaffee-Kohle-Abkommen*). The German government described the deal as a "loan secured by coffee" (*Kredit gegen Kaffeesicherheit*). The import/export firm Rudolf Petersen, which had negotiated the terms of the agreement with the German coal syndicate and the Brazilian government, was chosen to serve as the trustee for all the parties involved. Petersen also came up with a way to handle the sale of coffee that entered the country outside the framework of the currency control regulations.[22] The board of the Kaffee-Verein was "confidentially" asked to speak in favor of the coffee-coal deal, and the membership soon learned of the first coffee shipment. Suspicion arose, however, because the deal had been proposed by an association member, Edgar Bohlen, who had business dealings with the Petersen firm, "which was not involved in the coffee trade and which had secured Mr. Bohlen as an advisor on matters pertaining to coffee."[23] For the Kaffee-Verein, the most important thing was to make sure that the "legitimate coffee trade" had the right to handle the sale. The imported coffee should serve the interests of the community, not of an individual firm. For that reason, following the conclusion of the negotiations on the agreement in late 1931, the Kaffee-Verein established a "distribution committee" consisting of the chair of its board, Bohlen, and three association members. The committee would be responsible for ensuring that all association members had access to the merchandise. At that point the state, which felt no obligation to honor the Hamburgers' wish for exclusivity, intervened and insisted that importers from outside Hamburg be allowed to participate. A complaint that the Kaffee-Verein submitted to the Reich Ministry of Economic Affairs protested that "the inland trade is favored over port city wholesalers and is generously supplied with import quotas."[24] That this complaint had more to do with preserving the Hamburgers' exclusive status than with a competitive disadvantage is suggested by the fact that the foreign exchange quotas of the early 1930s were adequate and that there had not been much interest among the Hamburgers in the so-called barter coffee (*Kompensationskaffee*). The Kaffee-Verein's annual report for 1933 noted, with little enthusiasm, that the coffee-coal agreement had

[22] Memorandum (presumably Petersen to the Reich Ministry of Economic Affairs), Sep. 25, 1931, Bundesarchiv Berlin R 2–16606. The Foreign Office was likewise involved in the negotiations from the outset and was kept informed of developments. See Politisches Archiv des Auswärtigen Amtes R 244–654.

[23] Archiv der Handelskammer Hamburg (hereafter AHHH), 11.B.88.1.12, Bl. 20.

[24] Undated document (spring 1932), StAHH 612–5/8, Sign. 3, Bd. 6.

"met with varying interest on the part of the members. On the whole, this arrangement has been welcomed."[25]

For Hamburg's coffee traders, 1933 initially marked merely a change of government, not the start of a new political era. Their main concerns were the threat of tighter foreign exchange controls and autarky-oriented trade policies. It soon became clear that the Nazi state wanted to support the importation of coffee by maintaining the barter agreement and would actively pursue bilateral trade agreements with coffee-producing nations. Nazi trade policy sought to promote exports above all and to base import opportunities on the trade balances with individual trading partners. On June 14, 1934, Reichsbank president Hjalmar Schacht issued the "Decree on the Import of Goods" that would be the core policy component of the "New Plan."[26] From that moment on importers had to file an application, which included an import permit and purchase order, for each individual business transaction. Coffee traders received import permission so long as the producing country purchased German goods of equivalent value. Settlement was handled by the Ausländersonderkonten für Inlandsgeschäfte (Special Foreign Costs for Domestic Business) (ASKI). Payments for coffee imports were deposited – in Reichsmark – into special blocked accounts; the exporting countries, in turn, used their credit balances to purchase German goods. Under this setup the role of the currency control offices was simply to monitor credits issued by the ASKI. "Export policy by coffee imports" was how the *Hamburger Tageblatt* described this system. The newspaper noted that "despite the foreign exchange situation, for the time being only regulation (*Steuerung*), not limitation, of coffee imports is planned." Indeed, the volume of coffee imports hardly changed in the following years. However, on account of bilateral trade balances, the German government gave preference to particular trading partners, and those preferences were not always in line with the business relationships coffee importers had established or with the tastes of German consumers.[27] This policy was also thwarted in part by resistance on the part of the coffee-producing nations, which had protectionist interests of their own. Brazil, for example, fought against the reexport of coffee purchased through ASKI accounts from Hamburg to

[25] Printed annual report, 1933, StAHH 612–5/8, Sign. 3, Bd. 7.

[26] Michael Ebi, *Export um jeden Preis: Die deutsche Exportförderung von 1932–1938* (Stuttgart, 2004).

[27] *KATEKA* Nr. 5, 1935, 54.

Scandinavia. German consumers turned their noses up at Brazilian coffee and wanted coffee from countries that had a negative balance of trade with Germany.[28] Both Schacht's New Plan and Göring's Four-Year Plan that followed it turned out to be advantageous for Hamburg's importers. The volume of green coffee that passed through Hamburg rose from 1,564,359 *Doppelzentner* (two-hundredweights) (dz) in 1933 to 1,908,033 dz in 1938, an increase of nearly 30 percent.[29] Accordingly, 1938 was the best year Hamburg importers had had for quite some time.[30]

Although state regulation proved lucrative, the Hamburg coffee importers nonetheless saw a threat in the Nazis' attempt to dissolve the Kaffee-Verein and to integrate the coffee industry in the "organic rebuilding (*Aufbau*) of the German economy." They were at risk of being grouped as wholesalers together with inland importers and coffee roasters in disregard of their claims of exclusivity. Moreover, as subordinates in a hierarchical structure, they would be reduced to mere recipients of orders from on high. The association, the symbol of the Hamburg coffee trade's proud self-governance and its standing beyond Hamburg, would be downgraded to a mere department of a larger body. The Hamburgers' drawn-out battle with the Nazi bureaucracy cannot be recounted in detail here. The outcome was that the coffee importers were classed as a subgroup of the "Wholesale, Retail, and Overseas Trade" group within the Reich Trade Group (Reichsgruppe Handel). The coffee brokers were assigned to the "Brokerage Trade" group. The two groups could join forces, though, in the context of the "Working Group on Coffee," whose membership was nearly identical to the Kaffee-Verein's. The Hamburgers nonetheless continued to fight for the formal preservation of the Kaffee-Verein. In essence, the conflict was about the first paragraph of the association's bylaws, which defined its purpose as "to look after the interests of the coffee import trade and the coffee futures trade in matters of market regulation." By contrast, the Nazi-led chamber of commerce insisted that the Kaffee-Verein's mandate be limited to overseeing the

[28] *Financial News London*, Oct. 26, 1934, translated for the Hamburg importers by the Press Service Hansa (Hamburg).

[29] See the table on shipments of green coffee to and from the port of Hamburg, 1912 and 1925–38 in Wierling, *Mit Rohkaffee handeln*, 368–9.

[30] Ibid., table 5, "5: Jahreseinkommen einiger Hamburger Kaffeeimporteure/-makler 1931–September 1939," 150. Because the relevant business and tax records either no longer exist or are not available to researchers, this list had to be based solely on the statements importers made during denazification proceedings.

technical workings of the coffee exchange.[31] Although the struggle between the two sides dragged on until the war began and was thus left unresolved, the Nazis had long since achieved what mattered most to them: the adoption of the so-called Führer principle (*Führerprinzip*), the Nazification of the Kaffee-Verein personnel, the expulsion of Jews from the association and the coffee trade, and at least lip service to the regime in official statements. Beginning in 1934, Jews were no longer put forward for the association's numerous honorary offices, and those who already held such positions were "requested" to give them up. Elections for the board of directors were abolished and the chairman of the association was henceforth appointed by the *Gau*. The board rarely met, and general meetings of the membership were held merely to ratify already made decisions. Moreover, the Kaffee-Verein accepted a number of new, younger members who had no experience in the coffee industry but were well connected to Nazi officials in the city government. They sought to bypass the board and reported directly to the local Nazi administration.

The Hamburg coffee traders' personal and collective pride in their corporate identity as a guild had rested on four pillars: free trade as a guarantee of their economic strength and independence, the exclusiveness and internal cohesiveness of their community, a shared understanding of entrepreneurial honor and solidarity, and, finally, a *bürgerlich* lifestyle that combined affluence with discretion. Little of that was still in place by the end of the 1930s. The end of World War I had not brought about the hoped-for return to free trade. On the contrary: state prerogative and intervention, above all in the allocation of foreign exchange, were confirmed and consolidated. That intervention might have supported the coffee trade, but it did so at the cost of importers' freedom to decide where they obtained beans, in what quantities, and how much they were willing to pay for them. Importers ultimately had to clear every deal in advance with Berlin, and by the end of the interwar period the state was deciding how much – if any – coffee could be imported and from which countries. The Weimar Republic took account of the Hamburgers' claims to predominance in the import trade, but the Nazi state was happy to encourage competition with other import centers, like Bremen and the Rhineland, not least to keep the Hamburgers in their place. The subordination of the coffee trade to the Nazis' economic "order" – to the strictly hierarchical

[31] The arduous negotiations about the Kaffee-Verein's bylaws are documented, from the perspective of the Nazified chamber of commerce, in StAHH 612–5/8, Sign. 5 and AHHH V.50.1.1.

structure they imposed – also served that purpose. The Hamburgers managed to save the Kaffee-Verein, but the association was fully subordinated to the Nazi regime. Its self-governance practices became empty rituals and were eventually abandoned.

The Kaffee-Verein's membership likewise underwent a change during the interwar period. In the 1920s a new generation of firms that did not belong to old Hamburg families were already joining the association. The newcomers from outside who sought their fortunes in the city quickly adapted and integrated, however, and they proved themselves during the struggle for survival in the early 1930s. One of them, Bernhard Rothfos, was appointed head of the Kaffee-Verein by the Nazis in 1939. Rothfos was born in 1898 in Bremen, where he became part owner of a coffee import firm. He set off on his own for Hamburg in 1925 and, having founded his firm, joined the Kaffee-Verein. His appointment as the head of the association was initially opposed by the membership because on at least two occasions he had broken with Hamburg business conventions and had thereby secured a great advantage over other importers.[32] But they ultimately went along with the appointment, not least because they expected that Rothfos would not think of giving in to the Nazis on the decisive question of the association's independence.

The confident young Nazis who joined the Kaffee-Verein after 1933, by contrast, were of a different caliber. They were contemptuous of business and moral traditions, and they were willing to assert themselves within the association against the defenders of tradition. The outbreak of World War II put their ambitions on hold. Nonetheless, under the impact of financial struggle and Nazi policy, the communal values and practices of the coffee industry, the shared notions of honor, trust, and propriety, began to erode. Nowhere was that clearer than in the association's dealings with its Jewish members, who, denied access to foreign exchange, had to shut down their businesses in 1937. Within a few years their economic and social lives in Hamburg were at an end, and the community of coffee merchants had lost its proudly proclaimed honor. The Kaffee-Verein was by no means proactive in trying to meet the regime's expectations. The "non-Aryan gentlemen" were not expelled, and they were initially defended against the antisemitic insults of new members. At the same time, in the belief that the Nazis posed only a temporary threat, the association sought, often with the support of the Jewish members, to make concessions to the regime, as, for example, when it ceased to

[32] Ibid., 161–3.

consider Jews for honorary positions in 1934. But the association was clearly aware that its conduct was not honorable. In 1936, for instance, at the insistence of the local Nazi leadership, it excluded Jewish members from participating in an anniversary celebration. The chairman, who had in the meantime joined the Nazi Party, sent each of them a letter of thanks for their service to the association along with a bouquet of flowers. In 1937, as noted earlier, "Jewish" firms were denied access to foreign exchange; Jewish importers had either to close their businesses or to sell them at greatly reduced prices to partners or other traders. All of the Jewish members had left Germany by 1938; its owner in exile, the last "Jewish" firm resigned from the Kaffee-Verein in 1939.[33] In their struggle to defend their guild practices, the Hamburgers were most successful in maintaining the Hanseatic lifestyle. The newcomers' attempt to change or to imitate the *bürgerlich* habitus of the owners failed. Various comments in the board meeting minutes speak to the contempt of their established colleagues. And in 1936, on the occasion of the fiftieth anniversary of the Kaffee-Verein, the young Nazis were sidelined and obviously reported the snub to the SS, which published an offensive article about the celebration.[34] But the pride of the old guard had by no means escaped unharmed, and their sense of exclusivity increasingly rested on self-deception. And then came the war.

6.4 FREE TRADE AND ITS DISCONTENTS

In contrast to the situation during World War I, Germany's international coffee trade came to an immediate standstill in September 1939, and German importers were cut off from the international coffee market well into the postwar period. Twelve Hamburg firms were designated as so-called W-Firms (*Wehrmachtsfirmen*) to supply the armed forces. The distrust that aroused among other firms was short-lived: even the W-Firms, like all the others, soon found themselves without coffee and

[33] Wierling, *Mit Rohkaffee handeln*, 131–3, 167–9.

[34] In the seating plan for the celebration the most aggressive of the young Nazis, Werner Langloh, was relegated to the most remote table: Akte 50-jähriges Vereinsjubiläum, Deutscher Kaffee-Verband. For an example of negative reporting on the celebration see the article "Kalter Kaffee" ("Cold Coffee") in the SS publication *Das Schwarze Korps*, which deplored the coffee merchants' bourgeois condescension: "We do not like such gestures, as if National Socialism, after three years, was now socially acceptable even in the coffee trade." AHHH V.50.1.1 (Verein der am Kaffeehandel beteiligten Firmen, Allgemeines, 1911–37), Bl. 50.

were thus unable to do their job. The Hamburg coffee industry's most important place of business economically and symbolically, the Sandtorkai in the city's free port, was almost completely destroyed during a British air attack in 1943. Exporters searched for ways to stay afloat financially. Those who were not conscripted into the armed forces tried to shift to other goods, joined other firms, or filled civilian positions in the Hamburg municipal government, the Nazi Party, or the Wehrmacht.[35] The invasion of the Soviet Union in the summer of 1941 opened new opportunities for the marketing of agricultural goods seized in occupied territories in the east and delivered to the Reich after the Wehrmacht had taken its share. Exporters also made themselves available to serve as the "trustees" (*Treuhänder*) of industrial firms, especially in the food industry, that the regime had seized.[36]

The community of coffee traders collapsed in the early weeks of the war. The members who remained in the city, mostly older importers, thus tried all the harder to maintain a sense of belonging. They published a short fortnightly newsletter to keep their dispersed colleagues abreast of their varied doings, *Die Kaffeebohne. Familienblatt am Sandtorkai* (*The Coffee Bean: The Family Paper of the Sandtorkai*). The title of the newsletter made clear what was at stake: the guild community itself, communicated by product and place and, under wartime conditions, translated into the emotional (and biological) language of kinship. The response from the "family" was, however, disappointing. The "family paper" was the project of a few stalwarts, and after the bombing of the Sandtorkai in the summer of 1943 it appeared only irregularly.[37]

As the widely dispersed coffee traders made their way back to the Sandtorkai in May 1945, the spatial, material, social, international, and financial foundations of their businesses lay in ruins. Their normative self-understanding was called into question during denazification and restitution proceedings. The collective loss of honor was not discussed within the community, however, as the Kaffee-Verein's members focused on the practical goal of rebuilding their businesses. The May 1945 activity report of the board noted: "Next year, the Verein looks back on sixty years of

[35] A list of conscripts was published in *Die Kaffeebohne*: StAHH 612–5/8, Sign. 15.

[36] Wierling, *Mit Rohkaffee handeln*, 190–2. There is also the case of coffee broker Heinrich Christen, who found a position as "Regional Commissar" in the civilian occupation of Norway. He wrote a detailed diary of his experiences. See Dorothee Wierling, ed., *"Wenn uns die Norskes schon nicht lieben ... ": Das Tagebuch des Dienststellenleiters Heinrich Christen in Norwegen 1941 – 1943* (Göttingen, 2021).

[37] The last issue appeared on Dec. 10, 1944.

activity. Many friendly connections were formed during this time ... If today there is still no prospect of once again importing coffee, we nonetheless believe that one day we will build new bridges and that our Verein can begin a new and happier chapter of its history."[38] This outlook rested on great hopes for help from the Western occupying powers, who exercised considerable influence on foreign trade until the formal establishment of the Federal Republic and whose policies would have long-lasting effect. For the Hamburg coffee industry, those policies had major consequences – namely, the end of its functioning like a guild both externally and internally. Two developments contributed to that outcome. The first was the imposition of new currency controls along with government regulation of how foreign exchange was to be allotted among firms and of how much coffee would be imported from which countries. That was familiar territory for Hamburg coffee traders, and they worked in close collaboration with the state to create a system that would serve their interests. Within the framework of the Verwaltung für Wirtschaft des Vereinigten Wirtschaftsgebietes (Economic Council for the Trizone) (VfW), the precursor to the Federal Ministry of Economic Affairs, a new Fachstelle Kaffee (Coffee Office) was established in November 1948. The Kaffee-Einkaufs-Kontor (Coffee Purchasing Office) (KEK) set up earlier by coffee traders was merged into the new office, which was located on the Sandtorkai in Hamburg. The office had an advisory board (*Beirat*) consisting entirely of importers. At the ceremonial opening of the office the VfW was represented by *Regierungsrat* (councilor) Max Pheiffer, and the occupying powers were represented by an American official from the Joint Export-Import Agency (JEIA). Speaking on behalf of the KEK was Bernhard Rothfos, who had been named head of the Kaffee-Verein by the Nazis in 1939 and, after a short period of withdrawal from the association's affairs, was once again its leader. He explained the already familiar quota system based on prewar figures, so-called base rates (*Messzahlen*); quota allocations would be decided by a commission of influential coffee importers in consultation with Pheiffer. Import/export trading houses were not supposed to import coffee directly themselves but rather to purchase it from importers. In other words, the new quota system was an attempt to reestablish the community as a self-regulating cartel on the basis of the prewar status quo. This attempt was stymied, however, by the determination of US occupation authorities to put an end to this and other German cartels.

[38] StAHH 612–5/8, Sign. 3, Bd. 8, May 29, 1945.

In August 1949 two representatives of the decartelization department of the Bipartite Control Office (BICO) visited the Fachstelle in Hamburg. The spokesperson, a Mr. Barshey, "took a negative position toward the entire process." Apparently the disagreement over prevailing practices of the officials responsible for the coffee industry was so sharp that the meeting had to be adjourned. The next day Barshey argued for a fully open, egalitarian process whereby the import market would be open to all, but all importers would receive the same amount of coffee. He backed away from this "leveling" a day later, but he also asked why more import/export trading houses than importers had received allocations from the most recent tender from Colombia. The Hamburg officials explained that inland firms had traditionally handled the trade with Colombia and they wanted to help those firms reestablish their business connections. Barshey then asked why, among the inland firms, Theodor Wille had been assigned the highest base rate; the answer was that the Wille firm, as both a trading house and an importer, had a special status. Such special regulations were entirely alien to the free market advocate Barshey. Why, he continued to press, was the import trade represented on the Fachstelle's advisory board "almost exclusively [by] firms with high base rates ... He had the impression that the Fachstelle (i.e., Regierungsrat Pheiffer) took advice solely from the large firms." Barshey also thought that the so-called reserve fund, which was to be used to aid victims of Nazi persecution and newcomers to get (re)established in the coffee business, was too small. In the future, he insisted, 20 percent of all coffee allocations should go to newcomers. It seemed to Barshey that "the large firms received their base rates solely because their grandfathers had already been in the business." In his view, however, the standard should be "not what had been but rather what is."[39]

With his brusque outburst, Barshey summed up the coffee traders' thinking and conduct in a few direct words. His position ran counter to all the principles that had stood behind the founding of the Kaffee-Verein in the late nineteenth century, which had been the basis of the guild community and had, at least in theory, guided the coffee trade during the first half of the twentieth century: self-regulation in times of limited resources, the unchallengeable decision-making authority of an inner circle consisting largely of the most successful firms; the imposition of rules to preserve the existing hierarchy while leaving room to address imbalances arising from circumstances beyond firms' control. It was

[39] Bundesarchiv Koblenz, Z8, unpaginated, 21265, Niederschrift Besprechung Barshey.

a system that was supposed to hold the community together precisely by the careful and predictable treatment of unequal subgroups. Barshey, by contrast, espoused the "American" principle of open competition, not only as a matter of personal opinion but also as representative of a decision-making agency. By the summer of 1950, after the Federal Ministry of Economic Affairs had taken the American position as its own, it was clear that the coffee traders would not get the restrictions on new import licenses they had been seeking.

The policy of the BICO's Import Advisory Committee (IAC) was to open the German coffee industry up to newcomers, and that had unpleasant consequences for the Hamburg importers. The base rate system was given up in favor of identical allotments of available supplies. In the case of the last tender of Colombian coffee, 554 firms applied for a 2 percent share of the total allotment. The applicants included 195 roasters and wholesalers along with 167 "rank outsiders," as the chair of the Kaffee-Verein complained in the summer of 1950. Coffee traders could do nothing about this situation. They could, of course, demand that the purchasers be registered importers, "but that would be turned down by the [Allied] *observers* precisely because they wanted *newcomers*." Moreover, some of the outsiders had taken delivery directly from exporters – in other words, without the aid of intermediary agents – only to turn around and immediately resell the shipment.[40] According to the German experts, the opening of the import business to all was leading to chaos, unfairness, and oversubscribed tenders. The observers, they complained, understood nothing of a trading system that had functioned well for many years, especially for the long-established import firms.

The dissolution of the guild community went hand in hand with dramatic changes in the international coffee market. The center of the trade shifted to New York, and the US dollar became its operating currency. Despite rising consumption, vast overproduction resulted in steadily sinking prices and, before long, the end of state import controls in the Federal Republic. Since the end of free trade during World War I, Hamburg coffee importers had been calling for its reintroduction. But when it was announced in the early 1950s that free trade in coffee would resume in 1955, they panicked. For them, free trade had always meant that they had the freedom to restrict the import trade to a small group of firms and to enforce the rules of the trade themselves. Allowing all interested parties to import coffee, including wholesalers and roasters, made

[40] Ibid., Werner Ihnen to the BWiM, Jul. 21, 1950.

that enforcement impossible. With the end of state-supervised tenders and of predetermined allotments, everyone was free to compete in international markets for the purchase of any amount of coffee at the going price. That jeopardized not only the exclusiveness of the Hamburg import trade but also the carefully balanced and universally respected system of long-standing business relationships with firms in coffee-producing countries in addition to the division of labor among importers, agents, brokers, downtown firms, and inland firms. Unlike in the past, Hamburg importers were now often forced to compete among themselves in order to stay in business.

At the same time, there were many signs of revival. The area around the Sandtorkai, which had been leveled during the war, had been rebuilt by 1956. A new "Coffee Center" consisting of several modern office buildings replaced the destroyed neo-Gothic structures. New warehouses could store more coffee than ever before. A group of undamaged buildings across from the Coffee Exchange was renovated. That complex expressed in stone the determination to connect back to pre-World War I tradition and, at the same time, to look ahead to a promising future.[41]

The free trade of the nineteenth century had developed against a backdrop of cooperation and stability. The free trade of the twentieth century, by contrast, was inextricably bound up with domestic and international competition. As soon as the coffee trade was fully liberalized, the number of import firms in Hamburg began to decline, a development that accelerated in the 1960s. The process of concentration started in the food retail business. Large grocery store chains preferred to deal with large roasters. Large roasters started to import coffee beans themselves. They relied on the services of agents, who took over the whole business of buying, insuring, and shipping.[42] The number of traditional importers, brokers, and agents declined drastically during the 1960s.

Bernhard Rothfos personified this new type of coffee trader in a unique way. He operated on the principle of putting the interests of his own firm

[41] The Hamburg government's press department reported in November 1959 on plans to construct two new warehouses with a combined storage capacity of 35,000 cubic meters, one of which, with a capacity of 14,680 cubic meters, would be used primarily for coffee: Pressestelle des Senats, *Wochendienst* 47, Nov. 21, 1959. It was estimated that the facility could store enough beans to meet the needs of the entire population for two years; that calculation was based on the then current per capita consumption figure of 2.8 kilograms, which was still below the interwar peak reached in 1938.

[42] So-called cost-insurance-freight (CIF) agents had existed before, but alongside traditional brokers and agents.

ahead of any consideration of the interest of the guild community.[43] After briefly withdrawing from the Kaffee-Verein in 1945, he emerged from denazification proceedings categorized as "not compromised" (*unbelastet*) although he had participated in the "Aryanization" of a chocolate factory and, in connection with that deal, had arranged for a RM 100,000 donation to the Nazi Party.[44] In 1953 Rothfos exploited a loophole in the complicated coffee tender process for his own competitive advantage – much as he had before the war – and did so with the knowledge and obvious consent of the Federal Ministry of Economic Affairs. By that time he was a leading figure in the coffee industry, in terms of both influence and business success, and, short of outright criminality, he did not hesitate to break the old standards of honorable business conduct if there was advantage to be gained. In this way he was able to amass enough capital to invest in an international distribution network, in instant coffee production, in the new major roasters Jacobs, Eduscho, and Tchibo, and in ventures with those firms. At this time none of the other Hamburg import firms had dared to extend its activities beyond importing. A speech Rothfos gave before his German staff in the 1980s made clear that he actively encouraged the process of concentration after he had secured exclusive supply contracts with individual firms. Working behind the scenes, he thus systematically contributed to small importers' steady loss of customers. By the time Rothfos was praising his own success he was the leading figure in the coffee trade. By 1980 the number of coffee importers had declined from 145 in Hamburg alone in 1951 to 27 in all of the Federal Republic.[45] Bernhard Rothfos exemplified the type of businessperson who, going beyond personal business connections, focused on expansion and making his firm globally active. Such a firm stood on its own; it was not dependent on the protection and support of a community. Indeed, it systematically worked against the very idea of shared community interests. The tight rules of conduct imposed by the Hamburg Kaffee-Verein were less a help than a hindrance to such firms, and community disapproval did nothing to harm them. Their owners had a completely different end in mind – namely, unconditional success in the capitalist international coffee market.

[43] On Rothfos, see Wierling, *Mit Rohkaffee handeln*, 299–308.

[44] Rothfos's denazification file, addendum to questionnaire, Aug. 2, 1946, StAHH 221–11, I (SH) 968.

[45] Wierling, *Mit Rohkaffee handeln*, table on 372–3. The numbers exclude agents and brokers.

6.5 FROM GUILD TO CLASS

In September 1960 the members of the Kaffee-Verein were informed that the board had decided that the association's approaching seventieth anniversary the next spring "would not pass without festive commemoration."[46] At the very least, a morning reception for the members and their guests would be "unavoidable." Members were presented with three options and asked to state their preference: a "men's pub night" at the Rathaus, a ceremonial dinner in the Hotel Atlantic, or a dinner followed by a ball (with female guests). The majority chose the least expensive option, the men's pub night. The morning reception took place in the new Coffee Exchange, where, in fact, little business was now conducted. There was sparkling wine and a speech by the chairman of the association's board, Günter List. He opened by noting that, in contrast to the "luxuriant" celebrations of their predecessors, they had to be "brief" and "modest" on this occasion. Until 1914 the "coffee ship" had sailed "swiftly before the wind." Then began a stretch of hard times, but 1948 marked the start of "seven fat years" that were followed, however, by "seven lean years" after 1955, which, List added, "today we unfortunately have not yet put behind us." It was, in other words, the seven years of postwar state regulation of imports that List held up as the good years and the years since the liberalization of the coffee trade as the bad ones. Speaking after List, the president of the chamber of commerce likewise spoke of the coffee trade's "concerns" and located their cause in "structural transformation." Later, during the members-only "men's night," the deputy chair of the Kaffee-Verein, Werner Hass, did not hold back. It was a question not of appearances but of reality. The reputation of the Sandtorkai had declined "around the world and at home." That was a result not only of structural change but also of the Hamburg coffee trade's own mistakes. The foundation of the trade had always been agreement on "setting aside all selfish personal interests." That had been accepted without question until World War II. With the resumption of trade after the war and, in particular, since liberalization, the traditional code of conduct had disappeared. Many had put their own interests ahead of the collective good, but, Hass warned, "momentary advantage [is] deceptive."

Hass interpreted the changes that occurred solely from the perspective of the community. The Sandtorkai was the symbol of collective prestige.

[46] For this and the following quotes from speeches, see Vereinsjubiläum 1961, folder Archiv des DKV, unpaginated.

The reputation of individual firms depended on that prestige, and, in turn, their "respectability" strengthened the collective. Hass did not think, however, that the decline of the traditional outlook was inevitable, and he ended with a "vow": "Despite all difficulties, we will not capitulate." He could not yet grasp that international trade was moving into a new era of "global players" in which communal ties no longer played a role. He saw only moral decay, not the belated start of a process of modernization. The prophecy in *The Communist Manifesto* that "all that is solid (*alles Ständische und Stehende*) melts into air, all that is holy is profaned, and man is at last compelled to face with sober senses, his real conditions of life, and his relations with his kind" was finally becoming reality at the Sandtorkai.[47]

For many, the disappearance of the community also led, however, to strong feelings of nostalgia. The good old days stand at the forefront of memories of the coffee trade, and the communal past has been symbolically revived in the historically protected Speicherstadt and the ultramodern adjacent "Port City" development. This memorialization of the Hamburg coffee trade has been sponsored by the Neumann Coffee Group, which took over Rothfos in the late 1980s and is currently the world's largest trader in raw coffee. It is also the patron of the Kaffee-Verein, which lives on with a few remaining members.

The case of the Hamburg raw coffee trade offers insight into a little-studied history that extends beyond a particular product and place. Overseas traders operated within global networks from the outset. They had connections in the most important centers of finance, they had business partners in the exporting countries, and they dealt with insurance, shipping, and logistics firms the world over. In the days before the Internet the port of Hamburg was connected to international markets by cable, telephone, and telex. These international networks were inextricably linked with local networks, just as the logic of corporatism could not be separated from the logic of global capitalism. Well into the twentieth century, the corporatist principles of exclusivity and cooperation were an important prerequisite for dealing with risks such as uncertain conditions in producer countries, overproduction crises, and price fluctuations. Much as corporatist bodies like the Kaffee-Verein invoked tradition, they were in fact products of the

[47] Karl Marx and Friedrich Engels, *The Communist Manifesto*, ed. Gareth Stedman Jones (London, 2002), 223.

international capitalist trading system that sought to provide a degree of economic and social security.

When did the gradual move away from corporatist practices actually begin? The emergence of the state as a powerful actor in international trade provided incentive for individual firms to ally with the state for their own advantage. That practice was familiar to some traders – Theodor Wille, for instance – from their dealings with coffee-producing nations in Latin America, where the political and economic elites were closely associated. But although the German state operated as an independent actor during the interwar period, it was nonetheless dependent on the community members' expertise. There were also signs that some in the Weimar Republic saw the idea of democracy as an opportunity to call the traditional hierarchies within the community into question. But it was probably upheavals in the international market above all that undermined the tried-and-true strategies of the importers banded together in the Kaffee-Verein and that prompted (some) member firms to seek solutions on their own. The importers who actively and successfully set out on that course were mainly newcomers – that is, young firm owners who did not come from the old Hamburg merchant families (who viewed them with suspicion) and seemed to have few ties to the community. That background presumably reinforced their tendency to operate more as business proprietors than as members of a community, and thus they ruthlessly pushed their way forward in a time of currency controls and turbulence on world markets.

For the Hamburg importers who were so proud of their honor, the experience of having to submit to the despised Nazis presumably undermined their moral self-confidence. The records of the Kaffee-Verein and interviews with former importers make clear that the members of the Hamburg coffee community have never seriously attempted to address the question of their conduct in the period 1933–45, whether to defend themselves, to accept responsibility for injustices, or to apologize. Instead, they simply describe those years as a time of restrictions on their business and of struggling to survive. The Kaffee-Verein's records from the early postwar period clearly attest to a policy of silence about the recent past and a desire to adapt to the new political situation in the hope of continuity. The internal and external corrosion of the guild community was thus an important factor in the decision of the occupying powers, the United States above all, to open the German coffee trade up to market forces.

PART III

PROMOTING CAPITALISM

7

Between Criticism and Innovation

Beer and Public Relations in the Weimar Republic

Sina Fabian

In March 1922, the Social Democratic newspaper *Vorwärts* revealed the "brewing trust's war plan" (*Kriegsplan des Braukapitals*) when it reported on a top-secret meeting of the German Brewers Association (Deutscher Brauer-Bund) (DBB). The meeting was, according to *Vorwärts*, mainly concerned with the question of how brewing companies could influence public opinion in favor of beer consumption and effectively combat the growing influence of the anti-alcohol movement.[1]

Vorwärts had managed to obtain inside information on this important meeting of the DBB. At this gathering crucial public relations (PR), strategies were discussed that were to be implemented in the following years. Getting positive media coverage was seen as most important in combating teetotalism. The "propaganda" was supposed to be subtle rather than blunt, and the importance of "scientific experts" and "statistics" was also stressed.

This chapter takes a closer look at the challenges the brewers faced in the 1920s and their reactions to them. The brewing industry had to develop new strategies to secure its business, as the teetotalists' momentum in the early 1920s was surprisingly strong. Beer was suddenly widely perceived not as an everyday drink but as a threat to the nation's well-being. The brewers' turn toward PR was thus a reaction to morally charged criticism that was also anticapitalist. This chapter sheds light on how industries that were criticized for producing "bad" products reacted to such criticism and adapted to changing circumstances. The Weimar

[1] "Kriegsplan des Braukapitals," *Vorwärts*, Mar. 2, 1922. Cf. for a reply and correction by the brewing industry: "Kriegsplan des Braukapitals," *Vorwärts*, Mar. 5, 1922.

years were, therefore, not just marked by anticapitalist critique; they were also a testing ground for new capitalist strategies that businesses adopted voluntarily or involuntarily. In this case, for instance, the brewers adopted both established and new methods of influencing the public in their favor.

Since beer was a consumer good that was not regarded as a basic commodity in most parts of Germany, it was also prone to criticism as an "unnecessary" or "luxury" good. This criticism was linked to anticapitalist discourses in the Weimar Republic. Capitalism was widely criticized during the "crisis years" of the early 1920s and early 1930s,[2] and mass consumption, especially of seemingly superfluous goods, was an easy target.[3] To make matters worse, the alcohol industry, unlike most others, was confronted by a well-organized and outspoken enemy: the teetotalism movement, which gained immense influence after the war.[4] While criticism regarding consumption practices in general, and alcohol consumption in particular, during the 1920s has been at least partially analyzed elsewhere, the ways in which producers, in this case, the brewing industry, responded to the criticism is much less well understood.[5] In reaction to the

[2] Cf. for a critical assessment of the "crisis" narrative: Moritz Föllmer and Rüdiger Graf, eds., *Die "Krise" der Weimarer Republik: Zur Kritik eines Deutungsmusters* (Frankfurt, 2005).

[3] Claus-Christian Szejnmann, "Semantik der Kapitalismuskritik in Deutschland nach dem Ersten Weltkrieg," in Dariusz Adamczyk, ed., *Wirtschaftskrisen als Wendepunkte: Ursachen, Folgen und historische Einordnungen vom Mittelalter bis zur Gegenwart* (Osnabrück, 2015), 77–99; Claudius Torp, *Wachstum, Sicherheit, Moral: Politische Legitimationen des Konsums im 20. Jahrhundert* (Göttingen, 2012); Martin H. Geyer, *Verkehrte Welt: Revolution, Inflation und Moderne, München 1914–1924* (Göttingen, 1998). The importance of mass consumption as a stabilizing but also problematic factor for the Weimar Republic has been highlighted in recent studies: Claudius Torp, "Das Janusgesicht der Weimarer Konsumpolitik," in Karl-Heinz Haupt and Claudius Torp, eds., *Die Konsumgesellschaft in Deutschland 1890–1990. Ein Handbuch* (Frankfurt, 2009), 250–67; Moritz Föllmer, *Individuality and Modernity in Berlin: Self and Society from Weimar to the Wall* (Cambridge, 2013), 58–72.

[4] Claudius Torp, *Konsum und Politik in der Weimarer Republik* (Göttingen, 2011), 249–68; Elke Hauschildt, *Auf den richtigen Weg zwingen … : Trinkerfürsorge 1922 bis 1945* (Freiburg im Breisgau, 1995).

[5] Cf. for a similar case: Gideon Reuveni, *Reading Germany: Literature and Consumer Culture in Germany before 1933* (New York, 2006). Histories of individual breweries have either ignored this topic altogether or have looked at it only peripherally: Erich Borkenhagen, *125 Jahre Schultheiss-Brauerei. Die Geschichte des Schultheiss-Bieres in Berlin von 1842 bis 1967* (Berlin, 1967); Christian Schäder, *Münchner Brauindustrie: 1871–1945; die wirtschaftsgeschichtliche Entwicklung eines Industriezweiges* (Marburg, 1999); Roman Köster, "Konjunkturen, Krisen, Konzentration: Zur Entwicklung des deutschen Biermarkts vom ausgehenden 19. Jahrhundert bis zur Weltwirtschaftskrise – Dortmunder Beispiele," in Karl-Peter Ellerbrock, ed., *Zur Geschichte der westfälischen Brauwirtschaft im 19. und 20.*

public discourse, which was hostile to alcohol production and consumption, the brewers' association greatly expanded and professionalized its PR efforts.

Although the term *public relations* (*Öffentlichkeitsarbeit*) did not yet exist, companies had been making use of the concept since the nineteenth century.[6] To have a presence in the media and at exhibitions was viewed as an important PR strategy by the beginning of the twentieth century. Advertising films and cooperative advertising (*Gemeinschaftswerbung*) were introduced on a large scale starting in the 1920s.[7] In-house PR experts also became more widespread in the 1920s, along with advertising departments, but neither was yet a common feature even of larger companies.[8] Scholars have performed studies of PR in industrial organizations during the Weimar years.[9] They are, however, mainly concerned with internal processes and political lobbying, while promotional

Jahrhundert (Dortmund, 2012), 109–31; Richard Winkler, *Ein Bier wie Bayern: Geschichte der Münchner Löwenbrauerei 1818–2003* (Neustadt an der Aisch, 2016).

[6] Michael Kunczik, *Geschichte der Öffentlichkeitsarbeit in Deutschland* (Cologne, 1997); Hartmut Kaelble, *Industrielle Interessenspolitik in der Wilhelminischen Gesellschaft. Centralverband Deutscher Industrieller 1895–1914* (Berlin, 1967); Barbara Wolbring, *Krupp und die Öffentlichkeit im 19. Jahrhundert: Selbstdarstellung, öffentliche Wahrnehmung und gesellschaftliche Kommunikation* (Munich, 2000); Clemens Wischermann, Peter Borscheid, and Karl-Peter Ellerbrock, eds., *Unternehmenskommunikation im 19. und 20. Jahrhundert: Neue Wege der Unternehmensgeschichte* (Dortmund, 2000); Hartmut Berghoff, *Zwischen Kleinstadt und Weltmarkt: Hohner und die Harmonika 1857–1961: Unternehmensgeschichte als Gesellschaftsgeschichte* (Paderborn, 1997). For the British case, see David W. Gutzke, *Protecting the Pub: Brewers and Publicans against Temperance* (Woodbridge, 1989).

[7] Wolbring, *Krupp und die Öffentlichkeit im 19. Jahrhundert*; Thomas Großbölting, "*Im Reich der Arbeit*": *Die Repräsentation gesellschaftlicher Ordnung in den deutschen Industrie- und Gewerbeausstellungen 1790–1914* (Munich, 2008); Marius Lange, *Unternehmerische Öffentlichkeitsarbeit in Deutschland: 1929–1936: Zwischen Demokratie und Diktatur* (Frankfurt, 2010); Dirk Schindelbeck, "Werbung für alle? Kleine Geschichte der Gemeinschaftswerbung von der Weimarer Republik bis zur Bundesrepublik Deutschland," in Wischermann, Borscheid, and Ellerbrock, eds., *Unternehmenskommunikation*, 63–97.

[8] Bruno Fischer, *Werbung und Organisation – ihre Bedeutung für den Fabrikbetrieb* (Weida in Thüringen, 1929), 109–12; Pamela E. Swett, *Selling under the Swastika: Advertising and Commercial Culture in Nazi Germany* (Stanford, CA, 2013), 18–26; Alexander Schug, "*Deutsche Kultur*" *und Werbung: Studien zur Geschichte der Wirtschaftswerbung von 1918 bis 1945* (Berlin, 2011).

[9] Heinz J. Varain, ed., *Interessenverbände in Deutschland* (Cologne, 1973); Bernd Weisbrod, *Schwerindustrie in der Weimarer Republik* (Wuppertal, 1978); Reinhard Neebe, *Großindustrie, Staat und NSDAP 1930–1933: Paul Silverberg und der Reichsverband der Deutschen Industrie in der Krise der Weimarer Republik* (Göttingen, 1981); Matt Bera, *Lobbying Hitler: Industrial Associations between Democracy and Dictatorship* (New York, 2016).

strategies aimed at the public have not yet received much attention from scholars. Michael Kunczik has made some inroads into the field, but his work is focused mainly on the nineteenth century.[10]

The term *propaganda* had been used interchangeably with *advertising* since the late nineteenth century. During World War I, the term was politicized and militarized. *Propaganda* was considered more aggressive than *advertising*. Only in the 1930s, however, were the terms clearly separated, and *propaganda* came to be used solely in the political sphere.[11] Thus, in all likelihood, the DBB deliberately chose to rename its press department so as to emphasize its importance and to invoke the more aggressive meaning because the DBB felt it was in a fierce battle to counter the activities of the temperance movement.

7.1 BEER PRODUCTION AND CONSUMPTION AFTER WORLD WAR I: CHALLENGES AND REACTIONS

The Deutsche Brauer-Bund was founded in 1871. After its fusion with the Deutsche Brauer Union in 1911 it became the brewing industry's central organization.[12] Only shortly before World War I did the DBB begin to perceive the anti-alcohol movement as a threat; it established a press department in 1912, in response. The temperance movement, which propagated moderate drinking, had initially focused its attention on spirits and had seen beer as a preferable alternative to liquor. Due to the growing influence of teetotalists in the movement, however, it increasingly turned against beer consumption after 1900.[13] While some activities had started before 1914, after the war, the brewing industry faced a stiff challenge.[14]

[10] Kunczik, *Geschichte der Öffentlichkeitsarbeit in Deutschland*; Lange, *Unternehmerische Öffentlichkeitsarbeit in Deutschland*; Marius Lange, "Unternehmen im 'Dienst an der Öffentlichkeit.' Theorieverständnis und Organisation von Public Relations in der Weimarer Republik," *Jahrbuch für Kommunikationsgeschichte* 12 (2010): 101–20.

[11] Thymian Bussemer, Propaganda. Theoretisches Konzept und geschichtliche Bedeutung, Version: 1.0, *Docupedia-Zeitgeschichte*, August 2, 2013, http://docupedia.de/zg/bussemer_propaganda_v1_de_2013 (accessed Aug. 8, 2018).

[12] Erich Borkenhagen, *100 Jahre Deutscher Brauer-Bund e. V. 1871–1971: Zur Geschichte des Bieres im 19. und 20. Jahrhundert* (Bonn, 1971).

[13] Hasso Spode, *Die Macht der Trunkenheit: Kultur- und Sozialgeschichte des Alkohols in Deutschland* (Opladen, 1993); Heinrich Tappe, "Der Kampf gegen den Alkohomißbrauch als Aufgabe bürgerlicher Mäßigkeitsbewegung und staatlich-kommunaler Verwaltung," in Hans J. Teuteberg, ed., *Durchbruch zum modernen Massenkonsum: Lebensmittelmärkte und Lebensmittelqualität im Städtewachstum des Industriezeitalters* (Münster, 1987), 189–236.

[14] Borkenhagen, *100 Jahre Deutscher Brauer-Bund e. V. 1871–1971*.

Due to scarce resources, food rationing, which hit the brewing industry as well, had been introduced in Germany early in the conflict. Barley rationing was introduced in 1915, and quantities were successively reduced to less than 10 percent of prewar levels.[15] In 1918, however, breweries were still managing to produce half as much beer as they had in 1913. This was made possible by significantly reducing the percentage of alcohol in beer. Under the barley rationing that continued until 1921, beer's alcohol content had been limited in 1919 to a mere 0.75 percent of volume.[16] Rationing and beer's generally poor quality in these years were the main reasons for a significant drop in consumption. Although consumption rates started to increase after the restrictions ended, Germans were still drinking only 60 percent of prewar consumption by 1924.[17]

These difficulties led to a period of consolidation among breweries, mainly driven by takeovers of smaller breweries by larger ones and by mergers. Smaller breweries often sold their malt and brewing quotas to larger breweries, especially during the war when they encountered financial difficulties. Some of them then closed, while others were kept open by the larger breweries in order to broaden their range by retaining customers loyal to the established brand.[18] Takeovers and mergers were numerous in the 1920s. The number of breweries in Württemberg, for example, decreased by more than 50 percent between 1914 and 1922.[19] Larger breweries, with publicly traded companies often among them, were particularly adept at taking advantage of the situation to grow their business significantly. Germany's two largest breweries, Schultheiss and Patzenhofer, both based in Berlin, merged in July 1920. In the same year Löwenbräu, Munich's largest brewery, merged with Unionsbrauerei, Munich's third largest.[20] Large stock-market breweries were responsible for 60 percent of beer production by the mid-1920s. Despite this

[15] Cf. Dortmunder Actienbrauerei during World War I: Roman Köster, *Die Konzentrationsbewegung in der Dortmunder Brauindustrie 1914 bis 1924: Das Beispiel der Dortmunder Actienbrauerei* (Essen, 2003), 33–60.

[16] Winkler, *Ein Bier wie Bayern*, 95–8; Deutscher Brauer-Bund, *Mitteilungen des Deutschen Brauer-Bundes*, 8 (1922), Archiv des Deutschen Brauer-Bundes, Berlin, Z76, 220–1.

[17] Statistisches Reichsamt, ed., *Statistisches Jahrbuch des Deutschen Reiches 1923* (Berlin, 1924), 312.

[18] "Weitere Liquidationen von Klein-Brauereien," *Vossische Zeitung*, June 9, 1920.

[19] Köster, "Konjunkturen, Krisen, Konzentration," 110; Hermann Otto, *Die Konzentrationsbewegung in der deutschen Brauereiindustrie* (Cologne, 1923); "Rückgang der Brauerei-Industrie," *Vossische Zeitung*, May 8, 1923.

[20] Borkenhagen, *125 Jahre Schultheiss-Brauerei*, 112–19; Winkler, *Ein Bier wie Bayern*, 99–100.; cf. further mergers and takeovers in Munich's brewing industry in the 1920s: Schäder, *Münchner Brauindustrie*, 265–300.

consolidation, the number of small and medium-sized breweries in Germany remained considerably higher than in most other countries.[21] The turn toward PR, therefore, happened during a time in which the brewing industry was undergoing significant structural and organizational change. The new larger breweries were the ones that showed more interest in implementing PR strategies and had the financial means to do so.[22]

A second consequence of the severe food shortages during the war was the politicization of food, which persisted into the early 1920s. Consumers' organizations achieved mass membership, and protests against rising food prices were prevalent until 1924.[23] Activists agitated against a free market and demanded the reinstatement or continuation of price and supply controls on basic consumer goods, such as bread and milk, after they had mostly been lifted in 1921.[24]

After rationing ended and beer consumption started to increase again, criticism began to mount, not just from the teetotalism movement but also from a variety of social and political groups. The Sozialdemokratische Partei Deutschlands (SPD), the churches, and even the Bavarian government for a short time supported the restriction of alcohol production and consumption.[25] This anti-alcohol sentiment is best understood as part of the larger wave of consumer protest at the time. Protest against alcohol consumption combined two important strands: fear of not having sufficient basic consumer goods and criticism of superfluous luxury consumption. Alcohol was targeted because important resources such as barley, potatoes, and fruit were, according to critics, wasted on producing unnecessary luxury beverages such as beer, liquor, and sparkling wine. Protesters demanded that the government deal with this nuisance, especially after the end of food controls and the return of the free market had made the gap in access to consumer goods between the well-off and the poor plainly visible.[26]

[21] Borkenhagen, *100 Jahre Deutscher Brauer-Bund e. V. 1871–1971*, 125–7; Karl-Peter Ellerbrock, *Geschichte der deutschen Nahrungs- und Genußmittelindustrie 1750–1914* (Stuttgart, 1993), 291–4. There are still considerably more small and mid-sized breweries in Germany than in most other countries: William James Adams, "Beer in Germany and the United States," *Journal of Economic Perspectives* 20 (2006): 189–205.

[22] Cf. for Löwenbräu's advertising and PR in the interwar years: Bayerisches Wirtschaftsarchiv (BWA), F002-54; F002-8836; F002-1360.

[23] Belinda Joy Davis, *Home Fires Burning: Food, Politics, and Everyday Life in World War I Berlin* (Chapel Hill, NC, 2000); Martin H. Geyer, "Teuerungsprotest, Konsumpolitik und soziale Gerechtigkeit während der Inflation: München 1920–1923," *Archiv für Sozialgeschichte* 30 (1990): 181–215; Torp, *Wachstum, Sicherheit, Moral*, 40–52.

[24] Geyer, "Teuerungsprotest," 186–7.

[25] Torp, *Konsum*, 253.

[26] Geyer, "Teuerungsprotest," 187.

The government was flooded with letters and petitions from various local and national organizations as well as from individuals demanding restrictions on alcohol production and consumption.[27] The debate was morally charged, as indicated by the *Vorwärts* article mentioned in the introduction to this chapter. The consumption of luxury food was usually derided in more general terms as "feasting" (*Schlemmerei*) and "gluttony" (*Völlerei*), whereas alcohol was explicitly attacked. Alcohol producers were accused of wasting important resources – alcohol consumers of moral failings. According to the critics, Germany was in a fragile, "topsy-turvy" (*verkehrt*) state in the early 1920s. Society as a whole seemed out of joint after defeat and revolution, and the increase in alcohol consumption appeared to epitomize this instability.[28] Alcoholic drinks were therefore often associated with the "evils" of society such as "foreigners" (*Fremde*) and "profiteers" (*Schieber*) who, it was alleged, indulged in bingeing and feasting and exploited the needs of ordinary Germans.[29] "Usury" was criticized alongside alcohol and luxury food consumption and contributed to the feeling that German society was morally decaying. It is therefore no surprise that protest against alcohol consumption increased in parallel with the hyperinflation that began in autumn 1922.[30]

Newspapers from across the political spectrum were similarly critical in those years. They also claimed that the industry was wasting scarce resources and insisted that Germany's reputation for beer and alcohol consumption created a negative image of the country abroad. Among the critical voices were newspapers that had staunchly defended alcohol consumption against the temperance movement when it first appeared in the late nineteenth century.[31]

[27] "Nahrungsnot und Alkohol," *Vorwärts*, Oct. 23, 1922; "Alkohol, Amerika und wir," *Hamburger Echo*, Jan. 26, 1921; "Die Steigerung des Alkoholverbrauchs," *Soziale Praxis*, Sept. 27, 1921; cf.: letters and petitions to the government in "Entwurf eines Gesetzes gegen den Alkoholmissbrauch – Eingaben," Bundesarchiv (BArch), R 1501/116362.

[28] Geyer, *Verkehrte Welt.*

[29] Gerald D. Feldman, *The Great Disorder: Politics, Economics, and Society in the German Inflation, 1914–1924* (New York, 1997); Bernd Widdig, *Culture and Inflation in Weimar Germany* (Berkeley, CA, 2001), 85–7; cf. for contemporary images: *Simplicissimus*, Apr. 21, 1920; *Simplicissimus*, June 8, 1921; *Der wahre Jakob*, Jan. 14, 1921; "Denkschrift zur Wirtschaftslage," BArch, R 43 I/1493.

[30] Geyer, "Teuerungsprotest."

[31] "Alkohol, Amerika und wir," *Hamburger Echo*, Jan. 26, 1921; "Deutschlands Aufwand für Genußmittel," *Frankfurter Zeitung*, Jan. 27, 1921; "Das Anwachsen des Alkoholismus," *Deutsche Allgemeine Zeitung*, July 2, 1921; "Berliner Auslandsbilder. Wie sie hier leben," *Vossische Zeitung*, Nov. 30, 1921; "Vom Feldzug des Alkoholkapitals," *Deutsches Volkstum*, 7/1923. For harsh criticism of the temperance movement by the *Vossische Zeitung* and *Frankfurter Zeitung* in 1896, see

Gideon Reuveni has shown that similar debates raged about the consumption of other leisure goods such as books. According to the dominant public discourse, a "book crisis" unfolded after the war. As with alcohol consumption, public discourse did not correlate with actual practice.[32] The difference, however, was that, while books were generally perceived as a "good" commodity, alcohol was seen as a "bad" one. Therefore, behind the "book crisis" was a fear that *not enough* "good" books were being read, whereas in the "alcohol crisis" it was feared that *too much* alcohol was being consumed.

Reuveni argues that the "book crisis" was not primarily about books but about fears of social upheaval and change after the war. Therefore the "crisis" seemed especially acute during the unstable early Weimar years.[33] This was very similar to the debates on alcohol consumption. It confirms that consumer goods were charged with connotations and expectations that made it hard, on one hand, for the state to manage and control them. On the other hand, it was also difficult for producers to deal with these assumptions and to adjust their marketing and PR efforts accordingly.[34]

The brewing industry had not been prepared for the level of criticism it faced. Prewar criticism had focused more on the impact of alcohol on health and less on its economic significance; the criticism of the early 1920s was a result of the war and the growing hyperinflation.[35] This was a new situation for the alcohol producers, especially the brewers. At first, the DBB concentrated on "proving" scientifically that beer was nutritious and that – if not consumed in excess – it had only positive effects on body and mind. Statistical materials and conclusions drawn by scientific experts were believed to carry most conviction.[36] Posters and flyers were designed that made excessive use of numbers and statistics in

Heinrich Tappe, *Auf dem Weg zur modernen Alkoholkultur: Alkoholproduktion, Trinkverhalten und Temperenzbewegung in Deutschland vom frühen 19. Jahrhundert bis zum Ersten Weltkrieg* (Stuttgart, 1994), 347.

[32] Hasso Spode, "Thematisierungskonjunkturen des sozialen Problems 'Alkohol'," in Karl Wassenberg and Sabine Schaller, eds., *Der Geist der Deutschen Mässigkeitsbewegung: Debatten um Alkohol und Trinken in Vergangenheit und Gegenwart* (Halle, 2010), 180–204.

[33] Reuveni, *Reading Germany*.

[34] Föllmer, *Individuality*, 58–72; Claudius Torp, "Besser als in Weimar? Spielräume des Konsums im Nationalsozialismus," in Birthe Kundrus and Sybille Steinbacher, eds., *Kontinuitäten und Diskontinuitäten: Der Nationalsozialismus in der Geschichte des 20. Jahrhunderts* (Göttingen, 2013), 73–93, Hartmut Berghoff, "Träume und Alpträume. Konsumpolitik im nationalsozialistischen Deutschland," in Haupt and Torp, *Die Konsumgesellschaft in Deutschland*, 268–88.

[35] Tappe, "Kampf," 227. [36] "Kriegsplan des Braukapitals," *Vorwärts*, Mar. 2, 1922.

order to prove beer's nutritious and healthy nature. Scientists – physicians in particular – contributed to this strategy by publishing studies that were often commissioned or at least funded by the brewing associations.[37]

In this leaflet (Figure 7.1), the brewers argued that beer was more nutritious than pearl barley. They also highlighted the utility of the brewing process, which produced draff that was used to feed livestock and therefore contributed to the production of milk, which was very scarce after the war.[38] More interesting than the arguments were the style in which they were presented. As this leaflet shows, the brewing industry attached considerable importance to the presentation of hard data. That mixing units such as tons, grams, and even spoonfuls was not a sign of scientific rigor seemed irrelevant. This leaflet from 1920 is an early example of the industry's new PR strategy. It combined scientific argumentation along with fierce attacks on the teetotalists and their "blind fanaticism," which had been common before World War I. The poster therefore represents a transition phase between new and old tactics.[39]

In the late nineteenth century the anti-alcohol movement had already begun gradually to move from a purely moral condemnation of alcohol to a focus on health and social hygiene. While moral arguments were still important, they were couched in subtler terms, while scientific arguments were now thought to be most convincing.[40] The brewing industry adopted these tactics after the war, as we begin to see in this example. The brewers' shift away from attacks toward factual and scientific argumentation in public communication was complete by the mid-1920s.

Another main argument also presented in the leaflet was the brewing industry's economic significance to the country.[41] Before the outbreak of the war the brewing industry had been the second largest industrial branch in terms of production value.[42] The brewers argued that the German economy would be severely hit and hundreds of thousands of jobs in farming as well as in industrial brewing and the service sector

[37] Paul Bauer, *Das Bier und seine Bedeutung als Nahrungs-, Genuß- und Heilmittel* (Berlin, 1920).

[38] "Graupen-Bier-Milch," BArch, NS 5/VI 4865; Bauer, *Das Bier*.

[39] "Kriegsplan des Braukapitals," *Vorwärts*, Mar. 2, 1922.

[40] Spode, *Die Macht der Trunkenheit*.

[41] Cf. "Resolution des Großen Ausschusses des Deutschen Brauer-Bundes," Mar. 20, 1922, in Tätigkeitsbericht des Deutschen Brauer-Bundes, 1921/2, in Deutscher Brauer-Bund, Tätigkeitsberichte 1921–9, Archiv des Deutschen Brauer-Bundes, Berlin, G 20, 43–4.

[42] Köster, "Konjunkturen, Krisen, Konzentration," 111.

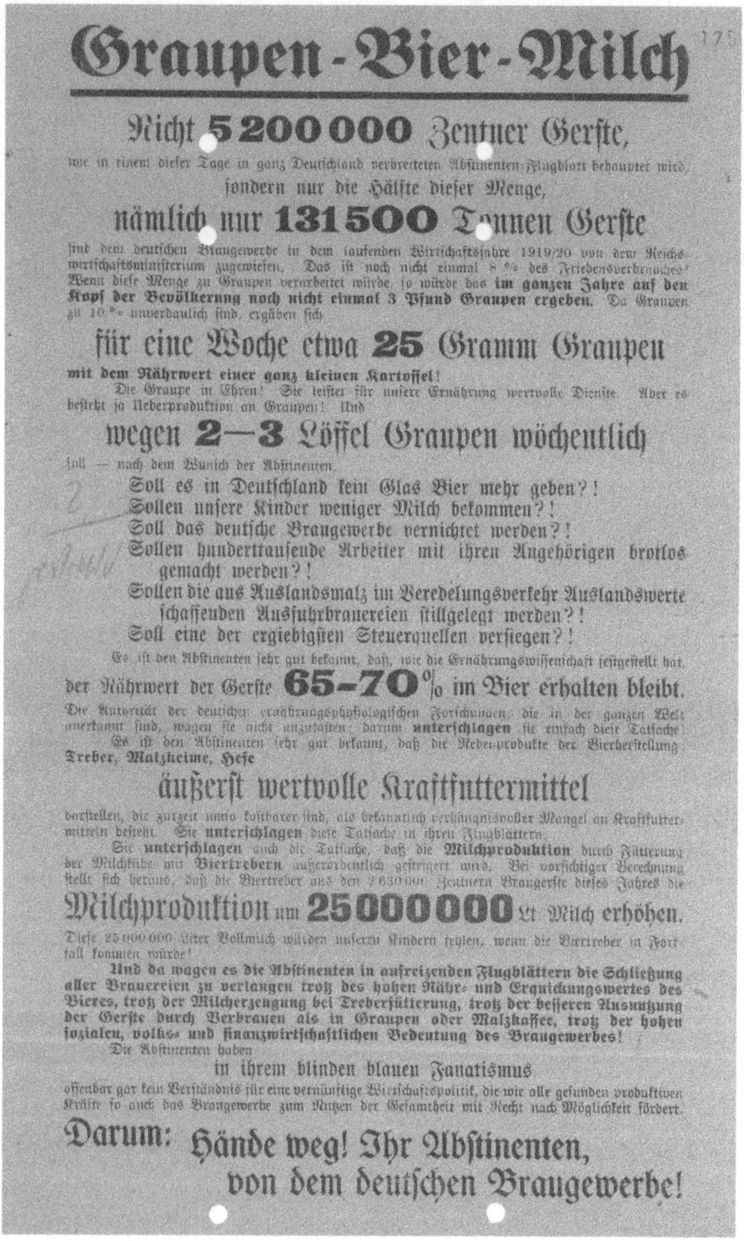

Graupen-Bier-Milch

Nicht 5200000 Zentner Gerste,

wie in einem dieser Tage in ganz Deutschland verbreiteten Abstinenten-Flugblatt behauptet wird,

sondern nur die Hälfte dieser Menge,

nämlich nur 131500 Tonnen Gerste

sind dem deutschen Braugewerbe in dem laufenden Wirtschaftsjahre 1919/20 von dem Reichswirtschaftsministerium zugewiesen. Das ist noch nicht einmal 8 % des Friedensverbrauches! Wenn diese Menge zu Graupen verarbeitet würde, so würde das **im ganzen Jahre auf den Kopf der Bevölkerung noch nicht einmal 3 Pfund Graupen ergeben.** Da Graupen zu 10 % unverdaulich sind, ergäben sich

für eine Woche etwa 25 Gramm Graupen

mit dem Nährwert einer ganz kleinen Kartoffel!

Die Graupe in Ehren! Sie leistet für unsere Ernährung wertvolle Dienste. Aber es besteht ja Ueberproduktion an Graupen! Und

wegen 2—3 Löffel Graupen wöchentlich

soll — nach dem Wunsch der Abstinenten.

Soll es in Deutschland kein Glas Bier mehr geben?!
Sollen unsere Kinder weniger Milch bekommen?!
Soll das deutsche Braugewerbe vernichtet werden?!
Sollen hunderttausende Arbeiter mit ihren Angehörigen brotlos gemacht werden?!
Sollen die aus Auslandsmalz im Veredelungsverkehr Auslandswerte schaffenden Ausfuhrbrauereien stillgelegt werden?!
Soll eine der ergiebigsten Steuerquellen versiegen?!

Es ist den Abstinenten sehr gut bekannt, daß, wie die Ernährungswissenschaft festgestellt hat,

der Nährwert der Gerste 65–70 % im Bier erhalten bleibt.

Die Autorität der deutschen ernährungsphysiologischen Forschungen, die in der ganzen Welt anerkannt sind, wagen sie nicht anzutasten; darum **unterschlagen** sie einfach diese Tatsache!

Es ist den Abstinenten sehr gut bekannt, daß die Nebenprodukte der Bierherstellung: **Treber, Malzkeime, Hefe**

äußerst wertvolle Kraftfuttermittel

darstellen, die zurzeit umso kostbarer sind, als bekanntlich verhängnisvoller Mangel an Kraftfuttermitteln besteht. Sie **unterschlagen** diese Tatsache in ihren Flugblättern.

Sie **unterschlagen** auch die Tatsache, daß die **Milchproduktion** durch Fütterung der Milchkühe mit **Biertrebern** außerordentlich gesteigert wird. Bei vorsichtiger Berechnung stellt sich heraus, daß die Biertreber aus den 2630000 Zentnern Braugerste dieses Jahres die

Milchproduktion um 25000000 Lt Milch erhöhen.

Diese 25000000 Liter Vollmilch würden unseren Kindern fehlen, wenn die Biertreber in Fortfall kommen würde!

Und da wagen es die Abstinenten in aufreizenden Flugblättern die Schließung aller Brauereien zu verlangen trotz des hohen Nähr- und Erquickungswertes des Bieres, trotz der Milcherzeugung bei Treberfütterung, trotz der besseren Ausnutzung der Gerste durch Verbrauen als in Graupen oder Malzkaffee, trotz der hohen sozialen, volks- und finanzwirtschaftlichen Bedeutung des Braugewerbes!

Die Abstinenten haben

in ihrem blinden blauen Fanatismus

offenbar gar kein Verständnis für eine vernünftige Wirtschaftspolitik, die wie alle gesunden produktiven Kräfte so auch das Braugewerbe zum Nutzen der Gesamtheit mit Recht nach Möglichkeit fördert.

Darum: Hände weg! Ihr Abstinenten, von dem deutschen Braugewerbe!

FIGURE 7.1 Leaflet that describes beer as more nutritious than pearl barley. Focusing on the nutritional value of beer was a direct reaction to the criticism that beer was a waste of resources. "Graupen-Bier-Milch," 1920, BArch, NS 5/VI 4865.

would be at risk if the brewing industry or beer consumption were regulated by stricter alcohol legislation. The DBB presented their case, for example, at the 1922 Magdeburg exhibition on the theme of "Settlement, Social Welfare, and Work." The brewers' exhibit focused on the economic importance of their industry and showcased export figures, tax revenues, and the number of men and women employed in the brewing industry as evidence for their value to Germany.[43]

Cultural or social arguments that had been brought forward before the war, such as beer's long tradition in German culture as well as its ubiquitous presence at most social occasions, were barely mentioned at all. No further arguments were made regarding the "pleasant side" of beer consumption. It was strictly promoted as food and not as a pleasure drink (*Genussmittel*) or leisure pursuit, hence the common comparison of its nutritional value with solid food such as bread.

The aftermath of World War I was a particular time in which moral arguments were valued more highly and were more influential than economic ones in political decision-making. While the teetotalism movement was successful with its mixture of moral and scientific argumentation, the brewing industry could only rely on economic and scientific arguments. The brewers, therefore, had only limited success in preventing the adoption of stricter legislation in the early 1920s.[44] This experience was nevertheless important for the brewing industry as it demonstrated that brewers' usual way of lobbying politicians and often getting their way by simply mentioning potential negative economic effects was not enough anymore. The brewers had to come up with new arguments, such as beer's nutritional value, and with new ways of communicating with the public.

Given the economic instability and general sense of crisis in these years, the critics of alcohol production and consumption had the momentum, speaking for wide sections of the population who supported stricter regulation, which, thanks to intensive lobbying efforts, was implemented by "emergency decree" alongside an anti-profiteering law in February 1923. It was the first nationwide legislation regulating alcohol distribution and consumption. It established, for example, a legal drinking age of sixteen for beer and wine and eighteen for liquor. Publicans were no longer allowed to serve alcohol to people who were already drunk. An

43 Tätigkeitsbericht des Deutschen Brauer-Bundes, 1921/2, in Deutscher Brauer-Bund, Tätigkeitsberichte 1921–9, Archiv des Deutschen Brauer-Bundes, Berlin, G 20, 63–4.

44 Tätigkeitsberichte des Deutschen Brauer Bundes 1922/3, in Deutscher Brauer-Bund, Tätigkeitsberichte 1921–9, Archiv des Deutschen Brauer-Bundes, Berlin, G 20.

alcohol license could now only be obtained if the person seeking it could prove that there was a need (*Bedürfnis*) for alcohol to be sold on the premises.[45]

A "pub law" (*Schankstättengesetz*) was discussed in the parliament at the same time. It aimed at even stricter regulations on the distribution and consumption of alcohol and was more detailed than the emergency law. The most important difference was that it also included a local option (*Gemeindebestimmungsrecht*), which meant that local communities could decide for themselves whether they wanted to be "dry" or "wet."[46] However, due to the turbulent events of 1923, no vote on the pub bill took place.

7.2 PROFESSIONALIZATION AND EXPANSION: THE CAMPAIGN AGAINST THE LOCAL OPTION

Although the DBB and the alcohol industry as a whole were not particularly successful in influencing the public debates of the early Weimar years in their favor, they were, at least partly, more effective in lobbying the government and members of the parliament in order to prevent even more severe restrictions.[47] Influence-peddling and political lobbying behind closed doors continued to be of great importance. However, the brewing industry also felt the need to stress publicly the importance of beer as Germany's national drink and to agitate openly against the Weimar Republic's "becoming dry" (*Trockenlegung*). Therefore, political lobbying and PR measures went hand in hand. This was especially the case with regard to the local option.[48] The "fight" (*Kampf*) for and against the local option peaked in 1925–6. Due to the efforts of the anti-alcohol movement,

[45] "Notgesetz vom 24.2.1923," in *Reichsgesetzblatt* (RGBl) I/1923, 147–51. Cf. government meetings and discussions beforehand: "Besprechung mit Vertretern der Gewerkschaften," Dec. 28, 1922, BArch, R 43 I/1493; "Aufzeichnung Staatssekretär Hamms über notwendige Maßnahmen der nächsten Zeit," Jan. 17, 1923, BArch, R 43 I/1493; "Ministerrat beim Reichspräsidenten," Jan. 9, 1923, BArch, R 43 I/1382.

[46] "Entwurf eines Schankstättengesetzes," June 6, 1923, *Verhandlungen des Reichstags* 378 (Berlin, 1924), 7114–19.

[47] "Kurzer Bericht über die Ergebnisse des Besuchs maßgebender Persönlichkeiten in Berlin in der Frage der Sonderbesteuerung des 8–9%igen Bieres," Jan. 26, 1922, Bayerisches Hauptstaatsarchiv (BayHStA), Bayerische Wirtschaftsstelle Berlin 83; Biersteuergesetz, BayHStA, MHIG 926.

[48] Cf. for political lobbying regarding this question: "Schankstättengesetzesentwurf Eingaben," BArch, R1501/116363; "Biersteuern," BArch, R 401/1294.

it was debated twice in the Reichstag, but this time the DBB was much better prepared to take up the fight.

It dramatically described its efforts to prevent the local option as a "question of life and death" for the industry and significantly increased the financial resources it devoted to the debate.[49] From the beginning of 1925 the breweries had to pay a "propaganda surcharge" of 300 percent of their membership fee. The DBB leadership defended the surcharge as necessary in light of the teetotalists' activities. The immense increase in financial and staff resources reflected the growing importance of PR. It also shows the advantage of having the support of a whole industry. The DBB was quickly able to acquire the money needed for its extensive PR strategy.

Most of the money raised was used to establish regional DBB offices in "endangered bigger cities," in order to react swiftly to teetotalist activities there.[50] While the DBB's annual report covered most topics in detail, it deliberately kept much of its propaganda activities under cover. The DBB explained the secrecy in the following way: "The propaganda department does not resort to methods which need to be hidden from the public in any way. But teetotalist fanatics have proven again and again that they reply to our openness with misrepresentation and distortion, even with deceit."[51]

One of the main targets of the campaign was the press. The DBB tried to influence media coverage by providing editors with propaganda material and favorable articles that stressed beer's long tradition and its importance for German culture and the economy. According to the DBB, these articles were supposed to relay a very subtle pro-beer message that even editors might not recognize. The articles were supposed to give the impression of neutrality and objectivity rather than to be easily identifiable as advertising. The DBB thus was making use of the strategies discussed at the 1922 meeting on which *Vorwärts* had reported.[52]

One example was a special edition of *Die Voss Berlin*, a weekly foreign paper, by the *Vossische Zeitung* in December 1921. It contained numerous articles focusing on precisely the topics the DBB had suggested: beer's

[49] Tätigkeitsbericht des Deutschen Brauer-Bundes, 1924/5, in Deutscher Brauer-Bund, Tätigkeitsberichte 1921–9, Archiv des Deutschen Brauer-Bundes, Berlin, G 20, 56.

[50] Ibid., 13. [51] Tätigkeitsbericht des Deutschen Brauer-Bundes, 1921/2, 104.

[52] "Kriegsplan des Braukapitals," *Vorwärts*, Mar. 2, 1922. The DBB denied the tactics made public by *Vorwärts*: "Der Kriegsplan des Braukapitals," *Vorwärts*, Mar. 5, 1922. However, the DBB's course of action reveals that it did largely follow these tactics. For the tactics see also: "Bericht über die Sitzung des Großen Ausschusses vom 28.6.1919," BayHStA, Bayerischer Brauerbund 408.

long history and tradition, as well as the modern, industrialized brewing process. Although the paper was in German, it was probably targeted at non-Germans, as it provided "insight" into German culture and resembled a travel guide to Germany. Max Osborn, the *Vossische*'s art critic, for example, wrote a long piece on "the city of art and beer" (*Die Stadt der Kunst und des Bieres*) in which he affectionately portrayed Munich's longstanding affinity for both.[53]

The brewers had to carefully choose the newspapers and editors to whom they offered their articles. If alcohol critics got hold of them, they made the public aware of the DBB's efforts to influence the media. Even before the war, the temperance movement had accused the "alcohol trust" (*Alkoholkapital*) of influencing the media by throwing its financial weight around with threats to withdraw advertisements. This was the temperance movement's explanation of the fact that critical voices had barely been heard in the media before the war. This accusation, combining anti-alcohol and anticapitalist arguments, was invoked again after the war.[54]

Although there is evidence that the brewers' associations did threaten to withdraw advertisements if papers published material in support of the teetotalism movement, it was not their main method of influencing content.[55] Significantly, more effort and money were put into supplying the media with positive reports about alcohol – beer, in particular. Although this was a major part of the DBB's propaganda activity, it was one of the topics deliberately omitted in the annual report.[56] This subtle method of influencing was also discussed in trade publications at that time, but reception was mixed. While some condemned it as "American methods" undermining professional journalism, others regarded it as a legitimate way of managing PR. Both sides agreed, however, that it was very effective.[57] Providing the media with favorable articles not

[53] *Die Voss Berlin. Auslands-Ausgabe*, Dec. 3, 1921.

[54] "Die Pressearbeit des deutschen Alkoholkapitals," *Neuland*, Jan. 10, 1926; Reinhard Strecker, *Der Kampf gegen das Gemeindebestimmungsrecht in Deutschland 1920–1930* (Berlin, 1930); Emil Kraepelin, "Alkohol und Tagespresse," in Deutsche Forschungsanstalt für Psychiatrie, ed., *Die Wirkung der Alkoholknappheit während des ersten Weltkrieges. Erfahrungen und Erwägungen* (Berlin, 1923), 197–209.

[55] "An die Fa. Rudolf Mosse," Aug. 26, 1925, BayHStA, Bayerischer Brauerbund 419.

[56] For discussion and practice of influencing the media, see "Deutsche Brauerbund an Bayerischen Brauerbund, Betrf.: Aufbringung eines Pressefonds," Oct. 19, 1919; "Bericht über die Sitzung des Großen Ausschusses vom 28.6.1919," BayHStA, Bayerischer Brauerbund 1068.

[57] Cf. for a critical view: Emil Dovifat, *Der amerikanische Journalismus*, first published 1928 (Berlin, 1990), 207–12. For a more positive view, see Herbert Wichmann, "Die

clearly marked as advertisements was quite common across many industries. The Weimar government even used the same method for its state-driven "wine propaganda" in the late 1920s.[58]

Usually, freelance writers were approached by the DBB and asked to write such articles and to offer them directly to the newspapers. Authors were paid a small sum by the newspaper, but they received much more from the organization on whose behalf the article was written.[59] The DBB called these writers "staff" (*Mitarbeiter*); they included "economists, physicians, and freelance writers who were disgusted by the teetotalists' demagogic activities."[60]

The temperance movement was furious that media coverage of alcohol had changed by the mid-1920s. The majority of newspapers were now critical of the local option and of stricter alcohol laws, in general, which contradicted their opinion of a few years earlier.[61] Alcohol critics attributed this change solely to the alcohol industry's meddling. In unusual accord, the DBB also claimed the shift as its own success.[62] But the change in attitude was not only a result of the brewers' PR efforts.

The reasons why the press no longer criticized alcohol consumption, as it had done in the early 1920s, were more complex. One reason was that the public perception that society was in crisis diminished after 1923. During the – in social and financial terms – relatively stable years of the mid-1920s, criticism of mass consumption, in general and of alcohol in particular decreased.[63] Alcohol was no longer regarded as a symptom of this disorder except by teetotalists. Most newspapers now argued, as they had done before the war, that it was more important to support the alcohol industries, especially the beer industry, as a vital economic engine and cultural touchstone.[64]

Bearbeitung der Presse," *Zeitschrift für Betriebswirtschaft. Vierteljahresschrift für betriebswirtschaftliche Forschung* 8 (1931–5): 307–11.

58 "Reichsausschuss Weinpropaganda," BArch, R 86/2013; Lange, *Unternehmerische Öffentlichkeitsarbeit in Deutschland*, 50–1.

59 Wichmann, "Die Bearbeitung der Presse."

60 Tätigkeitsbericht des Deutschen Brauer-Bundes, 1928/9, in Deutscher Brauer-Bund, Tätigkeitsberichte 1921–9, Archiv des Deutschen Brauer-Bundes, Berlin, G 20, 102.

61 Cf. media clippings in "Rauschgifte. Abstinenz – Allgemeines," BArch, NS 5-VI/4865; BArch, NS 5-VI/4866; BArch, NS 5-VI/4867.

62 Strecker, *Der Kampf gegen das Gemeindebestimmungsrecht in Deutschland 1920–1930*; "Sitzung der Schankstättenkommission am 16.9.1927," BayHStA, MHIG 6992; Tätigkeitsbericht des Deutschen Brauerbundes 1928/9, 101–3.

63 Torp, *Konsum*.

64 "Die Abstinenzbewegung und ihre Gefahren," *Tägliche Rundschau*, Apr. 4, 1926; "Gegen die Trockenlegung Deutschlands," Apr. 10, 1926, BArch, NS 5-VI/4867.

Another reason for the press's critical stance toward significantly stricter alcohol laws, including the local option, was that Prohibition in the United States was now mainly seen as a nuisance. While the majority of German newspapers had been in favor of Prohibition or had at least argued that positive effects outweighed negative ones in the early years of the experiment, by the mid-1920s most newspapers had concluded it was a failure.[65] As a consequence, support for the local option had also decreased significantly because it was seen as a crucial step toward Prohibition-like legislation. These two factors were more important for shaping the media's overall opinion of alcohol than the DBB's PR efforts. The latter, though, together with other alcohol industry association strategies, successfully popularized the argument that the local option was the first step toward Prohibition, which was key to its eventual abandonment by the public.[66]

Another battleground on which the "fight" for and against alcohol consumption was waged was exhibitions and fairs. They had become important mass media in the nineteenth century, combining economic and entertainment aspects in order to attract a large audience. This strategy worked well not only for world fairs but also for large national fairs. It did spark criticism too, however.[67]

Brewers' associations had taken part in exhibitions and fairs before the war, for instance, in the International Hygiene Exhibition in Dresden in 1911. But they significantly increased their activities in this area after the war. While the DBB or regional brewing associations regularly took part in exhibitions and fairs in the 1920s, their main focus was on the Exhibition for Healthcare, Social Welfare, and Physical Exercise (GeSoLei or Ausstellung für Gesundheitspflege, soziale Fürsorge und Leibesübungen), which took place in Düsseldorf in 1926. The Republic's largest exhibition attracted 7.5 million visitors and was mainly dedicated to health and hygiene issues, as indicated by its title. Public health (*Volksgesundheit*) had become an even more important topic after the war, not least because of Weimar's promise of a social welfare state.

[65] Cf. for example: "Das alkoholfreie Amerika," *Tägliche Rundschau*, Feb. 18, 1922; "Amerika wie es ißt und trinkt," *Vossische Zeitung*, Apr. 13, 1922; "Der Vormarsch der Nassen. 6 Jahre Prohibition," *Vossische Zeitung*, Feb. 28, 1926; "Die Abstinenzbewegung und ihre Gefahren," *Tägliche Rundschau*, Apr. 4, 1926.

[66] "Was ist das Gemeindebestimmungsrecht? Der Auftakt zu Trockenlegung Deutschlands," Staatsarchiv München (StAM), Pol. Dir. München 5424.

[67] Großbölting, "*Im Reich der Arbeit*," 123–68; Alexander C. T. Geppert, *Fleeting Cities: Imperial Expositions in Fin-de-Siècle Europe* (New York, 2010).

The exhibition was designed to showcase Germany's resilience and recovery after the war. For this reason, Düsseldorf, which had been occupied by French troops until the previous year, was chosen as its location.[68]

The DBB decided early on to use the exhibition as a major platform to "show the brewers' importance as producers of Germany's national drink and their importance for the national economy." It rightly identified the exhibition as an important arena to "defend beer against teetotalist attacks."[69] The GeSoLei was a friendly venue for alcohol critics, as they could relate to all three major exhibition topics. The DBB was determined to defeat the teetotalism movement on its home turf and therefore invested a lot of thought and financial resources into its exhibition appearance (Figure 7.2). The brewers' presence at the GeSoLei cost half a million Reichsmark, which, as before, was drawn from the membership surcharge. It amounted to more than 1,000 percent of the regular membership fee.[70] The bulk of the investment went toward creating a large exhibition space advantageously located at the entrance of the venue, so that every visitor had to pass it. The exhibition organizers had run into financial trouble and therefore welcomed the substantial sum the brewers paid to secure this prominent spot.

The anti-alcohol movement's displays, in contrast, were assigned a section in one of the permanent exhibition halls alongside other exhibitors.[71] The brewers' cheeky presence at the health and hygiene exhibition sparked heavy criticism even before it opened to the public.[72] The protest, however, was of no avail, as the organizers of the GeSoLei decided to combine the hygiene exhibition with a trade fair (*Gewerbeschau*) at which industries not directly connected to the exhibition's main themes could also exhibit.[73] The organizers hoped, on the one hand, to attract more visitors by presenting a broad spectrum and, on the

[68] Sebastian Weinert, *Der Körper im Blick: Gesundheitsausstellungen vom späten Kaiserreich bis zum Nationalsozialismus*, (Göttingen, 2017); Hans Körner and Gabriele Genge, eds., *Kunst, Sport und Körper: 1926–2002, GeSoLei* (Ostfildern-Ruit, 2002).

[69] "Deutscher Brauer-Bund auf der Gesolei," BayHStA, Bayerischer Brauerbund 447, 8.

[70] Tätigkeitsbericht des Deutschen Brauer-Bundes, 1924/5, 13–14.

[71] *Große Ausstellung für Gesundheitspflege, soziale Fürsorge und Leibesübungen. Amtlicher Katalog* (Düsseldorf, 1926), 55.

[72] "Gegen den Alkohol," *Vossische Zeitung*, Feb. 3, 1926; "Momentbilder der Düsseldorfer Ausstellung," *Vossische Zeitung*, July 24, 1926; Weinert, *Der Körper im Blick*, 136–8.

[73] Weinert, *Der Körper im Blick*, 136–8; Großbölting, *"Im Reich der Arbeit"*; Tätigkeitsbericht des Deutschen Brauer-Bundes, 1925/6, in Deutscher Brauer-Bund, Tätigkeitsberichte 1921–9, Archiv des Deutschen Brauer-Bundes, Berlin, G 20, 69.

FIGURE 7.2 The brewers' exhibition area at GeSoLei-Düsseldorf in 1926 comfortably surpassed the teetotalists' area in size. From "Der Deutsche Brauer-Bund auf der GeSoLei-Düsseldorf," s.l. 1926, p. 9. Source: Kunstbibliothek, Berlin.

other, to profitably offer exhibition space to industries wanting to take part.[74] The Brewers' Hall was the most elaborate of the temporary display spaces and won the exhibition's first prize. The DBB's presence at the GeSoLei also demonstrated the brewing industry's significantly larger financial power compared to that of the temperance organizations.

While the hall stood as a symbol of the brewers' power and importance in German society, the display inside was designed along the same lines. The exhibition's leitmotif argued that beer was an important factor in Germany's economic, social, and even physical well-being.[75] The materials presented referred directly or indirectly to arguments by alcohol critics and countered them with pro-beer text and images. This created a paradoxical situation for visitors. In one segment of the exhibition they were informed of the dangers of alcohol consumption, but they learned the exact opposite in the Brewers' Hall. This absurdity was magnified by the fact that the brewers had copied the temperance

[74] Weinert, *Der Körper im Blick*, 63–4.
[75] "Deutscher Brauer-Bund auf der Gesolei," BayHStA, Bayerischer Brauerbund 447.

movement's strategy of focusing on "scientific" proof. Both sides displayed statistics and graphs and quoted scientific "truth."[76]

The exhibition also stressed the "positive" and pleasurable aspects of beer consumption. In addition to arguments about beer's nutritional value, the DBB now also stressed its social value, citing Johann Wolfgang von Goethe's drinking poem "Ergo Bibamus" and pointing out the relaxing effects of beer when consumed after a day's work (Figure 7.3), as millions of Germans, including past luminaries such as Otto von Bismarck, already knew.[77]

This image is an example of the brewers' indirect fight against the anti-alcohol movement. Although teetotalism was not explicitly named as a threat, the poster suggested a danger that a well-deserved after-work beer might be taken away from hard-working men. It called upon workers to stand up for their custom of having a "Feierabendbier." The poster also propagated "responsible drinking" as it made clear workers should only drink *after* work.

The DBB reused but also repackaged long-established images. Beer had been marketed as a traditional drink since the nineteenth century. Print advertisements before 1900 often depicted preindustrial brewing methods and the monks who provided area residents with beer. The tomfoolery that often accompanied drinking to excess in the premodern era was also a favorite topic of nineteenth-century beer advertisements.[78] By the interwar period, however, drunkenness no longer featured in the industry's promotional efforts. Instead, the brewing industry argued for moderate drinking. But the definition of what exactly "moderate" consumption entailed differed greatly between the brewers and the temperance movement.[79]

[76] "Gesolei. Ein kritisches Nachwort zu der Ausstellung in Düsseldorf," *Vorwärts*, Oct. 17, 1926; compare, for example: "Alkoholismus und die deutsche Volkswirtschaft," Deutsches Hygiene Museum Dresden (DHMD), 2014/318.13; "Die Bedeutung der Brauindustrie als Steuerquelle für das Reich," in "Deutscher Brauer-Bund auf der Gesolei," BayHStA, Bayerischer Brauerbund 447, 30.

[77] "Deutscher Brauer-Bund auf der Gesolei," BayHStA, Bayerischer Brauerbund 447, 36–7.

[78] Heinrich Tappe, "Der Genuss, die Wirkung und ihr Bild: Werte Konventionen und Motive gesellschaftlichen Alkoholgebrauchs im Spiegel der Werbung," in Jürgen Teuteberg, Peter Borscheid and Clemens Wischermann, eds., *Bilderwelt des Alltags: Werbung in der Konsumgesellschaft des 19. und 20. Jahrhunderts* (Stuttgart, 1995), 228–9.

[79] See, for example, "Durchschnit. Verwendung von je 100 Mark Monatseinkommen," DHMD, 2014/318.12; "Biergenuß und Mäßigkeit," in "Deutscher Brauer-Bund auf der Gesolei," BayHStA, Bayerischer Brauerbund 447, 31.

FIGURE 7.3 Pro-beer poster for the Deutsche Brauer-Bund at GeSoLei-Düsseldorf. The exhibition called upon male workers to protect their after-work beer. From "Der Deutsche Brauer-Bund auf der GeSoLei-Düsseldorf," s.l. 1926, p. 65. Source: Kunstbibliothek, Berlin.

The DBB's propaganda department was very satisfied with its performance at the GeSoLei. One has to keep in mind, however, that the DBB also had to legitimize the large financial contributions by its members, so it naturally stressed its own success. Nevertheless, it also cited reports from alcohol critics complaining that the "brewery palace" had attracted considerably more visitors and attention than the temperance movement's exhibition.[80] The official exhibition catalogue supported the brewers' cause by describing their exhibit as very informative and objective. It even encouraged visitors to "pay as much attention to the brewers' exhibition as to the exhibition on alcohol abuse." It also dispatched criticism of their presence at the GeSoLei as the work of "fanatics." In both ways, then, the organizers of the health and hygiene exhibition defended their decision to include the pro-beer installation, demonstrating that the controversy over the brewers' presence at the GeSoLei remained evident.[81] In the end, the DBB claimed that it was satisfied with its participation: the organization had reached an enormous number of visitors and had presented its case in a sophisticated manner. Although they still felt the industry faced a tough opponent, the tide appeared to be turning.

Shifting attitudes were also visible in parliamentary debates in the mid- and late 1920s. Stricter alcohol laws and the local option were debated several times in the Reichstag. The debates became less morally charged over the years. Attitudes toward alcohol consumption could therefore be expressed more freely, and positive references to alcohol became acceptable again during the stable period following the revaluation of the currency.

In 1930, Emil Köster from the Wirtschaftspartei (Economy Party) made a speech in the parliament arguing against the "pub law" (*Schankstättengesetz*). Köster himself owned a pub (*Gastwirtschaft*) and was chairman of the German Publicans Association (Deutscher Gastwirts-Verband). His speech was witty, funny, and enriched with puns on drinking and drunkenness. Members of all parties reacted with cheers, laughter, and applause. Köster was even asked to continue speaking at the end of his lengthy monologue.[82]

A performance like this certainly would not have been possible during the early or mid-1920s. The DBB also cooperated closely with members of the parliament and provided them with background information. Speeches in the parliament were often based on the newest scientific research. The teetotalism movement and the DBB competed in providing their supporters with materials. The DBB had its own statistical

[80] Tätigkeitsbericht des Deutschen Brauer-Bundes, 1925/6, 61.

[81] *Große Ausstellung für Gesundheitspflege, soziale Fürsorge und Leibesübungen. Amtlicher Katalog*, 56–7.

[82] 151st session, Mar. 28, 1930, in *Verhandlungen des Deutschen Reichstags, vol.* 427 (Berlin 1930), pp. 4711–18.

department that was, among other things, responsible for providing this research.[83]

The DBB recognized this overall change in the climate with relief and satisfaction. The propaganda department's financial resources were reduced after the local option was rejected for the second time in the Reichstag in 1926. However, the importance of PR had been proven over the past several years; its value was acknowledged and plans for it to remain active in these ways were made. Even though the immediate danger of significantly stricter alcohol regulation was over, beer consumption remained below its prewar level.

The DBB consequently expanded its advertising portfolio in the coming years. Cooperative advertising (*Gemeinschaftswerbung*) was especially suited to the brewing industry because beer, as a widely accessible daily-use consumer product, served less as a marker of distinction than other consumer goods. Individual brewers also all aimed at the same target group and could therefore easily work together. Furthermore, through the DBB the brewing industry already had a professionalized propaganda machine in place that had been a pioneer of cooperative advertising before it became a common strategy in the mid-1920s.[84] Smaller breweries in particular benefited from it, as they usually did not have the necessary resources for large advertising campaigns.

The association focused especially on films. It produced *Vom Halm zum Glas* (*From the Stalk to the Glass*) in 1928, depicting the beer production process in a fifteen-minute silent film. It coupled the industrial nature of the process (close-up shots of large machinery) with clips of the rural and premodern stages such as the hop harvest. The film became quite popular and was still being shown in cinemas in the 1930s.[85] In addition, the DBB also produced funny animated films aimed at "ridiculing the teetotalists' exaggerated demands."[86]

The DBB decided in the early 1930s that it was time to create a sound film for the big screen. The aim was to produce a film that would be

[83] Tätigkeitsbericht des Deutschen Brauer-Bundes, 1929/30, in Deutscher Brauer-Bund, Tätigkeitsberichte des Deutschen Brauer-Bundes 1929–34, Archiv des Deutschen Brauer-Bundes, Berlin, G 20.

[84] For a definition of *Gemeinschaftswerbung*, see Schindelbeck, "Werbung für alle." On cooperative advertising in Nazi Germany, see also Swett, *Selling under the Swastika*, 82–5.

[85] "Vom Halm zum Glas," www.youtube.com/watch?v=usB1M5gE3UU (accessed Jan. 2018); Filmwerbung, BayHStA, Bayerischer Brauerbund 426.

[86] Tätigkeitsbericht des Deutschen Brauer-Bundes, 1928/9, 107. "Filmwerbung," BayHStA, Bayerischer Brauerbund 426. Unfortunately, none of these films seems to have survived.

entertaining and informative rather than a purely educational movie such as *Vom Halm zum Glas*. Convincing filmgoers was considered especially important because the rise of cinema culture in the 1920s was perceived as a main reason for the decline in beer consumption. Many people went to the movies instead of going to the pub after work.[87]

The DBB therefore decided to represent itself in cinemas through the movie *Hell oder Dunkel* (*Light or Dark*), which had a running time of twelve minutes. The DBB commissioned the Ufa production company. Ufa also guaranteed five thousand showings within the first year. The film was directed by Willy Prager and starred well-known actor Hans-Adalbert von Schlettow.[88] Von Schlettow's character traveled around the country and encountered various people including a physician, an athlete, a young woman, and a teetotalist. The dialogue between them served to communicate beer's positive "qualities" for the human body and soul. Once again the DBB spared no expense for this prestigious project, commissioning Germany's biggest and best-known production company and a well-known cast.[89]

7.3 CONCLUSION

Although the DBB's PR strategies got off to a rocky start, they were rapidly expanded and professionalized. By the late 1920s, PR was firmly established within the DBB and constituted an important part of its activities. Indeed, the DBB was a pioneer, establishing its propaganda department right after the war.

Its strategies corresponded to PR techniques discussed in trade publications. Long-established methods such as participation in exhibitions were combined with more recent innovations, such as cooperative

[87] Heinrich Tappe, "Alkoholverbrauch in Deutschland im 19. und 20. Jahrhundert. Entwicklung und Determinanten des Trinkverhaltens," in Hans J. Teuteberg, ed., *Die Revolution am Esstisch: Neue Studien zur Nahrungskultur im 19.–20. Jahrhundert* (Stuttgart, 2004), 291.

[88] Cf. for Prager, who was sacked by the Nazis: Kay Weniger, *Zwischen Bühne und Baracke: Lexikon der verfolgten Theater-, Film- und Musikkünstler 1933–1945* (Berlin, 2008), 281; cf. on von Schlettow, who was a Nazi supporter and starred in many films in the 1930s and 1940s: Ernst Klee, *Das Kulturlexikon zum Dritten Reich: Wer war was vor und nach 1945* (Frankfurt, 2007), 626.

[89] "Propaganda-Abteilung. Tätigkeitsbericht 1931/1932," in Deutscher Brauer-Bund, Tätigkeitsberichte des Deutschen Brauer-Bundes 1929–34, Archiv des Deutschen Brauer-Bundes, Berlin, G 20, 13–15; www.murnau-stiftung.de/movie/12129 (accessed Aug. 10, 2018).

advertising, film, and subtle opinion pieces in the press. The importance PR gained within the DBB can also be measured by the immense financial resources derived from surcharges made available for PR. However, many of the "propaganda activities" were deliberately kept under wraps in the annual report.[90]

In 1929, the propaganda department celebrated its tenth anniversary. It argued that it had made use of "all possible means of propaganda" throughout the decade. It was convinced that the propaganda department's work would always be needed going forward – and it was right in its long-term forecast.[91]

Public relations constituted a particular culture of capitalism, being a simultaneous reaction to anti-consumerist and anticapitalist discourses. Thus, this criticism initiated new forms of capitalist behavior. Before the war the DBB had not felt the need to put much thought or many resources into PR because criticism of alcohol, especially of beer, had been minimal. After the war, however, the brewing industry had to legitimize its very existence in the public discourse. What was initially regarded as a temporary and flexible reaction to the anti-alcohol discourse developed into an important long-term capitalist tool. The Weimar years, therefore, were not just a period of criticism and contempt of capitalism but also a time of innovation and a testing ground for new forms of capitalism, in particular, because many of its established aspects came under threat in the 1920s and early 1930s.

The brewing industry had to adapt to these changed circumstances. Influence-peddling, lobbying behind closed doors, and stressing the brewing industry's economic significance were no longer enough because public opinion had become hostile – at least for a short period of time – toward beer production and consumption. This made the industry something of a special case at that time, especially as public opinion toward beer "normalized" again over the course of the 1920s.

Several industries, however, faced the brewing industry's problems over the course of the twentieth century. The brewers' case therefore helps explain the dynamics that turned a widely accepted product into a condemned one.[92] Furthermore, it sheds light on the strategies these

[90] Tätigkeitsbericht des Deutschen Brauer-Bundes, 1924/5, 13–14.

[91] Ibid., 1928/9, 101–8.

[92] Nicole Petrick-Felber, *Kriegswichtiger Genuss: Tabak und Kaffee im "Dritten Reich"* (Göttingen, 2015); Eckart Conze, Martin Klimke, Jeremy Varon, eds., *Nuclear Threats, Nuclear Fear, and the Cold War of the 1980s* (New York, 2017).

industries used to deal with hostile public opinion, such as financing "scientific" research.[93] An analytical perspective on these businesses and industries can broaden our understanding of capitalist strategies in particular with regard to how industries adapt to economically, socially, or environmentally changed circumstances.

[93] Naomi Oreskes and Erik M. Conway, *Merchants of Doubt: How a Handful of Scientists Obscured the Truth on Issues from Tobacco Smoke to Global Warming* (New York, 2010); see also, despite its subjectivity: Robert N. Proctor, *Golden Holocaust: Origins of the Cigarette Catastrophe and the Case for Abolition* (Berkeley, CA, 2011).

8

Managing Consumer Capitalism

Artists, Engineers, and Psychologists as New Marketing Experts in Interwar Germany

Jan Logemann

Was interwar capitalism a creative chaos in need of order or a powerful machine requiring constant maintenance? Was the economy a growing organism that needed to be sustained, and did it have a soul that could be searched for? One way of approaching cultures of capitalism in Weimar and Nazi Germany is to ask about the concepts by means of which contemporaries tried to make sense of socioeconomic transformations, including their use of analogies such as engines and organisms for economic processes. Correspondingly, the forms of expertise – from economic expertise to engineering and psychological knowledge – deemed necessary to manage capitalist markets can also be revealing.

Contemporary debates on interwar capitalism, as other chapters in this volume demonstrate, engaged with the social inequalities inherent in capitalist economies as much as with its cultural implications for gender relations or national identity. One aspect of recurring concern for interwar commentators was the seemingly erratic and unpredictable character of markets in capitalist economies. Periods of extreme inflation, stock market swings, and speculative bubbles worried experts and laymen alike. It is therefore no surprise that the period saw an intensification of business cycle research among economists and that two of the most enduring interpretations of capitalism to come out of the interwar years emphasized the transformative power of markets in capitalist economies. Károly Polányi's *Origins of Our Time: The Great Transformation* locates "the origins of our time" in the socially destructive power of increasingly disembedded markets. Somewhat more upbeat, fellow émigré Joseph

Schumpeter posited the "creative destruction" brought about by market forces as the central dynamic of interwar capitalism.[1]

Whether the power of markets was to be managed and restrained or harnessed for future development, navigating capitalism increasingly appeared to require new experts during the 1920s and 1930s. This chapter focuses specifically on perceptions of expanding consumer markets in interwar Germany, looking at the diagnoses offered by different groups of professional experts engaged in shaping consumer practices and the world of goods. The rise of marketing experts in this era suggests contemporaries came to recognize consumers (particularly women consumers) as significant actors in shaping the dynamics of capitalist economies. While the degree to which Weimar Germany can be regarded as a "consumer society" remains contested, commercialized market-based consumption practices were increasingly at the forefront of contemporary discussions of capitalism and its cultural implications. Consumers, contemporaries noted, contributed to the volatile character of markets, and new experts sought to exploit this insight not only by appealing to their desires and emotions but also by attempting to make consumer behavior more calculable.

Debates about the department store during the first half of the twentieth century are a case in point.[2] Department stores signified broad transformations of market structures such as an increase in both sales volume and market concentration as well as their perceived social consequences, including conflicts over access to goods and increased retail competition. One aspect of the contemporary debate is particularly revealing for our discussion of interwar cultures of capitalism: department stores appeared to embody both the rational efficiency of modern markets and their fundamentally irrational characteristics. On one hand, department stores with their sumptuous, carefully arranged displays of merchandise underscored the sensual and emotional appeal of interwar consumer capitalism to contemporary observers. Much like advertisements and an expanding commercial entertainment culture, they represented the appealing

[1] Károly Polányi, *Origins of Our Time: The Great Transformation* (London, 1945), and Joseph Schumpeter, "The Creative Response in Economic History," *Journal of Economic History* 7 (1947): 149–59.

[2] See most recently Paul Lerner, *The Consuming Temple: Jews, Department Stores, and the Consumer Revolution in Germany, 1880–1940* (Ithaca, NY, 2016). On the contentious debate about department stores during this period see also Detlef Briesen, *Warenhaus, Massenkonsum und Sozialmoral: Zur Geschichte der Konsumkritik im 20. Jahrhundert* (Frankfurt, 2001).

surfaces and the barely veiled sexuality of Weimar-era consumption. Contemporaries frequently commented on these new aesthetic and emotional aspects of consumer markets as manifest in department store design.

Highlighting rationalization in distribution, by contrast, observers also marveled at large stores as expressions of modern, efficient mass distribution. Department stores were discussed as new "machines for selling." They neatly represented the very specialized or departmentalized nature of "modern" economies, and accounts of department store planning, work, or management emphasized the introduction of Taylorist elements to the realm of distribution. Such rational and functional aspects were no longer restricted to the realm of industrial production; instead, over the course of the 1920s, they came to be regarded as increasingly integral to forms of household consumption and to consumer marketing. Department stores were thus also part of an effort to make consumer markets more rational and predictable.

Experts in various marketing-related professions, from sales and advertising to market research and commercial design, consciously engaged these apparent contradictions of increasingly rationalized yet volatile and emotional interwar consumer markets. In this chapter, I explore the professional and intellectual debates about consumer capitalism during the 1920s and early 1930s. In particular, I ask about professional perceptions of interwar consumer capitalism among German marketing experts and market researchers as well as among product designers and graphic artists. In trade journals and professional publications of the era, we not only find contradictory analyses of the nature of consumer markets. Opinions also diverged over what type of expert was best suited to shaping consumer capitalism and whether engineers, artists, or psychologists ultimately held the key to understanding consumer markets. Whereas interwar artists and designers frequently stressed the importance of functionality and standardization, many market researchers emphasized the emotional and irrational dimensions of consumer capitalism. They all shared, however, a common emphasis on the newfound importance of consumption and of consumers as economic actors in Weimar-era capitalism.

8.1 WEIMAR CONSUMER CAPITALISM AND THE PARADOX OF INNOVATION

Rereading the classic historiographical debates about "organized capitalism" in interwar Germany, one finds that social historians during the

1970s paid scant attention to issues of consumption. Their focus was squarely on the role of finance and industry cartels, on the organization of labor markets, and on the production side of the economy.[3] The organization of consumer markets, by contrast, rarely came into view, despite the tremendous growth of retailing organizations, for example, or the various effects that producer organizations had on consumers.

Today, we know a great deal more about the importance of consumer markets during the interwar years.[4] The shortages of World War I had politicized questions of consumption and had raised expectations of the state regarding the organization of markets and the provision of consumer goods.[5] Marred by economic crises, consumer politics took center stage during the Weimar Republic, as Claudius Torp has shown.[6] Basic subsistence needs and the public management of housing, food, and energy markets were of primary importance in this still less than affluent society. Discretionary forms of consumption remained embedded in moral economies, and paternalist regulation restricted consumer choice when it came, for example, to alcoholic beverages or consumer credit. The "consumer as citizen" did not yet play a dominant or even prominent role in Weimar politics, which continued to privilege the interests of producers, retailers, and workers.[7] Still, the interwar era was marked by growing expectations of future consumer affluence with new forms of commercial entertainment and mass-produced consumer goods. Inexpensive household items such as beauty products became increasingly widespread, even if the accessibility of more expensive durable goods lagged behind levels in other Western European economies or the United States. Novel consumer goods from vacuum cleaners to automobiles remained out of reach for the vast majority of Germans, but they became something to aspire to and part of the consumer imagination. This consumerist promise, as Hartmut Berghoff and

[3] Heinrich August Winkler, ed., *Organisierter Kapitalismus: Voraussetzungen und Anfänge* (Göttingen, 1974).

[4] On the rise of consumer markets since the late nineteenth century see, for example, Heinz-Gerhard Haupt, *Konsum und Handel: Europa im 19. und 20. Jahrhundert* (Göttingen, 2003) and Uwe Spiekermann, *Basis der Konsumgesellschaft: Entstehung und Entwicklung des modernen Kleinhandels in Deutschland 1850–1914* (Munich, 1999).

[5] See Belinda Davis, *Home Fires Burning: Food, Politics, and Everyday Life in World War I Berlin* (Chapel Hill, NC, 2000).

[6] Claudius Torp, *Konsum und Politik in der Weimarer Republik* (Göttingen, 2011).

[7] See, for example, Hartmut Berghoff, Ingo Köhler, and Harald Wixforth, "Navigation im Meer der Interessen," in Carl Ludwig Holtfrerich, ed., *Das Reichswirtschaftsministerium der Weimarer Republik und seine Vorläufer: Strukturen, Akteure, Handlungsfelder* (Berlin, 2016), 421–516.

others have argued, was later extensively employed by the National Socialist regime.[8] Both the Weimar years and the Nazi era, historians of consumption suggest, were characterized by significant discrepancies between everyday experiences of deprivation on one hand and omnipresent expectations of consumerist lifestyles on the other.

Despite prevailing experiences of scarcity, however, the metropolitan centers of Weimar Germany, in particular, saw a dramatic expansion of commercial practices aimed at individual consumers that transformed everyday life. Historian Janet Ward has described an emerging consumer culture characterized by seductive "surfaces" – the aesthetic appeals of an "electric [and electrifying] modernity."[9] New forms of advertising permeated newspapers, journals, and urban spaces, touting product innovations, stimulating experiences, and increasingly rapid cycles of changes in fashion.[10] Theaters and cinemas presented what many contemporaries perceived as an indulgent entertainment culture, which reflected changing social norms and redefined gender roles especially among young, metropolitan consumers.[11] The "New Woman" emerged as a cultural symbol of a growing number of more emancipated female consumers with their own money to spend and catered to by magazines and advertisers. Carefully prepared by professional window dressers, the display windows of Weimar-era department stores presented aestheticized dreamscapes of goods. Much like the movies of the era, these were read by contemporaries as expressions of sensual and feminized consumer markets driven by emotions and desires, and they raised questions about the morality of such

[8] Hartmut Berghoff, "Enticement and Deprivation: The Regulation of Consumption in Pre-war Nazi Germany," in Martin Daunton and Matthew Hilton, eds., *The Politics of Consumption: Material Culture and Citizenship in Europe and America* (Oxford, 2001), 165–84. See also Wolfgang König, *Volkswagen, Volksempfänger, Volksgemeinschaft: "Volksprodukte" im Dritten Reich. Vom Scheitern einer nationalsozialistischen Konsumgesellschaft* (Paderborn, 2004) and the recent survey by Tim Schanetzky, *"Kanonen statt Butter": Wirtschaft und Konsum im Dritten Reich* (Munich, 2015).

[9] Janet Ward, *Weimar Surfaces: Urban Visual Culture in 1920s Germany* (Berkeley, CA, 2001).

[10] Peter Borscheid, *Das Tempo-Virus: Eine Kulturgeschichte der Beschleunigung* (Frankfurt, 2004), esp. 320–6. On advertising see Alexander Schug, "Werbung und die Kultur des Kapitalismus," in Heinz-Gerhard Haupt and Cornelius Torp, eds., *Die Konsumgesellschaft in Deutschland, 1890–1990: Ein Handbuch* (Frankfurt, 2009), 355–69.

[11] See, for example, Detlev Peukert, "Das Mädchen mit dem 'wahrlich metaphysikfreien Bubikopf.' Jugend und Freizeit im Berlin der zwanziger Jahre," in Peter Alter, ed., *Im Banne der Metropolen: Berlin und London in den zwanziger Jahren* (Göttingen, 1993), 157–75.

spending (Figure 8.1). Indeed, efforts to stimulate and modify (especially female) consumer needs and desires (*Kauflust*) have recently been the focus of emotional histories of early consumer capitalism in Germany.[12]

FIGURE 8.1 This 1921 cover of the advertising magazine *Das Plakat* alludes to contemporary notions of "irrational" (consumer) markets and perhaps morally questionable consumption in the turbulent years following World War I. *Das Plakat* 12.1 (1921), cover design by Walter Schnackenberg, printed by Kunstanstalt Oscar Consée. © 2021 Artists Rights Society (ARS), New York / VG Bild Kunst, Bonn.

[12] Anne Schmidt, "From Thrifty Housewives to Shoppers with Needs: On a Capitalist Program of Education," in Schmidt and Christoph Conrad, eds., *Bodies and Affects in Market Societies* (Tübingen, 2016), 167–87.

A very different image emerges, by contrast, when we focus on the organizational rigors and the functional forms that dominate interwar consumerism and on "rationalized" mass production as a defining characteristic. Weberian notions of the bureaucratization of capitalism were already a prominent element of "organized capitalism," but, in his classic interpretation of this historiographical concept published in 1974, Jürgen Kocka hinted only in passing at discourses of scientization and their glorification of efficiency.[13] Subsequent studies have since identified a spirit of technocratic "social engineering" as a pervasive force in mid-twentieth-century "high modernity," which left a mark on debates about consumer capitalism as well.[14] Efforts to systematically engineer a more efficient production, distribution, and consumption of goods were motivated both by commercial profit motives and by reform efforts to improve standards of living across society. The Fordist model of standardized mass production was widely debated among Weimar-era students of consumer markets. To its proponents, the "American" model promised heightened efficiency in production and in consumption alike as Taylorist principles could be applied to both the factory and the household.[15] Indeed, observers began to see consumer households as an integral part of the national economy, which needed to become more predictable and efficient.[16]

Efforts to subject the household and consumers to the principles of modern engineering abounded during the interwar years. The introduction of norms and product types, Anne Sudrow has shown, spoke to a widespread effort to standardize consumer goods in an era bookended by two war economies.[17] The organization of distribution too witnessed a great degree of rationalization with new retailing formats, the advent of

[13] Jürgen Kocka, "Organisierter Kapitalismus oder Staatsmonopolistischer Kapitalismus?" in Winkler, *Organisierter Kapitalismus*, 19–35, here 23.

[14] On social engineering and the era of high modernity see Thomas Etzemüller, ed., *Die Ordnung der Moderne: Social Engineering im 20. Jahrhundert* (Bielefeld, 2009), and Lutz Raphael, "Ordnungsmuster der 'Hochmoderne'? Die Theorie der Moderne und die Geschichte der europäischen Gesellschaften im 20. Jahrhundert," in Lutz Raphael and Ute Schneider, eds., *Dimensionen der Moderne: Festschrift für Christoph Dipper* (Frankfurt, 2008), 73–92.

[15] See especially Mary Nolan, *Visions of Modernity: American Business and the Modernization of Germany* (Oxford, 1994).

[16] The home economy had taken on a particularly central role since World War I. See Nancy Reagin, *Sweeping the German Nation: Domesticity and National Identity in Germany, 1870–1945* (Cambridge, 2007), esp. chapter 3.

[17] Anne Sudrow, "Der Typus als Ideal der Formgebung: Zur Entstehung der professionellen Produktgestaltung von industriellen Konsumgütern (1914–1933)," *Technikgeschichte* 76 (2009): 191–210.

systematic market research, and the rise of advertising as a profession.[18] Recently the proliferation of various economic experts and professionals has become a central focus of a history of knowledge of modern capitalism. From this perspective, interwar consumer capitalism was defined by a spirit of systematic professionalism and increased functional efficiency.

This drive for functional efficiency stood at odds with dynamics impelled by desires and changing fashions.[19] The ensuing tension, I argue, represents a core characteristic of the interwar culture of consumer capitalism, and it relates to what sociologist Andreas Reckwitz has described as the "paradox of innovation" in late capitalism.[20] On one hand, Reckwitz argues, this stage of capitalist development was characterized by a Weberian emphasis on formal rules and predictable standards. The importance of bureaucratic and technical rationality was most clearly exemplified by the rise of scientific management as an ideal and by the model of the large, Fordist corporation that succeeded through standardized production and employing economies of scale. On the other hand, Reckwitz continues, we find a countervailing, Schumpeterian impulse that emphasized the "creative destruction" inherent in modern capitalism. While companies became more predictable with regard to their internal processes, external markets became more unpredictable. New technologies, dynamic markets, and a logic of continuous capital accumulation forced companies into constant change and innovation, according to Reckwitz. This led not only to the establishment of R&D units for technological innovation, but also to design units specialized in aesthetic innovation combined with an increased use of market research.

Conflicting needs for standardization and predictability on one hand and for continuous change and novelty on the other, Reckwitz argues, gave rise to organizational attempts to make innovation permanent and paved the way for an aesthetization of economic processes. It also opened the door for new groups of experts and professionals. The advertising and fashion industries as well as the design field served as pioneering sectors of a new, creative economy emerging in the interwar years. New, overwhelmingly male consumer experts in these fields engaged in an elite discourse during the 1920s and early 1930s, which directly addressed

[18] See Spiekermann, *Basis*, and Gerulf Hirt, *Verkannte Propheten? Zur "Expertenkultur" (west-)deutscher Werbekommunikatoren bis zur Rezession 1966/67* (Leipzig, 2013).

[19] See also Sudrow, "Der Typus als Ideal der Formgebung," 195–7.

[20] *Late capitalism* is the term used by Reckwitz. Andreas Reckwitz, *Die Erfindung der Kreativität: Zum Prozess gesellschaftlicher Ästhetisierung* (Berlin, 2012), esp. 133–45.

the very paradox Reckwitz identifies. In their analysis of consumer capitalism and in their attempts to manage the markets, some experts fashioned themselves as engineers while others looked at art and psychology to understand the dynamics of new consumer markets.

8.2 THE ARTIST AS ENGINEER: THE AESTHETICS OF FUNCTIONALISM IN CONSUMER CAPITALISM

Aesthetics played a profound role in 1920s debates on consumer capitalism. Trade journals of the advertising industry such as *Die Reklame* not only discussed new trends in graphic and industrial design; they were also full of ads themselves promoting the services of designers, printers, color specialists, and other professionals with backgrounds ranging from more traditional crafts to modern art. Periodicals committed to covering design and the applied arts similarly paid a great deal of attention to new forms of commercial application in advertising and industrial production. Many commercial artists, however, stressed the importance of a rational and functionalist aesthetic in their work.

Advertising experts were frequently enthusiastic about the potential role of "the artist" within the economy. Artistic creation for commercial and advertising purposes (*Anbietarbeit*) was thought to pose special challenges because purely aesthetic considerations were restricted by the client and the product as well as by the specific sales function and intended audience reception of the artwork. Yet, the financial resources along with the quality materials and new technologies available to commercial artists also opened up new creative possibilities; to some they even promised an "ecstasy of artistic realization" (*Rausch der Verwirklichung*).[21] Art schools in Düsseldorf and elsewhere had begun to integrate advertising into their curricula after World War I, combining graphic design with practical insights from advertising professionals.[22] At the same time modernist artists saw an opportunity to tie their artistic agenda to recent technological developments. Artists, Bauhaus teacher Georg Muche warned in 1926, had to contend with a technological age that seemed to "only need engineers." While art and technology would never quite follow the same logic, he observed, the imperatives of technical and

[21] Werbwart (Johannes) Weidenmüller, "gestaltende anbiet-arbeit," *Bauhaus* 2(1) (1928): 1. On the call for more artistic advertising see also Josef Wilden (Handelskammer Düsseldorf), "Reklame und Wirtschaft," *Die Reklame* 19 (1926): 457.

[22] Rudolf Albrecht, "Kunstakademie und Reklame," *Die Reklame* 19 (1926): 458.

organizational functionality and of economic profitability were producing a new aesthetic sensibility: "the genius of the inventor and the spirit of commercial competition are becoming creative factors" in contemporary industry.[23] In short, many artists were eager to produce new commercial designs for the "machine age."

Debating the relationship between art and industry was not an entirely new development of the interwar years. The efforts of the Werkbund, an association of German artists, craftspeople, architects, and industrialists founded in 1907, to connect art and industry, like the industrial design work of Peter Behrens, provide important earlier examples.[24] Now, however, the urgency of artistic production for a "machine age" came ever more prominently to the fore, spurred on in part by the experience of the war effort.[25] When the Werkbund newsletter was relaunched as *Die Form* in 1925, Walter Curt Behrend's editorial essay emphasized the need to find new forms and artistic expressions for a world of production transformed by new industrial processes, machines, and materials. Design had become a problem of construction, which required collaboration between the entrepreneur, the engineer, and the artist.[26] Functional forms, architect Hugo Häring added, could fulfill aesthetic and creative needs and serve to achieve a "planned economy of our intellectual life."[27] Elaborate craft production was not entirely a thing of the past, as metal artist Georg Mendelssohn observed, because, for example, "a lavishly decorated scarf [was] clearly a piece of capital" in which artistic labor was preserved and could be used for conspicuous consumption. In industry, however, the ornamental forms were deemed obsolete as machines and affordable mass production demanded efficiency and "smooth surfaces."[28]

Modern capitalism required commercial artists to adopt the mindset of the engineer – this was a recurring theme among 1920s design professionals. Graphic designer Jan Tschichold introduced his widely received

[23] Georg Muche, "Bildende Kunst und Industrieform," *Bauhaus* 1(1) (1926): 5–6.

[24] On the Werkbund see Frederick Schwartz, *The Werkbund: Design Theory and Mass Culture before the First World War* (New Haven, CT, 1996). On Behrens's work see especially Tilmann Buddensieg, *Industriekultur: Peter Behrens and the AEG, 1907–1914* (London, 1984).

[25] On advertising art during the war see, for example, Gudrun König and Anne Schmidt, "Moderne Ambivalenzen: Konsumkultur und Propaganda im Ersten Weltkrieg," in Thomas Schleper, ed., *Aggression und Avantgarde: Zum Vorabend des Ersten Weltkrieges* (Essen, 2014), 250–62.

[26] Walther Curt Behrendt, "Geleitwort," *Die Form* 1(1) (1925): 1–2.

[27] Hugo Häring (Berlin), "Wege zur Form," *Die Form* 1(1) (1925): 3–5.

[28] Georg Mendelsohn, "Industrie und Ornament," *Die Form* 1(2) (1925): 1–2.

handbook *The New Typography* (1928) by stating: "the engineer shapes our age." Dispensing with out-of-date artistic traditions, which only led to "complete cultural chaos" at a time of rapid technological innovation, new mass-produced goods from typewriters to light bulbs and marvels of engineering from airfields to department stores defined a new, functional aesthetics.[29] Artists in various fields strove to abide by the engineering paradigm. Graphic artists and printing professionals worked to develop standardized universal typefaces with a clean, modern look in order to economize printing and to organize layout by clear and calculable standards.[30] Especially in advertising and industrial design, graphic designer Max Buchartz noted, aesthetic design required the use of the latest "economically progressive techniques and organizational methods," such as standardized norms, biotechnical and psychological research, and Wilhelm Ostwald's color nomenclature. Advertising art, Buchartz believed, had to be "engineered like a motor."[31] Others saw advertising graphics as analogous to turbines – in other words, responsible for the transformation of economic energy from production to consumption ("Propaganda-mechane"), a "techno-scientific" process based on the laws of optics and mechanics. The brand design and form of the product not only had to be economical; they had to be optimized through the insights of modern science and engineering.[32]

Few modern artists were as focused on the importance of functional form and design for mass production as the protagonists of the Bauhaus school.[33] After 1926 their monthly periodical *Bauhaus: Zeitschrift für Gestaltung* (*Bauhaus: Magazine for Design*) portrayed design work for mass production and advertising devised at the school. Graphic designer Herbert Bayer wrote about advertising as a new driving force in industry and culture that required sound training based primarily not on aesthetics but on the laws of different sciences: "compared to the mathematical certainty of the work of the engineer, it becomes apparent that the attempts of the ad man are [still] haphazard."[34] Josef Albers noted that

[29] Jan Tschichold, *The New Typography: A Handbook for Modern Designers*, orig. ed. 1928 (Berkeley, CA, 1995), 11.

[30] See Tschichold, *New Typography*, and the overriding interest in issues concerning norms and types in the paper and printing industry, for example, issues of the *Archiv für Buchgewerbe und Gebrauchsgraphik* throughout the late 1920s.

[31] Max Buchartz (Bochum), "Neuzeitliche Werbung," *Die Form* 1(7) (1926): 136–41.

[32] Johannes Molzahn, "Ökonomie der Reklame-Mechane," *Die Form* 1(7) (1926): 142–5.

[33] On Bauhaus commercial ties see Frederic Schwartz, "Utopia for Sale: The Bauhaus and Weimar Germany's Consumer Culture," in Kathleen James-Chakraborty, ed., *Bauhaus Culture: From Weimar to the Cold War* (Minneapolis, MN, 2006), 115–38.

[34] Herbert Bayer, "typografie und werbesachengestaltung," *Bauhaus* 2(1) (1928): 10.

an economically minded era required economical forms and that the school had to cater to "the need for functional design."[35] Bauhaus artists strove to reform both art and consumer capitalism, and their journal documented attempts to scientifically explore consumer marketing and advertising while promoting Bauhaus training and Bauhaus goods as the proper artistic expression for Weimar consumerism.[36]

The Bauhaus was not alone in this venture. During the 1920s the work of Bauhaus artists frequently appeared in journals for design such as *Die Form* as well as in advertising periodicals. The journal *Offset: Buch- und Werbekunst* (*Offset: The Art of Books and Advertising*), for example, dedicated a special issue to the Bauhaus's attempts at functional design, even changing its traditional layout to embrace modern forms and typography. Here, the Bauhaus was portrayed as a "laboratory" or "center for experimentation" (*Versuchszentrale*) aiming to produce types and standardized forms by "combining the work of the engineer, the businessman, and the artist."[37] In Frankfurt, another center of design and urban reform, the journal *Das Neue Frankfurt* similarly engaged topics of modern advertising and styling beginning in 1927. While competitive advertising had added a sense of chaos to metropolitan life, observers noted, functionally designed ads and commercial signs could actually improve modern urban aesthetics.[38] Most crucial to the Frankfurt efforts, however, were attempts at standardized housing under Ernst May's urban planning office, which were replete with uniform designs for doors and windows, furniture and ovens created by Ferdinand Kramer, Grete Lihotsky, and others.[39] Much like airships, cars, dams, and other achievements of contemporary engineering, such furnishings, architect-designer Franz Schuster argued, had to catch up with "technological modernity" in order to fit the needs of people.[40]

Consumers, however, still needed to be sold on new functionalist forms, as Grete Lihotsky – one of the few prominent women in this

35 Josef Albers, "werklicher formunterrich," *Bauhaus* 2(2) (1928): 3–4.

36 See, for example, "die wissenschaftliche arbeitsstelle des vdr," *Bauhaus* 2(1) (1928): 14.

37 "Das Bauhaus," *Offset: Buch- und Werbekunst*, issue 7 (1926): 358–60.

38 Walter Dexel, "Reklame im Stadtbilde," *Das Neue Frankfurt* 1(3)(1927): 45–56, and Adolf Behne, "Kultur, Kunst und Reklame," *Das Neue Frankfurt* 1(3) (1927): 57–60.

39 See Wilhelm Lotz, "Möbeleinrichtung und Typenmöbel," *Die Form* 3(6) (1928): 161–76, and Ernst May, "Grundlagen der Frankfurter Wohnungsbaupolitik," *Das Neue Frankfurt* 2(7/8)(1928): 113–24. On Kramer see, for example, Bauhaus Archiv, ed., *Ferdinand Kramer: Architektur und Design* (Berlin, 1982).

40 Franz Schuster, "Die neue Wohnung und der Hausrat," *Das Neue Frankfurt* 1(5) (1927): 123–7.

debate – observed with regard to her efforts at household rationalization including the design of the famous "Frankfurt kitchen." Female consumers, in particular, appeared to most designers not only as susceptible to advertising and irrational fashion appeals but also as inherently conservative in their taste and consumption habits. The continued prominence of gaudy decorations, Lihotsky explained, was mainly due to women's lack of openness to new ideas and their preference for a traditional "cozy" home. The city of Frankfurt thus assembled exhibitions and displays to persuade female consumers to make use of new functional furniture and labor-saving household designs, which, despite the promotions, were widely regarded as "too sober" by consumers.[41] Much like home economists at the time, design experts sought to mold the consumption habits of women to fit their normative ideals of rational and proper consumer behavior within the household. Here, designers tapped into a broader discourse on household rationalization sustained by Weimar industrialists, social reformers, and bourgeois feminists alike.[42] Teaching (especially female) consumers how to consume, they hoped, would ultimately make interwar markets more efficient, more predictable, and more manageable.

Whenever designers listened too closely to the voice of the engineers (embodied most concretely in the Deutscher Normenausschuss [German Standardization Committee]), the resulting emphasis on norms and functionality was often at odds with consumer desires for fashion and decorum.[43] To those who likened artists to engineers, such as Walter Gropius of the Bauhaus or Frankfurt's Ernst May, it was not simply products and advertising, but consumers themselves who were in need of (social) engineering. Modern housing, Gropius believed, required the principles of engineering because "building entailed the shaping of life and everyday living (*Gestaltung von Lebensvorgängen*)." As most people had similar life needs (*Lebensbedürfnisse*), he argued, it made economic sense to satisfy these uniform mass needs in a standardized manner. Standardized

[41] Grete Lihotzky, "Rationalisierung im Haushalt," *Das Neue Frankfurt* 1(5) (1927): 120–3.

[42] Mary Nolan, "'Housework Made Easy': The Taylorized Housewife in Weimar Germany's Rationalized Economy," *Feminist Studies* 16 (1990): 549–77.

[43] See Sudrow, "Der Typus als Ideal der Formgebung." The committee was originally founded in 1917 as the Normenausschuss der deutschen Industrie and renamed in 1926 to reflect its growing scope. Its impact on graphic design and printing came especially through the work of Walter Porstmann. See Robin Kinross, introduction to Tschichold, *New Typography*, xxvii–xxxviii.

materials and styles would eliminate "waste and wrongheaded markers of individuality." Whether for suitcases or clothing, standardized forms would improve quality and eventually further cultural development.[44]

In the minds of reformers like Gropius, the merging of domains between the artist and the industrial engineer would allow the initiative of the artist to predominate more than the other way around. Artists who engaged in the design of functional goods were in a position to "open up and expand" the narrow and "materialistic mindset" of leaders of industry.[45] Bauhaus commentators such as Ernst Kallai also made clear, furthermore, that while modern artists – following the lead of the United States and (more recently) the Soviet Union – recognized the necessity of practical design and advertising, one needed to remain critical vis-à-vis the noisy sensationalism of popular consumer culture. This required a pedagogical approach, which would highlight distinctions between the modern and practical work-mindedness of the artist and the equally modern and practical "commodity-mindedness of capitalism."[46]

In the end, emphasizing the role of the artist as an engineer of consumer capitalism served not only the interests of an emerging design profession but also a larger reform agenda. Faced with an interwar reality of widespread scarcity, most advocates of functional design aesthetics hoped to influence consumer capitalism in ways that improved the consumption standards of the population at large through rationalized production, efficient consumption, and improved products.[47] On one hand, artists such as Mart Stam put the consumer and "the human scale" at the center of their new engineering-inspired approach to design: they paid increasing attention to the physiological needs (ergonomics) and perceived psychological needs of their

[44] Walter Gropius, "systemische vorarbeit für rationellen wohnungsbau," *Bauhaus* 1(2) (1927): 1.

[45] Walter Gropius, "Wo berühren sich die Schaffensgebiete des Technikers und des Künstlers," *Die Form* 1(6) (1926): 117–24.

[46] Ernst Kallai, "das bauhaus lebt!" *Bauhaus* 2,2 (1928): 1–2, and Ernst Kallai, "sie wundern sich," *Bauhaus* 3(3) (1929): 11. Such pedagogical efforts directed at consumers had a longer history dating back to the nineteenth century. See, for example, Jennifer Jenkins, "*The Kitsch Collections* and *The Spirit in the Furniture*: Cultural Reform and National Culture in Germany," *Social History* 21 (1996): 123–41.

[47] Next to the Frankfurt developments, housing exhibitions by the Congrès internationaux d'architecture moderne (*International Congresses of Modern Architecture*) (CIAM) or by cities such as Cologne speak to this vision of "modern" and democratic consumer standards during the last years of the Weimar Republic. See, for example, Ernst Jäckh, "Diskussion der Ausstellung 'Die neue Zeit' – Köln 1932," *Die Form* 4(15)(1929).

customers.[48] On the other hand, these "artists as engineers" frequently betrayed an overly simplistic understanding of the consumer economy as analogous to a machine with standardized, interchangeable, and largely predictable parts. Like Gropius, they assumed a nearly uniform *homo consumens* with homogenous needs and tastes. In their view, an efficiency-minded artist (or an engineer with aesthetic sensibility) presented the ideal expert equipped to understand and reform interwar capitalism.

8.3 RATIONALIZATION AND ITS LIMITS: THE MARKETING PROFESSIONAL AS PSYCHOLOGIST

This vision of a rationalized economy did not go unchallenged at the time, with critics pointing to the limits of such a functionalist analysis of the dynamics of consumer markets. "Humans," an editorial in *Die Form* observed in 1927, "are to a high degree typical beings with uniform desires and needs." Yet, the editorial continued, the ensuing standardization, "although a necessity, evokes a growing disgust in everybody who pauses to think about it."[49] Well attuned to seemingly irrational rejections of standardization and to consumer desires for elements of novelty and individuality, a growing group of marketing professionals rejected the simple *homo consumens* of the designers as much as the equally simplistic *homo oeconomicus* devised by economists. Instead, they pointed to the unpredictable and inherently psychological dynamics of consumer markets, which largely defied rational calculation.

To be sure, interwar marketing in Germany was characterized by an overarching trend toward professionalization.[50] From window dressers and salespersons to advertisers, the era saw the emergence and proliferation of professional organizations and standards. While many German marketing professionals still tended to emphasize the individual genius of instinct-driven advertising men, their practices were increasingly informed by specialized education and early efforts in advertising science.[51] The

[48] Mart Stam, "Das Mass – Das richtige Mass – Das Minimum-Mass," *Das Neue Frankfurt* 3(2)(1929): 29–30.

[49] "Qualität oder Quantität? Eine Kultur- und wirtschaftspolitische Betrachtung," *Die Form* 2(8) (1927): 225–7.

[50] Ingo Köhler and Jan Logemann, "Towards Marketing Management: German Business and Marketing in the Nineteenth and Twentieth Centuries," in Brian Jones and Mark Tadajewski, eds., *The Routledge Companion to Marketing History* (London, 2016), 371–88.

[51] On the development of the advertising profession see especially Hirt, *Verkannte Propheten?* See also Christine Lamberty, *Reklame in Deutschland 1890–1914:*

establishment of German subsidiaries of American advertising agencies helped introduce systematic advertising research as part of a more comprehensive approach to managing consumer markets.[52] "Modern" advertising, Mannheim-based advertising scholar Edmund Lysinski explained in 1924, meant influencing the "masses" in an "organized" manner. To avoid disruptive chaos, "planned" advertising could reconcile existing differences, structure emotions and desires, and achieve "unity" in society and the economy.[53]

Marketing experts too sought to "rationalize" distribution and "engineer" it better. One prominent venue for the professionalization of sales practices was the trade journal *Verkaufspraxis* (*Sales Practice*), which began publication in 1925. Its editor, Victor Vogt, was particularly interested in bringing American sales and marketing innovations to a German-speaking audience of retailers and corporate managers, including attention to consumer psychology. Next to topics such as brand goods or chain store distribution, contributions to the journal analyzed the motivations of consumers, discussed the psychology of sales pitches, and looked at the ways advertising impacted sensory perception.[54] Uwe Spiekermann has argued that Vogt was representative of early proponents of systematic "consumer engineering," a new form of consumer-focused marketing management based on careful analysis of consumer markets that would become a more widespread practice during the middle decades of the twentieth century.[55]

Market and consumer research became a crucial element in engineering consumer markets, and the 1920s and 1930s saw early systematic developments in this area. Interwar consumer markets had been particularly erratic and, much like other forms of economic observation at the time, consumer market research consequently sought to anticipate, stabilize, and control cyclical swings. A series of scientific publications and handbooks began to

Wahrnehmung, Professionalisierung und Kritik der Wirtschaftswerbung (Berlin, 2000), and Claudia Regnery, *Die Deutsche Werbeforschung, 1900–1945* (Münster, 2003).

[52] On the practice of "full-service" agencies see Alexander Schug, "Wegbereiter der modernen Absatzwerbung in Deutschland: Advertising Agencies und die Amerikanisierung der deutschen Werbebranche in der Zwischenkriegszeit," *WerkstattGeschichte* 34 (2003): 29–51.

[53] Edmund Lysinski, *Die Organisation der Reklame* (Berlin, 1924), esp. 12–14.

[54] See, for example, "Kauf-Motive," *Verkaufspraxis* 1(9) (June 1926), 3–7, or "Die fünf Sinne und die Werbung," *Verkaufspraxis* 2(5) (Feb. 1927), 265.

[55] See Uwe Spiekermann, "German Style Consumer Engineering: Victor Vogt's Verkaufspraxis, 1925–1950," in Jan Logemann, Gary Cross, and Ingo Köhler, eds., *Consumer Engineering: Marketing between Planning Euphoria and the Limits of Growth* (New York, 2018), 117–45.

delineate the contours of a specialized body of market research knowledge, and several institutions promoted practical advances in business research. In Vienna, Paul Lazarsfeld's Wirtschaftspsychologische Forschungsstelle (Research Center for Economic Psychology) had begun to conduct sophisticated market surveys for Austrian, Swiss, and German companies by the early 1930s. Even earlier, Wilhelm Vershofen's Institut für Wirtschaftsbeobachtung der Fertigware (Institute for the Economic Observation of Finished Goods) had been established in Nuremberg. It was a precursor to the later Gesellschaft für Konsumforschung (Consumer Research Company) (GfK) which after 1934 began to conduct nationwide consumer surveys for marketing purposes.[56] The journal *Markt der Fertigware* (*Finished Goods Market*) publicized the Nuremberg efforts in market research and analysis beginning in 1929 – systematic surveillance was offered to make export markets and domestic consumption predictable and manageable. Market research, marketing scholar Erich Schäfer explained, fulfilled a complementary function to advertising in shaping consumer desires, in that it helped discover those needs and desires in the first place. Market observation and analysis, he believed, demonstrated that "the rationalizing tendencies of today are slowly arriving in the marketing process."[57]

Despite this belief in the potential for rationalization, however, market researchers also recognized challenges and limitations to such efforts to engineer capitalism. Consumers as economic actors in many ways confounded attempts to manage consumer markets. Wilhelm Vershofen, for example, wrote about the "limits of rationalization" in a 1927 manifesto against what he perceived to be a seemingly ubiquitous fascination with Fordism and efficiency in Germany. Economic life, to Vershofen, was hardly rational, and the "technical reasoning" that permeated Fordist efforts to increase efficiency and optimize mass production, he believed, ran into

[56] On the Vienna research institute, see Jan Logemann, *Engineered to Sell: European Émigrés and the Making of Consumer Capitalism* (Chicago, 2019), chapter 2, and Ronald Fullerton, "Tea and the Viennese: A Pioneering Episode in the Analysis of Consumer Behavior," in Chris Allen and Deborah John, eds., *Advances in Consumer Research* (Provo, UT, 1994), 418–21. On the Nuremberg center, see Georg Bergler, *Die Entwicklung der Verbrauchsforschung in Deutschland und die GfK bis zum Jahre 1945* (Kallmünz, 1960) and on the GFK Wilfried Feldenkirchen and Daniela Fuchs, *Die Stimme des Verbrauchers zum Klingen bringen: 75 Jahre Geschichte der GFK Gruppe* (Munich, 2009), as well as Jonathan Wiesen, *Creating the Nazi Marketplace: Commerce and Consumption in the Third Reich* (Cambridge, 2011), 153–60.

[57] Erich Schäfer, *Grundlagen der Marktbeobachtung* (Nuremberg, 1928), esp. 11.

problems in the consumer sector. Here, irrational consumer behavior was driven by urges and impulsive or emotional needs. Indeed, Vershofen noted, the same technological reasoning that had given rise to Fordist mass production also furthered a sensual consumer culture craving speed and constant innovation.[58]

This dialectic created a fundamental dilemma for consumer capitalism, which mirrors the "paradox of innovation" Reckwitz described. Any attempts by engineers to design the "most rational" good and to create standardized product types for mass consumption, Vershofen believed, were bound to run up against powerful consumer desires for social distinction and emotional needs for fashionable colors and patterns. In Germany, even more than in the United States, he cautioned, it was unlikely that consumer markets would decide in favor of the most rationalized or standardized products.[59] Instead, companies had to anticipate and manage consumer expectations and produce a diverse and ever-changing array of products to meet dynamic demand.

This made the expertise of marketing and advertising professionals particularly valuable. More than engineering, however, the study of psychology emerged as a primary source of professional inspiration for this group during the 1920s. Psychotechnics, inspired by Taylorist efforts in scientific management, had received a great deal of attention in human resource management since the war, but marketing quickly emerged as a second major field of practical psychology in business. Many contemporaries saw advertising as just that, a form of "applied psychology."[60] Reflecting this widespread interest, Theodor König's introductory volume on advertisement psychology quickly went through three editions between 1924 and 1926. König too noted the tension between rational, intellectual reasoning and impulsive sensuality in motivating consumer behavior, and he stressed the importance of psychological experiments (rather than market statistics) in understanding consumer markets.[61] A certain psychological uniformity, König admitted, could be discerned among consumers, and there were universal cognitive and behavioral patterns that professional advertising could take advantage of (Figure 8.2). Generally, however, diversity among consumers owing to region and nationality or gender

[58] Wilhelm Vershofen, *Die Grenzen der Rationalisierung* (Nuremberg, 1927).
[59] Ibid., 52–6.
[60] Alfred Gellhorn, "Reklame und Stadtbild," *Die Form* 1(7) (1926): 132–5.
[61] Theodor König, *Reklame-Psychologie*, 3rd ed. (Munich, 1926).

Abb. 380. Betrachter einer Juwelenauslage in charakteristischer Haltung

FIGURE 8.2 Shoppers inspecting a jewelry store display window in "characteristic poses." Experts tracked their eye movement, posture, and expressions. Studying consumers, their psychology, and their desires, they believed, would help make markets more manageable. Rudolf Seyffert, *Allgemeine Werbelehre* (*General Theory of Advertising*) (Stuttgart, 1929).

and class required a highly differentiated, segmented, and localized psychological approach.[62]

While marketing experts set out to study the dynamics of consumer capitalism by scientific means, most looked for social-psychological patterns rather than natural laws or mechanical processes. In the eyes of 1920s advertisers, psychology offered a way to rationalize an aestheticized and emotional world of consumption.[63] According to Rudolf Seyffert, professor of advertising at the University of Cologne, advertising was much more a cultural science than an economic one.[64] Seyffert emphasized the importance of psychology as an auxiliary field in his 1929 handbook for the advertising profession. Perception studies (e.g. on optical illusions) as pursued by Gestalt psychologists, for example, allowed insights into the cognitive

[62] Ibid., esp. chapter 3.

[63] Stefan Haas, "Psychologen, Künstler, Ökonomen: Das Selbstverständnis der Werbetreibenden zwischen Fin-de-Siecle und Nachkriegszeit," in Peter Borscheid and Clemens Wischermann, eds., *Bilderwelt des Alltags: Werbung in der Konsumgesellschaft des 19. und 20. Jahrhunderts* (Stuttgart, 1995), 78–89, esp. 82–3.

[64] Rudolf Seyffert, *Allgemeine Werbelehre* (Stuttgart, 1929), 12.

processes of consumers that advertisers could exploit. Observing the eye movements of individuals viewing posters or testing their recall of slogans and brand names offered quantifiable data that marketing professionals could utilize in planning campaigns. Still, examples of artwork and creative design also take up a significant portion of Seyffert's handbook. Planning, clarity, and predictable uniformity were portrayed as important to successful advertising, but so were originality and novelty. Going beyond economic rationality, Seyffert urged that attention should be paid to the artistic design of advertising and packaging. This took on a particular importance for products such as cigarettes or lipstick or in spontaneous sales situations and other cases in which an appeal to senses and emotions – a conscious or subconscious emotional impact – was essential.[65]

Advertising and market research experts of the 1920s thus frequently portrayed consumer markets as driven by emotions and difficult to predict. While they believed that professional marketing could make them more manageable, the very presence of humans as consumers made them quite unlike machines or abstract economic models. To argue that consumers were simply seen as an irrational mass by interwar marketing experts does not fully do them justice, however.[66] In many ways they betrayed a much more nuanced understanding of the complex dynamics at the heart of consumer capitalism than many of their contemporaries. By the 1930s, for example, market researchers avoided stereotypically coding consumers as women, and they consciously differentiated consumer habits according to gender as much as to region and income.[67] To them, psychologists rather than engineers or, more precisely, commercial artists versed in psychology and marketing professionals who were able to see the cognitive, behavioral, and social boundaries of rational action, presented the ideal experts for navigating dynamic consumer markets. While marketing experts generally believed in the social benefits of a well-regulated economy, their primary goal – in contrast to many of the artists discussed earlier in this chapter – was to maximize sales rather than to reform German capitalism.

[65] Ibid., 56–61.

[66] See, for example, Nepomuk Gasteiger, *Der Konsument: Verbraucherbilder in Werbung, Konsumkritik und Verbraucherschutz* (Frankfurt, 2010).

[67] Jonathan Wiesen, "National Socialism and Consumption," in Frank Trentmann, ed., *Oxford Handbook of the History of Consumption* (Oxford, 2012), 433–50, here 442–3.

8.4 CAPITALISM CURTAILED: REVIVING DEMAND IN AN "ORGANIC" ECONOMY

The Great Depression did not spell an end to the fledgling consumerism of the Weimar years, but it did further exacerbate its inherent tensions and shortcomings. Apart from a few national brands, actual marketing practice during the interwar decades mostly fell short of either the rational planning or of the intricate aesthetic and psychological appeals demanded by the experts discussed earlier in this chapter. The crisis underscored, furthermore, that scarcity rather than affluence remained the primary reality experienced by most Weimar-era consumers. Overcoming the economic slump, many marketing experts now believed, required a more broad-based access to consumer goods. Much like proto-Keynesian advocates of mass marketing in the United States, Wilhelm Vershofen argued in 1933 that the key to "reviving" the economy lay in strengthening consumers and in shoring up and channeling purchasing power.[68] Under National Socialism many experts furthermore expressed increased interest in curtailing the market dynamics of consumer capitalism by limiting competition among producers and retailers and by managing consumer behavior. To this end, market research along with an increased associational organization of retail and advertising companies could, experts and Nazi policy makers believed, help improve the functioning of consumer markets by measuring needs and directing behavior.[69] They strove to resolve what they regarded as the core contradiction of modern consumer capitalism: that it had pitted calculating, rational businesses against the increasingly unpredictable "habits," "fashions," and "fancies" of consumers – that is, "fate on the market" (*Marktschicksal*).[70]

Organic metaphors for the economy gained prominence among marketing experts during the 1930s. To overcome the crisis, the popular image of "cranking" the economic engine was misleading, Vershofen argued, because the consumer economy was not a machine but rather a living organism, which had to be "revived" by fostering and directing the growth of consumer activity.[71] The image of the organism, of course,

[68] Wilhelm Vershofen, *Produktionsankurbelung oder Belebung des Verbrauchs?* (Nuremberg, 1933). Vershofen argued for income increases and public credit to spur on consumer activity.

[69] Institut für Wirtschaftsbeobachtung, ed., *Marktanalyse und Marktbeobachtung* (Stuttgart, 1933), with introductory comments by Verhofen and Schäfer.

[70] Vershofen, *Produktionsankurbelung*, 4–6.

[71] Ibid., 3.

resonated with Nazi ideology and the purge and exclusion of Jewish retailers, advertisers, and commercial designers from the economic body of the nation. More specifically, however, an understanding of the consumer economy as an organism allowed for "irrational" aspects of consumption; it served to integrate them into a controlled and coherent "biological phenomenon."[72] After 1933 advocates of *Bedarfslenkung* (consumption engineering) such as Victor Vogt now argued that consumer impulses should be disciplined and subordinated to the needs of the larger economic organism while associational organizations would tame overly unruly consumer markets and a competitive distribution sector.[73] The organic metaphors helped legitimize the concept of a "hedged in" and organized consumer economy that Jonathan Wiesen has dubbed the "Nazi marketplace."[74]

Liberal capitalism, none other than Nuremberg consumer expert Ludwig Erhard explained in 1937, had been riddled by fundamental problems. Traditional economics, focused on the competition between rational actors in the productive sphere had, he argued, ignored the problems of the consumer. An economy made up of people was "not a machine," Erhard noted, and an ever-growing supply of goods did not automatically create its own demand. Problems of distribution were therefore "inherent to market economies," which had been dominated by the "addictions" and "whims" of instinct-driven consumers. Now that capitalism had been overcome by a more organic model, however, the later architect of West Germany's social market economy continued, a new economic ethics would allow for more collective methods of directing consumption. Psychologically informed advertising and market research could aid in steering both production and consumption in a more effective fashion.[75] Consumer psychology, experts argued increasingly, could be used to diffuse the contradictory dynamics of consumption in a more organized and less competitive (or less capitalist) marketplace.

Still, the rhetorical transition in expert discourses between the Weimar and Nazi years was in many ways more a nuanced shift than a clear break.

[72] See, for example, Otto Schäfer, "Vorwort," in Internationaler Ausschuss für Absatzwirtschaft, ed., *Absatzforschung und Absatzpraxis in Deutschland* (Stuttgart, 1937), xii.

[73] Spiekermann, "German Style Consumer Engineering."

[74] Wiesen, *Creating the Nazi Marketplace*, esp. 6–7.

[75] Ludwig Erhard, "Verbrauchsforschung, ihr ökonomischer Ort, ihre wissenschaftliche Begründung und ihre wirtschaftspolitische Zielsetzung," in Internationaler Ausschuss für Absatzwirtschaft, ed., *Absatzforschung und Absatzpraxis in Deutschland*, 124–33.

This reflected strong continuities in marketing practice, as Pamela Swett has shown with regard to advertising throughout the 1930s.[76] In addition, the new professional expertise of architects and designers as well as of advertisers and consumer analysts was of great interest to a regime that made both the mass production of standardized consumer goods ("people's products") and emotional propaganda appeals hallmarks of its political strategy. Even if the political framing of economic policies changed, consumer experts continued to struggle with similar problems of channeling distribution before and after 1933. They furthermore engaged in efforts to social-engineer consumer markets for both private and political gain, which fundamentally resembled the approaches developed during the 1920s.

Whether they took their cues from engineering or psychology, marketing professionals of the interwar decades put forward analyses that put an increasing emphasis on managing the dynamics of markets and paid close attention to the role of consumers in modern capitalism. They uncovered fundamental cultural contradictions in consumer capitalism, but also promised to provide professional tools to overcome these contradictions. In Germany this eventually contributed to the construction of a "Nazi marketplace" in which the dynamics of capitalism were at least partially curtailed. Many of the protagonists of the 1920s debates on modern consumer capitalism, however, found themselves forced into exile after 1933.

In the United States, their ideas about commercial design and the psychological dynamics of consumer markets would fuel a powerful post-Depression current of "consumer engineering." As I have demonstrated elsewhere, US experts in "consumer engineering" systematically sought to employ market research, consumer psychology, and commercial design to navigate and engineer consumer markets.[77] Market researchers set out to make markets more "rational," legible, and predictable to corporations. At the same time market psychologists and industrial designers engaged in understanding and manipulating the emotional and aesthetic appeal of goods, stimulating an incessant desire for novelty and continuous change. Here too we find the tension between the rationalizing aspects of interwar marketing and its more emotional and disruptive

[76] Pamela Swett, *Selling under the Swastika: Advertising and Commercial Culture in Nazi Germany* (Stanford, CA, 2013).

[77] Logemann, *Engineered to Sell*. See also Jan Logemann, "Consumer Modernity As Cultural Translation: European Émigrés and Knowledge Transfers in Mid-century Design and Marketing," *Geschichte und Gesellschaft* 43 (2017): 413–37.

side, which, I argue, is crucial for understanding the characteristic dynamics of consumer capitalism in the United States as well as in Europe. As émigrés, many Weimar artists and academics later found themselves employed by Madison Avenue advertising agencies and by a growing number of corporate design and market research departments. They helped unleash the full cultural and economic potential of mid-century American consumer capitalism. After the war their work would find its way back to postwar Germany, now – somewhat misleadingly – perceived as part of an "Americanization" of European consumer capitalism.

What, in the end, can we learn about the culture(s) of interwar capitalism from contemporary consumer experts? As demonstrated, their diagnoses of market dynamics revealed at once the rational, functional, and efficient aspects of capitalism and its emotive, creative, and ultimately often disruptive side. The interplay between emotional aspects of consumer markets and professional efforts to manage them through forms of "scientific" marketing provides a promising vantage point for further research on the cultural dynamics of capitalism at the intersection of a history of knowledge and a history of emotions. Reflecting the increased significance of knowledge and of the knowledge sector within the economy, studies on professionalization and the rise of expert cultures, as well as on the increasing "scientization" of market practices, have already contributed to a history of knowledge of interwar economic processes.[78] Studying the consumer sector raises additional questions about the emotional dimensions of such developments. What accounts for the apparent and growing commercial demand for novelty and sensual experience? How did the motivations and attitudes of consumers and other economic actors change and how likewise did the moral economies in which their actions were embedded?

As we map the transformation of economic knowledge onto economic actors and their behavior we can make connections to changing emotional regimes that governed everyday economic practices and experiences. New pleasures derived from aesthetics, novelty, and change – contemporary experts on consumer capitalism understood – were closely linked to fears about chaos and crisis as much as to rationalization processes and a search for predictability through systematic standardization in markets. Such contradictory dynamics can be found in consumer markets across the twentieth century, but what set interwar cultures of capitalism apart was that they appeared so novel and so intensely palpable and urgent at the time.

[78] See, for example, Hirt, *Verkannte Propheten?*

9

A Society Safe for Capitalism

Violent Crowds, Tumult Laws, and the Costs of Doing Business in Germany, 1918–1945

Molly Loberg

9.1 INTRODUCTION: PROCESSING TUMULT

In its first two years of operation, 1919–21, Berlin's newly established Tumult Bureau received sixteen thousand claims seeking compensation for damages and injuries caused by domestic unrest.[1] Such claims had flooded government offices across Germany since the end of World War I and the early days of the November Revolution. They varied widely in nature of injury and scale of demand. They included petitions from farmers whose crops had been pillaged by soldiers and workers, pedestrians wounded by urban street fighting, and town dwellers with homes vandalized by politically hostile neighbors. Even the widow and the daughter of socialist leader Karl Liebknecht sued for compensation after his murder by Freikorps troops.

But petitions from businesses dwarfed all other claimant categories. Like the personal tragedies just described, these compensation claims provide a mirror image of political violence but through the lens of liability for property crime. From major cities to small towns, businesses itemized their losses for the authorities. Hermann Tietz, head of Warenhaus Tietz, the department store chain, complained to the Berlin Magistrat that successive waves of violence had struck the company's Alexanderplatz location in the early months of the republic. According to Tietz, "insurrectionists" broke four display windows on November 9 and 10, 1918. Far greater damage occurred from early to mid-January,

[1] "16 000 angemeldete Tumultschäden in Berlin," *Berliner Tageblatt und Handelszeitung*, Jun. 1, 1921.

when exchanges of gunfire between government troops and Spartacists shattered glass panes up to the third story and riddled with bullet holes the silk jackets and gowns on display.[2] The city of Dortmund assessed the damages resulting from unrest between November 1918 and March 1920 at 17 million marks.[3] During hyperinflation food manufacturer Knorr reported catastrophic losses in macaroni noodles and soup mixes after crowds ravaged its warehouses in Essen.[4] Fluctuating currency values in fact magnified losses, especially as petitions languished for months and even years in bureaucratic channels.

Businesses did not frame their losses as individual tragedies but rather as threats to local and national economies. They mobilized professional associations and political parties to lobby government at all levels on their behalf. In no small part because of such efforts, the Weimar government committed itself in principle to make good on a law that preceded its existence, the 1850 Prussian Tumult Law (*Tumultgesetz*). In so doing, the nascent republic accepted liability for the violence that precipitated and accompanied its foundation. Its authoritarian successor, the Nazi regime, found it more challenging than expected to revoke these legal obligations. While most other claim categories subsided, retailers as well as their insurance companies aggressively invoked the Tumult Law throughout the Weimar Republic and into the Nazi period, even in the aftermath of *Kristallnacht*.

As the largest claimant category, businesses seeking redress for "tumult" shaped expectations about the role of government in an era of capitalism and mass politics. A significant body of historical research assesses how political violence both established and undermined the foundations of the Weimar Republic. That said, much of this work focuses on violence against persons – for example, assassinations, street brawls, attempted coups, and crowd suppression.[5] Certainly, focusing on this kind of violence makes sense. It helps historians track the brutal

[2] Correspondence of Hermann Tietz with Magistrat, Nov. 1918 and Jan. 1919, Landesarchiv Berlin (LAB) A Rep. 010–01–01, Nr. 462.

[3] Stadtverwaltung Dortmund to Reichsminister des Innern, Nov. 15, 1920, Bundesarchiv Berlin (BArch) R 1501/116433.

[4] Knorr to Stadtverwaltung Essen, Nov. 7, 1923; Knorr to Reichswirtschaftsminister, Jan. 19, 1924, BArch R1501/116431.

[5] A few examples: Mark Jones, *Founding Weimar: Violence and the German Revolution of 1918–1919* (Cambridge, 2016); Dirk Schumann, *Political Violence in the Weimar Republic: The Fight for the Streets and the Fear of Civil War, 1918–1933*, trans. Thomas Dunlap (New York, 2009); George Mosse, *Fallen Soldiers: Reshaping the Memory of the World Wars* (Oxford, 1990).

legacies of World War I, compare the founding of the German republic with other revolutionary examples, and draw attention to the ways National Socialists diverged dramatically from (but in some instances remained consistent with) the actions and attitudes of their predecessors. Nevertheless, the largest and most pervasive category of violence during the Weimar Republic was property crime. Property crime rates rose from the end of World War I and peaked in 1923 at three times the prewar level. Rates then fell off in the mid-1920s before climbing again with the onset of the Depression.[6] Taken individually, some incidents resembled "normal crimes," not unlike examples of vandalism, theft, and arson from before 1914. Taken together, however, property crime on this scale could not be separated from politics, in terms of either motive or consequence. The Tumult Law itself elided such distinctions.

This chapter considers the following questions: What promises did the Weimar Republic and later the Nazi regime make to insulate business from "tumult" and why? Did these promises bolster or undercut the legitimacy of these governments? How did businesses appraise state guarantees compared with their other options such as security systems or private insurance? In so doing, this chapter explores the complex ways in which pervasive interwar violence threatened capitalism and, with it, the stability of state authority. At the same time, it contends that pervasive violence prompted businesses to articulate the obligations of the state, in particular the state's responsibility to protect property and provide a society safe for capitalism.

9.2 THE 1848 REVOLUTION AND AFTER: A PUNITIVE PRECEDENT

In 1918, citizens and the incipient republic inherited a body of German laws. It was not clear yet which would remain and which would pass away. To make their claims for compensation, petitioners drew upon the seventy-year-old Prussian Tumult Law and thus a precedent that predated the 1918 revolution and even the founding of the German nation. Prussia had adopted the Tumult Law in the wake of the failed 1848 revolution. Indeed, officials drew inspiration from measures the French government had passed in 1795 in order to quell riots and rebellion as the state turned

[6] Peter Wagner, *Volksgemeinschaft ohne Verbrecher: Konzeptionen und Praxis der Kriminalpolizei in der Zeit der Weimarer Republik und des Nationalsozialismus* (Hamburg, 1996), 28–42.

from revolution toward reaction.[7] The 1850 Prussian Tumult Law dealt with crimes of scale, in other words, damage to property and persons caused by violent crowds. In the midst of a riot, the size of the crowd provided anonymity and thus protected perpetrators from identification, prosecution, and punishment. Moreover, the destructive potential of a crowd far exceeded that of an individual. The law therefore shifted liability for injuries and damages from unidentified perpetrators to the *Gemeinde* – that is, the specific municipality, district, or parish where the unrest began. The distinction between the geographic origin of agitation and the actual scene of violence mattered in a society divided by class, as property owners often lived apart from workers. Compensation covered the destruction inflicted by crowds as well as collateral damage caused by the measures used by the military or police to suppress crowds.

Two competing legal principles underpinned this displacement and reassignment of liability under the Tumult Law.[8] The first understood the *Gemeinde* as a community whose members bore collective responsibility for a riot either by participating in it or by failing to stop it. On this principle, the law functioned as a preemptive and punitive measure. It assumed that, if threatened with higher communal taxes, communities would police themselves better or expose perpetrators. By assigning damages to the community as a whole, the law was intended to act as a deterrent against agitation and collective action and thus preserve both monarchy and property. The second principle understood the *Gemeinde* as the local authority and administrative body, acting through institutions of enforcement such as the police. From this perspective, the law compensated victims for institutional failures to protect and preserve order. Most

[7] Prussia had passed a less extensive Tumult Law in 1835 that the 1850 law built upon. Reichsminister des Innern to Finanzamt, Feb. 8, 1919, BArch R 5/6149.

[8] A number of dissertations and legal tracts from the early Weimar Republic provide overviews of both the history and the central issues of the law: Kurt Bertram, "Das preussische Tumultgesetz vom 11. März 1850," Rechts- und Staatswissen. Diss., Universität Greifswald, 1919; Erich Pilz, "Die zivilrechtliche Haftung der preussischen Gemeinden für Vermögensschäden nach dem Tumultschadengesetz," Rechts- und Staatswissen. Diss., Universität Greifswald, 1919; Bruno Friedlaender, *Das preussische Tumultschadengesetz* (Berlin, 1919); Heinrich Metz, "Tumultschadenshaftung," Rechtswissen. Diss., Universität zu Köln, 1923; Arthur Röhring, "Die Grundzüge der geschichtlichen Entwicklung und der heutige Stand der Tumultschadensgesetzgebung," Rechts- und wirtschaftswissen. Diss., Thüringische Landesuniversität Jena, 1926. See also Christiane Kimmel, *Staatshaftung für Tumultschäden: Historische Entwicklung, Zustand und Reformperspektiven einer staatlichen Einstandspflicht für Tumultschäden in Deutschland unter vergleichender Berücksichtigung der französischen Rechtslage* (Berlin, 2003).

legal scholars concurred that the framers of the Prussian law backed the first understanding of liability, that is to say that it was based on communal guilt or passivity.[9] Still, the phrasing was ambiguous and allowed for either or both understandings.

Two key historical developments over the course of the nineteenth century undercut the idea of community liability and made state liability for tumult more plausible. As urban areas grew and grew together, it became difficult to speak of distinct civic units, much less ones united across class and political lines. Furthermore, the broadening of the tax base dispersed risk and cost and thus weakened the punitive effect of the law and the incentive for individual citizens to take a stand, especially against an agitated crowd. As a parallel development, the state asserted and expanded its monopoly on the legitimate use of force. It assumed greater responsibility for ensuring domestic safety and tranquility. It managed the collection and dispersal of revenues for public administration. Bureaucracy swelled. By the second half of the nineteenth century, European countries instituted modern police forces for the suppression, investigation, and prosecution of "normal crime."[10] But the state did not compensate victims of everyday occurrences of theft, vandalism, arson, or assault. Instead, the perpetrators, insurance companies, or the victims themselves had to assume this burden. The widening distance between the original intent of the Tumult Law and historical developments, including urban growth and the corresponding expansion of administration and policing, allowed for a wider range of legal interpretations. In Breslau in 1906 and Berlin in 1910, for example, workers seized upon the law *to accuse police* of using excessive force by severely wounding and disfiguring bystanders with the sabers they used for crowd control during strikes and protests.[11]

On one hand, the 1850 Tumult Law normalized a limited level of violence as part of daily life. On the other, the law established parameters for acceptable levels of violence and cast the state as the defender and

[9] Friedrich Caro offers a slightly different interpretation from the aforementioned legal dissertations and tracts by emphasizing that when lawmakers first discussed the issue in 1848–9, their intent was not to prevent revolutionary acts as such but rather mob disturbances. See his work *Haftung der Gemeinden für Revolutionsschäden* (Berlin, 1919), in LAB A Rep. 001–02, Nr. 2095.

[10] Albrecht Funk, *Polizei und Rechtsstaat: Die Entwicklung des staatlichen Gewaltmonopols in Preussen 1848–1918* (Frankfurt, 1986).

[11] "Die Entschädigung für die abgehackte Hand," *Volkswacht*, Oct. 30, 1906, 57. and 58. Sitzung, Mar. 24 and Mar. 27, 1911, *Verhandlungen, Preussischer Landtag, Haus der Abgeordneten* (Berlin, 1911).

restorer of peace when circumstances deviated from normal. And yet, because the law addressed exceptional cases, it remained exceptional in application. The Berlin municipal government documented only a few dozen relevant incidents between 1850 and 1914.[12] Most claims proved unsuccessful.[13] As one jurist explained regarding the Tumult Law, "It is not material that has the same significance attached to it at all times. It is much more a kind of 'occasional law' (*Gelegenheitsgesetzgebung*) that will only be of general interest in times of domestic unrest and revolution."[14] This made the law, as one observer later recounted, a "sleeping beauty" roused from its long dormancy by the outbreak of World War I.[15]

9.3 THE WEIMAR REPUBLIC: THE PRICE OF REVOLUTION

By war's end in 1918, Germans were invoking the Tumult Law on an unprecedented scale. Postwar political and economic instability upended definitions of "normal" crime and violence. The pivotal events of the early Weimar Republic – the Spartacist Revolt, the toppling of the Bavarian Soviet Republic, the Kapp Putsch, the suppression of the Rhineland separatists, and hyperinflation – all produced a surge of claims. Street violence caused severe collateral damage. Bystanders suffered injury and death. Grenade splinters marred the facades of buildings and bullets shattered shop windows. At the same time citizens sought recompense for petty acts of theft, vandalism, and assault. These incidents cumulatively assumed such breadth and tenacity in the postwar period that they blurred the boundaries between normal crime and national crisis. Robberies and lootings frequently accompanied protests. But they also flourished in a general atmosphere of insecurity and conflict. Perpetrators targeted a wide range of stores: groceries, bakers, clothiers, opticians, and tobacco stores. Jewelry stores were a particular favorite.

As claims piled up, municipalities grappled with the overwhelming burdens imposed by an old law that suddenly had become relevant again. Their financial position was precarious. According to the Tumult Law, the cost of reparation fell on the community where the violence began. Yet cities and towns were already struggling with substantial wartime debt. Growing welfare demands further drained their coffers.

[12] Stadtverordneten-Versammlung, LAB A Rep. 000–02–01, Nr. 1648, 1649.
[13] See Berlin notice, *Der Israelit*, Aug. 17, 1881, 819.
[14] Röhring, "Grundzüge," 1.
[15] Metz, "Tumultschadenshaftung," 11.

In May 1919, the state Prussian Budget committee surveyed the situation and reported that "unanticipated consequences of the law" might lead to the "ruin of a community."[16] Berlin's mayor warned that the city's finances would collapse if it paid reparations for street fighting.[17] And Berlin was just one of many sites that reported crushing costs resulting from the unrest that spread across Germany, from towns like Gotha and Stolp (Słupsk), to major urban centers such as Munich and Hamburg.

In response, local officials sought loopholes to extricate themselves from their legal obligations. Some simply claimed insolvency and forwarded itemized lists of damage to their superiors at the next level of government. Others disputed the geographic origins of the tumult and shifted blame to their neighbors. As one example, in July 1920, seven men in uniform looted a textile shop in Pankow, a district on the periphery of Berlin. According to Pankow officials, the looters had declared *in mid-act* that they came from the neighboring district of Weissensee.[18] Pankow officials therefore demanded payment from their Weissensee counterparts. Other officials simply refused to accept a specific geographic origin for tumult and instead characterized incidents as part of a "civil war" (*Bürgerkrieg*) or a "broad grassroots movement" (*eine allgemeine Volksbewegung*).[19] In other words, despite specific local manifestations, the violence had a geographic origin that encompassed the whole nation. Other officials wondered if disregarding uncomfortable laws was simply a privilege of victory. Should a revolutionary movement have to pay if (unlike in 1848) it wins? The law provided a practical incentive to ascribe specific historical meanings to the emerging Weimar Republic. By redefining the violence as general domestic unrest and a national problem, local officials diverted political pressure and liability upward through administrative channels. As the boldest strategy to dodge spiraling costs, municipalities appealed to the emerging republic to change the law and accept compensation claims as a national burden.

In their lobbying efforts, municipalities found disgruntled but willing partners in the business owners who had initiated the Tumult Law claims. True, local officials had often rejected these claims. Yet, because of this, businesses shared with municipalities a common interest in getting

[16] Staatshaushalts-Ausschuss, 5. Sitzung, May 2, 1919, BArch Berlin R 5/6149.
[17] Rettkowski, *Wer haftet für die Tumultschäden nach Ausbruch der Revolution im November 1918?* (Berlin, 1919).
[18] Gemeindevorstand Pankow to Gemeideverwaltung Weissensee, Jul. 26, 1920, R 1501/116428.
[19] Magistrat Charlottenburg, Mar. 25, 1919, R 1501/116425.

national help. Municipal governments advocated in support of their business communities. Addressing the Ministry of the Interior on behalf of "extraordinarily damaged tradespeople" in his town, Hamborn's mayor described a bleak economic landscape: "With their boarded-up windows, entire streets offer a picture of a city devastated by war."[20] The mayor of Remscheid wrote of the "understandable agitation," particularly among the "lower middle classes," who now threatened to stop paying taxes.[21]

At the same time, businesses recognized the problems towns and cities faced. They conceded that the scale of damage exceeded the capacities of municipal budgets. After the Berlin Municipal Assembly refused to pay, the Berlin Association of Textile Retailers turned to Chancellor Philipp Scheidemann. They lamented in a letter, "During the recent Spartacist Uprising in Berlin, a substantial part of our membership suffered significant damage through robbery, looting, and constant shooting. The businesses sit either empty or with completely ravaged salesrooms .... Some small shops are on the brink of catastrophe."[22] By addressing their appeal to the chancellor, retailers made a local issue into a national one. A number of professional associations called for a comprehensive legal resolution. Writing to the Ministry of the Interior, the German Chamber of Commerce sympathized with municipalities but argued that failure to compensate would lead to "the destruction of valuable economic existences" that would disturb "the entire circle of trade and businesspeople."[23] The two hundred and fifty thousand members of the Property Owners Association of Germany held that, although the revolution had broken out in individual cities, as soon as it led to a "complete transformation of the political relationships of the German nation," its battles became "a matter for the Reich."[24]

As a key feature, petitions detailed losses sustained by individual business or property owners but also connected these hardships to a spiral of collective misfortune that might end in economic disaster for all. Many once flourishing businesses faced "ruin," according to the common phrasing. "Yesterday they were still well-to-do people, today they are without the smallest means of subsistence or shelter," as one official described the

[20] Oberbürgermeister, Hamborn am Rhein, Feb. 5, 1920, BArch R 1501/116426.
[21] Oberbürgermeister, Remscheid, Jan. 3, 1924, BArch R 1501/115439.
[22] Verein der Textildetaillisten Gross-Berlins, Mar. 27, 1919, BArch R 1501/116424.
[23] Deutscher Industrie- und Handelstag, Apr. 1, 1919, BArch R 1501/116424.
[24] Zentralverband Haus- und Grundbesitzer-Vereine Deutschland, Feb. 12, 1919, R 43I/2695.

situation.[25] Furthermore, as the letters explained, looting without restitution posed a particular type of threat to a retail economy that had become increasingly reliant on the structures of capitalism and mass consumption, even though the businesses themselves varied in size and scale of integration. Simply put, stores drained of operating and investment capital or denied credit by banks or wholesale distributors could not replace stolen or damaged goods and therefore had nothing to sell. They could not stay in business, much less rebuild. In the aggregate, looting interrupted the retail cycle, particularly with respect to the sale of food since crowds heavily targeted grocers, bakers, and butchers. When pleading his case to the local police, Alois G. of Mainz provided a personal example of the larger economic and social dilemma.[26] After the war the disabled veteran had invested all his savings in a fruit and vegetable stall. On his first day at market, a disturbance erupted and the agitated crowd stole many of his goods and forced him to sell the rest cheaply. Having lost all his capital, he turned to work as a day laborer even though he hoped to return to selling. In the National Assembly, Representative Jacob Astor (Catholic Center Party) explained how violence upended merchants' long-term spending and venture strategies. Repeated lootings drove merchants to shut stores and turn employees out into the street. They withheld payments to distributors and other creditors in order to avoid becoming beggars. Astor reminded the Assembly that "no one should forget that the German economy is on the brink of collapse and needs credit from abroad."[27] But it would never occur to foreigners to invest in German businesses if they feared unrest and loss without restitution. The mayor of Hamborn pleaded for "any form of help, perhaps interest-free loans," so business could resume.[28] The city of Duisburg also described the looming downward economic spiral: the city rejected compensation claims, businesses could not get private credit, members of the middle class went bankrupt, prices for goods continued to rise, and the strain on the consumer intensified. Rejected compensation claims weighed heavily on "economic life in its entirety."[29] The Chamber of Commerce of Düsseldorf protested that retailers could no longer serve as

[25] Der Reichs- und Staatskommissar für den Befehlsbereich des VII. A.-K., Feb. 14, 1920, BArch R 1501/116426.

[26] Ausschuss zur Feststellung von Entschädigungen für Aufruhrschäden in der Provinz Rheinhessen, Jan. 11, 1921, R 1501/116434.

[27] 87. Sitzung, Sep. 30, 1919, *Verhandlungen der verfassungsgebenden Deutschen Nationalversammlung* (Berlin, 1920), 2770.

[28] Oberbürgermeister Hamborn, Feb. 1920, BArch R 1501/116426.

[29] Report Duisburg, Aug. 3, 1920, BArch R 1501/116433.

the "victims of the people's rage" and persevere "without protection" and "insufficient compensation."[30] Retailers and their representatives wanted a functioning capitalist economy. If denied this, they sought a financial buffer against the ravages of volatile politics.

The National Assembly bowed to pressure from municipalities and business interest groups and contemplated a revision of the Tumult Law in early spring 1919, even as it faced the much greater challenge of drafting the constitution of the Weimar Republic. Officials and delegates acknowledged at the outset the awkwardness of the task. In remarks before the assembly on behalf of the Ministry of the Interior, Theodor Lewald admitted the law's conservative origins that harked back to "the dying days of the French Revolution" and "the reactionary period."[31] Nevertheless, the ministry supported reviving and expanding the law "within the new democratic Germany" and helped formulate a draft. The ministry eschewed punishment as the basis of the law, a foundation the ministry and "all freedom-minded circles" deemed "irreconcilable" with "universal legal principle."[32] Ministry officials understood that the foundation of the Weimar Republic depended on the actions of defiant crowds. Still they feared rising social tensions and political discontent because of unpaid damages. The process of legislative compromise dragged on for a year. In an April 1920 reading of the law before the National Assembly, Hans Herschel (Catholic Center Party) made an urgent case for its passage: "What would happen if this does not become law? The answer is simple: an unbearable situation would arise." He called upon the Assembly to "heal the wounds that the revolution wrought."[33]

A new law "regarding damages from internal unrest" passed on May 12, 1920.[34] The revision process had transformed the meaning and purpose of the Tumult Law from the punishment of crowds to the restitution of citizens. Moreover, it entailed a major shift in scope and practice. Since 1918, many parts of Germany had resented and protested the 1850 Tumult Law because it excluded them. Despite the shared experience of postwar violence, the old law only applied to Prussia.[35] The new law

[30] Handelskammer zu Düsseldorf, Jul. 17, 1920, BArch R 1501/116428.

[31] 87. Sitzung, Sep. 30, 1919, *Nationalversammlung*, 2774.

[32] Correspondence with "die Herren Staatsminister," Apr. 9, 1919, R 5/6149.

[33] 175. Sitzung, *Nationalversammlung*, Apr. 29, 1920, 5616.

[34] Gesetz über die durch innere Unruhen verursachten Schäden, *Reichsgesetzblatt*, 1920, Nr. 106. It was informally referred to as the *Tumultschädengesetz* or *Tumultschadengesetz*.

[35] Bavaria, Baden, Württemburg, Hessen, Saxony had similar laws with parallel yet distinctive histories and formulations.

encompassed the entire Reich. Rather than burden a specific community with the costs of unrest, the national government paid the majority of costs out of general taxation funds. It took on one-half (six-twelfths) of the burden. The state in which unrest took place paid four-twelfths, and the municipality or community saw its share of any compensation reduced to two-twelfths.

The law thus fostered national unification, albeit through its registration and potential indemnification of public unrest. It represented a tense compromise among disparate stakeholders: bankrupt municipalities, recalcitrant private insurers, irate citizens, and apprehensive finance ministers. Despite its eventual passage, the debate over the law also revealed foundational differences of opinion among the political parties. When presenting the revised law to the assembly, Georg Theobald Alexander, Graf zu Dohna (German People's Party) confessed, "It is fully clear to the committee, that the proposed regulations will satisfy none of those involved … Perhaps the strange harmony of discord is proof that the law follows the only possible line of resolution among the clashing interests."[36]

Controversy centered on Section 2 of the new law, which tied compensation to *need* as a strategy to contain financial burdens on the government. When evaluating claims, review boards were required to consider the victim's overall wealth and employment situation and only to approve compensation if the damages "unduly impeded the affected person's means of making a living."[37] This provision incensed business and property owners. It galvanized their lobbyists, sympathetic newspapers, and political parties. New interest groups such as the National Association of Victims of Civil Unrest (Reichsbund der Tumultgeschädigten) organized beside older trade associations like the German Chamber of Commerce and specific retailers' unions. In the early postwar period the *Berliner Tageblatt und Handelszeitung* newspaper gave extensive coverage to issues of civil unrest, property crime, police failures, and liability. A regular column, "The Insecurity in Berlin," catalogued countless robberies, break-ins, and lootings. Opinion pieces in this newspaper and trade-specific journals and newsletters (*Der Konfektionär*, *Deutsche Kolonialwaren und Feinkost-Rundschau*) took regular aim at the limits

[36] 175. Sitzung, Apr. 29, 1920, *Nationalversammlung*, 5615.

[37] *Reichsgesetzblatt*, 1920, Nr. 106. Authorities at the state level established committees on an ad hoc basis. The minister of the interior, along with state and local governments, appointed members to represent their interests. Local representatives often had ties to commerce and industry. Chairs were required to have experience in the judiciary or high civil service.

of the law. They emphasized that attacks on property harmed the middle classes above all, first as the targets of violence and second as the taxpayers most burdened with the cost of restitution. They refused to concede the authority to define and pass judgment on a subjective category like financial ruin to a government committee.

According to critics of the provision, needs-testing would exacerbate social division and intensify class conflict. As if to prove this point, they disagreed about which tier of the propertied classes suffered most. Some believed that the law imperiled the lower middle classes (*minderbemittelt, klein Mittelstand*) with their want of credit. Characterizing the new law as antisocial, Fritz Warmuth of the conservative German National People's Party insisted that the wealthy could afford the private insurance premiums, but the "little man" (*der kleine Mann*) needed help from the state.[38] Others thought the provision endangered the rich. According to Representative Moritz Baerwald of the left-liberal German Democratic Party, rioters would ransack villas and castles if they believed such acts had financial consequences only for the victims. "Quite possibly, the person who receives full compensation might be a common black market and war profiteer, while the other who receives nothing might have worked hard for twenty or thirty years for what he lost in a day of unrest," he chided.

Nevertheless, whether advocating for the lower or higher tiers of property owners, critics of needs-based compensation found common ground in the language of universal rights. They cited constitutional principles such as "All Germans are equal before the law."[39] Therefore, the state should not exclude them from the benefits of the taxes they paid while entitling others. Appropriating the language the left had once used against them, bourgeois parties and interests decried the new Tumult Law as a "class law." Protecting citizens and their property was the "essence" of the state. If the state failed in this regard, it was obligated to compensate. Whether it could afford to do so was immaterial. According to critics, the state could not simply shift the burden of its own insolvency onto the well-to-do.

The debate over compensation thrust lawmakers into an essential dilemma of democracy within a capitalist society, although they may not have fully understood it as such at the time. The state could not guarantee an equal right to restitution without accepting and, indeed,

[38] See debate 87. Sitzung, *Nationalversammlung*, Sept. 30, 1919, 2766–77.
[39] See debates 87, 88, 175, *Nationalversammlung*.

even preserving social inequality. Payouts in full or in part to the wealthy de facto contributed to the maintenance of their status within a hierarchy. Yet, the state could not deny the right of compensation to the wealthy while granting it to the less fortunate without breaching the universality of law. While means-testing forms the foundation of many welfare states and poverty relief programs, critics at the time perceived a meaningful distinction between the state granting benefits to the needy as opposed to owing compensation to the injured. Despite the vast sums paid out, all sides considered the settlements at best an unsatisfactory or unjust compromise.

On a more practical level, officials from the Ministry of the Interior and the Ministry of Finance saw comprehensive compensation as an impossibility because of current budget shortages as well as an uncertain future. Although officials sought resolution under the law, suspicions lingered that revolutionary violence might continue. Undersecretary Lewald from the Ministry of the Interior cautioned the National Assembly: "We do not know what lies ahead of us." Under the circumstances, the government could not replace every window broken in the villas of "very rich people."[40] Between the initial debates on the law and its passage, the right-wing Kapp Putsch shocked Berlin and ignited a left-wing uprising in the Ruhr. In the final debate before the vote, Representative Herschel, who supported the compromise legislation, nonetheless pointed out the strangeness of the situation: "We cannot even find out the approximate sum of damages caused by the unrest, even before the outbreaks in the Ruhr. People mention fantastic sums like seventeen billion marks and then twelve billion, and then for a change, one billion. The truth is likely somewhere in the middle."[41] The assembly hall erupted with laughter.

The joke, however cynical, lost its absurdity as the costs of the damage quickly became untethered from recognizable numbers. Once local committees formed to investigate and assign value to claims according to the new law, they forwarded astonishing bills to the national government. In just one example, officials from Düsseldorf submitted 2,019 claims in October 1920. They asked for 5 million marks as a starting point. In the meantime the national budget deteriorated under myriad postwar pressures. In May 1921, the Allies presented the final reparations bill. Budget conversations often wove together war and tumult burdens. Furthermore, worsening inflation wreaked havoc with compensation payments. Committees constantly had to recalculate sums. After a crowd of five

[40] 87. Sitzung, *Nationalversammlung*, 2774–5.
[41] 175. Sitzung, Apr. 29, 1920, *Nationalversammlung*, 5615.

thousand unemployed people looted grocery stores at the height of hyperinflation in 1923, the town of Remscheid asked for 60 billion marks. That same month Hamburg told the Ministry of the Interior to stop the transfer of paper money altogether. "The number of unsatisfied people is so high and the damages so extensive, that one has to use means that still have meaning," the committee grumbled.[42] Düsseldorf asked for future payments in US dollars. At the same time, inflation unleashed a new wave of consumer unrest, especially in the Rhineland and Ruhr. Even the small town of Overath witnessed the looting of 140 to 150 stores and one death. Denied restitution because an outbreak of looting in Essen in October 1923 did not threaten the company's "existence," Knorr warned that it might withdraw from the region entirely and abandon the "population of the Ruhr," whom the company had tried to supply with goods despite all the dangers and difficulties of doing business in occupied territory.[43]

The same pressures compelled the national government to limit its exposure further. As part of emergency budget measures, a 1924 revision to the law capped compensation at 75 percent of the calculated loss.[44] Moreover, it extricated the national government from the scheme. Instead, compensation fell to the state and municipality where the unrest took place in a ratio of two to one. At the local level, committees enforced frugality in smaller ways – for example, by insisting that shopkeepers accept smaller panes of glass to replace large display windows as officials deemed the latter a mere luxury. The German Chamber of Congress reported "outrage" in their circles, described the law as a "direct invitation to loot," and predicted a devastating effect on credit, trade, and retail.[45] Nevertheless, these provisions, alongside growing stability, served their purpose. In 1928, the Ministry of the Interior reported no outstanding claims and considered the matter of tumult damage "concluded," at least in terms of the national budget.[46]

The issue came back to life when property losses spiraled again with the onset of the Great Depression and the so-called latent civil war between National Socialists and communists during the late Weimar Republic. In this tense economic and political climate, acts of vandalism and theft

[42] Reichskommissar, Ausschuss zur Feststellung von Entschädigungen für Aufruhrschäden, Nov. 23, 1923, BArch R 1501/116438.
[43] Knorr, Jan. 19, 1924, BArch R 1501/116431.
[44] *Reichsgesetzblatt*, Mar. 31, 1924, 381.
[45] Deutscher Industrie- und Handelstag to Reichswirtschaftsministerium, Feb. 21, 1924.
[46] Reichshaushaltsrechnung 1928, *Verhandlung des Reichstages* (Berlin, 1929), 671.

occurred not only in direct connection to demonstrations but also in the midst of everyday urban life. In October 1930, Nazis shattered display windows of the Wertheim department store and the Isidor Dobrin coffeehouse to celebrate their newly won seats in the Reichstag. *The Clothing Manufacturer* trade journal covered the incident in several issues and used it to frame the position of retailers across Germany in the context of rising levels of public violence. The article "Full Compensation for Tumult!" criticized the limitations of the current law. Indeed, the publication eagerly championed a return to the previous standard of the Prussian Tumult Law: "This kind of legal regulation is the state's most important duty to the taxpayer, namely the preservation of public order. Moreover, given enough publicity, full compensation by either the state or the community would perhaps serve as a lesson to the public to act against all forms of unrest, because the damages come out of the pocket of the taxpayer."[47] The German Retail Association similarly described the Tumult Law as too full of "clauses and exceptions" to be of much use. The association cheered on a sympathetic representative from the Economic Party (Wirtschaftspartei) who had demanded an answer on the floor of the Prussian State Parliament to the question, "Is the government prepared to provide adequate police protection in all shopping streets or to provide tax relief to victims for looting damage?"[48] Retailers detected "carelessness" among the authorities, who no longer feared the high costs of preventing violence.[49] They complained that if the state refused to pay damages, then it should at least deploy "its power sufficiently" to keep unrest away from commerce. Calls for greater compensation often went hand in hand with appeals for more aggressive policing. Each demand implied that the state had failed.

Even as they challenged the state to provide security and relief, business and property owners pursued "self-help" throughout the interwar period.[50] They took common security techniques and devices and enhanced their visibility and durability to correspond to the greater threat of violence. Shop owners might sleep in display windows at night. During particularly tense moments they might close entirely, pull heavy iron

[47] "Voller Schadenersatz des Staates bei Tumultschäden," *Der Konfektionär*, Nov. 1, 1930.

[48] "Strassentumulte und Plünderungen," *Deutsche Einzelhandels-Zeitung*, Nov. 1931.

[49] Pressedienst des Einzelhandels, "Vom Boykott zum Terror!" Aug. 26, 1932; Hauptgemeinschaft des Deutschen Einzelhandels to Reichswirtschaftsministerium, Aug. 31, 1932, R 3101/13859.

[50] For more on private security measures, see Molly Loberg, *The Struggle for the Streets of Berlin: Politics, Consumption, and Urban Space, 1914–1945* (Cambridge, 2018), chapter 4.

blinds down over the store windows and doors, and flee the area. Some merchants signed up for citizen militias, although such groups typically used rhetoric that was more aggressive than what they were prepared to back with action. Provisions of the Versailles settlement formally banned these groups in 1921. Businesses that could afford to do so hired private security such as watchmen and store detectives. Shops at the cutting edge of technology installed telephones to alert police to disturbances. Others in particularly unstable areas locked goods behind metal bars or shutters and encased sales counters in glass. When choosing security strategies, business owners carefully weighed risk against cost. These determinations depended, of course, on the political and economic context across Germany and within their own local community.

Private security measures aimed to preempt violence and thus substitute for insufficient or failed policing – that is, one type of state failure. Similarly, businesses turned to private insurance firms to fill the gaps in the Tumult Law. In 1929 and 1930, the Association of German Department Stores and Large Retailers insisted that in "politically and economically uncertain times" private riot insurance had become an "absolute necessity," especially because the state rejected so many claims for damages.[51] Yet private policies were problematic. Many fire and theft insurance policies explicitly excluded the consequences of war or riots. The categorization of the crime mattered, much as victims of a hurricane today might only receive payment for wind damage but not for damage due to flooding. Some German insurers perceived in postwar insecurity a window of opportunity and offered special policies to cover "civil commotion." They evaluated risks in terms of time and space and designed policies accordingly. Customers could purchase high-priced, short-term policies with a three-to-six-month term to cover moments of economic or political crisis. Insurers divided Germany into three zones with premiums based on the predicted level of hazard. Display windows required a special "riot risk" surcharge.

The experiment with private riot insurance, however, brought poor returns. Violence of this kind wreaked havoc upon the risk calculations of actuaries. Insurers found it difficult to charge premiums low enough to entice customers during more stable times and outside of the most precarious districts and, at the same time, charge premiums high enough to keep the private insurer afloat in the event of riot. Only particularly wealthy or

[51] *Jahresbericht des Verbandes Deutscher Waren- und Kaufhäuser*, 1929, 60; *Jahresbericht* 1930, 36.

fearful retailers took on such policies. In 1919, the German Association for the Protection of Insurance Customers complained that companies exploited customers' anxieties and ignorance of their legal rights to charge excessive premiums for riot insurance, just as they had during the war with aerial bombardment insurance.[52] Moreover, the premiums customers had paid evaporated if an insurer went under. By the late 1920s, German companies had largely retreated from this market and left the field open to foreign insurers, primarily Swiss and British firms.

Finally, the Tumult Law gave private insurers an excuse not to pay. A British insurance company dropped the Butter Landau grocery store chain after a series of lootings in 1931. The insurer encouraged the retailer to sue the city instead. A lawyer for Butter Landau described the situation as a national embarrassment because the insurance company had remarked that it could not do business "if such African conditions prevail in Berlin."[53] Retailers accepted and paid for market solutions to violence, but these too disappointed them.

The Tumult Law thus compelled constant reassessment of mass violence and the resulting obligations of the state within the context of shifting historical circumstances. The sense of diminishing law and order at the end of the Weimar Republic was twofold: an inability of the state to police the streets and a reluctance to compensate for this failure. Citizens did not simply endure violence but rather remained actively committed to legal and financial redress. Through their frustrations and disappointments, retailers articulated a clearer vision of the preconditions that the state must provide in order for businesses to survive. Free market solutions offered little relief against economic crisis and political turmoil.

9.4 NATIONAL SOCIALISM: THE UNEXPECTED COSTS OF "PUBLIC RAGE"

National Socialists often characterized high crime rates and political violence in public space as pathologies of the Weimar Republic. According to their own statistics, streets became safer once they assumed power. In 1934, the new director of the criminal police attributed the

[52] Deutscher Versicherungs-Schutzverband to Rat der Volksbeauftragten, Jan. 21, 1919, R 1501/116424. See also Ernst Nord, *Die Entwicklung des Deutschen Versicherungswesen in seiner Beziehung zum Weltkriege und Dessen wirtschaftlichen Wirkungen* (Berlin, 1922), chapter 4; Gerald Feldman, "Civil Commotion and Riot Insurance in Fascist Europe, 1922–1941," *Financial History Review* 10 (2003): 165–84.

[53] Butter Landau, Sep. 25, 1931, LAB A Pr.Br.Rep. 030, Nr. 7538.

decline in crime to the "perceptible revitalization of public morals in National Socialist Germany."[54] Of course, statistics and rhetoric of this kind neglected the violence caused by the party now in power. Even more than the Weimar Republic, the Nazi regime identified crowd sentiment as a source of its legitimacy. Yet, the very collective rage that the Nazis incited and instrumentalized brought their government into legal jeopardy under the Tumult Law.

Indeed, the law laid bare the contradictions between the Nazi Party's invocations of law and order and its valorization of violence. In the early months of 1933 professional associations that had advocated for the rights of retailers during the Weimar Republic faced an even more daunting challenge: to persuade the new National Socialist government to stop the violence and intimidation carried out by party members.[55] When attacks on Jewish shops erupted in March 1933, the German Chamber of Commerce perceived a broad economic danger in them. It warned key government ministries of the damage to state authority and to economic recovery if the government did not "revive trust." The Association of German Department Stores and Large Retailers expressed "extreme concern" after Hermann Göring snidely dismissed the need for police protection for Jewish shops facing such attacks.

Yet, like its predecessor the Weimar Republic, the Nazi regime inherited the legacy of the Tumult Law. Some Jewish business owners successfully petitioned for compensation for the March actions. The National Economic Court (*Reichswirtschaftsgericht*) decided in December that "domestic unrest" was the cause of damage to display windows and thus the Tumult Law applied.[56] Political ideology clashed with legal precedent, and the Nazis had not yet coordinated all areas of government, including the judiciary. Nazi leaders called for an organized nationwide boycott of Jewish shops on April 1, in part to channel their SA activists away from physical destruction and toward psychological intimidation. In the course of 1933–4, the Ministry of Economic Affairs repeatedly forbade destructive acts against Jewish shops by Nazi groups like the SA or the Combat League of the Commercial Middle Classes. Orders to

[54] "Seit der Machtübernahme durch die Nationalsozialisten ständiger Rückgang der Kriminalität," *Der Angriff*, Oct. 26, 1933.

[55] Deutscher Industrie- und Handelskammertag to Reichswirtschaftsminister, Mar. 10, 1933; Verband Deutscher Waren- und Kaufhäuser, Mar. 11 and 28, 1933, BArch R 3101/13859.

[56] Peter Longerich, *Politik der Vernichtung: Eine Gesamtdarstellung der nationalsozialistischen Judenverfolgung* (Munich, 1998), 34.

cease large-scale actions were issued with the aim of improving public perceptions of the regime and its supporters. These orders also protected the government and private insurers from compensation claims. But the assault on the rule of law was well underway. A 1934 decree for the "Settlement for Claims in Civil Law" enabled the minister of the interior to quash lawsuits by Jews against the state at will.[57]

Despite the chicanery that legalized the Nazis' ever-broadening antisemitic persecution, the Tumult Law lingered as a source of frustration. As late as 1938, officials faced a tangle of unintended legal and insurance problems caused by mass violence. On November 9, 1938, during the anniversary celebrations of the 1923 Hitler Putsch, the Nazi elite signaled their approval of collective reprisals against Jews for the assassination of junior diplomat Ernst vom Rath by Herschel Grynszpan in Paris. That night, SA troops and members of the Hitler Youth devastated synagogues, businesses, and residences across the country. They destroyed eight thousand stores. Fifteen hundred were looted. Losses in broken glass totaled between 8 million and 10 million RM.[58]

The government sought to create the impression that the *Kristallnacht* pogrom was a "spontaneous" outburst of popular rage. Such an impression was essential to Nazi propaganda. Orders instructed perpetrators to dress in civilian clothing rather than their uniforms. In Berlin, police arrested onlookers who dared to suggest that the perpetrators were party activists acting under orders. Yet, despite the value of such a performance for propaganda purposes, the impression of a popular crowd action meant that public and private schemes to compensate for rioting applied. The government would still be liable – not because of the instigation by party leaders or because of party members' participation – but because, if officials claimed that crowds caused the damage, this would trigger the provisions of the Tumult Law. Furthermore, it would affect private insurance payments. By 1938, few businesses possessed riot insurance, in part because both private insurers and the state had curbed policies that referred to any kind of public disorder. Nevertheless, some businesses maintained full coverage. One such example, a jewelry store in Berlin, estimated its losses at 1.7 million RM. And if the government denied that "tumult" had occurred, this would further open and

[57] Feldman, "Civil Commotion and Riot Insurance," 175.

[58] SD-Hauptamt, "Bericht für November," Dec. 7, 1938, in Otto Kulka and Eberhard Jäckel, eds., *The Jews in the Secret Nazi Reports on Popular Opinion in Germany, 1933–1945* (New Haven, CT, 2010), 340–3.

complicate the scope of claims. Private insurance companies would be compelled to pay benefits according to their regular policies on fire, theft, or vandalism. Moreover, an intricate set of separate policies might cover a single location. For example, an "Aryan" property owner might have a policy covering the glass, a Jewish retailer one that covered the shop interior, and a foreign distributor one that covered the goods. Insurance companies were anxious to avoid such payments. The regime would not concede either form of state liability, for starting or for failing to stop the violence. Nazi leaders certainly did not want Jews compensated for the violence.

It took more than a year for officials and insurance companies to work their way out of the legal and financial morass the regime had created. While these meetings and the correspondence were often tense, they happened quietly and behind closed doors. The first exchange between Nazi leadership and insurers happened on November 12, just days after the *Kristallnacht* pogrom. Representing the Ministry of the Interior, Wilhelm Stuckart settled the debate over the categorization of the unrest: "We do not acknowledge tumult." Hermann Göring interjected, "Absolutely right."[59] Following the meeting, officials invented a new law to recast victims as perpetrators and perpetrators as victims. The government ordered Jews to pay to the state an "atonement tax" of 1 billion RM to compensate for the loss of national wealth. The Law for the Restoration of the Appearance of the Street required Jewish proprietors to rapidly repair any damages to windows and facades and surrender any insurance payments to the state. Yet other, more complicated matters remained. While the 1934 decree effectively prohibited German Jews from suing the state, a significant amount of the damaged property belonged to other parties. Potential claimants included non-Jewish landlords, owners of recently "Aryanized" businesses, foreign business and property owners, Jews with foreign citizenship, and otherwise mistaken targets. These victims and their insurance companies were well aware of the Tumult Law. Even if the government could extricate itself from liability

[59] "Stenographische Niederschrift von einem Teil der Besprechung über die Judenfrage, Nov. 12, 1938," in *Trial of the Major War Criminals before the International Military Tribunal, Nuremberg, 14 November 1945–1 October 1946, v. 28* (Nuremberg, 1945–7), 1816-PS; "Verordnung über eine Sühneleistung der Juden deutscher Staatsangehörigkeit vom 12. November 1938," "Verordnung zur Wiederherstellung des Strassenbildes bei jüdischen Gewerbebetrieben vom 12. November 1938," *Reichsgesetzblatt*, Nov. 14, 1938, 1579–81. See also Gerald Feldman, *Allianz and the German Insurance Business, 1933–1945* (Cambridge, 2001), 190–235.

by citing the law's restrictions (e.g., need) or issue a decree to protect private insurers, this would certainly feed domestic discontent and foreign hostility. In December 1938 Heinrich Himmler, head of the SS and the increasingly coordinated and nationalized police force, ordered municipalities to report businesses that fell into this category for the purpose of compensation. These orders referred only to "*Kristallnacht* damage" without specifying the legal category of the disturbance or referring to the relevant law.[60] Although German Jews received no compensation, some foreigners and "Aryans" who suffered collateral damage did, mostly from private insurers. Since the government did not legally acknowledge tumult, traditional policies regarding fire, theft, and vandalism applied. German insurers agreed to these sums because the state compelled them to do so. At the same time they escaped the staggering sums owed to Jewish clients. Historians have described the decrees that followed *Kristallnacht* as examples of the cynical, brutal, and perverse nature of Nazi ideology because they recast victims as perpetrators. This is certainly accurate. But legal and bureaucratic precedent shaped these measures and made them both financially pragmatic and politically necessary.

9.5 FINAL THOUGHTS

The evolution of the Tumult Law marked a conceptual shift that took place over the course of the nineteenth and twentieth centuries as traditional notions of the state as a bulwark against threatening crowds gave way to ideals of the state as constituted by the aggregate of citizens and their rights. In Germany, governments that emerged through the upheavals of the early twentieth century were compelled to quantify and monetize not only the destruction of the preceding order but also the collective violence of their own citizens.

The Weimar Republic and the Nazi regime both staked their legitimacy on their ability to provide security and preserve orderly daily life, including an environment secure enough to conduct business. They went so far as to assume financial liability for "domestic unrest." The history of compensation thus reveals a continuity across revolutionary ruptures and different political systems in that the legitimacy of each state depended on its exclusive ability to both instigate and prevent violence.

[60] Reichsführer SS und Chef der Deutschen Polizei, Dec. 12, 1938, in Joseph Walk, ed., *Das Sonderrecht für die Juden im NS-Staat: Sammlung der gesetzlichen Massnahmen und Richtlinien, Inhalt und Bedeutung* (Heidelberg, 1981), 266.

The application of the 1850 Tumult Law and its subsequent iterations, however, created an expectation that the state would compensate for failed security and a deficient capitalist order. Moreover, these laws provided a framework through which citizens could pursue their challenges. This framework was powerful enough to undercut the revolutionary foundations of the Weimar Republic and, for certain protected classes of claimants, hold the Nazi regime liable for antisemitic violence. For very different reasons, neither the Weimar nor the Nazi state could fully meet its obligations under the Tumult Laws. But these governments dared not fully abandon their obligations for fear of undermining their legitimacy. Instead, the regularity of public violence compelled each government to limit its liabilities. In so doing, they retreated from their obligations through exceptional measures of their own: the Weimar Republic by invoking its financial instabilities and the National Socialist regime by shifting liability to the victims.

The Tumult Law shows the unexpected influence of insurance, law, and finance in shaping the meanings and consequences of violence, especially violence on a large scale. Definitions of domestic unrest evolved through the aggregation of claims. The Tumult Law reveals efforts to quantify the individual and societal costs caused by the collapse of states, economies, ideologies, and the rule of law. Such costs were meant to deter future violence. For their part, businesses assessed political risk when deciding whether to spend or invest. Businesses experienced violence during the interwar period under very different political systems. This compelled them to articulate the conditions that must exist for industry and commerce to function and flourish. They mobilized individually and collectively to call upon the state to provide these. Yet, their demands frequently failed.

PART IV

RACIALIZING CAPITALISM

10

Völkisch Banking?

Capitalism and Stuttgart's Savings Banks, 1933–1945

Pamela E. Swett

> The first savings banks in the world were founded in Germany. One of these savings banks was the Württembergische Landessparkasse in Stuttgart, the oldest saving institute in Württemberg. Although the founding of the WLsp coincided with the beginning of industrialization and the economic unfolding of the modern, so-called economic age, its founders were in no way "capitalist" in their motives. Their savings bank did not have its origins in profit; rather it was a social institution in the best sense of the word.[1]

This passage comes from a 1943 article in the *NS-Kurier* celebrating the 125th anniversary of the Württembergische Landessparkasse (WLsp). Ever since the 1931 banking crisis, banking, in general – big banks in particular – had been viewed warily by Germans, and the *Sparkassen* (savings banks) had worked tirelessly to emphasize that they were different – more trustworthy, more supportive of community interests over selfish, individual profit. In other words, the *Sparkassen* were, according to their most ardent supporters, "in no way 'capitalist'."[2] While this basic assertion had been central to the self-image of the *Sparkassen* before 1933, once the National Socialists came to power, it became even easier (and more politically prudent) to promote the perceived *völkisch* (nationally or ethnically distinctive) nature of these local public institutions. The *Sparkassen* had stood for *Gemeinnutz vor Eigennutz* (the common good over individual interests) for generations. Now was their chance to shine.[3]

[1] Wirtschaftsarchiv Baden-Württemberg, Stuttgart, Bestand: B 101 Bü 1111, "125 Jahre Württembergische Landessparkasse," *NS-Kurier*, Jun. 1, 1943.

[2] Ibid.

[3] Christoph Kopper agrees, calling the *Sparkassen* "the national-'socialist' ideal model of a credit institution that operated under public supervision and did not serve private profit-making

Embedded in this anticapitalist rhetoric we also find a much older, potent antisemitism that was revived during the Depression.[4] The greed of the large, private banks and other profit-driven capitalist ventures was conflated with "Jewish business practices." As party commentator Gottfried Feder explained in 1933, "the idea to control a people through money and with money accords perfectly with the mentality of the Jews."[5] And so, the *Sparkassen* were quick to proclaim that their business model was anything but "Jewish." Indeed, they insisted that the savings banks protected and fostered Germany's best values: hard work, thrift, and community spirit. The public relations campaign, long in the making but more confident after 1933, worked well. Party leaders like Interior Minister Wilhelm Frick applauded the savings banks for having nurtured "the most noble of German virtues [frugality and industry] since their founding, even in the hardest times."[6]

As Germans made their way back to employment in the mid-1930s, vast amounts of money found its way into institutions like the WLsp and its rival, the Städtische Sparkasse und Girokasse Stuttgart (Municipal Savings and Clearing Bank Stuttgart). Deposits increased still further under the conditions of severely restricted personal consumption and high labor productivity that marked the war years.[7] Adam Tooze concludes that about 1 billion RM were deposited each month during 1941 by

interests." *Zwischen Marktwirtschaft und Dirigismus: Bankenpolitik im Dritten Reich, 1933–1939* (Bonn, 1995), 21.

[4] On the Depression-era backstory see Martin H. Geyer, "What Crisis? Speculation, Corruption and the State of Emergency during the Great Depression," *Bulletin of the GHI* 55 (2014): 9–35.

[5] Gottfried Feder, *Die funktionelle Bedeutung des Geld- und Kreditwesens* (Berlin, 1933), 6; for another example of the same sort of praise for the history of public banking in Germany, in contrast to "Jewish" private banking, see Arthur Herrmann, *Zweihundert Jahre öffentliches Bankwesen* (Berlin, 1935).

[6] Bundesarchiv Berlin, NS6/492. Special edition of the *Deutsche Sparkassen-Zeitung*, Oct. 3, 1933. For more on the history of the *Sparkassen* see Pamela E. Swett, "Mobilizing Citizens and Their Savings: Germany's Public Savings Banks, 1933–1939," in Mary Lindemann and Jared Poley, eds., *Money in the German-Speaking Lands* (New York, 2017), 234–49. Also Hans Pohl, *Wirtschafts- und Sozialgeschichte der deutschen Sparkassen im 20. Jahrhundert* (Stuttgart, 2005), and Jens Piorkowski, *Die deutsche Sparkassenorganisation, 1924–1934* (Stuttgart, 1997).

[7] Two periods of consolidation at the end of 1933 and again in 1938 had reduced the number of *Sparkassen* in Württemberg from seventy to sixty-four and then to thirty-seven. The WLsp and the SSGS remained the two largest in the state. Manfred Biehal, *Der Württembergische Sparkassenverband, 1916–1982* (Berlin, 1984), 100, and Kopper, *Zwischen Marktwirtschaft und Dirigismus*, 75–7. Paul Thomes notes that in 1905 Württemberg was already the state most densely served by the *Sparkassen* network, with "a savings bank for every 1197 inhabitants or 10 square km." Paul Thomes, "German Savings Banks As Instruments of Regional Development up to the Second World War," in

individual account holders, and that much of this sum was then redirected toward the war effort by the state through the purchase of government bonds. This process has been termed "the silent financing of the war," though it was never kept secret from the population.[8] As one speech delivered during a rally for Saving-Week in 1942 at the Städtische Sparkasse Stuttgart explained:

> Without a doubt, work and saving are of decisive and critical importance during war. Still today the well-known word that is essential to leading the war is money, money, and again money. Because money is only another word for raw materials, tools, and labor, which are indispensable to the war effort, and which the individual, instead of taking and using himself, through saving – and that means renouncing immediate consumption – turns over to the state as a loan.[9]

Putting all this together, from the long history of the *Sparkassen* in towns and cities around the country to the central role they played during the war, it is clear these institutions were vital to individual Germans and to the national economy in peace and war. They also had a special position in the cultural fabric as particularly representative of perceived German virtues – hard work, thrift, community – the appraisal of which was heightened during the Third Reich. However, we know little about this sector.[10] How did these "most *völkisch*" of institutions operate during the Nazi era? In particular, how were National Socialism and capitalism intertwined in *Sparkassen* decision-making and self-representation? In what follows, I demonstrate that the logics of capitalism remained paramount in the minds of the savings bank managers: market competition; the belief in objective, evidence-based decision-making as the key to profit; and personal enrichment. However, their belief in capitalist principles did

Youssef Cassis, Gerald Feldman, and Ulf Olsson, eds., *The Evolution of Financial Institutions and Markets in Twentieth-Century Europe* (Aldershot, 1995), 146–7.

[8] Adam Tooze, *Wages of Destruction: The Making and Breaking of the Nazi Economy* (London, 2006), 354–5, including figure 15 on page 355.

[9] Wirtschaftsarchiv Baden-Württemberg, Stuttgart, Bestand B102, Bü 461 "Sparwoche Betriebsappel," Oct. 26, 1942. For a more public entreaty, see the speech by state secretary (Finance) Fritz Reinhardt on the eve of National Saving Day, Oct. 31, 1941. Complaints about *Kriegssparen* (war savings) also turn up in the SOPADE reports; see *Deutschland-Berichte der Sozialdemokratischen Partei Deutschlands (SOPADE)*, 1934–1940, vol. 7, *March 1940* (Salzhausen, 1980), 186–91.

[10] The focus in the literature has been firmly on the "big banks." See Harold James, *The Deutsche Bank and the Nazi Economic War against the Jews* (Cambridge, 2001), and *The Nazi Dictatorship and the Deutsche Bank* (Cambridge, 2004); Lothar Gall, *Der Bankier: Hermann Josef Abs* (Munich, 2004); Klaus-Dietmar Henke, ed., *Die Dresdner Bank im Dritten Reich*, 4 vols. (Munich, 2006); and Ludolf Herbst and Thomas Weihe, eds., *Die Commerzbank und die Juden* (Munich, 2004).

not make them any less useful to the regime, nor did it mean they did not support the aims of the dictatorship. It did, however, provide ways for these men to rationalize their own behavior and legitimize their support for the dictatorship as good for business and their customers.

10.1 SPARKASSEN IN THE NATIONAL SOCIALIST ECONOMY

Owing to the affinity between Nazi ideology and the savings banks' self-representation and status as public institutions, the *Sparkassen* were quickly brought into line and would go on to fulfill several essential roles in the Nazi economy. First, as spokesmen for the WLsp and other savings banks liked to trumpet, since their founding they had offered a way for Germans of meager means to grow their wealth, prepare for emergencies, and achieve long-term personal financial goals. In this way, on a micro level they were essential to the capitalist economy. These saving accounts were the sole financial investment for a large portion of the population. Over time, German men and women could see some growth to their savings that was either put toward private needs and wants – everything from Christmas presents and educational expenses to household goods and holidays – or left to accumulate, providing some sense of security for whatever lay ahead. No account was too small. And in 1930s Germany, the vast majority of individual accounts indeed remained small. In 1936, three-quarters of all personal savings accounts held less than 300 RM, and more than 50 percent held between 20 RM and 100 RM. However, by 1938, there were about 35 million of these accounts, which means about half of all Germans, including children, had a *Sparkasse* booklet in their name.[11] Despite the limited size of most accounts, they were promoted as a way for "Aryans" to participate in the material abundance that the regime promised was just around the corner. Few would enjoy it in the mid-1930s, but thanks to the *Sparkassen* everyone could prepare for its arrival.[12]

The second role the *Sparkassen* had always played in Germany's capitalist economy was as an affordable lender to small business. Since their founding in the nineteenth century, these public institutions had turned

[11] "Entwicklung der Spareinlagen der deutschen Sparkassen von 1924–1937," *Die Deutschen Sparkassen und ihre Organisation* (1938), 10.

[12] See further Pamela E. Swett, "Private Life in the People's Economy: Spending and Saving in Nazi Germany," in Elizabeth Harvey, Maiken Umbach, and Johannes Hürter, eds., *Private Life and Privacy in Nazi Germany* (Cambridge, 2019), 135–55.

community members' savings into loans for local businesses, safeguarding them in rough times and allowing for expansion in good times. The *Sparkassen* also helped finance public infrastructure and social projects and thereby served their communities in substantial ways. But they were also big business. By the interwar period their operations had expanded, making them in reality full-service banks. Savings, lending, payment transfers, even mortgages – *Sparkassen* did it all. Germans could avail themselves of fourteen thousand such deposit sites around the country, employing about fifty-six thousand men and women in the mid-1930s.[13]

However, the *Sparkassen* also faced challenges, which pushed their business model in new directions. First, owing to the high levels of debt many *Gemeinden* (municipalities) carried during the Depression, an emergency decree of 1931 prohibited *Sparkassen* from making further municipal loans and, with that change, the connection to community projects and social services declined dramatically.[14] Second, after 1933 private sector investment also declined as local businesses struggled first because of the Depression and then as a result of Reich policies that prioritized heavy industry. The number of new mortgages dried up as well, as home building slowed markedly. Finally, while public savings banks had always fallen under the authority of the ministries of the interior in each respective state, after 1933 the *Gauleiter* intervened regularly and local party leaders were moved into managerial roles with control over decisions large and small.[15] This concentration of power in the hands of party functionaries meant the *Sparkassen* came to play a key role in the nepotism, racial exclusion, and financial corruption later seen as hallmarks of the Nazi economy and society.[16]

Cut off from municipal lending and struggling to find adequate private-sector lending as the economy shifted away from consumer manufacturing, particularly after the introduction of the Four-Year Plan in 1936, the savings banks increasingly invested in government debt in order to respond to the Reich's unquenchable thirst for cash – a trend that culminated during

[13] Rudolf Lencer, "Der Mitarbeiter in der Sparkasse als der Träger der Sparidee," *Die Deutsche Volkswirtschaft*, no. 15 (1938), 551.

[14] Kopper, *Zwischen Marktwirtschaft und Dirigismus*, 149.

[15] What we see happening here with regard to state intervention in these communal banking institutions is reflective of a larger picture of declining municipal autonomy after 1933. Jeremy Noakes, "Die kommunale Selbstverwaltung im Dritten Reich," in Adolf M. Birke and Magnus Brechtken, eds., *Kommunale Selbstverwaltung/Local Self-Government: Geschichte und Gegenwart im deutsch-britischen Vergleich* (Munich, 1996), 65–81.

[16] Among others, Frank Bajohr, *Parvenüs und Profiteure: Korruption in der NS-Zeit* (Frankfurt, 2001), chapter 1.

the war years. For example, the WLsp's directors reported that historically only about 33 percent of the bank's portfolio had been invested in bonds, but by 1945, that figure had almost doubled to 63 percent.[17] These figures mirror trends at the state and national levels.[18] At the end of 1945 the WLsp also reported that it held about 420 million RM in savings deposits – 23 million more than the previous year – despite temporary periods of high withdrawal shortly before occupation and again in the fall of 1945 as denazification proceedings heated up.[19] In other words, rates of deposit at the nation's *Sparkassen* continued to climb throughout the Nazi era. Although some anxiety about the safety or accessibility of deposits was voiced in the last stage of the war and in the months that followed, the *Sparkassen* generally retained the trust of most Germans through the life and death of the regime.[20]

What follows explores examples of bank behavior, using primarily the WLsp but also the other large Stuttgart-area savings bank, the Städtische Sparkasse und Girokasse Stuttgart (SSGS), as a case study.[21] I examine the ways in which the banks' leaders, who, after 1933, increasingly supported regime policies, responded to changing circumstances and worked to stabilize their own institutions while also tolerating or profiting from corruption. Focusing briefly on three issues – *Gleichschaltung* (Nazification) within the *Sparkassen*, competition between the two *Sparkassen* and with other banking institutions in the area, and the banks' participation in regime policies, including the "Aryanization" of Jewish-owned property – it becomes clear that by championing an image

[17] Wirtschaftsarchiv Baden-Württemberg, Stuttgart, Bestand B101, Bü 97, Vorsteherrats-Sitzung, Nov. 21, 1945, 5–6.

[18] Biehal, *Der Württembergische Sparkassenverband*, 158–9. For a discussion of regional variation in the *Sparkassen* market, see Thomes, "German Savings Banks," 143–62. On *Sparkassen* and saving in the occupied territories and among foreign laborers in Germany, see Ingo Loose, *Kredite für NS-Verbrechen* (Munich, 2007), 187–208.

[19] Wirtschaftsarchiv Baden-Württemberg, Stuttgart, Bestand B101, Bü 1111, "420 Millionen RM Spareinlagen bei der Württembergischen Landessparkasse," *Stuttgarter Zeitung*, Jan. 9, 1936.

[20] Philipp Kratz makes the argument that stable deposit rates demonstrate trust in the regime. I am less confident that such an assertion can be made. What sound alternatives did people have? After all it was illegal to hoard funds and downright silly once mass bombing began. Kratz, "Sparen für das kleine Glück," in Götz Aly, ed., *Volkes Stimme: Skepsis und Führervertrauen im Nationalsozialismus* (Frankfurt, 2006), 59–79.

[21] The two banks joined forces to create the Landessparkasse-Girokasse on Apr. 1, 1975. After several further amalgamations, its current name is Landesbank Baden-Württemberg (LBBW). For another case study, see the Bavarian example by Frank Finzel, *Spuren: 175 Jahre Sparkasse Coburg: Hauptwege, Nebenwege, Irrwege* (Stuttgart, 1996).

of their work as firmly rooted in the support of local community members, the role of the *Sparkassen*'s leadership in abetting the regime and in personal corruption remained muted. It is not surprising that bank managers continued to seek the best deal for their customers. My point is that the presumption that business success should trump other considerations (such as the bank's own charter) shows the very strength of a capitalist mentality and the ways such a worldview could also aid the regime.

Not all of these men chose to get rich personally off of victims of the dictatorship, though some did. Others, however, looked the other way, in part at least because they believed that keeping the banks afloat somehow mitigated the crimes that were committed. As Roman Köster argues, capitalism's *Pathosgehalt* (emotional content) means individuals can "live in" it.[22] For these Stuttgart bankers, capitalism was a way of life. At the war's end these men publicly insisted that bank decisions had been based on a rational mathematics of impersonal and apolitical gains versus losses. At first glance this excuse seems a simple postwar fabrication, but behind closed doors over the preceding decade we can see this self-understanding at work.

Given the public nature of the *Sparkassen*, each institution was required by the recently enacted Law for the Restoration of the Civil Service to purge Jewish employees and those who held adversarial political positions in the spring of 1933. On April 27, a meeting was held of the Städtische Sparkasse's committee for *Beamten* (employees who had been granted status akin to that of civil servants). Present also were the director, Oesterle, and his deputy, Jetter. Representing the party, the Nazi city councilor, Hugo Kroll, had been invited as a guest to the meeting, but was absent owing to illness. Hermann Pfahler, a *Beamte* from the credit office, took the floor at the outset to declare that there are "people present in the firm, who do not belong to the party in power, and about whom the Directors are continually receiving [inflammatory] information." Oesterle shot back that "such things belong to the past" and that everyone should work to stop such gossip. Nonetheless, the next item on the agenda was the release of a "non-Aryan employee" named Gunz.[23] Oesterle pointed out quite plainly that the law must be followed, while Pfahler added his

[22] Roman Köster, "Transformationen der Kapitalismusanalyse und Kapitalismuskritik in Deutschland im 20. Jahrhundert," *Geschichte und Gesellschaft*, Special Issue 24 (2012), *Kulturen der Weltwirtschaft*, ed. Werner Abelshauser, 284–303, here 285.

[23] Wirtschaftsarchiv Baden-Württemberg, Stuttgart, Bestand B102, Bü 81, "Niederschrift über der Sitzung des Beamtenausschusses," Apr. 27, 1933. Since Gunz was an *Angestellte*, there was no legal requirement that he be let go.

personal dig that in Gunz's case "retirement" was especially warranted because he had not served in the Great War.

From there they moved quickly to non-Jews who might fall under the proscriptions of the legislation owing to their political views. Once again Pfahler was quick off the mark in declaring that one colleague, Götz, had supported an organization to fight antisemitism "and as such is to be viewed as an enemy of the National Socialist movement." Götz had also once allegedly used the term "Nazi oaf" at work, thereby demonstrating his antipathy to the movement and new regime. But Oesterle was hesitant about making the decision to fire Götz. He insisted on checking whether the directors had the authority to remove *Beamten*. Moreover, Oesterle explained that he was unfamiliar with Götz's political liaisons. While he did admit that Götz had a tendency to "scandalize and shock" his colleagues, Oesterle accepted the behavior as "just his way." Eventually Oesterle clarified his position: firing was too harsh a penalty, given that Götz was "a capable man with a fund of ideas." His skills trumped his political unreliability. In the end, the men decided to keep an eye on their colleague, but not remove him. Sidelined for the moment, Pfahler promised to take an active role in surveillance.

Two further *Beamten* were then discussed. One had been a member of the Republic-supporting Reichsbanner (a multiparty center-left organization); another had championed the Catholic Center Party. Pfahler insisted that "all be removed and that it be recommended to them that they draw a line under their pasts and begin to work in a national socialist sense." But the chair of the committee argued that the removal of Knospe, the Center Party supporter, "was hardly possible, since he is, as an advertiser for the building and loan association, at present irreplaceable."[24] We see in these examples the competing priorities that businesses, even publicly owned corporations, experienced in this period. Managers were not averse to *Gleichschaltung*. Some were enthusiastic about cleaning house, while others had at least reconciled themselves to following the law. There was no sense that they felt that the targeted men should somehow be defended or protected because the legislation was unjust. Rather they balked when their colleagues' present value as bright and productive contributors to the Sparkasse's capitalist aims was outweighed by the potential financial disadvantages of retaining the services of non-Nazis.[25] It is worth repeating,

[24] Ibid., Sitzung des Beamtenausschusses, Apr. 27, 1933.

[25] Pohl cites other instances in which so-called political enemies retained their *Sparkassen* positions or, as in one case, regained a position after first being let go during

however, that no one declared Herr Gunz's service to the bank more valuable than the consequences of keeping a Jewish colleague on staff.

Hermann Pfahler would go on to be an instrumental player in the *Gleichschaltung* of both of Stuttgart's *Sparkassen*. In fact, in July 1933, he requested leave from his normal duties at the Städtische Sparkasse until October 1, in order to take up an opportunity offered by the body coordinating *Gleichschaltung* in savings banks at the national level to lead the process for the state of Württemberg.[26] But even for men like Pfahler who were ideologically committed to the new regime, politics and business were intertwined and indeed capitalist aims could be used to achieve political ends. Later that summer, Pfahler wrote to city councilor Kroll, his party colleague and personal friend. He noted that, in his new position for the Württembergische Sparkassen und Giroverband (Association of Wurttemberg Savings and Clearing Banks) (WSGV) he had been to a meeting of the national association in Berlin. There he had heard about some financial irregularities within the Stuttgart *Girokasse*. He relayed the information to Kroll, thrilled that the accounting errors might lead to the downfall of Oesterle and Jetter, who had overruled him two months earlier.[27] Unfortunately for Pfahler, that never came to pass, which could explain why he left the SSGS when his work for the WSGV came to an end, taking up a position as a director at the WLsp, where he would stay until 1938.[28]

That the SSGS wanted to hold onto its best adman, Knospe, despite his troublesome political views should not come as a surprise. Regardless of the image of these banks, which was bolstered by Nazi ideals of *bodenständige* (down-home) institutions that provided a public service and rejected selfish capitalist interests, the *Sparkassen* were locked in

Gleichschaltung. The Catholic man was considered to have an "above average skill set" and was rehired, even though he still refused to sign his memos with "Heil Hitler." Pohl, *Sparkassen*, 171.

[26] Wirtschaftsarchiv Baden-Württemberg, Stuttgart, Bestand B102, Bü 81. Letter from Pfahler to the Direktion der Stätdtischen Sparkasse Stuttgart, Jul. 1, 1933.

[27] Wirtschaftsarchiv Baden-Württemberg, Stuttgart, Bestand B102, Bü 81. Letter from Pfahler to Kroll, Jun. 29, 1933. Always scheming, Pfahler also refers to Oesterle's "property speculation and other risky business in the sum of 15 to 20 million RM" in a letter to Minister President Mergenthaler on the same day.

[28] At this point, Pfahler took a pay cut to return to his original employer, the SSGS. His former colleagues speculated that "personal reasons" were at play as well as the fact that Oesterle was near to retirement from the Städtische Sparkasse in 1938, and the younger Pfahler probably strategized that a return offered "better chances" of advancement. Wirtschaftsarchiv Baden-Württemberg, Stuttgart, Bestand B101, Bü 96-I, Vorsterrats-Sitzung, Mar. 19, 1938, 14.

a highly competitive market with one another and with other types of banks. The two *Sparkassen* discussed in this chapter were no exceptions. The WLsp and SSGS tried to differentiate between themselves in order to carve out market niches that offered the appearance that each was above competition. As the oldest bank in the state, the WLsp always returned to its 1818 founding and its promise to serve even the poorest in the region. The SSGS had a foothold in the city center among the more upwardly mobile. In private, however, the WLsp leadership cast aspersions at all "other" *Sparkassen*, especially the SSGS, for courting the "middle classes."[29] The WLsp leadership believed that these other public institutions had always regarded the WLsp enviously, because of its historic market dominance, and sought to dilute its influence through control of the regional association, the WSGV.[30]

An obvious way to compete in this tight market was to attract more customers by opening more branches and deposit stations, and both *Sparkassen* sought to expand in this way as the economy stabilized in the mid-1930s.[31] However, the WLsp claimed that the other *Sparkassen* and the WSGV worked together through "anti-*Landessparkasse* business politics ... to impede [its] ability to set up full-time branches in larger cities."[32] And there seems to be some truth to these claims. In 1934, the Nationalsozialistische Deutsche Arbeiterpartei (National Socialist German Workers' Party) (NSDAP) city councilman and friend of Hermann Pfahler, Hugo Kroll, wrote to Stuttgart's mayor and charged the WLsp with sales practices that belied "truth and good faith" and were directed squarely against the SSGS. He went on to demand that the WLsp's request to open new branches be prohibited and that the mayor apply for permission from the Württemberg and Reich economics ministries for the Städtische Sparkasse to open branches in all provincial towns within twenty kilometers of Stuttgart.[33] Two years later, after Gauleiter

[29] Wirtschaftsarchiv Baden-Württemberg, Stuttgart, Bestand B101, Bü 996. Letter to Johannes Metzler from the WLsp, Jun. 17, 1938.

[30] Wirtschaftsarchiv Baden-Württemberg, Stuttgart, Bestand B101, Bü 96-II, WLsp Vorsteherrats-Sitzung, Dec. 20, 1940, 1–13 (quotation from 6–7; emphasis in the original). The WSGV was founded in 1886.

[31] Wirtschaftsarchiv Baden-Württemberg, Stuttgart, Bestand B101, Bü 424. Letter from the SSGS Verwaltungsrat to the WSGV requesting permission to establish new deposit sites, Dec. 21, 1935.

[32] Wirtschaftsarchiv Baden-Württemberg, Stuttgart, Bestand B101, Bü 96-II, WLsp Vorsteherrats-Sitzung, Dec. 20, 1940, 1–13 (quotation from 10).

[33] Wirtschaftsarchiv Baden-Württemberg, Stuttgart, Bestand B101, Bü 1114. Letter from Stadtrat Kroll to Oberbürgermeister, Stuttgart, Nov. 14, 1934.

Murr threatened to close the WLsp altogether, precipitating the integration of more party functionaries into the bank's leadership to satisfy Württemberg's top Nazi, the two banks settled on a plan in which each promised not to encroach further on the other's prime markets.[34]

Although that agreement may have mollified the situation to some extent, an article about the state of Württemberg published at the very end of 1938 in the national journal *Sparkasse* noted that the competition among the region's savings banks and between them and the private banks was "not to be underestimated" and had led to "many selfish business methods," which cast a shadow of "disrepute" on the entire industry.[35] Jockeying for position in the crowded field continued into the war – for example, the Städtische Sparkasse sent unsolicited letters to wives of servicemen encouraging them to open accounts at SSGS branches if they found they had extra income now that their husbands had left for war. The WLsp fired off an angry communiqué to its cross-town rival after realizing some of these letters were going to their own account holders, demanding that the SSGS halt the practice, which contravened fair competition rules.[36]

While the climate in Stuttgart may have been particularly contentious, there is no reason to believe conditions were much better elsewhere. In 1935 and 1936, there were repeated reminders of Reich-level regulations meant to curb competition among banks. For example, *Sparkassen* wishing to implement a pick-up service (*Abholverfahren*) were reminded that banks could only offer to pick up the deposits of *existing* customers. In other words, banks were not allowed to poach one another's clients by showing up at their homes. The regularity with which such instructions were circulated before and during the war indicates this measure was likely frequently violated.[37] Competition between the public savings banks and private banks also continued unabated, and it was often Nazi officials who flouted laws and regulations. Christoph Kopper notes that in some towns, the overlap in personnel between Nazified city bureaucracies and *Sparkassen* management meant coordinated pressure was applied to

[34] Wirtschaftsarchiv Baden-Württemberg, Stuttgart, Bestand B101, Bü 424. WLsp memo, Aug. 28, 1936.

[35] Wirtschaftsarchiv Baden-Württemberg, Stuttgart, Bestand B102, Bü 59, "Württemberg," *Sparkasse* (Dec. 12, 1938), 402.

[36] Wirtschaftsarchiv Baden-Württemberg, Stuttgart, Bestand B101, Bü 424. Letter from the WLsp to the SSGS, Aug. 29, 1940.

[37] Wirtschaftsarchiv Baden-Württemberg, Stuttgart, Bestand B102, Bü 85, "Wettbewerbsabkommen und Zwecksparaktion," no date, likely 1940.

funnel business away from private banks. In at least one municipality, the result of such efforts was that city workers were prohibited from setting up automatic wage deposits to any accounts other than those held at the town's *Sparkasse*.[38]

10.2 CAPITALISM AND CORRUPTION

The *Sparkassen* were competing for customers who would entrust their savings to their institutions, but they were also competing increasingly among themselves for investment opportunities for those funds. The credit market was drying up as the regime pushed the economy toward war, leading to a retraction in consumer goods manufacturing, retail, and local building. Given the rather slim gains to be made in their traditional areas of engagement, the *Sparkassen* sought to diversify their portfolios in new directions. Offering a so-called *Arisierungskredite* (Aryanization credit) to local businessmen, financing ventures that did not fit their small-business mandate, and partnering on state-funded industrial projects provided opportunities for new investment, but such strategies also meant more involvement by state and party officials. As public institutions, the *Sparkassen* had always been regulated by the ministries of the interior of the *Land* (state) in which they were established, but the *Gauleiter* (alongside the interior minister and his representatives) played an increasingly active role in Stuttgart's *Sparkassen* as the 1930s wore on. Although the forced retirement and termination of some bank employees in the early days of the regime had led to the inclusion of more party-friendly voices throughout all levels of the institution, in 1936, the WLsp leadership shifted quite substantially in favor of the regime.[39] In July of that year, as part of a Ministry of Finance proposal to rationalize Württemberg's banking industry, the WLsp was threatened with closure. Otto Weiss, handpicked by Württemberg Gauleiter and Reich governor (Reichsstatthalter) Wilhelm Murr, despite having no prior banking experience, was hired into the bank's leadership as part of a deal to keep the bank open. As soon as Weiss was voted in by the board of directors, the chairman wrote to Murr directly, confirming Weiss's appointment and

[38] Kopper, *Zwischen Marktwirtschaft und Dirigismus*, 90.

[39] Wirtschaftsarchiv Baden-Württemberg, Stuttgart, Bestand B101, Bü 1070/1. The WLsp circulated a spreadsheet among its branches asking managers to comment on a variety of categories for each employee, such as party affiliation or worldview, before January 30, 1933, and to add other "political comments." One branch manager in Balingen was cited, for example, for refusing to raise the swastika flag on the Day of Potsdam.

asking in return for "his protection on the matter of the bank's continued existence," adding solicitously that the WLsp has "always fulfilled its duties to the people and state and will continue to do so in the future."[40]

In 1937, the supervisory board was expanded with the addition of several party functionaries "so that the ties between the WLsp and the party can be expressed anew."[41] In 1938, there was another major reshuffling of the leadership. Pfahler was leaving once again for the SSGS, and it was decided that the bank management would go from a team of four directors to two. The proposed leaner structure, and the decision to promote the state and party favorite, Weiss, to work alongside Otto Hill, was brought to the board, already approved by the interior minister and Gauleiter Murr. As one board member, Herr Mailänder, answered when asked whether he supported the changes: "The Gauleiter has given his support as well as the supervising authorities. So what, indeed, can one man like me say about it?"[42] "And yet," Mailänder added, "I would like to make a conscientious and independent decision, if I am going to be a member of this board," and would therefore request that such "information [in future] be circulated among the members at least one week before the meetings." In addition to his concerns about process, Mailänder also wondered aloud about the amount of money paid out to those involved in the shake-up, including Pfahler, who was receiving 4,000 RM even though he was leaving of his own accord for the WLsp's

[40] Wirtschaftsarchiv Baden-Württemberg, Stuttgart, Bestand B101, Bü 997. See the memo dated July 28, 1936, and Murr's follow-up on October 30, 1936, reassuring the WLsp that the Sparkasse was out of the woods for the time being. Murr was an "old fighter" who remained loyal to Hitler until the end. Murr killed himself in 1945. He had received the post of Gauleiter in 1928 and Reichsstatthalter in 1933. Besides his loyalty to Hitler, Murr was known for his limited intelligence and the ruthless administration of his offices with the help of a small "Gau-clique." For a short biographical sketch, see Joachim Scholtyseck, "'Der Mann aus dem Volk' Wilhelm Murr, Gauleiter und Reichsstatthalter in Württemberg-Hohenzollern," in Michael Kissener and Joachim Scholtyseck, eds., *Die Führer der Provinz: NS-Biographien aus Baden und Württemberg* (Konstanz, 1997), 477–502 (quotation from 489). To get a sense of how he operated, see Hartmut Berghoff and Cornelia Rauh, *The Respectable Career of Fritz K.* (New York, 2015).

[41] Wirtschaftsarchiv Baden-Württemberg, Stuttgart, Bestand B101, Bü 96-I "Vorsteherrats-Sitzung," Jul. 7, 1937, 14. See also the meeting of February 24, 1937, for the addition of Gau Propaganda Chief Adolf Mauer as board member. Another example would be Walter Reihle, who was both Gauwirtschaftsberater for Württemberg and a director at the SSGS, as noted in Gerhard Kratzsch, *Der Gauwirtschaftsapparat der NSDAP* (Münster, 1989), appendix.

[42] Wirtschaftsarchiv Baden-Württemberg, Stuttgart, Bestand B101, Bü 96-I "Vorsteherrats-Sitzung," Mar. 19, 1938, 15.

cross-town rival.[43] Finally, he echoed the words of another member of the committee who had also doubted the efficacy of having two directors share authority equally. Who ultimately would be in charge? Or as Mailänder put it, referencing the zeitgeist of 1938, the new design "contradicts the *Führerprinzip* (leader principle). If that rule is to be followed, there should only be one."[44]

In the following months, with its new Gau-approved, leaner management structure in place, the WLsp became a clear business partner for the regime and a conduit for personal gain by bank managers and local party leaders. The WLsp was quickly given the opportunity to become a chief lender to Stuttgart's consumer cooperative of more than fifty thousand members. As security for credit amounting to more than 1 million RM, the bank received the mortgages on more than a dozen properties in the city and its environs. The buildings were in good condition and were of mixed use, including residential and commercial properties. The prize possession was the address that held a state-of-the-art, industrial-sized bakery that "could meet the needs of military headquarters in three or four days." While the opportunity was welcome, Mailänder raised the potential of "political consequences." He was not worried about the past links between Marxist politics and consumer co-ops; those days were long gone. Rather he feared that small business owners, the WLsp's traditional customer base, would see this partnership as a betrayal. Weiss noted that in Heilbronn, working with the local co-op had only led to an increase in customers for the lending *Sparkasse*. Mailänder, however, reiterated that the bank's small and middle-sized businesses must be prioritized. He even wondered aloud whether working with such a large business partner would contravene the institution's charter. But Weiss insisted that, given the credit freeze, it was important for the *Landessparkasse* to find "alternative advantageous places for their money beyond government bonds."[45] Moreover, their rivals at the

[43] In postwar testimony Gustav Himmel, a member of the WLsp board at the time, claimed that "the outsider" Weiss had been foisted on the bank by Gauleiter and state president of Württemberg Wilhelm Murr and that his arrival signaled to those outside the bank that the "institution was now fully in the hands of the party." Wirtschaftsarchiv Baden-Württemberg, Stuttgart, Bestand B101, Bü 970, Gustav Himmel, Apr. 29, 1948, p. 5. According to the 1947 testimony of board member Otto Hill, Weiss had worked for Reichsleiter Max Amann as the head of the NS-press for Württemberg. Wirtschaftsarchiv Baden-Württemberg, Stuttgart, Bestand B101, Bü 970, Otto Hill, Oct. 23, 1947, p. 4.

[44] Ibid., p. 17.

[45] Wirtschaftsarchiv Baden-Württemberg, Stuttgart, Bestand B101, Bü 96-II, "Vorsteherrats-Sitzung," Dec. 15, 1938. A ban on municipal loans by *Sparkassen* was put in place in 1931 and remained in effect until 1941. Biehal, *Der Württembergische Sparkassenverband*, 101.

Städtische Sparkasse had been lenders to the co-op, and that hadn't hurt their reputation. The board consented to the deal. In this case, the party's man, Weiss, made a purely capitalist argument about staying competitive through investment, even if the object of investment pulled them away from their more traditional customer base. This is not to say that Weiss did not also have the party's long-term goals in mind. Rather it illustrates the point that capitalist arguments remained both convenient and compelling in this context.

While the case of the co-op caused some controversy among the supervisory board, because at first glance, it was a decision that prioritized financial gain over the WLsp's traditional *völkisch* focus on small businesses, there were also new opportunities to combine Nazi ideology and profit-making. The local financial market may have been shrinking throughout the decade, but there was new business to be done in extending credit to firms "Aryanizing" Jewish-owned companies. At the start of November 1939, the supervisory board received data on the current standing of fifteen loans the banks categorized as *Arisierungskredite* totaling more than 3 million RM. Some were paid out to private investors directly, including to Director Otto Weiss (300,000 RM), and others went to business owners who hoped to snap up Jewish-owned competitor firms, or companies in related industries, at a fraction of their value. After presenting the status of each loan, Chairman Hill remarked that at interest rates around 5 percent, the bank was doing very well with these investments. No discussion followed.[46] Toward the end of the war, the WLsp still held the majority of these loans amounting to a sum of 2.5 million RM. Several of the loans had been recently refinanced with the assistance of military or civilian authorities.[47] Beyond making the theft of Jewish property financially possible, the WLsp also approved personal and business loans and mortgages to friends and officials – individuals with connections to the party – some of which were granted without collateral. Weiss, Hill, Pfahler, even Gauleiter Murr, and several others from the bank personally benefited from such arrangements, receiving tens of thousands of Reich marks each in personal loans.[48]

[46] Wirtschaftsarchiv Baden-Württemberg, Stuttgart, Bestand B101, Bü 96-II, "Vorsteherrats-Siztung," Nov. 2, 1939. Weiss's loan went to the "purchase" of the Kahn brothers' linen mill between Stuttgart and Ulm in the village of Laichingen.

[47] Wirtschaftsarchiv Baden-Württemberg, Stuttgart, Bestand B101, Bü 96-II "Vorsteherrats-Sitzung," Jun. 15, 1944, p. 13.

[48] Wirtschaftsarchiv Baden-Württemberg, Stuttgart, Bestand B101, Bü 386. See the spreadsheet compiled by the bank in 1947 that is divided into three categories: "Party-linked loans," "Aryanization loans," and "House loans." It is not clear whether the "House

One set of loans stands out among the rest – those for the establishment of a concrete plant southwest of Stuttgart in Dotternhausen. The WLsp entered into this first direct business partnership with the regime in December 1938. In the discussions about the venture, the language of financial capitalism masked the political and military objectives of the site, even as the investment was found to be a failure. Ambitious local businessman and leader of the Gau bureau for technology (*Amt für Technik*) Rudolf Rohrbach was seeking sizable funds to build and operate a cement factory, a (strictly confidential) project that "is in accordance with the Four Year Plan and has the support of General Inspector Dr. Todt."[49] Rohrbach also had approval from the Reich Ministry of Economic Affairs, and his financial plan called for an investment of 3.8 million RM, 1–1.5 million of which was to come from the WLsp. There was a current shortfall in cement production, the board was told, and Dr. Todt estimated that cement needs would outpace existing production for the next fifteen years – so profit from this site was "undoubtedly assured." Rohrbach also believed that fuel could be refined from the oil shale reserves on the land, leading to even greater profits.

A joint-stock company was created with Rohrbach as individually liable, though the Württembergische Bank, the Handels- und Gewerbebank in Heilbronn, the Heinrich Taxis firm, and three other construction companies all held stock. The biggest single investor would be the WLsp. Articulating his support for the project, Weiss explained that the interest rate for this massive loan would be set high (5.5 percent), so the bank stood to gain handsomely. For those colleagues who may have been worried that such a large deal strayed from their *völkisch* mandate, Weiss again reminded them that the interest generated would allow the WLsp to continue supporting the bank's small savers – the customers "of lesser means." Some of the board members remained skeptical, given that a similar project in Holzheim in 1930 had ended in failure. But Rohrbach and Weiss promised that this location was better, bigwigs like Todt were

loans" are mortgages on new properties or renovations of existing dwellings. In the case of new properties, some addresses may be the former homes of Jewish émigrés – "Aryanization" of a different sort.

[49] Wirtschaftsarchiv Baden-Württemberg, Stuttgart, Bestand B101, Bü 96-II "Vorsteherrats-Sitzung," Nov. 7, 1938, 3–13. Rohrbach plays a substantial role as a member of the regional party and business elite in Berghoff and Rauh's study of Fritz Kiehn. As they report, Rohrbach was "a young, ambitious, and educated party functionary, full of moral rigor and a socially motivated ideological enthusiasm for education." Berghoff and Rauh, *Respectable Career of Fritz K.*, 89.

enthusiastic, and new technologies would make production more efficient. The board gave its consent.[50]

At the beginning of 1942, the board was told that the construction was complete, though production data were not yet disclosed, and (more alarmingly) an additional 3.5 million RM was needed to complete the mechanics to produce fuel and to counter rising industrial costs associated with the war. This sum was to be shared by the two banks (WLsp and Württembergische Bank) as the rest of the investor group declared its inability to raise more funds.[51] By September the total needed more than doubled from 3.5 million RM to more than 7.5 million RM, with the WLsp expected to pay two-thirds of the total. Cement and lime production were now underway, but the problems with the fuel refinery meant the project was still deep in the red.

Rohrbach, who was given the floor to explain the situation to the supervisory board, blamed the lack of a trained workforce for some of the early difficulties. He had since turned to Soviet POWs who had impressed him, and he declared that his long-term plan was to run the plant "exclusively with Russian POWs." The initial shortcomings in staff meant the machinery was not closely monitored, he added, which had led to "almost daily" breakdowns. Rohrbach remained insistent, however, that in the coming year, the situation would turn around. The Reich government still stood behind the operation, securing 4.1 million RM of the newly requested funds and providing additional tax relief. Alongside Rohrbach's presentation, some members of the board described the positive impressions they had taken from a visit to the site. Others noted that Rohrbach seemed on top of the situation and trusted his view that profit was just around the corner. What was never under discussion were the political and military reasons for the loans. The shortages the German war machine faced were not mentioned. The calls by the nation's leaders for increased production were not repeated. Nor was a patriotic exhortation ever made to support this seemingly troubled project despite its difficulties. Rather the board discussed the proposal as it might have done a loan for a shopkeeper hoping to expand in 1935: Was the expertise present to make the project successful? Would the bank see a profit from its investment? Rohrbach seemed to have a way forward, and so the board voted to

[50] Wirtschaftsarchiv Baden-Württemberg, Stuttgart, Bestand B101, Bü 96-II "Vorsteherrats-Sitzung," Nov. 7, 1938, 3–13.

[51] Wirtschaftsarchiv Baden-Württemberg, Stuttgart, Bestand B101, Bü 96-II "Vorsteherrats-Sitzung," Jan. 27, 1942, 13–15.

back the additional credit requested.[52] Did the men really believe Rohrbach's arguments about the potential profitability of the project? It is impossible to know. They may have recognized the project was as unlikely to succeed as other German strategies in the latter half of the war. What interests men more is that the men found it easier to articulate their support for the project by marshaling capitalist arguments than by invoking the language of defensive war. In the summer of 1944, six years after the first loan had been extended, the factory was still losing money for its investors.[53]

10.3 CONCLUSION

What sorts of conclusions can we draw from small financial institutions like the WLsp and SSGS? It is really no surprise that the two banks discussed here competed in the market, despite their anticapitalist, pro-little-man rhetoric. It does, however, speak to the misgivings many Germans harbored about capitalism that their financial institutions would be wary of admitting that they participated in a competitive market with all its attendant bad behaviors. In fact, the public's anxieties about the security of their hard-earned money were increasing in the lead-up to the war, effecting changes in customer behavior. Even though most account holders continued to deposit their "excess earnings" in the local *Sparkassen* after 1939, they increasingly chose short-term savings plans, despite lower interest rates – wary of inflation and the banks' increasing reliance on government paper.[54] In these decisions, German savers remained loyal to the regime and kept a stake in a war most hoped would be won, but avoided unnecessary risk – a capitalist calculation indeed.

The focus of this chapter, however, has been the ways in which the actions of leaders within these financial institutions followed a similar

[52] Wirtschaftsarchiv Baden-Württemberg, Stuttgart, Bestand B101, Bü 96-II "Vorsteherrats-Sitzung," Sep. 15, 1942, 1–14.

[53] Wirtschaftsarchiv Baden-Württemberg, Stuttgart, Bestand B101, Bü 96-II "Vorsteherrats-Sitzung," Jun. 15, 1944, 13–15.

[54] Wirtschaftsarchiv Baden-Württemberg, Stuttgart, Bestand B101, Bü 96-II, Vorsteherrats-Sitzung, Dec. 20, 1940, 14. The WLsp reported that before the war two-thirds of account holders chose long-term plans and one third chose short, but from the onset of the war these figures had reversed. *Sparkassen* holdings in government paper increased from 2.27 billion RM in 1933 to 8.1 billion RM in the summer of 1939. The amount had risen to almost 50 billion RM by September 1944. Figures from Pohl, *Sparkassen*, 207 and 209.

calculus. Decisions were fashioned as rational, apolitical choices – good if they benefited the financial outlook of the banks, bad if they did not. When regime supporters like Pfahler or Weiss presented a choice based on ideology, like firing an anti-Nazi colleague, they faced resistance if the value the person represented to the bank outweighed his liabilities. When discussions were held about whether to pour more funds into the unprofitable cement factory, the conversation never turned to the desperation of the government and military to produce more fuel, cement, and lime. Rather the arguments for and against supporting the production site revolved solely around the financial outlook of the deal. We should not conclude that these men were apolitical. They were well aware of the subtext for the concrete firm as critical to the war effort. And yet, neither the military conflict nor their duty to the nation was ever mentioned in discussions of the project. Instead, capitalism gave them a framework within which to live and work that allowed them to make decisions with criminal implications without further reflection on their behavior and its consequences.[55]

Did that capitalist framework transform over time? In other words, did the definition of what was "good for the bank" differ in 1942 from what it had been in 1932, or 1902? The answer is certainly yes in each instance. And these shifting boundaries are, in part, what makes capitalism so adaptable and ultimately so robust in times of crisis. In the case of *Sparkassen* strategy after 1933, the goal lines had clearly been moved. External pressure or coercion played a part at times, but, alongside such intervention, the definition of acceptable capitalist behavior had been extended to include actions formerly considered illegal or immoral.[56] It was still capitalism – the long-term aims of investing in local individuals and businesses remained – but the strategies for achieving such aims had expanded markedly. Furthermore, it would appear that individuals brought in to represent the party, like Otto Weiss, whose background in

[55] Ingo Köhler makes the point that reinterpreting Jewish property as "plundered national property" helped legitimize the expropriation. Similarly, evaluating political decisions in terms of profit also legitimized actions taken by these men. Köhler, "The Dispossession of the Jews and the Europeanization of the Holocaust," in Hartmut Berghoff and Jürgen Kocka, eds., *Business in the Age of Extremes* (Cambridge, 2013), 172–203, here 201.

[56] Thomas Welskopp makes a similar argument about the fluid nature of the boundary between legal and illegal behavior when discussing capitalist strategies during Prohibition in the United States, for example. See Thomas Welskopp, "Zukunft bewirtschaften. Überlegungen zu einer praxistheoretisch informierten Historisierung des Kapitalismus," *Mittelweg* 36 (1: Praktiken des Kapitalismus): 81–97, here 93.

finance was negligible, actually grew into the role of capitalist agents. In other words, while coercion and fear undoubtedly remained part of the business culture, during the mid-1930s the party officials who had moved into the *Sparkassen* also demonstrated that they could be valuable in the increasingly competitive financial marketplace.

If profit for the bank was seen only in positive terms, regardless of whether that profit was the result of the dispossession of Jewish property or pursued through the exploitation of POW labor, how did the men understand the personal benefits of corruption that resulted from the granting of loans to party friends and bank employees? (There was, of course, significant overlap between these two categories.) Corruption at the WLsp did come to light after the war. In 1947, the bank's executive was charged first by the local *Gewerkschaftszeitung* (trade union newspaper) and shortly thereafter in a similar manner by Stuttgart's Sozialdemokratische Partei Deutschlands (German Social Democrat Party) (SPD) newspaper, the *Volkswille,* with having given preferential credit arrangements to themselves and local party bigwigs before 1945.[57] The bank's managers, some of whom survived the war (Otto Weiss died on the eastern front in the last months of the conflict), defended their actions and denied all charges of corruption.[58] They did so once again by defending the capitalist value of these arrangements, which could only have been based on rational, value-neutral decision-making, if they were good for business. Otto Hill, chair of the supervisory board from 1937, insisted in postwar testimony, for example, that it had been a very competitive moment in the market and that all banks had to work hard to win customers. Moreover, Hill continued:

> All credit applications were evaluated in the credit office by experienced staff and reviewed by the management team, and only after thorough discussion were they approved .... All personal factors were put aside, and only purely objective considerations were evaluated. Beyond the required guarantees, the political position of the creditor was in no way taken into consideration.[59]

[57] Copies of the *Volkswille* article "Gemeinnütz – wie Sie ihn sahen ... " (Jul. 26, 1947) and the first article that offered substance to the rumours of corruption, "Wir fordern Aufklärung!" *Die Gewerkschaftszeitung* (Apr. 15, 1947): 108, can be found in Wirtschaftsarchiv Baden-Württemberg, Stuttgart, Bestand B101, Bü 386.

[58] Weiss was called to Wehrmacht service on June 16, 1942. The notice of his death circulated at the bank on December 14, 1944. Wirtschaftsarchiv Baden-Württemberg, Stuttgart, Bestand B101, Bü 84.

[59] Wirtschaftsarchiv Baden-Württemberg, Stuttgart, Bestand B101, Bü 970, Otto Hill, Oct. 23, 1947, p. 11. Hill replaced Gustav Himmel as chair of the supervisory board in 1937. Wirtschaftsarchiv Baden-Württemberg, Stuttgart, Bestand B101, Bü 96-I "Vorsteherrats-Sitzung," Feb. 24, 1937.

It is easy to see why Hill would hide behind this rationalization of his complicity in the confiscation of Jewish property, personal enrichment, and financial support of the war machine. However, given the bank's actions during the 1930s and early 1940s, there is no reason to believe that he simply fabricated this defense after the war. Instead, Hill and many of his colleagues had seen their work through this capitalist lens – had indeed chosen not to evaluate "the personal factors" that lay at the heart of "Aryanization," the use of forced labor at the cement factory, or the other crimes in which they engaged. In other words, while the capitalist intentions of the bank were never voiced, in fact, were repudiated, before 1945, times had now changed. In the new climate that marked the postwar era, capitalism and its supposed objective, value-free perspective were held up as evidence that the bank had not been corrupt or racist in its previous business decisions. The most *völkisch* bank had been capitalist all along.

11

Völkisch Capitalism

Himmler's Bankers and the Continuity of Capitalist Thinking and Practice in Germany

Alexa Stiller

11.1 INTRODUCTION: CAPITALISM AND THE NAZI REGIME

This chapter argues that the Nazi regime produced a specific variety of capitalism, referred to here as *völkisch* capitalism. The focus is on the contradiction between National Socialist settlement policy, imbued with anticapitalist rhetoric, and the capitalist settlement practice in the annexed territories of the Third Reich during World War II. This chapter shows that the settlers were conceived of as capitalist subjects, that the state compensation for the property of the resettled "Volksdeutsche" ("ethnic Germans") was organized by the Deutsche Umsiedlungs-Treuhandgesellschaft mbH (German Resettlement Trust Company) (DUT) as a private enterprise, and that the DUT implemented this practice by means of both private-sector auditing techniques and a partnership with private banks on behalf of the public sector. In this chapter "settlement" is primarily understood as the creation of German family farms on annexed Polish land. The Nazi regime managed its settlement policy by means of a large-scale robbery of the local population in the annexed areas, illustrated here using the example of German-occupied Wielkopolska (Greater Poland), the so-called Wartheland.

Since the economic and social system in Germany between the years 1933 and 1945 is referred to here as capitalist, I define capitalism briefly. The criteria for determining a capitalist economic order are the existence

For the discussion of earlier versions of this chapter I would like to thank Joachim Söder-Mahlmann, Moritz Föllmer, Pamela Swett, Jonathan Zatlin, Marc Buggeln, Armin Nolzen, Kim Christian Priemel, Christian Gerlach, Roman Köster, Volker Berghahn, and Mischa Suter.

of private ownership of means of production and of production factors such as capital and land, wage labor, and the existence of market mechanisms (demand and supply). Whether or not free (i.e., unregulated) markets are intrinsic to it remains debatable. Within the framework of this basic definition, various priorities are set with regard to the origins of the capitalist system. For Karl Marx and many of his successors, the main criterion was "double free wage labor" (that is, labor "free" of the means of production and reproduction, so that, apart from his or her labor as a commodity, a worker has nothing else to offer on the market) and, in connection with this, the emergence of specific classes and capital accumulation by means of the "surplus value" created by labor.

For Immanuel Wallerstein and other world system theorists, on the other hand, the production of and trade in goods on the world market with the aim of maximizing profit was the decisive motivation that led to the emergence of the capitalist world system. At first glance, neither view seems to fit Nazi Germany, which shifted its economic production more and more to forms of forced labor, especially during the war, and which had already disconnected itself from the world market in the 1930s in its efforts to achieve autarky. The theories of Marx and Wallerstein, however, also offer a fundamental critique of capitalism, which, depending on one's point of view, is based either on the absorption of the surplus value created by labor (i.e., on exploitation) or on the achievement of the surplus value created by unequal exchange (i.e., on appropriation).[1]

At this point it is important to add another "ingredient" of capitalism: structural racism. W. E. B. Du Bois, C. L. R. James, and Eric Eustace Williams pointed out the close connection between slavery/the slave trade and capitalism in the first half of the twentieth century. Cedric J. Robinson created the term *racial capitalism* when discussing their research.[2] Here I follow their insight that the capitalist world system is inherently racist. *Völkisch* capitalism is a variation of this. How exploitation and appropriation took place within the framework of nationalist and racist thought and action in the field of settlement policy, and how the Nazi authorities in question used the profit gained from it is the subject of this chapter.

[1] See, in greater detail, Alexa Stiller, "Völkischer Kapitalismus. Theoretische Überlegungen anhand des empirischen Beispiels der Deutschen Umsiedlungs-Treuhandgesellschaft 1939–1945," *Zeitschrift für Geschichtswissenschaft* 66 (2018): 505–23.

[2] Cedric J. Robinson, *Black Marxism: The Making of the Black Radical Tradition*. Foreword by Robin D. G. Kelley with a new preface by the author (Chapel Hill, NC, 2000).

What is the state of scholarly debate on the question of whether the Nazi economy, especially the war economy, fit the capitalist criteria? There is agreement that the Nazi regime, shortly after taking power, began to organize the German economy as a war economy. This meant that the Nazi economy had certain special features as compared to the regular market economies of the time: production targets were fixed, the production of war material had priority over goods for export or private consumption, resources were also managed according to plan, foreign exchange was state-controlled in order to be able to import the necessary raw materials, and price controls were put in place to counteract inflation. Accordingly, the classic market principles were no longer valid.[3] The question of whether the National Socialist economic order was based on market-economy or planned-economy principles has therefore been debated for decades.

However, this question has far less to do with capitalism than is commonly assumed. It goes without saying that the Nazi regime organized its war economy according to a plan, but in certain areas it allowed market structures to apply and also acted opportunistically in relation to the private sector. The usual scope for supply and demand was severely limited by price policy and the allocation of raw materials, which meant that producers could no longer achieve higher profits by increasing prices or quantities. As a result, competition – that is, the pursuit of profit – had to focus on reducing production costs, as Franz Böhm had already observed in 1942.[4] The Ordoliberals, such as Böhm and Walter Eucken, recommended themselves to the National Socialists "as opponents of classical liberalism and the planned economy," as Ludolf Herbst has explained. Nevertheless, the theoretical conceptions behind their economics corresponded to the Nazi regime's interest in state control and

[3] Cf. Adam Tooze, *The Wages of Destruction: The Making and Breaking of the Nazi Economy* (London, 2006); Hans-Erich Volkmann, *Ökonomie und Expansion: Grundzüge der NS-Wirtschaftspolitik. Ausgewählte Schriften*, ed. Bernhard Chiari (Munich, 2003); Alan S. Milward, *War, Economy and Society: 1939–1945* (London, 1977); Friedrich Forstmeier and Hans-Erich Volkmann, eds., *Kriegswirtschaft und Rüstung, 1939–1945* (Düsseldorf, 1977); Friedrich Forstmeier and Hans-Erich Volkmann, eds., *Wirtschaft und Rüstung am Vorabend des Zweiten Weltkrieges* (Düsseldorf, 1975); Dietmar Petzina, *Autarkiepolitik im Dritten Reich: Der nationalsozialistische Vierjahresplan* (Stuttgart, 1968); Berenice A. Carroll, *Design for Total War: Arms and Economics in the Third Reich* (The Hague, 1968).

[4] Franz Böhm, "Der Wettbewerb als Instrument staatlicher Wirtschaftslenkung," in Günther Schmölders, ed., *Der Wettbewerb als Mittel volkswirtschaftlicher Leistungssteigerung und Leistungsauslese* (Berlin, 1942), 55–98, here 65–6.

economic management of the market.[5] The price fixing in 1936 inevitably entailed a rationalization of industrial and, in some cases, agricultural production.[6] Consequently, it cannot be said that in the Nazi economic system no market mechanisms functioned at all.

Returning to the question of market economy versus planned economy, Franz L. Neumann observed during World War II that economic systems are often mixed economies and that this also applied to the Third Reich: "The German economy of today has two broad and striking characteristics. It is a monopolistic economy – *and* a command economy. It is a private capitalist economy, regimented by the totalitarian state."[7] Therefore, an analytical separation of Nazi politics from capitalist economy takes us no further, nor are there sufficient arguments against calling the economic and social system in the Nazi regime capitalist, even if there are deviations from the liberal ideal type of capitalism.[8]

This chapter is divided into three sections. The first examines theoretically and empirically the relationship between property and expropriation in the Third Reich intertwined with the antisemitism and antiliberalism of the Nazi Party and the practice of so-called Aryanization. The second begins with a brief explanation of the institutional and power-political context of the Nazi settlement policy in annexed western Poland, which was shaped by the special authority of the Reichskommissar für die Festigung deutschen Volkstums (Reich Commissioner for the Strengthening of Germandom) (RKF) under Heinrich Himmler's leadership. It then analyzes in detail the activities of the DUT, in particular the attitude of its protagonists – Himmler's bankers – toward expropriation, their concept of the "ethnic German" settlers as capitalist subjects, and their entrepreneurial thinking and actions. The

[5] Ludolf Herbst, *Der totale Krieg und die Ordnung der Wirtschaft: Die Kriegswirtschaft im Spannungsfeld von Politik, Ideologie und Propaganda 1939–1945* (Stuttgart, 1982), 148–9.

[6] See Joachim Lehmann, "Mecklenburgische Landwirtschaft und 'Modernisierung' in den dreißiger Jahren," in Frank Bajohr, ed., *Norddeutschland im Nationalsozialismus* (Hamburg, 1993), 335–46; Tilla Siegel and Thomas von Freyberg, *Industrielle Rationalisierung unter dem Nationalsozialismus* (Frankfurt, 1991); Rüdiger Hachtmann, *Industriearbeit im "Dritten Reich": Untersuchungen zu den Lohn- und Arbeitsbedingungen in Deutschland, 1933–1945* (Göttingen, 1989); Martin H. Geyer, "Soziale Sicherheit und wirtschaftlicher Fortschritt," *Geschichte und Gesellschaft* 15 (1989): 382–406.

[7] Franz Neumann, *Behemoth: The Structure and Practice of National Socialism, 1933–1944* (Toronto, 1944), 261.

[8] Eike Henning, *Bürgerliche Gesellschaft und Faschismus in Deutschland. Ein Forschungsbericht*, 2nd ed. (Frankfurt, 1982), 287–8, also 70–2, 86–95.

third section investigates the postwar career of one of the main protagonists of the DUT in the Federal Republic of Germany until the mid-1960s. The conclusion takes up the concept of *völkisch* capitalism and relates it to the previously presented empirical findings.

11.2 PRIVATE OWNERSHIP AND EXPROPRIATION IN NAZI GERMANY

In 1920 the Nazi Party declared in its twenty-five-point program that its supposed anticapitalist aims were "breaking the interest bondage," "nationalizing" trusts, "profit-sharing in large enterprises," and "expropriating land" (point 17).[9] However, the prominent use of the term *expropriation* in the party program was to prove an obstacle to the rise of the Nationalsozialistische Deutsche Arbeiterpartei (National Socialist German Workers' Party) (NSDAP). Therefore in 1928 Adolf Hitler declared an official addition to point 17 of the party program: "Since the NSDAP stands on the ground of private property, it follows automatically that the passage about 'expropriation without compensation' refers only to the creation of legal possibilities to expropriate, if necessary, land that was illegally acquired or is not being administered in accordance with the common good. This is primarily directed against Jewish real estate speculation companies."[10]

Later, Hitler explicitly acknowledged private property and major landownership in Germany, which assured him the support of the East Elbian Junkers and large sections of the German business community. As a result, the Nazis enacted only one decidedly anticapitalist law after they came to power in 1933: the Reichserbhofgesetz (Reich Hereditary Farm Law) of the same year. Although the law took some privately held land out of the market by regulating inheritance, it was less directed against large landowners than the Reichssiedlungsgesetz (Reich Settlement Act of 1919) had been.[11] Another ideologeme from 1920, on the other hand, was to be successively

[9] Twenty-five-point program of the National Socialist German Workers' Party, Feb. 24, 1920.

[10] Hitler's speech on Apr. 13, 1928, printed in *Völkischer Beobachter*, Apr. 19, 1928. I would like to thank Armin Nolzen for drawing my attention to this supplementary statement. See also Jan Schleusener, *Eigentumspolitik im NS-Staat: Der staatliche Umgang mit Handlungs- und Verfügungsrechten über privates Eigentum 1933–1939* (Frankfurt, 2009), 41–57.

[11] Cf. Uwe Mai, *"Rasse und Raum": Agrarpolitik, Sozial- und Raumplanung im NS-Staat* (Paderborn, 2002).

expanded in the future with the annexation of territory during the World War II: "Only German citizens may own German land."[12]

Some historians suggest, by referring to Joseph Goebbels's diary entry of 1924 in which he described the existing economic system as "Jewish capitalism," that the Nazis inextricably linked *anticapitalism* and antisemitism in their ideology.[13] However, it is more apt to say that the Nazis linked their rejection of *liberalism* to antisemitism. The anticapitalism of the Nazis was only a facade. In 1938, for example, Herbert Backe described the "occidental" conquest of the world as "purposeful free trade" that was opposed to the "selfish" free trade, with which he associated the "Jews."[14] The construction of a difference between "money grubbing" and "creative" capital (*raffendes* and *schaffendes Kapital*) in Nazi ideology also served this purpose.[15] The Nazis' attitude to capitalism was thus not fundamentally negative, but rather ideologically antiliberal, nationalist, antisemitic, and at the same time quite pragmatic.

The question of how, precisely, antiliberalism and the capitalist economic and social system were connected in Nazi Germany requires further detailed theoretical analysis. For this I would like to draw on Herbert Marcuse's thoughts. As early as 1934, he stated that the Nazi regime carried out its struggle against "liberalism" solely on an ideological level, and not on a practical level, because "it was largely in agreement with the basic structure" of liberalism/capitalism – namely, the sanctity of private property. In the Third Reich the "private initiative of the entrepreneur" and private property in general alongside the "private organization of the society" remained the basis of the state.[16] According to Marcuse, the antiliberal ideology turned "against the capitalist *Ungeist* (demon), against the bourgeoisie and its 'greed for profit.'" The bourgeoisie was presented in the form of the "small and petty *Händlertum* (merchant class)"; capitalism was associated with the "type of free competition of independent individual capitalists": "The new *Weltanschauung* reviled

[12] Twenty-five-point program of the National Socialist German Workers' Party, Feb. 24, 1920.

[13] Horst Möller, *Regionalbanken im Dritten Reich* (Berlin, 2015), 6.

[14] Herbert Backe, *Das Ende des Liberalismus in der Wirtschaft* (Berlin, 1938), 46–7. See also Willi A. Boelcke, *Deutschland als Welthandelsmacht 1930–1945* (Stuttgart, 1994), 31–5.

[15] See Henning, *Bürgerliche Gesellschaft*, 234, 281.

[16] Herbert Marcuse, "Der Kampf gegen den Liberalismus in der totalitären Staatsaufassung," in Wolfgang Abendroth, ed., *Faschismus und Kapitalismus: Theorien über die sozialen Ursprünge und die Funktion des Faschismus* (Frankfurt, 1967), 39–74, here 45. The essay was first published in 1934 in *Zeitschrift für Soziologie*.

the 'merchant' and celebrated the 'ingenious business leader.'"[17] The Nazi fight against the bourgeoisie was less important in practice, as we know today, than Marcuse had assumed in 1934 and when his essay was reprinted in 1967.

Following Marcuse, I would like to put forward the thesis that the Nazis constructed "greed for profit" and "petty *Händlertum*" primarily as "Jewish" and were thus able to externalize all allegedly negative aspects of capitalism using antisemitic stereotypes. The *Volksgemeinschaft* (people's community), which was to remove all class conflict and class barriers, was its counter image. This ideologeme of the "classless society on the basis of and within the framework of the existing class society," as Marcuse so aptly describes it, could – and this is also my extension of his thoughts – only function on the basis of the exclusion and expropriation of the German Jews.[18]

In practice, the expropriation of Jewish Germans took place first, followed by the expropriation of Jewish Austrians, through so-called Aryanization (the Nazis did not need this special form of expropriation of the Jews living in the occupied territories). "Aryanization" was not based on the legal institution of expropriation (although it can be called "expropriation" in the figurative sense – that is, meaning "robbery," as Marx also used the term). "Aryanization" was political pressure and measures such as forced sale (after a considerable depreciation in value), forced transfers, and seizure without compensation of personal property.[19] The legal process of the expropriation of property by the state, as it developed with the emergence of the bourgeois nation-state in the nineteenth century, on the other hand, had been connected from the start with compensation, for in liberal thinking property is regarded as a universal freedom *and* human right, which cannot be denied or taken without restitution.[20] Although the legal institution of expropriation continued to exist under the Nazi regime, it no longer applied universally. While opponents of the regime and Jewish Germans were increasingly

[17] Ibid., 46–7. [18] Ibid., 55.

[19] See Schleusener, *Eigentumspolitik*, 201–81. For "Aryanization," see, for example, Christiane Kuller, *Finanzverwaltung und Judenverfolgung: Die Entziehung jüdischen Vermögens in Bayern während der NS-Zeit* (Munich, 2008); Frank Bajohr, *"Arisierung" in Hamburg: Die Verdrängung der jüdischen Unternehmer 1933–1945* (Hamburg, 1998); Angela Verse-Herrmann, *Die "Arisierungen" in der Land- und Forstwirtschaft 1938–1942* (Stuttgart, 1997).

[20] See Dieter Schwab, "Eigentum," in Otto Brunner, Werner Conze, and Reinhart Koselleck, eds., *Geschichtliche Grundbegriffe: Historisches Lexikon zur politisch-sozialen Sprache in Deutschland*, 8 vols. (Stuttgart, 1979), 2: 65–115.

deprived of their rights from 1933 onward, the law only continued to apply to "desired" members of the *Volksgemeinschaft*.

At the same time, nevertheless, the regime did extend the state's jurisdiction over private property. The Reichsautobahn Act of 1933, for example, allowed the universal expropriation of private real estate. In return, regulations concerning reparation, which had previously been handled differently in the German states, were standardized. For the first time the law introduced a new type of compensation: the expropriated landowner would not receive money, but an equivalent piece of land.[21]

What applied to the construction of the highways was also implemented for military purposes two years later: the Landbeschaffungsgesetz (Land Procurement Act) of 1935 further expanded the legal basis for expropriation and the state's scope for action in this respect. The law gave the Wehrmacht the opportunity to expropriate land for necessary construction projects, such as proving grounds. In 1935 the demand for military training areas was estimated to be as high as 158,000 hectares (ca. 390,426 acres).[22] Until well into the war, the Wehrmacht made use of the Land Procurement Act and, with the help of the limited-liability Deutsche Ansiedlungsgesellschaft (German Settlement Company) (DAG), relocated families to other estates.

Later Hermann Göring made use of the Land Procurement Act in building the industrial conglomerate Reichswerke Hermann Göring. The third authority entitled to apply the law was the Reich Commissioner for the Strengthening of Germandom from October 1939 onward. Nevertheless, since it combined expropriation with compensation, the Land Procurement Act only applied within the borders of the *Altreich* (i.e., Germany, Austria, and the Sudetenland).[23] A general law of expropriation was discussed during the Nazi era but was never realized.[24]

The robberies that took place in the annexed and occupied territories were consistently based on measures of confiscation connected with a constructed crime – namely, that of being the "enemy of the *Volksgemeinschaft* and the Reich." Which state agency or special authority was responsible for confiscation and liquidation in the various annexed and occupied territories varied. In annexed western Poland (*eingegliederte Ostgebiete*), to which the Wartheland belonged, the Haupttreuhandstelle

[21] Schleusener, *Eigentumspolitik*, 96–8. [22] Ibid., 98–102.

[23] See Alexa Stiller, *Völkische Politik: Praktiken der Exklusion und Inklusion in polnischen, französischen und slowenischen Annexionsgebieten, 1939–1945* (Göttingen, 2022).

[24] Schleusener, *Eigentumspolitik*, 103–36. See also Werner Schubert, ed., *Akademie für Deutsches Recht 1933–1945: Protokolle der Ausschüsse*, 22 vols. (Berlin, 1995), 3.7: 523–86.

Ost (Main Trustee Office for the East) (HTO), under Göring's aegis, was in charge of the liquidation and disposition of urban and commercial Polish and Jewish property.[25] However, the RKF was responsible for confiscating and distributing rural and agricultural property. Göring had thus prevailed over the Reich Minister of Food and Agriculture (who nonetheless maintained control over the yields and management of the large agricultural estates during the war). Thus, the RKF was the main beneficiary of the German annexation of West Poland along with the HTO. Five million hectares (approx. 12.3 million acres) of agricultural land were henceforth under the control of the RKF. By the end of the war the RKF had confiscated 250,000 hectares (approx. 617,763 acres) of it.[26] Who, then, was this Reich Commissioner for the Strengthening of Germandom? What was his program? And how did he implement it?

11.3 HIMMLER'S BANKERS, COMPENSATION FOR "ETHNIC GERMAN" ASSETS, AND THE SETTLER FAMILY AS A VÖLKISCH CAPITALIST SUBJECT

Shortly after the Nazi invasion of Poland, Hitler commissioned Himmler with the so-called Festigung deutschen Volkstums (strengthening of Germandom), concentrating initially on the so-called incorporated eastern territories or annexed western Poland. However, Himmler's mandate as Reichskommissar für die Festigung deutschen Volkstums and his apparatus became continuously broader and more complex in the course of the further expansion of the Greater German Reich. In addition to the planning of settlements, the tasks of the RKF consisted in the relocation of "ethnic German" groups to the Reich and the "creation of space" for these groups – that is, the expulsion of "undesired" locals from the declared settlement zones. The RKF also sought to extend its mission to the field of *Eindeutschung* (Germanification) and naturalization, an aim that was achieved when Himmler took over the Reich Ministry of the Interior at the end of 1943.

The *völkisch* policy of the RKF was constituted by the interdependence of the "strengthening of Germandom" and the expulsion and

[25] See Bernhard Rosenkötter, *Treuhandpolitik: Die "Haupttreuhandstelle Ost" und der Raub polnischer Vermögen 1939–1945* (Essen, 2003).

[26] See Allgemeiner Überblick über die vermögensrechtlichen Verhältnisse des Reichskommissars für die Festigung deutschen Volkstums, National Archives and Records Administration (NARA), RG 242, BDC Administrative Records, Box 26, Binder 88/1.

extermination of all groups that were allegedly "harmful to the German people" (*volkstumsschädlich*) or "alien to the *Volksgemeinschaft*" (*volksgemeinschaftsfremd*). The RKF implemented about 70 percent of its settlement activities during the war in the Wartheland.[27] In the following I examine how the rural settlement of "ethnic German" resettlers (*Umsiedler*) was carried out and what economic thinking guided the actions of the heads of the responsible organization.

The "strengthening Germandom" program, implicitly announced by Hitler in his speech to the Reichstag on October 6, 1939, focused on national minorities in the East Central European countries – primarily Jews and "ethnic Germans." The Jews were to be excluded and expelled; inclusion and "homecoming" awaited the "ethnic Germans." The program began with their bilaterally negotiated so-called resettlement from Estonia and Latvia. This was followed in the winter of 1939 by their resettlement from Soviet-occupied eastern Poland, a result of the secret additional protocol of the Hitler-Stalin Pact (further resettlement from the Soviet "area of interest" in Southeastern Europe followed). The bilateral treaties secured reparation for the property of the "ethnic German" resettled families. In order to clear the assets of the *Volksdeutsche*, the RKF initiated the establishment of the Deutsche Umsiedlungs-Treuhandgesellschaft mbH (German Resettlement Trust Company) (DUT).

Himmler mandated Wilhelm Keppler, who, besides holding other positions, was head of the Deutsche Revisions- und Treuhand-Aktiengesellschaft (German Auditing and Trusteeship Company), an accountancy firm, to establish the limited liability company known as the DUT.[28] Its task was to regulate all property matters concerning the "ethnic German" resettlers on the RKF's or the German state's behalf. Based in Berlin, the DUT was explicitly founded not as a government agency, in contrast to Göring's Main Trustee Office for the East (*Haupttreuhandstelle Ost*), which was responsible for confiscating, administering, and liquidating Polish and Jewish urban and business

[27] See Stiller, *Völkische Politik*.

[28] Letter from Himmler to the Deutsche Revisions- und Treuhand-Aktiengesellschaft, Nov. 2, 1939, Sammlung der Arbeitsgrundlagen der DUT, Bundesarchiv (BArch), R 186/38. For the Deutsche Revisions- und Treuhand AG, see Ute Pothmann, *Wirtschaftsprüfung im Nationalsozialismus: Die Deutsche Revisions- und Treuhand AG (Treuarbeit) 1933 bis 1945* (Essen, 2013). For Keppler, see Peter Longerich, *Heinrich Himmler: Biographie* (Munich, 2008), 268–9.

property in the "incorporated eastern territories."[29] As a company under the private law of the Reich, its share capital amounted to 1 million Reichsmark and was raised by the Deutsche Revisions- und Treuhand AG and the Garantie-Abwicklungsgesellschaft mbH (Guarantee Processing Company Ltd.). The Reich Commissioner for the Strengthening of Germandom reimbursed the day-to-day expenses of the DUT from the Reich's resources.[30] The first managing director of the DUT, Dr. jur. Karl Schmölder, stated after the war that when he was recruited by Keppler he had asked "for the company to be set up purely privately as a GmbH, so that I could keep political influence as far away from it as possible."[31] Ulrich Greifelt, the head of the RKF, stated in 1947 that the Reich Ministry of Finance had also had an interest in a limited liability company "in order to keep the budget clean and not upset the Reich's financial regulation."[32] Accordingly, the new trustee office was set up as a private company to compensate for the state's fiscal weakness. As a limited liability company, the DUT was able to take out loans from banks without expanding public debt, which in turn resulted in the creation of a shadow budget for the Reich.

Technically, the DUT was a credit institution, albeit a special one.[33] Its main task was to deal with economic and property matters arising from the removal and subsequent settlement of the *Volksdeutsche*. The DUT was therefore not so much the "house bank of the RKF" through which Himmler was able to raise funds, as Götz Aly has put it, but rather a clearinghouse.[34] In other words, the DUT's banking business was limited to interim financing; its core tasks were the identification of mutual receivables and payables as well as the settlement of the resulting financial transactions.[35]

[29] See Announcement of the German Press Agency about the foundation of the DUT, Nov. 11, 1939, BArch, R 43/II/1412. Cf. Karl Stuhlpfarrer, *Umsiedlung Südtirol 1939–1940*, 2 vols. (Vienna, 1985), 1: 262.

[30] "Die DUT berichtet," *Neues Bauerntum* 33 (1941): 171–2.

[31] Schmölder, Jan. 22, 1948, Interrogation No. 2585a, NARA, RG 238, M-1019, Reel 65: 2.

[32] Greifelt, Mar. 14, 1947, Interrogation No. 872, NARA, RG 238, M-1019, Reel 22: 26; Greifelt, May 5, 1947, Interrogation No. 1147b, ibid.: 2–6.

[33] So also Raul Hilberg, *Die Vernichtung der europäischen Juden: Die Gesamtgeschichte des Holocaust*, 9th ed. (Frankfurt, 1999), 256.

[34] See Götz Aly and Susanne Heim, *Vordenker der Vernichtung: Auschwitz und die deutschen Pläne für eine neue europäische Ordnung* (Hamburg, 1991), 154; Götz Aly, *"Endlösung": Völkerverschiebung und der Mord an den europäischen Juden* (Frankfurt, 1995), 66, 129–30.

[35] Cf. Stuhlpfarrer, *Umsiedlung*, 268, 355; Ingo Loose, *Kredite für NS-Verbrechen: Die deutschen Kreditinstitute in Polen und die Ausraubung der polnischen und jüdischen Bevölkerung 1939–1945* (Munich, 2007), 246.

The main protagonists at the DUT were all qualified financial experts. Its first managing director or chairman, Karl Schmölder, was born in Bochum in 1895 and followed in the footsteps of his father (most recently the senate president of the Berlin Appellate Court) by becoming a lawyer. From the mid-1920s to 1933 he had been a civil servant in the Reich Ministry of Justice. Under the Brüning and Papen governments, he participated in cabinet and ministerial meetings. In 1931 – the year of Germany's great banking crisis – he was involved in drafting the Emergency Decree on Payment Transactions (*Notverordnung über den Zahlungsverkehr*), the Capital Flight Decree (*Kapitalflucht-Verordnung*), and the Decree on Joint Stock Companies and Limited Partnerships (*Verordnung über Aktiengesellschaften und Kommanditgesellschaften*).[36]

The stock corporation law reform of 1931, in which Schmölder had played a leading role, introduced the mandatory independent audit of annual financial statements for stock corporations and limited partnerships.[37] This was two years earlier than in the United States, for example.[38] Schmölder had cocreated the institution of the external audit and thereby had a decisive influence on the new regulation of banks and companies in the aftermath of the global economic crisis. Brüning's cabinet is actually known for having relied on the liberal theories of prominent economists such as Friedrich August von Hayek, Ludwig von Mises, and Wilhelm Röpke to cope with the economic crisis, especially with

[36] Tilman Koops, ed., *Akten der Reichskanzlei. Die Kabinette Brüning I und II*, 3 vols. (Boppard am Rhein, 1982), 2: 1382, 1662, 1679, 1685, 1693, 1706, 1770; Karl-Heinz Minuth, ed., *Akten der Reichskanzlei. Das Kabinett von Papen*, 2 vols. (Boppard am Rhein, 1989), 1: 31, 2: 637.

[37] Karl Schmölder, "Die amtliche Enquete zur Vorbereitung der Reform des Aktienrechts," *Juristische Wochenschrift* (1929): 1338–45; Karl Schmölder, "Der Entwurf eines Gesetzes über Aktiengesellschaften und Kommanditgesellschaften auf Aktien," *Juristische Wochenschrift* (1930): 2623–33; Leo Quassowski and Karl Schmölder, *Verordnung über die Rechte der Schuldverschreibungsgläubiger vom 24. September 1932 nebst der preußischen Durchführungsverordnung* (Berlin, 1932); Franz Schlegelberger, Leo Quassowski, and Karl Schmölder, *Verordnung über Aktienrecht (Verordnung des Reichspräsidenten über Aktienrecht, Bankaufsicht und über die Steueramnestie) vom 19. September 1931 nebst den Durchführungsbestimmungen* (Berlin, 1932). See also Werner Schubert, ed., *Quellen zur Aktienrechtsreform der Weimarer Republik (1926–1931)*, 2 vols. (Frankfurt, 1999), 2: 953; Reni Maltschew, *Der Rückerwerb eigener Aktien in der Weltwirtschaftskrise 1929–1931: Eine Untersuchung zu den Hintergründen und Zielen der Notverordnung des Reichspräsidenten vom 19. September 1931* (Berlin, 2004), 98.

[38] See Securities Act of 1933: An Act to provide full and fair disclosure of the character of securities sold in interstate and foreign commerce and through the mails, and to prevent frauds in the sale thereof, and for other purposes, May 27, 1933.

regard to savings in the state budget.[39] Nevertheless, Schmölder gained experience in state intervention in the economy during this period.

After the NSDAP came to power, Schmölder moved to the Prussian Ministry of Economics and Labor as a ministerial councilor (*Ministerialrat*) in May 1933 on the recommendation of Otto Schniewind.[40] He stayed there only briefly and in 1935 moved to the private sector. He became a member of the board of directors of the Rheinische Hypothekenbank (Rhineland Mortgage Bank), which absorbed the Berliner Hypothekenbank (Berlin Mortgage Bank) by merger in 1935.[41]

In addition, he held further positions in the Nazi regime. As bank director and retired ministerial councilor, he was also a member of the Advisory Council of the Section of Private Mortgage Banks, of the Akademie für Deutsches Recht (German Law Academy), of the State Committee at the headquarters of Dresdner Bank and the admission board of the Berlin Stock Exchange, of the supervisory boards of Reichs-Kredit-Gesellschaft AG (Reich Credit Company), and of the Stramberg-Witkowitzer Cement Works in Ostrava.[42] In the German Law Academy, Schmölder was a member of the Mortgage Law and the Real Estate Credit Committees.[43] After 1935, he combined his expertise in international finance and currency transfer with the mortgage and loan business. This made him exactly the right person to organize the asset clearing of the *Volksdeutsche* from 1939 onward.

[39] Harald Winkel, "Der Glaube an die Beherrschbarkeit von Wirtschaftskrisen (1933–1970): Lehren aus der Wirtschaftskrise," in Gerhard Schulz, ed., *Die Große Krise der dreißiger Jahre: Vom Niedergang der Weltwirtschaft zum Zweiten Weltkrieg* (Göttingen, 1985), 17–43, here 22–5. Cf. Jan-Otmar Hesse, Roman Köster, and Werner Plumpe, *Die Große Depression: Die Weltwirtschaftskrise 1929–1939* (Frankfurt, 2014).

[40] Schmölder, Oct. 8, 1947, NARA, RG 238, M-1019, Reel 65: 2. See also Reinhold Zilch and Bärbel Holtz, eds., *Die Protokolle des Preußischen Staatsministeriums 1817–1934/38*, 12 vols. (Hildesheim, 2004), 12.2: 689; Lothar Gruchmann, *Justiz im Dritten Reich 1933–1940: Anpassung und Unterwerfung in der Ära Gürtner* (Munich, 2001), 243.

[41] Schmölder, Jan. 22, 1948, Interrogation No. 2585a, NARA, RG 238, M-1019, Reel 65: 1.

[42] "Compass," *Finanzielles Jahrbuch* 7 (1943): 511. See also Harald Wixforth, "Expansion durch 'Arisierung'? Die Geschäftsausweitung der Reichs-Kredit-Gesellschaft in die 'Provinz,'" *Bankhistorisches Archiv* 35 (2009): 1, 1–24; Jonas Scherner, "Staatliche Förderung, Industrieforschung und Verfahrensentwicklung: Die Tonerdeproduktion aus deutschen Rohstoffen im 'Dritten Reich,'" in Sören Flachowsky, Rüdiger Hachtmann, and Florian Schmaltz, eds., *Ressourcenmobilisierung: Wissenschaftspolitik und Forschungspraxis im NS-Herrschaftssystem* (Göttingen, 2016), 383–422.

[43] Schubert, *Akademie für Deutsches Recht*, 3.7.

Schmölder was the DUT's chairman from its founding in November 1939 until the end of 1940 (officially until March 1941) and subsequently a member of the supervisory board until the end of the war.[44] His successor as chairman was Alfred Kulemann (born 1897). Kulemann had been a corporate lawyer at the Deutsche Hypothekenbank Berlin (German Mortgage Bank Berlin) since 1926 and a member of its board of managing directors since 1934. He joined the DUT's board of managing directors in February 1940 and remained with the trust company until the end of the war. Dr. jur. Kurt Kleinschmidt (born 1904) from the Mecklenburgische Hypotheken- und Wechselbank (Mecklenburg Mortgage and Exchange Bank) served as the second managing director from November 1939 to May 1945. Kleinschmidt, who had first worked as an in-house lawyer before his promotion to general counsel of the Deutsche Zentralbodenkredit-Aktiengesellschaft (German Central Land Credit Company) in Berlin from 1929 to 1937, was nominated by Schmölder as the second managing director specializing in real estate and mortgage matters. Kleinschmidt and Kulemann both joined the Nazi Party in 1933. Kleinschmidt also joined the SS (*Schutzstaffel*) in the same year; both received the rank of SS officers in 1940.[45] As was common in the banking sector at the time, the management in Berlin later included six other directors, including two auditors, a retired state's attorney, and a former board member of the mortgage department of the Creditanstalt-Bankverein, a Viennese credit bank.[46]

The tasks of the DUT were entirely determined by the RKF's field of activity. Specifically, these consisted of recording and valuing the assets left behind by resettled persons, liquidating and transferring these assets, providing financial support for the resettlers after their arrival in the Greater German Reich, carrying out the so-called asset compensation (*Vermögensausgleich*) procedure, and valuing and clearing the objects allocated to the resettled persons by the RKF. Later, the task of estimating

[44] Letter from Keppler to Himmler, Mar. 13, 1941, BArch, NS 19/809; Kleinschmidt, Jun. 4, 1947, Interrogation No. 1388, NARA, RG 238, M-1019, Reel 35: 4.

[45] Kulemann, Jul. 16, 1947, NARA, RG 238, M-1019, Reel 39: 1–2; Kleinschmidt, Jun. 4, 1947, Interrogation No. 1388, ibid., Reel 35: 2–4.

[46] Umdruck Nr. 9 der Dienststelle des RKF, Jul. 31, 1940, Geschäftsverteilungsplan der DUT, Jul. 1, 1940, BArch, R 49/2573; Geschäftsverteilungsplan der DUT, Jun. 1, 1941, BArch, R 49/34; Organigramm des Geschäftsverteilungsplanes der DUT, Jan. 1942, ibid.; Bericht der DUT über das Geschäftsjahr 1941, BArch, R 49/2316; Geschäftsbericht für das Jahr 1942 der DUT, Mar. 1943, BArch, R 43/II/1411a.

the assets of relocated "Germanizable" people from the annexed territories of Alsace, Lorraine, Luxembourg, and Slovenia and relocating members of groups III and IV of the German People's List (*Deutsche Volksliste*) from the "incorporated eastern territories" was added, as well as, in some regions, the administration of the property of these persons. Since those identified as potentially "Germanizable" were to be integrated into the *Volksgemeinschaft*, the DUT was also responsible for the transfer of their assets.[47] At the end of 1942 the DUT was looking after a total of 806,106 "ethnic German" resettlers, 271,804 of whom were considered asset holders.[48]

The clearing of the assets and real estate left behind by the resettled ethnic Germans was not only a virtual financial transfer, it took place in the middle of the war and the Nazi regime's "conquest of living space." The reparations to be paid to ethnic Germans were therefore inextricably linked with the violence and robbery perpetrated against the "undesired" population groups in the annexed and occupied territories. Himmler, Greifelt, and Keppler agreed with the DUT's management that "the reimbursement of assets should take place as far as at all possible through the transfer of real values in the eastern regions."[49] The guiding principle of the DUT's assets compensation was therefore the "restitution in kind" (*Naturalrestitution*) of the resettlers – in other words they were compensated for the property they had left behind by means of goods confiscated from Poles, Jews, French people, Slovenians, and others displaced from the annexation areas.[50]

The DUT staff at the regional offices of the RKF in the annexed western Polish territories were also responsible for commercial and urban settlement. Together with the *Volksdeutsche*, DUT staff selected appropriate companies, previously taken away from Polish and Jewish owners without compensation.[51] The head of the DUT branch office in Poznan and a member of the management board, Dr. Ferdinand Bang, explained the

[47] "Die DUT berichtet," 171; Kleinschmidt, Jun. 4, 1947, Interrogation No. 1388, NARA, RG 238, M-1019, Reel 35: 5f.; Hoffmann, Aug. 18, 1947, ibid., Reel 28: 6. See also Geschäftsbericht für das Jahr 1942 der DUT, Mar. 1943, BArch, R 43/II/1411a.

[48] Geschäftsbericht der DUT für das Jahr 1942, Mar. 1943, BArch, R 43/II/1411a.

[49] Note by Greifelt, Feb. 5, 1940, about a meeting with Himmler, Keppler, and Kleinschmidt, BArch, R 49/614. Cf. Ulrich Greifelt, "Die Festigung deutschen Volkstums als zentrale Ostaufgabe," *Reichsverwaltungsblatt* 62 (1941): 509–14, here 512.

[50] Kleinschmidt, Jun. 16, 1947, Interrogation No. 1388a, NARA, RG 238, M-1019, Reel 35: 2; Affidavit Kulemann, Jul. 23, 1947, ibid., Reel 39: 4.

[51] Cf. Geschäftsbericht für das Jahr 1942 der DUT, Mar. 1943, BArch, R 43/II/1411a.

"principle of restitution in kind" in the *Reichsverwaltungsblatt* (*Reich Administration Journal*) as follows: "As far as possible, no cash funds from the Reich budget are to be used. Rather, the resettler is to be satisfied in kind from the mass of spoils available in such a way that, after a certain period of transition, he will be living in conditions similar to those he would have experienced if he had not been resettled."[52] The employees of the RKF apparatus and the DUT were well aware of the fact that Nazi settlement policy functioned only through wartime expansion and a widespread expropriation of "undesired" local inhabitants.

In addition to the deprivation of the expelled persons, the DUT and RKF employees restructured the social and economic conditions of the "ethnic German" resettled groups within the framework of assets compensation. On one hand, the resettlers, who had been classified as "A-cases" (i.e., those who were limited to settling within the 1938 borders of Germany and Austria), were only compensated in the form of claims under the Reich's debt register – irrespective of the amount of their cash assets or the value of their property in their country of origin.

Edgar Hoffmann, the DUT employee who handled these cases, admitted after the war that several resettlers who had received an "A" decision complained about this classification.[53] On the other hand, the RKF apparatus provided farms to "racially valuable" resettlers ("O-cases") in the "incorporated eastern territories," even if they had not previously owned agricultural land.[54] Greifelt and the DUT management did not agree with this system of determining assets compensation primarily according to racial criteria. However, there was no way around it because Himmler was convinced of the benefit of "racial selection" as a principle.[55] Not only by robbing the locals, but also in the way it selected settlers for the "new territories," the RKF created social divisions among "ethnic Germans." In this system the DUT had the task of securing the property claims of the *Volksdeutsche* and reordering the economic and social structure of the annexed regions according to racial criteria.

Although the RKF apparatus handed over companies and factories to "Baltic German" entrepreneurs, especially in the Wartheland, its main

[52] Ferdinand Bang, "Die Deutsche Umsiedlungs-Treuhand-Gesellschaft," *Reichsverwaltungsblatt* 62 (1941): 177–80, here 179. Cf. Adalbert W. Schürmann, *Der deutsche Osten ruft. Wirtschaftsraum und Wirtschaftskräfte der wiedergewonnenen Ostgebiete* (Hamburg, 1942), 49.

[53] Hoffmann, Aug. 18, 1947, NARA, RG 238, M-1019, Reel 28: 5.

[54] See Bang, "Deutsche Umsiedlungs-Treuhand-Gesellschaft," 179.

[55] See Stiller, *Völkische Politik*.

focus, as already mentioned, was on rural settlement. The DUT employees recognized their work in asset compensation benefited the "ethnic German" resettlers, but they also understood how their task aided the Reich. The granting of compensation in kind assisted in the development (*Aufbau*) of economic structures in the "incorporated eastern territories." This "development" was characterized by harsh Germanization methods, which included "Aryanization," expulsion, seizure, and robbery, alongside common financial policies such as tax breaks and loans for resettlers, local *Volksdeutsche*, and *Reichsdeutsche* trustees or entrepreneurs. In using such measures, the Nazi regime pursued the political goal of "integrating" the annexed territories into the economic area of the Greater German Reich, and also redirected the flow of capital. For example, the DUT directed investment into the economy of the "new territories" by granting development loans (*Aufbaukredite*) to "ethnic German" settlers. A postwar quote from Schmölder is to be treated with caution because he was undoubtedly interested in whitewashing his own role, but it nevertheless illustrates the economic thinking of the DUT's bank managers:

> I went about the business as a banker. Now I have prepared the following account for myself, and this way of calculating things is correct: Anything that happens during the war is only provisional. If the war is lost, the Polish owner will return to his property. If I now grant a loan on the property, the business will be preserved for the ultimate owner. That's better than the property being devastated. There were two things I was really concerned about, first that a resettler, a resettler who knew what he was doing, should come into the business to avoid losses of material assets. Second, that people who were only out to make a profit should be kept out. The credit action also stemmed from this thought.[56]

The quotation refers to two other important aspects of Nazi capitalist thought and action – a positive assessment of efficiency and a rejection of profit for its own sake – which I discuss later in this chapter. First, let me explain the so-called credit action that Schmölder spoke about.

Initially the DUT granted loans from the RKF or state budget to settler families to enable them to establish a new livelihood in the annexed regions, but Schmölder and Kleinschmidt changed this practice to private funding.[57] The DUT established bank consortia in which all major German banks, savings banks, and cooperative banks were involved. Kleinschmidt stated after the war that the inclusion of the banks had

[56] Schmölder, Jan. 22, 1948, Interrogation No. 2585a, NARA, RG 238, M-1019, Reel 65: 6–7.

[57] "Die DUT berichtet," 172.

been "a thought that came naturally" to Schmölder, Kulemann, and himself because all of them came from a mortgage bank background and were familiar with long-term lending.[58]

The first bank group created in 1940 was the Eastern Consortium (*Ostkonsortium*). It had a loan volume of 100 million Reichsmark (reduced to 85 million in 1943) and was alternately led by the Dresdner Bank and the Deutsche Bank. According to Kleinschmidt, ten to twelve banks were involved, including the Commerzbank. Schmölder recalled after the war that none of these banks had declined the DUT's invitation to the first meeting to discuss the establishment of the consortium in late November 1939. The meeting was chaired by Keppler and lasted two to three hours. Fifty to sixty gentlemen from various German banks took part. "The only controversial point was the matter of refinancing," said Schmölder. The banks wanted to be able to reclaim their money from the Reichsbank, which Keppler initially rejected. In the spring of 1940 a guarantee by the Reich was finally agreed upon, as this was the only way to achieve a low interest rate of 4.5 percent at the beginning and 4 percent later on.[59]

The amount of each individual bank's loan fund was precisely regulated in the syndicate agreements.[60] The decision to grant so-called development loans (*Aufbaukredite*) was reserved to the DUT, with loans in excess of 30,000 Reichsmark requiring the additional approval of the head of the RKF office, Greifelt (who was, together with Keppler, the most important decision maker on the supervisory committee of the DUT).[61] By the end of 1942, DUT had lent the resettlers a total of approximately 157 million Reichsmark, while the bank loans guaranteed by the Reich only amounted to approximately 52 million.[62] The extent of the banks' lending services within the framework of the total costs shows that, for the RKF apparatus, the participation of bank consortia in development loans for settlement was not necessary but was practical.[63]

[58] Kleinschmidt, Jun. 25, 1947, Interrogation No. 1492, NARA, RG 238, M-1019, Reel 35: 14.

[59] Schmölder, Oct. 8, 1947, NARA, RG 238, M-1019, Reel 65: 9–13 (quotation on 11); Kleinschmidt, Jun. 25, 1947, Interrogation No. 1492, ibid., Reel 35: 5–14. See Loose, *Kredite*, 250–4.

[60] Bang, "Deutsche Umsiedlungs-Treuhand-Gesellschaft," 178.

[61] Nachweisung der im 4. Vierteljahr 1940 von der DUT an volksdeutsche Umsiedler ausgegebene Kredite, BArch, R 49/29; Kleinschmidt, Jun. 25, 1947, Interrogation No. 1492, NARA, RG 238, M-1019, Reel 35: 7, 11.

[62] Geschäftsbericht für das Jahr 1942 der DUT, Mar. 1943, BArch, R 43/II/1411a.

[63] That is also Loose's assessment; see Loose, *Kredite*, 254, 257.

But what interest did the banks have in participating? They undoubtedly earned money from the interest received on the loans granted in connection with the RKF's settlement policy. However, with an interest rate of 4–4.5 percent, in reality they could expect a profit margin of only 0.25 percent, according to Ingo Loose's study of German banks in occupied Poland.[64] The granting of development loans ended once the compensation for assets had been concluded, which was to be completed by the DUT approximately two to three years after resettlement. The banks' interest from granting loans, however, was not the main reason for their participation in the RKF's *Volkstum* policy.

After the war Kleinschmidt assessed the motivation as follows:

> The banks naturally had a certain interest in acquiring a certain number of customers later on among the resettlers, especially the industrial and agricultural resettlers ... In my opinion, there was a certain amount of competition among banks for the new business in the East. I recall, for example, that public-sector banks developed a keen interest in not being excluded from this business by the major private banks.[65]

In other words, the banks pursued a long-term strategy. It was about competition for segments of this future market.[66] However, competition was limited by the DUT and other governmental organizations to asset management in the annexed and occupied territories.

Instead of a completely "open" competition, then, the Nazi regime promoted something else: initiative and commitment. In the field of settlement policy, the RKF apparatus and the DUT implemented this principle as follows. Although the resettlers usually acted as trustees of the confiscated businesses, they were granted the "right to self-management" (*Recht auf Eigenbewirtschaftung*).[67] In some cases there were even transfers of property, although the Nazi regime postponed all transfers of ownership until after the end of the war (to ensure that "war profits" were distributed fairly among soldiers' families). In particular, the RKF considered "Baltic German" land barons, who had received large agricultural enterprises in the Wartheland, for transfer of ownership. This was done because the fiduciary use of the managed properties had not led to

[64] Ibid., 251.

[65] Kleinschmidt, Jun. 25, 1947, Interrogation No. 1492, NARA, RG 238, M-1019, Reel 35: 19.

[66] See also Loose, *Kredite*, 252; Harald Wixforth, *Die Expansion der Dresdner Bank in Europa* (Munich, 2006), 513–16, 523, 614.

[67] Affidavit Kulemann, Jul. 23, 1947, NARA, RG 238, M-1019, Reel 39: 3.

the desired yield targets being achieved, as Kleinschmidt admitted after the war.[68] Bang publicly explained the reasoning behind the decision during the war: "In the interests of the economic development of the new East, it seemed desirable as well to bring the entrepreneurial initiative of the resettlers to full effect by concluding the interim stage of provisional administration as soon as possible."[69] This shows that the RKF apparatus, through the DUT bankers and in the course of its settlement policy, promoted central elements of the capitalist social and economic order: property, entrepreneurship, and productivity. The special Nazi component was that these capitalist elements were only promoted in the interest of the *Volksgemeinschaft* and strictly in accordance with nationalist and racially exclusive criteria. The primacy of these inclusionary and exclusionary criteria meant that the capitalist economic and social order under the Nazi regime can only be described as *völkisch* capitalism.

But to what extent can the capitalist thought and action of Himmler's bankers and RKF apparatus be applied, as I have just done, to the entire Nazi regime? To this end, it is necessary to define the actual components of what the Nazis understood to be the spoils of war to be divided later. This cannot be discussed in its entirety in this chapter, nevertheless a thesis will be presented here. In addition to short-term looting and labor exploitation in the occupied territories, a medium-term shift of property took place *during the war* above all in the annexed territories: western Poland, Alsace-Lorraine, and Slovenia. Of the individual new provinces, the Wartheland had by far the largest agricultural sector. It is not without reason that the RKF conducted more than 70 percent of its settlement policy during the war there. So, if annexed western Poland was not only an important "battlefield" for Nazi organizations but also for private economic interests in the distribution of the spoils of war after the war – though some distribution began secretly during the war – then it is crucial to examine what happened there and how the RKF and the DUT were involved. After the war, Schmölder described the situation in the "incorporated eastern territories" from the DUT's perspective as follows:

> In the *Ostraum*, we found a fait accompli insofar as the confiscation of Polish property had already been completed, and the entire holdings had been placed in trust administration by representatives of the *Treuhandstelle Ost*. In that sense, I accepted the fact and said to myself: If these businesses are already being made

[68] Kleinschmidt, Jul. 15, 1947, Interrogation No. 2816, NARA, RG 238, M-1019, Reel 35: 10.

[69] Bang, "Deutsche Umsiedlungs-Treuhand-Gesellschaft," 179.

over to persons of German origin during the war, then they should be given to resettlers and not to people from the Reich. I therefore set store by the decree on the order of priority (*Rangfolge-Erlass*). At that time, there was a sort of race for profits in the East. There were any number of interested parties from the Reich coming forward who wanted to get their hands on something.[70]

That in 1948 Schmölder laid the entire responsibility for the confiscation of property from Poles and Jews at the door of Göring's HTO, thereby exonerating himself, is not surprising. More interesting here, however, is that Schmölder regarded the work of the DUT as being purely for the benefit of resettlers, whose financial interests needed safeguarding against the alleged greed of some *Reichsdeutsche*. This was also the aim of the HTO and the RKF's so-called Decree on the Order of Priority. The decree stipulated that in the case of trusteeship and transfer of property, priority was to be given to "ethnic German" resettlers and the local *Volksdeutsche* (later only the "higher-ranked" members of the *Deutsche Volksliste* groups I and II), followed by the former German residents of the old eastern Prussian provinces who emigrated to Germany between 1918 and 1939, and only then to the Germans from the Reich who had no connection to the region.[71] The two Nazi organizations were probably pursuing the goal of creating a stable *Volksgemeinschaft* in the annexed territories in the long term, reducing socioeconomic dissatisfaction by a state-imposed division of the spoils of war. That does not mean, however, that they were actually pursuing the goal of a "classless society." The compensation of the "ethnic German" resettlers shows that the social positions of individuals in a class society were generally not changed by the RKF apparatus and the DUT – unless the individual resettler family was "racially particularly valuable" as a future farming family.

The Nazi regime excluded "the stranger" and "the other" from "their own" – that is, the Jews from German society and the native Slavic populations, Poles, Slovenes, etc., in the annexed and occupied territories. However, the Nazi regime also stratified the members of the *Volksgemeinschaft* not only according to their social position but also according to nationalist and racist criteria. This is particularly evident in the RKF's *völkisch* policy toward "ethnic German" immigrant families.[72]

[70] Schmölder, Jan. 22, 1948, Interrogation No. 2585a, NARA, RG 238, M-1019, Reel 65: 4–6.

[71] See letter from Himmler to Winkler, Feb. 3, 1940, enclosed: decree from Dec. 19, 1939, Archiwum Państwowe w Poznaniu (APP), 800/161; Note of the Office of the RKF, Dec. 18, 1939, BArch, R 186/37.

[72] See Stiller, *Völkische Politik*.

It is this policy of exclusion and inclusion from which I extrapolate the attribute *völkisch* to make up the concept of *völkisch* capitalism presented here.

11.4 HIMMLER'S BANKERS IN THE GERMAN FEDERAL REPUBLIC

Schmölder, Kulemann, and Kleinschmidt were interrogated in the course of the trial of Greifelt et al., Case 8 of the Nuremberg Military Tribunals (NMT) between June 1947 and January 1948.[73] At no point was the trial about holding them accountable for their actions. Instead, the US investigators questioned them only about the structures and procedures involved in the resettlement of the *Volksdeutsche*, including the expulsion of locals from the annexed territories and the confiscation of their possessions, in order to obtain incriminating evidence against the defendants in Case 8. As shown earlier in this chapter, all three men worked actively to wash their hands and those of the Reichskommissar für die Festigung deutschen Volkstums; instead, they declared the Haupttreuhandstelle Ost responsible for the robbery of Poles and Jews. Schmölder described the former head of the HTO, Max Winkler, as the "promoter of the Third Reich in the East."[74] Rather than admitting their own contributions to the expulsion and settlement policies, they emphasized their affinity to the conservative German resistance. This is especially true of Schmölder, who mentioned his support for Hans von Dohnanyi and claimed to have been known as an "opponent of the regime" among entrepreneurs as early as 1934.[75] Whether the latter is true can hardly be verified, but Dohnanyi and Schmölder did know each other from the Reich Ministry of Justice, where Dohnanyi had worked with Schmölder since 1929 as an assistant consultant, and the two men and their wives socialized on a regular basis. Despite Dohnanyi's critical attitude toward the Nazi regime, Schmölder supported him professionally and privately. Dohnanyi also seemed to trust Schmölder. In March 1940, he put him

[73] These statements have been used here as a source. For Case 8 of the Nuremberg Military Tribunals, see Alexa Stiller, "Die Volkstumspolitik der SS vor Gericht: Strategien der Anklage und Verteidigung im Nürnberger 'RuSHA-Prozess,' 1947–1948," in Ministry of Justice of North Rhine-Westphalia, ed., *Leipzig–Nürnberg–Den Haag: Neue Fragestellungen und Forschungen zum Verhältnis von Menschenrechtsverbrechen, justizieller Säuberung und Völkerstrafrecht* (Düsseldorf, 2008), 66–86.

[74] Schmölder, Jan. 22, 1948, Interrogation Nr. 2585a, NARA, RG 238, M-1019, Reel 65: 7.

[75] Ibid.; Schmölder, Oct. 8, 1947, NARA, RG 238, M-1019, Reel 65: 3 (quotation).

on a list of potential members of a new government after Hitler. Schmölder's willingness to help, however, did not go beyond his close friend: when Dohnanyi came to Schmölder seeking a job at the Rheinische Hypothekenbank in Berlin for the legal advisor of the Confessional Church, Friedrich Justus Perels, Schmölder failed to offer support.[76]

After the war, Schmölder continued to be in great demand among the new West German government, banks, and companies as an expert on currency issues. As the head of the legal department in the Office for Currency Affairs (Büro für Währungsfragen) (BfW), he was the general secretary and commentator of the Deutsche Mark Opening Balance Law (*DM-Eröffnungsbilanz-Gesetzes*), responsible for valuing the monetary and tangible assets of companies.[77] This was based on the following process: as part of the currency reform, all entrepreneurs had to disclose the value of their assets as on the date of the opening balance sheet of the *Deutsche Mark*. This valuation determined future tax calculations, depreciation options, and the measurement of equalization of burdens (*Lastenausgleich*) obligations due to war damages and postwar expulsions.[78]

As early as 1970 political scientist Hans-Hermann Hartwich came to the conclusion that the Deutsche Mark Opening Balance Law was primarily a political instrument that enabled the private sector to make an "almost loss-free transition" to the new state and economic order.[79] As already mentioned, Karl Schmölder was responsible for drafting this law, which was of great importance for the West German private sector.[80] But Schmölder was by no means the only former Nazi to play a leading economic role in the young Federal Republic. Schmölder's superior at the Office for Currency Affairs, for example, was ministerial director Rudolf Harmening. Like Schmölder before 1933, Harmening had worked in the Reich Ministry of Justice. Between 1934 and 1945 he was in the Reich Ministry of Food and Agriculture, where he dealt with questions of

[76] Marikje Smid, *Hans von Dohnanyi – Christine Bonhoeffer: Eine Ehe im Widerstand gegen Hitler* (Gütersloh, 2002), 120–1, 163, 173, 205, 241, 284.

[77] "Gratulation zu Schmölders 65. Geburtstag," *Zeitschrift für das gesamte Kreditwesen* 13 (1960): 933. See also Hans-Dieter Kreikamp, ed., *Akten zur Vorgeschichte der Bundesrepublik Deutschland, 1945–1949*, 5 vols. (Munich, 1981), 5: 241, 264, 448–9.

[78] Hans-Dieter Kreikamp, "Einleitung," in Kreikamp, *Akten zur Vorgeschichte der Bundesrepublik Deutschland*, 5: 27.

[79] Hans-Hermann Hartwich, *Sozialstaatspostulat und gesellschaftlicher Status quo* (Cologne, 1970), 111.

[80] See also Karl Schmölder, Ernst Gessler, and Franz Merkte, *Steuerliche Richtlinien zum DM-Bilanzgesetz (DMBR)* (Stuttgart, 1950).

the management of rural enterprises in annexed western Poland during the war.[81]

In addition to his government positions, Schmölder continued to work in the private sector. He was a member of the board of directors of the Rheinische Hypothekenbank from 1935 to 1963 until he took over as chairman of the supervisory board from his predecessor Otto Schniewind, another German banker with a Nazi past.[82] And in the Federal Republic of Germany too, he again held a number of different supervisory board and committee positions: he was the sole chairman of the Association of Private Mortgage Banks, a board member of the Federal Association of Private Banks, a member of the Central Capital Markets Committee, and an honorary professor at the University of Mannheim. On his sixty-fifth birthday, the *Zeitschrift für das gesamte Kreditwesen* (*Journal for the Entire Credit System*) paid tribute to his life's work with the following words:

> Karl Schmölder is one of the most distinguished, well-known, and influential experts in the banking industry of the Federal Republic of Germany. ... Thanks to his wide-ranging professional career and his activities in economic and financial policy sustained by loyalty to liberal (*freiheitlich*) principles, Karl Schmölder has won himself a large circle of friends, who are attached to him by bonds of both professional and personal appreciation, thanks to his extensive professional career.[83]

His activity at the DUT in the RKF apparatus went unmentioned, but Schmölder's thinking and acting between the 1920s and the 1960s, including during the twelve years of National Socialism, had always been *freiheitlich* in the sense of being based on a belief in the market economy.

11.5 CONCLUSION

The main protagonists of the DUT belonged to the bourgeois financial elite before 1933, between 1933 and 1945, and after 1945. They were able

[81] See Stiller, *Völkische Politik*.

[82] Manfred Pohl, *Baden-Württembergische Bankgeschichte* (Stuttgart, 1992), 274, 309.

[83] "Gratulation zu Schmölders 65. Geburtstag," *Zeitschrift für das gesamte Kreditwesen* 13 (1960): 933. Cf. Karl Schmölder, "Der Kapitalmarkt in gesamtwirtschaftlicher Schau," *Vortrag, Verhandlungen des Allgemeinen IX. Deutschen Bankiertages* (1958): 100–19; Karl Schmölder, "Rechnungslegung, Prüfung und Publizität der Aktiengesellschaft," *Zeitschrift für handelswissenschaftliche Forschung* 2 (1950): 279–302; Kurt Kleinschmidt, "Die Banken und die Schuldscheindarlehen," *Zeitschrift für das gesamte Kreditwesen* 16 (1963): 20, 950–9.

to integrate their German national (*deutschnational*) thoughts and their business values relatively well into the settlement policy of the RKF. No break in their economic thinking and activity can be detected. Schmölder's career continued in the Federal Republic of Germany unhampered by his involvement in the Nazi regime. When he retired, the financial community sang the praises of his "loyalty to liberal principles." How can this continuous narrative from the world economic crisis to the economic miracle, in which the Nazi era and World War II apparently played no disruptive role, be explained?

Dieter Ziegler has pointed out that denazification had hardly any effect on the continued employment of former bank directors.[84] Financial and administrative networks survived the war largely untouched. Even a superficial look at the early Federal Republic reveals a renewed encounter between Schmölder, Schniewind, and Harmening, all of whom had worked in the Reich Ministry of Justice before 1933 and were active in the Nazi regime afterward. A detailed investigation would most likely reveal further facts about reestablished networks. Historians often ask how it was possible for former Nazis to become democrats with such rapidity after 1945. Perhaps this was much easier than we think. In the light of the results of this study, I would offer the following thesis: they were able to "return" so easily to the liberal social and economic order because the Nazi regime had never abandoned certain fundamental capitalist principles, but had continued to use them, even though it had not maintained a liberal stance in its political and legal thinking.

Karl Schmölder's example shows that people like him were powerful intermediaries in public-private partnerships from the early 1930s to the 1960s because of their multiple functions in government and the private sector. Public-private partnership includes not only the mobilization of private capital for public projects but also cooperation in terms of commercial law and other forms of mediation. Even under the Nazi regime, fostering and maintaining public-private partnerships remained

[84] The discontinued employment of persons such as Karl Rasche and Carl Luer "formed the exception to the rule," Ziegler stated. In contrast, Gall and Scholtyseck assumed that a deep personnel caesura was the rule. See Dieter Ziegler, "Strukturwandel und Elitenwechsel im Bankwesen 1900–1957," in Volker R. Berghahn, Stefan Unger, and Dieter Ziegler, eds., *Die deutsche Wirtschaftselite im 20. Jahrhundert: Kontinuität und Mentalität* (Essen, 2003), 187–218, here 216–17; Lothar Gall, "Hermann Josef Abs," in Hans Pohl, ed., *Deutsche Bankiers des 20. Jahrhunderts* (Stuttgart, 2008), 1–12; Joachim Scholtyseck, "Otto Schniewind," in Pohl, *Deutsche Bankiers des 20. Jahrhunderts*, 373–85, here 377.

a fundamental function of the state within capitalism, as had been the case since at least the end of the nineteenth century, becoming increasingly so in the twentieth. The most striking characteristic of cooperation between the public sector and private enterprise under the Nazi regime, in contrast to the Weimar Republic and the Federal Republic of Germany, lay in the definition of the "common good" in contradistinction to "profit," whereby, in practice, the Nazis used Montesquieu's formula "the common good before the self-good" (*Gemeinnutz geht vor Eigennutz*) to bring about the exclusion and deprivation of "undesired" groups, including Jews, Poles, and others. Even if in our perception today the mass murder of Europe's Jews was the central act of the Nazi regime, and is thus at the center of today's assessment of the Third Reich, the Nazi system was not based on a radical break with capitalist principles.

The empirical study of the economic actions and thinking of the DUT's managers has brought to light many capitalist elements. State administration and the reimbursement of the assets of the "ethnic German" resettler groups were carried out under the authority of a private company; the DUT managed a public-private partnership between the RKF or the German state and private banks; the private property of the "desired" population, the members of the *Volksgemeinschaft*, was generally recognized (but again hierarchically differentiated according to racial, political, and other selection criteria); the Nazis only deprived "undesired" population groups of their property rights; there was a strong interest in the economic development of the annexed territory (including investments in the new market); the image of "ethnic German" resettler families was that of hard-working groups of incomers regarded as capitalist subjects for the economic growth of the allegedly backward "East"; entrepreneurial initiative and competition were emphasized as long as both served the interests of the *Volksgemeinschaft* rather than merely individual profit. Like the social order in Nazi Germany, the economic order was strongly influenced by dichotomies: "racially" valuable vs. inferior, German vs. non-German, hard-working vs. "work-shy," productive vs. unproductive etc. – but this did not mean that there were no gray zones in between.

Völkisch capitalism was a variety of capitalism. Ideologically the Nazi regime condemned the political and legal aspects of liberalism but not its economic principles. It allowed private ownership of the means of production and production factors as well as market mechanisms, albeit in a very limited and regulated form. *Völkisch* capitalism was inclusive and exclusive – the exploitation of the "undesired" groups was to some extent so thoroughgoing that it led to their death – but the mass murder of the

European Jews can and should not be explained in economic terms alone. Antisemitism and racism in the context of occupation counterbalanced the promotion of the *Volksgemeinschaft* during the war. The managing directors of the German Resettlement Trust Company followed this *völkisch* thinking and practiced it to the best of their capitalist knowledge.

Index

CPSIA information can be obtained
at www.ICGtesting.com
Printed in the USA
LVHW080903050222
710357LV00003B/50